Muriel Ostriche
Princess of Silent Films

Muriel Ostriche
Princess of Silent Films

and
Early American Film Production

by Q. David Bowers

FOREWORD BY ANTHONY SLIDE

Published Simultaneously By:
The Vestal Press, Ltd.
320 North Jensen Road, Vestal, New York 13850

and
Bowers and Merena Galleries, Inc.
Box 1224, Wolfeboro, New Hampshire 03894

Library of Congress Cataloging-in-Publication Data

Bowers, Q. David.
   Muriel Ostriche: princess of silent films, and early American film production.

   Bibliography: p. 235
   Includes index.
     1. Ostriche, Muriel, 1896-   .   2. Moving-picture actors and actresses--United States--Biography.
I. Title.
PN2287.073B69   1987   791.43'028'0924   [B]   87-1981
ISBN 0-911572-63-5
ISBN 0-911572-64-3 (pbk.)

Published simultaneously by:

The Vestal Press, Ltd.
320 North Jensen Road, Vestal, New York 13850
and
Bowers and Merena Galleries, Inc.
Box 1224, Wolfeboro, New Hampshire 03894

All rights concerning this book are reserved by the author, Q. David Bowers. Written permission is required for the reproduction of any information in this book, except for brief excerpts used in a review in a newspaper or magazine. *Muriel Ostriche: Princess of Silent Films and Early American Film Production* is a cooperative production of The Vestal Press, Ltd. and Bowers and Merena Galleries, Inc.

© 1987 by Q. David Bowers

Contents

Acknowledgments 8
Foreword
    By Anthony Slide 11
Preface 15

Chapter One
    Beginning at Biograph 19
Chapter Two
    The Eclair Experience 29
Chapter Three
    The Road to Thanhouser 49
Chapter Four
    The Little Princess 67
Chapter Five
    Thanhouser in Decline 115
Chapter Six
    Moxie and More Movies 141
Chapter Seven
    The World Years 159
Chapter Eight
    Later Films 197

Appendix One
    Filmography 223
Appendix Two
    Muriel Ostriche Chronology 233
Bibliography 234
Index 235

Acknowledgments

The author expresses appreciation to the following for help in the ways indicated:

Muriel Ostriche Copp, for her friendship, kindness, and recollections. Mary K. Valley, for transcribing voluminous research notes, setting the manuscript into type, and for correspondence with dozens of individuals and institutions. Anthony Slide, for writing the foreword and for the inspiration provided by his published works, especially *Aspects of Film History Prior to 1920* and *Early American Cinema*. Edward Wagenknecht, for reviewing the manuscript and for many valuable suggestions, including the title of the book. Kevin Brownlow, for reviewing the manuscript and for help and suggestions in several areas.

Academy of Motion Picture Arts and Sciences, for Vitagraph information. Rita Ecke Altomara, of the Fort Lee (New Jersey) Public Library, for information. Elizabeth Arlin, for compiling research notes. George M. Barringer, of the Georgetown University Library, for several images of Muriel Ostriche. Bebe Bergsten, of Historical Films, for the identification of several film titles and for suggestions. The Bettmann Archive, for photograph searches. Eileen Bowser, of the Museum of Modern Art, for Biograph information and for locating a film title. Michael Corenthal, for supplying certain publications. Mrs. Calvin S. (Mollie) Demarest, daughter of Muriel Ostriche, for information. Mariette DiChristina, of the New Rochelle (New York) *Standard-Star*, for publicizing the search for Muriel Ostriche and Thanhouser information. Billy H. Doyle, for a newspaper clipping. Geraldine Duclow, curator of the Theatre Collection, Free Library of Philadelphia, for illustrations and trade magazine information, and for locating several film titles. Doug Duijan for photographs. Morris Everett, for suggesting information sources. Mrs. Charles (Jean) Geoly, daughter of Muriel Ostriche, for information. Lorraine Gillman, for research in the UCLA Film Library, Los Angeles. Irvin R. Glazer, for suggestions and sources of information. David Hagen, of the Georgetown University Library, for photographs. Dr. Gerald Hamm for information. Tim Hawkins, of the Wisconsin Center for Film and Theatre Research, for clippings and photographs. Gloria Hewitt, daughter of Muriel Ostriche, for introducing me to her mother and for much help and information. William Hewitt, for providing a photograph. James R. Hobin, Albany (New York) Public Library, for a newspaper clipping. Dr. Jan-Christopher Horak, of the George Eastman House, for photographs and frame enlargements. Larry G. Horton, for a magazine article. Maxine Jacobs, for a photograph. Sidney Kingsley, husband of Madge Evans, for information concerning *The Volunteer*. Richard Koszarski, of the American Museum of the Moving Image, for information and for providing a number of important Thanhouser photographs. Linda Kowall, for enthusiasm, suggestions, and reviewing the manuscript. Joseph Lauro, of Archive Film Productions, Inc., for information. Jeannette W. Levitt, of the Nassau County (New York) Clerk's Office, for information. Library of Congress, Washington, D.C., for information. Robin Little, of *Films in Review*, for suggestions. Tom McGovern, for photography at the New York Public Library. Rick Moody, for information concerning Thanhouser and its players, and for furnishing many newspaper clippings relating to Thanhouser, especially items from the *New Rochelle Pioneer*. The New York Public Library Theatre Collection at Lincoln Center, for use of its archives. Marjorie Pepe, of the Harvard Theatre Collection, for a magazine article. Dr. Gerald Rose, for information. Samuel K. Rubin, of *Classic Images*, for publicizing the project. Eva M. Santelli, for research at the New York Public Library, New York City Hall, and Museum of Modern Art. Charles Silver, of the Museum of Modern Art, for Biograph information. Charles Smith, for an advertisement featuring Muriel Ostriche. Dale Stein, of the Kraus-Thompson Organization, for help in several ways. Gil Williams, of The Vestal Press, for proofreading and suggestions. Christine M. Wiltanger, for research in several New York and New Jersey institutions and for copy editing, proofreading, and suggestions.

Appreciation is also expressed to the staff members of the Graphic Arts Department, Bowers and Merena Galleries, Inc., for production of the volume: J.E. McCabe (manager), William Winter (assistant manager), Margaret Graf, Linda Heilig, Judy Bouchard, Lee Blythe Lilljedahl, and Cathy Dumont (manager, photography department).

Cover illustration: Portrait of Muriel Ostriche from the *New York Dramatic Mirror*, August 14, 1919.

Muriel Ostriche, center foreground, in a Thanhouser production, circa 1914. (Courtesy of the American Museum of the Moving Image, Lawrence Williams Collection)

A tragic moment on a Thanhouser set, circa 1914, with Muriel Ostriche shown to the left. (Courtesy of the American Museum of the Moving Image, Lawrence Williams Collection)

Foreword
By Anthony Slide

I have little doubt that the first thought which flashes through the mind of the reader is, "Why a book on Muriel Ostriche?" My response to such a question would be, "Why not a book on Alice Joyce, King Baggot, Florence Lawrence, Arthur Johnson, Maurice Costello, or Florence Turner?" In 1913 *The Motion Picture Story Magazine* organized a popularity contest to discover the favorite female and male stars of their readers. Muriel Ostriche came second in the former category, reason enough for a book-length study. But what of the winners, Romaine Fielding of the Lubin Company and Alice Joyce of the Kalem Company? Why are there no volumes on their careers? Why, indeed, has almost nothing been written on them even in article form in recent years? Just as Muriel Ostriche is deserving of recognition, in book form, for her contributions to the early motion picture industry in this country, so are many other actors and actresses of the period in need of similar documentation.

Q. David Bowers is to be congratulated for having the courage to compile a book such as this, not to mention the tenacity to track down Muriel Ostriche and to elicit such a wealth of fascinating, first-hand observations from her. Bowers uses Muriel Ostriche's career as a springboard from which to discuss the activities of various companies with which she was associated, most notably the Thanhouser Company of New Rochelle. As a historian, he is not much concerned with analysis, but rather with a straightforward recitation of the facts. He is not here to criticize, largely because the films in which Miss Ostriche appeared are no longer available for contemporary viewing and analysis, but to provide us with the basic documentation available from a thorough reading of the trade papers and house organs of the period. I suspect Q. David Bowers would designate himself a historian rather than a critic. Perhaps he understands that the two are different professions. The historian should go about his task and leave the in-depth analysis to a first-rate critical scholar such as Dudley Andrew.

Here is film history as it should be considered: taking the primary source materials and reporting the evidence which they provide.

However, the purpose of this foreword is not merely to praise Q. David Bowers or Muriel Ostriche, an actress about whom I must confess I knew little prior to reading this volume. I would like to discuss the greater ramifications of a book such as this, which is, I believe, the first to concern itself solely with a detailed chronology of the career of an actress or actor from the teens years of filmmaking. Of course there were a few volumes published at the time—Pearl White's highly romanticized autobiography, *Just Me*, in 1919; Oren Clayton Reel's *The Life of Earle Williams* from 1915; and J. Warren Kerrigan's 1914 effort, *How I Became a Successful Moving Picture Star*, in which he gave full credit to his mother. But on the whole, the lives and careers of the players of the period have only been covered through a handful of career articles by such fine researchers as DeWitt Bodeen, Harold Dunham, George Mitchell, and Jack Spears in the pages of *Films in Review*, when that journal was under the editorship of Henry Hart and Charles Phillips Reilly.

One major problem for the casual observer is that our perception of stardom and star billing is tarnished by current celebrities attaining such heights of glory, not through public acclaim or recognition, but through the negotiations of their agents. Everything today is contingent upon agreed credits and billing. There are no featured players or supporting casts in television productions; everyone is a star in some capacity. It would be impossible to recreate today the artistic qualities of early movie posters. Contemporary posters must give credit to all and sundry, because all have stipulated billings in their contracts.

It is difficult to appreciate there was once a time—in the teens and twenties—when being a "star" really meant precisely that. It took a while for early producers to accept the reality of public appeal, which they saw as going hand-in-hand with demands for salary increases; but once companies, such as Vitagraph and Kalem, realized audiences could and did identify with certain stars, they were quick to promote their players through lobby displays in theatres (as early as 1910) and through the establishment of the screen's first "fan" magazine, *The Motion Picture Story Magazine* (in 1911). Stars became identified with specific companies—

John Bunny was Vitagraph's comedian, Pearl White was Pathé's serial queen and Muriel Ostriche was Thanhouser's leading lady of Princess films—and so it was very necessary for companies to nuture and promote the players which they had under contract. (Indeed, as Bowers notes, Thanhouser was so protective of its leading lady that it was happy to create a unique brand name, Princess, to designate her films.)

Randolph Bartlett, writing in a 1919 issue of *Motion Picture Magazine* (previously *The Motion Picture Story Magazine*), summed it up when he commented, "The star is inevitable. Drama is the result of conflicting forces acting upon an individual, but can be interesting only when one is interested in the individual involved."

Scholars and historians today tend to concentrate more on the films than their stars, in direct contrast to what Bartlett wrote almost seventy years ago—and perhaps because scholars and historians are too divorced from the audiences for whom this entertainment medium creates its films. It is arguable that the problem lies in it being easier to analyze a film than to analyze a performance within that film. Less arguable is that there is much academic snobbery involved in the film history movement. Critical studies have taken priority over historical documentation. Yet without the latter, the first is not a viable proposition. To analyze the past, we must have it fully documented, and as far as the American film industry is concerned, we are a long way from that goal.

Back in 1977, in my introduction to *Aspects of American Film History Prior to 1920*, I wrote something which seems as relevant today as then: "President John Adams, in 1807, commented that a complete history of the American Revolution could not be written until all the state histories were known. It is my firm belief that much the same statement could be applied to the history of the American cinema today. There can be no complete history until the work of every company, however obscure, every technician, and every actor has been examined and recorded."

I have often wondered why it is not possible for at least one of the countless film schools in this country to establish a program whereby students, as part of the curriculum, are required to undertake filmed or videotaped interviews with the survivors of the film industry's early years. The project need not be limited to those active in the studios, but could and should include musicians, theatre owners, and exchangemen. It is tragic enough that many performers and technicians considered minor by today's standards have never been the subject of audio-taped oral histories. It is doubly tragic that there is neither funding nor incentive to produce audio *and* visual oral histories with these pioneers—true documentaries in which an individual's career is documented by the filmmaker. This is what I tried to do a few years ago with my 30-minute documentary, *Portrait of Blanche Sweet*, and I am presently involved in two similar projects, on actress Viola Dana and cinematographer Karl Brown.

Time is running out for the pioneers of the American silent film industry. Ours is the last generation to have the privilege of knowing these wonderful individuals. Posterity will blame us for not having the foresight to capture a record of their lives and careers on film or tape.

There is so much left to do in the field of film history, and yet so many academics—so-called film scholars and film historians—spend their time in considering the methodology of film history. The time for methodology is later. The time is *now* for getting the job done, regardless of the methodology used. What if Iris Barry or Henri Langlois had spent their early years at the Museum of Modern Art or the Cinémathéque Francaise, not in the acquisition of films in urgent need of safeguarding and preservation, but in discussions as to the best methods to be used in going about their tasks? To be sure, these pioneers in the archival field made mistakes, but they accomplished much because they understood the need for immediate action. Far too much and too many have already been lost to the film historian because he has been slow to recognize the need for concerted efforts to document the past while the living artifacts of that past are still with us. Consider Lewis Jacobs' brilliant 1939 history of *The Rise of the American Film*, and consider how much greater it would have been had Jacobs interviewed all the pioneers of the film industry who were still around when he wrote his book.

I recently received a communication from a society "to promote the study of early cinema." I was told it had taken the society a year to find my address. I could not help but ponder how these people could ever track down a Muriel Ostriche when they could not even locate an address for someone who is listed in a number of volumes of *Who's Who*. Here is an organization which has been in existence for more than a year, and all it has accomplished is the printing of a four-page bulletin indicating the group's primary concern to be rules and regulations and the listing of the activities of its members. Nowhere was there any indication of what needed to be done and what, if anything, the group had accomplished. Yet again, restoration and research takes second place to methodology. We are, regretfully, in an age where the bureaucracy of film history is paramount, and documentation is little more than a sideline. It seems as if academic stature rather than creative research is what matters.

Q. David Bowers has accomplished something which few academics will ever accomplish. He has tracked down a pioneer actress of the silent era. He understood the detective work involved in such a search, and he knew what was involved. He has painstakingly documented Muriel Ostriche's life and career. He knew where to look and the research techniques involved in such documentation. He has the tenacity to get his work published. He understands the bias of many publishers against books devoted to silent cinema, and has the persuasive ability to talk a publisher into undertaking such a project. He has not sought grants from the likes of the National Endowment for the Humanities or the National Endowment for the Arts to enable him to study the feasibility of his project.

No! Q. David Bowers went out and he did it. I, for one, salute him for what he has accomplished. And I congratulate Muriel Ostriche for having such a dedicated and trustworthy biographer.

Thanhouser melodrama, circa 1914. (Courtesy of the American Museum of the Moving Image, Lawrence Williams Collection)

A Princess Film still, circa 1914, taken by Lawrence Williams, a Thanhouser staff photographer of the era. Muriel Ostriche (right) stands near her leading man, Boyd Marshall, and holds in her arm some file folders and two books by Bulwer Lytton. A descendant of Lawrence Williams donated a number of Thanhouser stills to the American Museum of the Moving Image, Astoria, Long Island, New York, where they remain today. (American Museum of the Moving Image, Lawrence Williams Collection)

Preface

I first became aware of Muriel Ostriche many years ago, in connection with searching for memorabilia pertaining to Moxie, the famous old-time soft drink. At the time I was engaged in research which eventually led to the publication of *The Moxie Encyclopedia*, a 760-page volume which told the reader all he wanted to know about this beverage, and probably much that he never dreamed of asking about. Muriel was the Moxie Girl, and from 1915 until about 1920 she was featured in Moxie advertising, with her image reproduced on china plates, hand-held cardboard fans, cloth jackets, baseball scorecards, posters, placards, and other items. By a stroke of luck I acquired the records and historial archives of the Moxie Company, including scrapbooks of advertisements and press clippings from the 1880s onward. In one particular volume were dozens of magazine and newspaper clippings about Muriel Ostriche—her films, her public appearances, and various aspects of her life.

Seeking to learn more about Muriel, I turned to historical files of film trade and fan magazines, including *Moving Picture World*, *Moving Picture News* (name later changed to *Motion Picture News*), *Motion Picture Story Magazine*, *Photoplay*, *Motion Picture Classic*, *Billboard*, *Variety*, *New York Dramatic Mirror*, *Exhibitors Herald*, *Motography*, and others. I learned that in 1913 Muriel Ostriche came in second (after Alice Joyce) among actresses in a nationwide popularity poll conducted by *Motion Picture Story Magazine*, capturing about twice as many votes as Mary Pickford. I learned that in 1913 Thanhouser, one of the most respected and successful film studios of the era, created a special division, Princess Films, to feature her in a series of weekly comedies. The more I delved into the subject, the more it became apparent that among actresses in the early teens Muriel Ostriche was in or near the front row of the motion picture industry.

In recent decades, the silent film era has occupied the attention of many film historians and biographers. Such famous personalities as Charles Chaplin, Mary Pickford, D.W. Griffith, and the Gish sisters have been the subjects of fine studies, and deservedly so. Indeed, one can fill an entire bookshelf with volumes on Chaplin alone. However, many other personalities from the pre-1915 era, a time which one writer has characterized as the archaeological period of American film history, have been overlooked, at least as subjects of detailed biographies. Such actors and actresses as Romaine Fielding (who was named as the most popular actor in the previously-cited 1913 popularity contest), G. M. Anderson (who starred in Western films and who was an owner of Essanay, one of the most prominent of the early companies), John Bunny (America's most popular comedian prior to the rise of Chaplin), Pearl White (the Pathé star of *The Perils of Pauline* serial episodes), Mary Miles Minter (who was one of the most heavily advertised stars of the teens), King Baggot (president and founder of the Screen Club and one of the top actors of the 1910-1915 span), Gene Gauntier (one of the most acclaimed actresses of the early period), Clara Kimball Young (a talented actress who suffered from poor business decisions and who was the subject of much wanted as well as unwanted publicity during the 1915-1920 years), several famous Florences (Lawrence, Turner, LaBadie), and others are largely forgotten today. Perhaps the present Muriel Ostriche biographical effort will inspire others to investigate this fascinating period of film history and to give other stars, major and minor, the recognition they deserve.

Happily, there are a number of scholars who do care about the obscure figures of the formative years of the motion picture in America and who, if they have not written separate biographical books, have devoted from a few paragraphs to a chapter or so on numerous personalities. Anthony Slide, for example, has produced several excellent books, with one of my favorites being *Aspects of American Film History Prior to 1920*. In this volume is to be found an entire chapter devoted to the Thanhouser Company, another to Ethel Grandin, and others to still further semiforgotten subjects and personalities. The magnificently illustrated works of Kevin Brownlow and John Kobal illumine many dark corners of early motion picture history. And, I cannot help but admire Edward Wagenknecht, whose life has embraced the field from the early years of the motion picture industry onward. He was there nearly at the beginning—and was corresponding with *Motion Picture Story Magazine* as early as 1912. By the 1920s, he was personally acquainted with the Gish sisters and other prominent personalities. Fortunately for all of us, he became a prolific historian and writer. His *The Movies in the Age of Innocence*, published in 1962, stands today as a classic in the field.

Still, it seems to me that there is much to be done. The more dusty issues I read of *Moving Picture World, Motion Picture News, Motion Picture Story Magazine*, and other early publications, the more I realize how vast the historical field of pre-1920 filmdom is and, in particular, how many revelations await the patient researcher studying the first two decades of the public exhibition of motion pictures in America, 1896-1916.

Imbued with the spirit of discovery, I decided to contribute a small stone to the foundation of early film history by writing the biography of Muriel Ostriche. The clippings kept by the Moxie Company revealed that she was born on March 24, 1896, and that her film career spanned the years from 1911 to 1921. The last clipping about her was dated 1925. By that time she had two daughters and was living in Great Neck, Long Island. What happened to her after that point I had not the faintest idea, nor did any film historians with whom I was in contact. Numerous advertisements were placed in general and specialized magazines and newspapers seeking further data. Fortune smiled, and early in 1986 one of Muriel's daughters, Gloria, contacted me—with the news that Muriel Ostriche was still living! I lost no time in contacting and eventually meeting Muriel, who was delighted to share her recollections of the years when she was one of the best-known actresses in America. A modest and kind woman, Muriel Ostriche attributes much of her success to being in the right place at the right time and to being associated with such fine studios as Eclair, Thanhouser, and World, not to overlook her initial hiring by the grand master of early directors, D.W. Griffith. The same modesty and lack of self-praise characterized Muriel during the height of her career, as numerous interviews reproduced in the following pages demonstrate. It is to Muriel's credit that she did not attempt to influence me in any way concerning the direction of the present book. Rather, she patiently answered questions, amplified obscure details, and helped in every way she could.

Had Muriel Ostriche's height of popularity occurred in the 1920s or 1930s, instead of the early teens, the present volume could contain critical reviews of her screen performances as interpreted by modern historians and critics. However, that option is not open. Virtually all of her films have disappeared. What we know of them today is gleaned primarily from trade reviews, advertisements, news articles, and photographic stills. Often, contemporary reviews were contradictory, sometimes so much so that it seems to a later reader that different reviewers must have been watching different films! On numerous occasions, *Moving Picture World* would praise one of her films, while *Motion Picture News, Variety*, or another periodical would find fault with it. The same is true, of course, of the reviews given to thousands of other films of the era. Thus, the biographer can, by selectively reprinting various items, craft a work to "prove" a particular point. Virtually any actor or actress of the period can be painted as either famous or forgettable, depending upon the intent of the writer. In the present instance, I have endeavored to use historical material evenly. Generally speaking, a reprinting of *all* of the press clippings and reviews I came across would portray Muriel Ostriche as being with scarcely a flaw. However, occasionally there were pejorative comments made by reviewers, and these have been included to balance the story.

Hired by D. W. Griffith for $5 per day, Muriel Ostriche first worked as an extra at the Biograph studios. After several studio changes she became a star with Eclair, then Thanhouser and World, with the height of her public acclaim coming during the 1913-1916 period. As you read about the career of Muriel Ostriche, it is my hope that you will experience a "you are there" feeling—that you will relive the spirit of the early era and will gain an insight into the life of a pretty, young actress and the studios and era of which she was a part.

This book includes the work of many writers. Rather than paraphrase or interpret early trade journal notices, I have quoted them, with occasional light editing (but with the meaning unchanged) and correction of typographical errors. In this way, the present-day reader can absorb the flavor of the times and events—just as readers of *Moving Picture World* and other journals did in the decade of Muriel's screen activity. My comments within quotations are set apart by brackets [ ]. In addition to material specifically pertaining to Muriel Ostriche, I have included numerous sidelights, incidents, and contemporary observations of the motion picture scene—to provide the setting and to relate the spirit of the era.

When Muriel entered the film industry in 1911, the "star system" had not yet been born, Mary Pickford and D. W. Griffith were virtually unknown to the American public, Lillian and Dorothy Gish had yet to cross the portals of Biograph, and Charles Chaplin was three years away from making his first film. The Trust companies were battling the Independents, and film companies of both sides considered it standard to turn out subjects, typically of one reel in length, at the rate of one every few days. Motion picture production was centered in New York City and the adjacent northern areas of New Jersey. Few people had heard of Hollywood, but virtually everyone knew of Fort Lee.

When Muriel left films in 1921, the industry was one of multi-million dollar deals, the one-reel film was an anachronism, certain players were earning over a million dollars a year, virtually all of the studios which had been prominent a decade earlier were out of business, Hollywood was known the world over, and Fort Lee was forgotten.

Here, then, is the story of Muriel Ostriche—the Moxie Girl—"the daredevil of the movies"—Thanhouser's little Princess—an actress who in her day brightened the lives of millions who saw her on the silver screen.

CHAPTER ONE

Beginning at Biograph

It was a warm day in the autumn of 1911. On New York City's Riverside Drive the trees had just begun to change color, and Muriel Ostriche, 15 years of age, was enjoying a walk not far from her home. A stranger approached her, introduced himself as Christy Cabanne, told her he was with the Biograph motion pictures studio, and said that she was attractive. "We are looking for pretty girls in the movies. Would you be interested?"

A conversation ensued, and Muriel, who had just entered the tenth grade, made plans to go downtown to Biograph at 11 East 14th Street. She was not a stranger to motion pictures at the time, for the Pickford family lived near her, and Jack Pickford especially was a close friend, often taking her for rides on the handlebars of his bicycle. His sister, Mary, worked at Biograph beginning several years earlier and was achieving a measure of acclaim for her acting abilities.

1911 was a busy time for the Biograph Company, and by November D.W. Griffith had directed or supervised the production of over 50 films since the beginning of the year. Later historians were to ascribe special merit to *The Lonedale Operator*, filmed in California by Biograph's traveling company in January, although at the time of release it was simply another in a long string of "two reel a week" Biograph issues, taking its place alongside such titles as *Madame Rex*, *Enoch Arden*, *The Jealous Husband*, *The Adventures of Billy*, and *The Miser's Heart*.

The American Mutoscope and Biograph Company, later familiarly known as Biograph, was founded in 1895. In 1896, Biograph films were exhibited for the first time to a paying public. By 1900, Biograph and its competitors, Edison, Vitagraph, and Lubin among them, enjoyed an active business supplying short motion picture subjects to vaudeville houses and lyceums for use as fillers between acts or other entertainment. By the year 1902, Biograph had over 2,500 films to its credit.

By 1907, Biograph films were considered to be "rotten," according to historian Terry Ramsaye, whose *A Million and One Nights*, published in 1925, chronicled the early motion picture industry. Biograph was in financial trouble, and Jeremiah J. Kennedy had been sent by a creditor, the Empire Trust Company, to study the situation and either to liquidate the company or breathe new life into it. Kennedy was set up as president, with Henry Marvin, an original 1895 Biograph partner, serving as general manager and vice president.

In 1908, David Wark Griffith, who used the assumed first name "Lawrence," an actor of uncertain fortunes, was hired by Biograph. His first screen appearance was earlier with Edison in the leading part in *Rescued From the Eagle's Nest*, which depicted Griffith as a mountaineer who climbed to a remote aerie, struggled with a fierce eagle, and rescued a hapless infant. Subsequently, Biograph offered him the chance to direct a film, mainly because he was at the right place at the right time, and no one else stepped forward to do it. His first directing challenge was *The Adventures of Dollie*, produced in June 1908. From then through early December 1909, Griffith was the only director at Biograph. Later, Griffith gradually attained a supervisory capacity, and when he left the company in the autumn of 1913, six directors were busy with various projects.

Under Griffith, Biograph films improved markedly, and by the time Muriel Ostriche was invited to visit the studio in 1911, his work was recognized throughout the industry, although the Biograph policy of not mentioning the names of those involved with films resulted in his name and those of Biograph players being unknown to the general public.

By the time Griffith left Biograph, he had earned the admiration of his peers and was respected in the industry. In 1915, his magnum opus, *The Birth of a Nation*, opened to audiences in large cities, with some theatres posting a two-dollar admission charge for the best seats during an era in which a nickel or a dime was standard. More so than any previous American-made film, *The Birth of a Nation*, which portrayed the spectacle of the North against the South in the Civil War and the complications of the Reconstruction era which followed, gripped the emotions of the public, caused controversy, and involved the audience in a detailed, lengthy film production.

In recent years, many film historians, particularly those writing for popular audiences, have focused on Griffith, to the virtual exclusion of other directors of the pre-1920 era. This is due to several reasons. First, Griffith's accomplishments in portraying an emotional story were considerable, especially against the backdrop of the unimaginative filming and editing of many of his peers. Second, Griffith recognized the value of publicity, and as soon as he left Biograph, the entire motion picture profession was made aware of his accomplishments, past and present. Editorially, the trade publications of the era largely agreed with what he said about himself.

The existence of the records of the Biograph Company, preserved at the Museum of Modern Art, New York City, has enabled historians to study in detail the background of the various films of the 1908-1913 Griffith era, a situation not possible with the products of Kalem, Vitagraph, Eclair, Thanhouser, and a host of other competitors. Similarly, the survival rate of Biograph films of the era is higher than that of its contemporaries, making it possible to analyze them today.

After assimilating information published about Griffith during recent decades, a reader might conclude that if one could travel back to 1911 when he hired Muriel Ostriche, his name would have been omnipresent. Also, one might conclude that just about every Griffith film exhibited dazzling virtuosity of technique and direction. Not so. In *Moving Picture World*, for example, Biograph was mentioned infrequently in comparison to its competitors. At a time when the Thanhouser Company, located in New Rochelle, New York, was the darling of the printed page—the movements of Thanhouserites, as they were called, were minutely detailed, and even social events were described—scarcely a word could be found about individual Biograph personnel or players, unless they had departed for greener fields and had included "formerly with Biograph" as part of their resume.

Some Biograph films were enthusiastically reviewed, some were described as being so-so, and still others were noted as screen failures. The editorial opinions expressed concerning Biograph films in general were neither more nor less laudatory than for certain of its competitors. Of course, trade paper reviews and commentary must be taken with large grains of salt. First, such periodicals could print only what they knew about, and if a rather obscure event was documented in a news release and sent to the editor of the *New York Dramatic Mirror*, *The Billboard*, or *Moving Picture World*, chances were good that it would be dutifully printed. Conversely, if no publicity release was sent out—as was usually the case with Biograph—nothing would be printed. So, what appeared in print in 1912, for example, depended on what was created by those desiring publicity. Furthermore, editors were careful to lay an even hand on everyone. Such topics as poor direction, financial mismanagement, and the human failings of players were not popular subjects for discussion in print, particularly since the success of the publications was predicated upon the advertising placed by the larger film producers and distributors.

Concerning Griffith's Biograph films themselves, one can view surviving prints and go long stretches without noticing anything out of the ordinary so far as exceptional film techniques are concerned, as Edward Wagenknecht has pointed out. This is not to dim the memory of Griffith, for he was respected by his peers at the time, and after he came to Biograph, the level of film quality was seen to improve greatly, as were the financial fortunes of the firm. Unquestionably, by 1915 he was the most acclaimed director in the land. However, it is not fair to divide movies, production techniques, and the quality of 1908-1915 era films into just two categories: Griffith and Biograph on one side marked "superb," and everyone else on the other side marked "also ran." In their day, the screen productions of Kalem, Thanhouser, Eclair, Solax, and many other studios were widely acclaimed and brought success not only to those who made them but to the exhibitors who screened them.

Accepting W. Christy Cabanne's invitation, Muriel Ostriche went to the Biograph studios at 11 East 14th Street, New York City, in October or early November 1911. Upon arrival, she was introduced to Griffith, who startled her by saying, "Those are quite some lamps!" Not knowing what he meant, she asked him, and he told her that she had very big eyes. Griffith asked her to take a screen test with Wilfred Lucas, one of Biograph's stock players. While Billy Bitzer turned the camera crank, young Muriel went through several parts. She was hired on the spot as an extra, at the going rate of $5 per day.

An account of the Biograph Studio is provided by Louis Reeves Harrison, in *Moving Picture World*, February 24, 1912:

"An air of mystery affects one upon entering the portals of the Biograph Studio, like that of an exclusive club or an old manse of Knickerbocker days. Once greeted by Mr. Daugherty, the atmosphere is warmed, but it is still fragrant with the spirit of other times. Mr. Daugherty is a gentleman of the old school, grave and dignified, yet the essence of genial courtesy. He is the friend-maker of the company, attracting all who come to know him well so that they feel an interest in the organization he has so long and faithfully represented at the point where it touches the outer world. It may readily be seen that I have a soft spot in my heart for this gentleman, although we have disagreed on many occasions."

The writer went on to say that he had recently seen a very unsatisfactory Biograph picture and was determined he could write a better scenario. He visited Daugherty at Biograph for some pointers, subsequently wrote a story and sent it in, and was rewarded by receiving $25. He noted that a number of Biograph comedies were anemic and that he could not believe that either Griffith or Daugherty was responsible for them. He considered earlier films to be better than current productions, and noted: "Biograph comedies were at one time delightful and, if those of today fail to provide diversion, I can only ascribe the lowering of their characteristics to extraneous influences."

The first Biograph production in November was *A Terrible Discovery*, filmed at the studio at 11 East 14th Street and in Fort Lee, New Jersey. On November 4th, production was completed, and attention was directed to the next effort, *A Tale of the Wilderness*, which was filmed by Billy Bitzer and which employed a stockade setup in Coytesville, New Jersey. Muriel Ostriche recalled that this was her very first film, and that her duties consisted of continually reloading a gun to aid in the defense of the fort against Indians on the warpath. Filming took place on the 8th, 13th, 14th, and 20th of the month, a particularly long time, considering that numerous contemporary productions took just a day or two.

Released on January 8, 1912, *A Tale of the Wilderness* was described by a Biograph publicity sheet:

A TALE OF THE WILDERNESS

In the Pioneer Days of Kentucky

IN THE WILDS of the Kentucky hills two brothers, the elder an outlaw, view from a distance the approach of a party of settlers moving forward to a new home in the vast wildness. The younger brother is overwhelmed by the sight of the pioneers, and, unknown to his elder brother, joins their party. The settlers build a stockade home and the outlook is most rosy, until the outlaw brother meets a girl from the stockade at the spring, he, of course, not knowing his brother is among the party. He forces his attentions upon her, which she repulses, rushing back to the stockade for help. The outlaw's influence with the neighboring Indians arouses them in his plan for vengeance. They attack the stockade, and when the settlers' chance seems hopeless they dig a tunnel from the back of the stockade to the hillside. Most of them have effected an escape, but among the few captured is the younger brother, so the outlaw regrets his action and uses again his influence with the Indians, but with a different effect.

 BIOGRAPH

Released Jan. 8, 1912

Muriel Ostriche's screen debut was made in *A Tale of the Wilderness*, a Biograph picture released on January 8, 1912. The stockade shown in the *Biograph Bulletin* page reproduced here was set up in Coytesville, New Jersey, a popular spot for motion picture production. (From the book, *Biograph Bulletins*, edited by Eileen Bowser)

"In the wilds of the Kentucky hills, two brothers, the elder an outlaw, view from a distance the approach of a party of settlers moving forward to a new home in the vast wilderness. The younger brother is overwhelmed by the sight of the pioneers and, unknown to his elder brother, joins their party. The settlers build a stockade home, and the outlook is most rosy, until the outlaw brother meets a girl from the stockade at the spring, he, of course, not knowing his brother is among the party. He forces his attentions upon her, which she repulses, rushing back to the stockade for help. The outlaw's influence with the neighboring Indians arouses them in his plan for vengeance. They attack the stockade, and when the settlers' chance seems hopeless they dig a tunnel from the back of the stockade to the hillside. Most of them have effected an escape, but among the few captured is the younger brother, so the outlaw regrets his action and uses again his influence with the Indians, but with a different effect."

In keeping with Biograph policy at the time, the names of the players were not featured in advertising or other publicity. Indeed, the anonymity demanded by Biograph was a standing joke in the field, with *Moving Picture World* noting in its inquiries column that questions concerning Biograph players could not be answered, ruefully lamenting that the British distributor of Biograph films was more generous with information, and much of what was known on the American side of the Atlantic had come to the press by way of England! The British distributor of Biograph was quite clever and invented names for the players. Thus, Blanche Sweet became Daphne Wayne to British viewers, and Mabel Normand was known as Muriel Fortescue! Later, Biograph mellowed its stand, and when *A Tale of the Wilderness* was reissued in October 1916, the cast was made public, and it was revealed that Dorothy Bernard was featured as a young woman, Charles Hill Mailes as the outlaw, Edwin August as the outlaw's younger brother, William J. Butler as the leader of the pioneers, and Dark Cloud as the Indian chief.

Nowhere mentioned was Muriel Ostriche, an extra along with a swarm of other actors and actresses. A Biograph advertisement showed a stockade made of vertical logs of an uneven length, cross-braced, enclosing a settlement. The same stockade was used the following month for *Billy's Stratagem*, featuring other players.

Moving Picture World, which regularly published reviews as a guide to exhibitors, covered *A Tale of the Wilderness*:

"The chief interest in this picture is in the elemental struggle, the growing danger of the band of immigrants, driving into a country which, as we see it, swarms of Indians, and their final escape from the savages when attacked in overwhelming numbers. The dramatic thread, telling of the relationship of two backwoodsmen, brothers, with each other, and, later of the one with the caravan and of the other, a renegade, with the Indians, affect us deeply. There are too many 'Indians by courtesy.' Large crowds of them are kept in view and, while there are extremely well-pictured incidents, there are also places where the illusion wears very thin. The background is a thin wood, leafless as in late autumn. The photographs are good. The picture falls short of being a good feature, but will serve well as a program filler."

In the same issue, a reviewer was considerably kinder to a competing Edison film, *Please Remit*, a review of which immediately followed the Biograph summary. The Edison production was noted as, "A very welcome comedy . . . [with] the characters clearly set forth by good players. . . . The audience plainly liked the picture. . . . No bill can be a poor one that includes it."

Other films of the day, such as *The Course of True Love* (Vitagraph), *An Old Excuse That Worked* (Lubin), *The Tramp and the Bear*, *The Evils of Impure Literature*, and even an educational film titled *Codfish Industry*, fared better in the hands of reviewers. Apparently *A Tale of the Wilderness* did little to advance either the reputation of Griffith or Biograph. However, as the launching platform for Muriel Ostriche's career, it is memorable as a footnote in film history.

Muriel Henrietta Oestrich was born on March 24, 1896, the only child of Miriam and Abram Oestrich. By 1911, Muriel was just over five feet tall, had gray eyes, and light golden brown hair. After entering the movies, Muriel toyed with her name and took the "e" from its place as the second letter and put it at the end, thus creating "Ostriche." The surname was a difficult one for typographers to assimilate, and many were the misspellings she received in print, most common being dropping the "e" altogether. She liked the name Elsie, and another idea, never adopted, was to style herself as Elsie Murad, the "Mur" coming from Muriel. Murad was the name of a popular cigarette of the time.

Her father was a salesman for boys' and children's clothing. He reported to an office and worked on the road. Born on Christmas day, in Lockport, New York, he was 50 years old when he died of diabetes in 1920.

Muriel's paternal grandfather, who came to America from Germany as a young boy, was a cotton farmer in the South during the Civil War. When the Yankees came he burned his crops. In the conflict, he suffered from shell shock, and after the war he traveled with his wife around the country in search of a cure. Muriel's mother, the former Miriam Rose, was from Pine Bluff, Arkansas. Miriam and Abram met in New York City when her brother brought Abram home from a social club meeting. The attraction was immediate, and he visited frequently.

At the time Muriel was born, her parents were living in New York City on 113th Street, in fancy premises, complete with crystal chandeliers and velvet trappings left over from an earlier use as a gambling parlor. Her education included attendance at Public School 186 and Wadleigh High School. "Then I quit, once I began working steadily in the movies," Muriel recalled. "I guess I was a dropout, as they call it nowadays." Her father disapproved of her acting interests, but her mother was enthusiastic. Often she accompanied Muriel to the studio or to filming on location.

Prior to her memorable encounter with W. Christy Cabanne, Muriel had acted in several school plays, including one in which she received local acclaim by portraying the part of a French doll. Echoing a line in the play, neighbors who had seen it would greet Muriel on the street with, "I am the French dollie," in their best French accent. Muriel had an outgoing personality, vibrant, and with an infectious enthusiasm. She had many friends and was well liked by her school chums.

Following her bit part in *A Tale of the Wilderness*, Muriel acted in at least two other Biograph productions, in one of which she played the part of a young lady. She later recalled a scene with Priscilla Dean and a young man at her side, walking down a road. Policemen mounted on horses came into view, and the pedestrians had to step aside.

Another part was played in *A Blot in the 'Scutcheon*, filmed in New York City in October 1912. She and Priscilla Dean each played pages in the dramatization of the 17th-century setting portrayed in a poem by Robert Browning. Released on January 29, 1912, the script was by Linda Arvidson Griffith, the soon-to-be-separated wife of the director, a recognized actress in her own right. When Biograph reissued the film in September 1916, the players, earlier not acknowledged, were identified as Charles Hill Mailes, Dorothy Bernard, Edwin August, Claire McDowell, William J. Butler, Charles H. West, Edna Foster, Edward Dillon, Harry Hyde, W. Christy Cabanne, Joseph Graybill, and J. Jiquel Lanoe. Muriel Ostriche, Priscilla Dean, and other bit players were not mentioned.

The earlier condemnation of *A Tale of the Wilderness* by *Moving Picture World* was in contrast to an enthusiastic review of *A Blot in the 'Scutcheon* by the same publication:

"An excellent two-reel picture of a very interesting poem. Browning's scenario stands out clearly, as shown, and the story is intensely dramatic. The play has been produced several times, but has never been very popular. Perhaps it is due to Browning's peculiar style, for the picture has the elements of popularity in a marked degree. The Biograph producer has also made a scholarly production in it and deserves high commendation. Not only did the three principals act in it with much intelligence and suggestiveness, but the choice of the scenes, their management, and their choice of backgrounds and settings are very satisfactory.

"The story is well known. . . . Browning's philosophy is a little hard, puritanical, and the story is apt to leave a slightly unpleasant taste in thoughtful spectators. But the story is very famous and the situation is poignantly intense. It is the week's greatest feature picture. It should be advertised among schools and teachers and people of culture. It is just the picture to win new recruits to the photoplay patrons. No exhibitors should regret having put it on; it ought to be a business getter."

The *New York Dramatic Mirror* reviewed the film in its January 31, 1912 issue:

"Since year one of motion picture uplift, Biograph has been a synonym of the word 'masterpiece,' and the film subject illustrated on this page and just released sustains, even adds to, this eminent reputation. Picture lovers who recall such exceptional productions as *Pippa Passes, The Three Fishers, Romola*, and others will find *A Blot in the 'Scutcheon* equal, if not greater, art than in previous Biograph efforts along the line of higher endeavor. They will also find what was lacking in some of the earlier art efforts—a most absorbing, intense, and sustained dramatic interest. The story as produced in this film, without losing any of the poetic and artistic tone, becomes actually thrilling—almost sensationally so. To this end the plot of the Browning poem lends itself remarkably well. When Thorold, Earl Tresham, sets out to kill the visitor to his sister, thus meaning to wipe out the stain of the family name, and not knowing that the clandestine caller is in reality his sister's fiance, the others of the household seek to follow and prevent the impending tragedy. It is here that the deft hand of the director has brought in the element of suspense, which he knows so well how to manipulate. And it seems not inartistic."

The reputation of *A Blot in the 'Scutcheon* has not survived the test of time, and today it is not considered to be among Griffith's more notable works. Indeed, in his book, *D. W. Griffith—An American Life*, biographer Richard Schickel mentioned it only in passing, as "more pretentious than satisfying."

Muriel Ostriche's work at Biograph received favorable comments from her mentor, W. Christy Cabanne, and from director D. W. Griffith. She would have stayed with the company, except that the Biograph production crew departed on its annual trip to California after the Christmas holidays. Muriel, not quite 16 years old, was too young to join the 50 regular players who headed westward to Los Angeles, where they subsequently spent the winter and spring, returning to the East toward the end of May. Muriel remained behind and continued her studies at Wadleigh High. Among her classmates was Miriam Cooper, who later became famous as an actress and married director Raoul Walsh. As the first days of the year 1912 approached, Muriel had yet to be flashed on the silver screen. Her three Biograph films were still being prepared for release.

By 1912, the year that theatregoers first viewed Muriel Ostriche's films, motion picture manufacturers in the United States were divided into two camps: those who distributed through the Motion Picture Patents Company, commonly referred to as the "Trust," and those who released their films through the Motion Picture Sales Company, the latter consisting of a loosely knit group of producers known as the Independents, led by Carl Laemmle. In the first camp were Biograph, Kalem, Lubin, Pathé, Selig, Vitagraph, Essanay, Edison, Cines, Urban-Eclipse, and Méliès.

The Trust companies had banded together earlier in order to share patents among themselves, and at the same time to exclude newcomers from the field. Edison, Selig, and other Trust members were deadly serious about the matter, and violators who dared to use a camera made with Trust-patented mechanisms were in danger of being roughed up by thugs or even shot by hired gunmen.

Distributing through the Motion Picture Sales Company were American, Champion, IMP (Carl Laemmle's Independent Moving Pictures Company), Nestor, Eclair, Itala, Majestic, Powers, Thanhouser, Ambrosio, Reliance, Solax, Rex, Bison, Lux, Great Northern, and Republic, with various members dropping out or being added from time to time. The Independents had to be ingenious, and often their filming was conducted in secret at unannounced locations, to escape spies for the Trust, who were ever on the lookout for misuse of cameras employing Trust-owned patents. The members of the Trust, the old guard in the film industry, rested on their laurels and were considerably less aggressive promoters than the Independents. Advertising in *Motion Picture World*, the leading trade paper of the time, strongly emphasized this point.

In January 1912, the Thanhouser Company, located in New Rochelle, New York, a town later memorialized in a musical stage show as being "45 minutes from Broadway," was releasing two films a week. Exhibitors were advised that forthcoming offerings included *Dr. Jekyll and Mr. Hyde, A Niagara Honeymoon, East*

Lynne, and *As it Was in the Beginning*. Founded by Edwin Thanhouser, the firm bearing his name devoted much of its efforts to reproducing classic melodramas and the stories of well-known novels, including much drawn from English literature. The company was widely admired and was considered a model of ethical conduct.

Not to be outdone, Essanay, a firm whose name was derived from the initials of its founders, Spoor and Anderson (S & A), proclaimed it was releasing four features a week. *For the Love of Mike* was billed as "a howling good comedy which will have your audience in hysterics," while *The Valley of Regrets* was stated to be "a drama as poignant and pathetic as the world-famous *East Lynne*," whereas *The Mail Order Wife* and *A Child of the West* were given other positive attributes.

The Eclair Film Company of America, a French firm with its studio and factory in Fort Lee, New Jersey, and with "branches everywhere," took out a double-page spread in the January 6th issue of *Moving Picture World* to proclaim several releases for the month, noting that a new series of comedies "makes possible a well-balanced program for the seventh day of the week and affords a clean and wholesome subject suited for Sunday audiences" and was to be inaugurated with the release on January 14th of *Jealous Julia*, with Gussie Hunt, late of the Vitagraph Company, in the leading role. Nestor Films, under the ownership of David Horsley, of Bayonne, New Jersey, offered three films a week, while the Solax Company, which did business from Congress Avenue, Flushing, New York, offered three films, including *Mignon*, billed as a "photoplay," a term which at the time was reserved for a serious dramatic performance, but which later became a generic name for any kind of action on the screen.

Vitagraph, one of the pioneer firms in the film industry, offered five pictures a week, featuring such titles in early January 1912 as *Romance of Wall Street*, *The Heart of the King's Jester*, *Destiny is Changeless*, and *The Course of True Love*. Vitagraph's main facilities were in Brooklyn, with branch offices in Manhattan, Chicago, Paris, and London.

At the same time, a news article related that two labor unions in Dallas, Texas passed resolutions requesting that the city fathers allow films to be exhibited on Sunday. In 1912, there was a sizeable faction of the American public against films of all kinds, and numerous articles in the public press told of their danger to citizens in general and children in particular. As a compromise to such sentiments, Sundays were kept free of film exhibition in many cities.

The *Chicago Daily News* told of a school teacher in that city who appreciated films. Her testimony was particularly welcomed by the movie industry, for Chicago was home to many who condemned the public showing of motion pictures. Many citizens proposed closing theatres down entirely. Picture show owners in the Windy City must have enjoyed reading the following:

"Imagination is being kindled in the Chicago child, and good books are for that reason more appreciated, according to one Chicago public school teacher. Motion pictures are given the credit. It seems a far cry from the 'nickelodeon' to the dramas and Shakespeare, according to this pedagogue, but the two go hand in hand, the one cultivating a taste for the other. 'When I first started English,' said she, 'I found it almost impossible to interest my pupils in books that really are worthwhile. For a long time I thought it was ignorance on their part, but I soon found that many of the pupils who did not seem to care for books were in reality a great deal brighter than I had ever been, were quick to learn, and had more retentive memories than I.

" 'Then I evolved a theory which I still hold—that only persons with good imaginations enjoy reading books. I talked to many of my pupils who did not enjoy reading, and in practically every case I found the difficulty the same—they regarded a book merely as so many pages; there was no 'human interest,' as the phrase is. . . .

" 'When the moving picture show came into popularity, however, it was interesting to note the change. As I remember, we had been studying Shakespeare's *Macbeth* and, as usual, the classes were making a dreary grind of the work. Then one morning my first class surprised me by manifesting a real interest in the play. My astonishment increased as each succeeding class manifested ever growing interest. Finally I asked one of the pupils what had caused his sudden interest, and I was informed that the Shakespearean drama was the subject of one of the reels at a nearby moving picture house the preceding night, and the majority of my pupils had taken advantage of the opportunity to get acquainted with the play. After that I was a motion picture convert.' "

The nickelodeon theatre, with its five-cent admission charge, was in its heyday, although evening performances sometimes cost a dime, and in larger cities admissions of ten cents to twenty-five cents were not unusual.

In the January 13, 1912 issue of *Moving Picture World* a correspondent told of a trip through the South: "Two reels form the usual show of a five-cent house in the cities, while a three-reel performance with a singer and good music is ten cents. A departure from this was found in Atlanta at the Vaudette, where a most extravagant program is presented for a nickel. It includes three photoplays, a singer or two, and a small orchestra.

"In Nacogdoches, Texas, a two-reel show costs five cents for children and ten cents for adults, and whenever an extra reel is offered the prices are raised to ten cents and fifteen cents. . . . The Lyric, the only moving picture in the town, has been instructing and amusing the people of Nacogdoches and vicinity for the past few years. Its genial manager finds it lucrative, and the motley attendance is orderly. While not much to boast upon in decorations, as we know such theatres in the East, the Lyric serves its purpose."

On balance, his trip through the South was satisfactory, and he concluded on a high note: "On every side I heard a good word for the motion picture industry—its educational, amusement and social values were considered an aid in uniting and uplifting humanity. College professors and those engaged in high literary pursuits, businessmen and factory workers, parents and children all spoke well of this enterprise which has now become a significant factor in the world's progress. The commercial side is encouraging, and consequently new managers are entering the field, with the result that very soon every little town will have its motion picture theatre."

Those reading trade papers in 1912 had many occasions for comic relief—such as with this notice in *Moving Picture World*:

"Brockton, Massachusetts exhibitors are handing out a very unusual story. During the Brockton Fair, the Edison Company took pictures of the best scenes. These pictures were exhibited at the Commercial Club of Brockton. It seems that a gentleman by the name of William Green was snapped by the Edison photographer. Said Mr. Green was sauntering down the midway. But the lady at his side was not Mrs. Green. Messrs. McCue and Cahill, the picture magnates of Brockton, decided to exhibit the reel in their house, and everyone came in to see Mr. Green and his mysterious companion. Mrs. Green came in—and the trouble began. At present every indication points to a divorce. Messrs. McCue and Cahill report the biggest week's business on record during the exhibition of the pictures, as the Green family is very well known in Brockton."

Later, the same magazine advised its readers of a problem:

"Bubbling over with indignation, a teacher in a deaf mutes' school in Louisville, Kentucky, left a moving picture theatre, charging that the characters were saying unspeakable things. This is the first instance of lip reading in Louisville. The reports from other cities have indicated that deaf mutes there also have objected to the lines spoken by characters in motion plays. It is evident that producers will have to do a little reforming before the animated pictures will prove popular in audiences composed of deaf mutes."

In the meantime *The Motion Picture Story Magazine*, the brainchild of J. Stuart Blackton, one of the guiding lights of the Vitagraph Company, was building an ever-widening readership by featuring detailed stories based upon movie plots and furnishing readers with lighthearted answers to their questions concerning pictures, the private lives and loves of the players, and various events, all presented in a highly readable manner.

Early in 1912, Muriel Ostriche went to the Powers Company, an independent producer. She later recalled that she was with Powers for but a brief time, and probably acted as an extra in just a single film. In its issue of February 17, 1912, the *New York Clipper* described the firm and its founder:

"P. A. Powers has been in the moving picture business since its very inception as a commercial proposition. His experience as an exchange man dates back about six years, and three years ago he became a manufacturer. You might say that his severe loss by fire last June has merely served to strengthen his determination, and that determination is represented today in his new duplex studio at 511 West 42nd Street, New York.

"This is one of the most modern of studios, embracing two stages with a novel scheme for shifting lighting apparatus so that while the director is working on one stage, his next set is being put up on the other. He has the distinction of having featured one of the most expensive Broadway stars in a moving picture, namely, Nat M. Wills, and now that his facilities are so highly perfected, he promises more to the trade. His film company is known as the Powers Motion Picture Company."

Pat A. Powers, who entered film production in October 1909, first set up shop in California, but soon he went to the center of action in New York and established a studio at Mount Vernon, north of New York City. Powers Picture Plays was the signature on his film posters. Subsequently, his company became affiliated with Universal.

Later, Powers became embroiled in a fight with Carl Laemmle over the control of the Universal Film Manufacturing Company, one of the world's leading producers of motion pictures. A number of important film distributors were dissatisfied with the way the Universal program was being released and the prices charged, and they met in secret to name Powers, a vice president of Universal, to represent them. In a melodrama worthy of being filmed, William Swanson and several of his associates, who allied with the Powers faction, "threw some of the books and corporate seal of the big film corporation out of the window Monday afternoon, June 16th, while a stockholders' meeting was in progress at 1600 Broadway in New York," according to an account in *The New York Clipper*. "It seems that the Pat Powers and Carl Laemmle conflict for the control of Universal reached a critical stage by the attempted expulsion of Mr. Swanson from the office of secretary by the Laemmle faction. All of the belligerents were discharged in a police court episode, which left matters practically as unsettled as they had been all along." Powers left Universal and became involved in other film matters, including Warner's Features, Inc., although the Powers Picture Plays designation continued to be used for a small segment of Universal's production.

Around the time of her short stint with Powers early in 1912, Muriel Ostriche's good friend, Jack Pickford, brother of Mary and Lottie, suggested that she go to Pathé Frères, in Brooklyn. Like Eclair, Pathé was an American branch of a French-based firm. Pathé, a pioneer in the French film industry, was also a leading manufacturer of phonographs and other items. In addition to studio facilities in Brooklyn and offices in Jersey City, a manufacturing plant was established in Bound Brook, New Jersey. In February 1912, leading members of the Pathé Freres stock company included Martha Spier, Red Wing, Billy Quirk, and Pearl White. *Pathé's Weekly*, a newsreel, was distributed to many theatres at the time and was designated by one writer as an "illustrated newspaper."

Muriel was directed to go to Brooklyn, where Pearl White was scheduled to star in a feature with Crane Wilbur. "One day Pearl White didn't show up, so I took her part," she remembered. Later, Pearl White returned, but by that time the film had been completed. "I was there for just a few weeks." Once again she was paid $5 per day for her efforts.

Pearl White, born in Missouri, began her career by acting on the stage, reciting Hamlet's soliloquy and, in particular, playing the part of Little Eva in *Uncle Tom's Cabin*. Signing with Pathé, she was featured in numerous "wild West" episodes, in which she demonstrated her riding ability. Her later *Perils of Pauline* serial adventures became famous and were followed by the highly successful *Exploits of Elaine* episodes. She remained with Pathé for many years, in contrast with many actors and actresses of the era who frequently switched studio affiliations.

Crane Wilbur, born in Athens, New York, in 1889, was a nephew of the noted stage actor Tyrone Power (who was the father of the 20th Century Fox star). He began his stage career at the age of 15. One day, while going to visit a friend in Fort Lee, New Jersey, who was recuperating from an illness, he witnessed a scene being photographed for a film. An actress was on a runaway horse, and the hero was supposed to save her, but the rescue failed, the damsel was in true distress, and Crane Wilbur, a bystander, grabbed the reins, subdued the beast, and lifted the fainting young lady from the saddle—thus inadvertently getting his first screen job. He subsequently appeared with Pearl White in *The Perils of Pauline*, but he noted in an interview that his favorite picture was *The Corsair*.

CHAPTER TWO

The Eclair Experience

While Muriel was with Pathé, a casting director from the Eclair Film Company saw her and asked for her name, address, and telephone number. Muriel Ostriche remembered:

"He called me up and asked me to meet him at the Fort Lee ferry. I did this, then I took the boat across the Hudson, and I was in a picture. They offered me $20 a week. I expected I would have a small part in my first picture, which was about a cooking school. We all had to wear cooks' hats and aprons. For some reason, the director sorted me out and paid particular attention to me. I guess I was good looking in those days. The director was Etienne Arnaud, a Frenchman who couldn't speak a word of English, so we had to use an interpreter. When the film came out, I realized I was the star of it, something no one told me at the time! I thought I was just an extra, not the lead. For the picture, my mother dressed me in a nice hat with a beautiful coat to match it. I remember the film very well.

"I must have pleased Etienne Arnaud, for he set me up as a star in the next film, which was the first in the Kid, Kit, and Kittie series. Later, when the war broke out in Europe, Mr. Arnaud was drafted. He returned to France with his wife and child. He was captured in action and was held as a prisoner of war by the Germans. After the war, he came back to the United States, and I remember seeing him at an exhibitors' ball. The group we were with all sang *Oh, You Beautiful Doll*, one of the most popular songs at the time. Etienne Arnaud once told me I had a face like an angel but eyes like a devil."

An article in *Moving Picture World* described the studio: "THE AMERICAN ECLAIR: The new American home of the Eclair pictures at Fort Lee, New Jersey is an education in itself to anyone fortunate enough to be allowed to visit it. It would hardly seem possible to visit a manufactory for moving picture films more thorough than this one. . . . The factory in itself is a model of its kind, the work of a French architect thoroughly schooled in cinematography; it is perfect in its adaptability for the production of the high-class work for which this company stands. The personnel of this American branch is most notable; while it would be difficult and perhaps unwise to give priority to any country or person, it is enough to say that every department is headed by 'a master in his line.' Wherein the French excel, there is a most capable Frenchman, and wherein the American may excel, there is to be found a native; as to the manner born, both noticeably working together in splendid harmony for their common good. Photographic art and chemical science are there found at their best. A detailed description of either department would show each to be a school of its kind.

"In the studio, artists of the first order are blending their abilities in preparing the scenes which shall amuse and edify thousands of people. It is pleasing to record that the Eclair management appreciates the importance of responsibility of their art and are determined to give the world only the best. This means that the educational picture is not going to be relegated to a minor place, but that it is going to have a leading position in Eclair productions.

"If the common test of character, 'from what sort of a home do you come?' is to be applied to the Eclair, it can certainly respond with credit; recreant, indeed will be any poor creature coming from such a source. Perfection in the higher realm of cinematography is certain. The only possible weakness is the usually uncertain human element which is to be found everywhere. The well-balanced, capable, courteous, and cultured staff of the American Eclair should be a guarantee of the strong, clean, moral, and educational qualities that affect your production."

At the same time, the writer of this laudatory description was undoubtedly hoping that Eclair would continue to use *The Moving Picture World* as a forum for its advertising, which, it developed, Eclair did.

The first film Muriel made for Eclair, about the cooking school, was titled *White Aprons* and was released on April 4, 1912. Written by Katherine G. Maher, the feature had a special attraction: "Pretty girls predominate in this film, and they are beautifully pictured," according to a press statement.

In March 1912, the time when Muriel joined the Eclair Film Company, *Moving Picture World* carried this notice: "You may have an ability and know all about acting, but you stand a slim chance of an engagement with Eclair directors if you don't wear

The cover of the 14th issue of *The Eclair Bulletin* featured Muriel Ostriche. At the time, the Eclair Film Company boasted of its lineup of "stunning" girls. (New York Public Library)

a pretty face. Out in Fort Lee, where the big Eclair establishment is located, they believe in beautiful girls and handsome men as magnets to attract the public. Girls with dimples are given first choice at all times. Of course, all applicants must possess acting ability along with beauty and form.

"Eclair boasts of nine 'stunners' and stands ready to wager a good dinner for the entire party if any other firm can produce an equal number of prettier girls. What any one of the nine contestants would do to the judges in the event of a decision could be imagined. Just the same, Eclair dotes on pretty girls, from the management down to the office help."

The Eclair Bulletin, published for distribution to exhibitors and film exchanges, described *White Aprons* as follows: "A domestic science school boasts of its pretty teacher and prettier pupils. Ralph Brown, the superintendent, falls victim to the charms of Miss Beth, the teacher. Ralph becomes a dyspeptic from eating delicacies made at the school, and his doctor prescribes a change of diet. Still the products of the school pour in, and the distracted superintendent decides to quietly bury them in the backyard. Miss Beth unfortunately uses the same plot of ground to promote the growth of celery plants, and when she and her class go to inspect them, finds on digging up the celery, a stack of the school's best mince pies adhering to the roots.

"Then the fun begins, and Ralph's troubles with it. The doctor's prescription is called in to save him from the ire of the pupils and tearful Miss Beth, who finally accepts the inevitable and Ralph."

The enthusiasm of the copy writer for *The Eclair Bulletin* had no counterpart in the opinion of the film given by the reviewer for the *New York Dramatic Mirror*: "One has the feeling that this film must have been written and edited by a schoolgirl and presented under the auspices of the school's dramatic club, for it shows very little mature thought in any respect."

Moving Picture World was a bit kinder: "The farce is not without pleasing quality, but it is very slight, and has no sharply indicated point. It will pass as a filler, or as a lightener to a program." A reviewer in *The Billboard* said about the same thing.

Muriel's second film produced by Eclair, but the first to be released (on April 2, 1912), *The Letter With the Black Seals*, was billed as Series I in the "Kid, Kit and Kittie" series by Etienne Arnaud, who devised the story and directed the action.

"When Uncle Bill passed away in a little cabin out west, all his old comrades and friends mourned his death, especially his little pal, Kid, whom he loved as his own child," noted an Eclair publicity release. "Before he died, the old man entrusted to Kid the delivery of his will to his niece, Kittie, in New York. This will disinherits an ungrateful nephew and leaves the old man's wealth to the girl.

"The nephew, learning of his ill fortune, tries to marry Kittie, and when she refuses, carries her off to the rendezvous of the Silk Mask Band, where she is finally traced by Kid and his pal Kit, who have reached New York with the will. By a clever ruse, the boy hero places a decoy and rescues Kittie, the Silk Mask Band escaping in an auto, which, owing to a disengaged brake, plunges into the Hudson River, after a wild dash down the Palisades."

Moving Picture World reviewed *The Letter With the Black Seals* as "an exciting drama full of life and action." The same publication a week later related that the film "will be found entertaining," and that "it presents a number of interesting situations." *Moving Picture World*, issue of April 27, 1912, stated in response to an inquiry that John Troyano, George Larkin, and Muriel Ostriche had the leads in *The Letter With the Black Seals*. With few exceptions, trade reviews of the period did not mention actors or actresses, and identification of them was often a matter of chance, to be learned in a questions and answers column, or to be noted when mentioned in passing in a separate biographical sketch. In 1912, before the "star system" was in effect, advertisements for most films were likely to mention the nature of the production, such as "drama" or "comedy," but it was felt that the names of the participants were not important. Within a year, the situation changed dramatically.

On the heels of Muriel Ostriche's first two Eclair film vehicles came a highly acclaimed production, *Oh, You Ragtime!* Created and directed by Etienne Arnaud, the picture was released on April 18, 1912. *Moving Picture News* gave a synopsis:

"Signor Olivero [played by Guy Oliver], a famous Italian pianist, is moving into his new apartment, when he discovers a copy of *Alexander's Ragtime Band*, which he immediately tries upon his piano as soon as the husky van-men push it into the room. The lilting ragtime melody is so pleasing to the professor that he becomes too engrossed to observe the antics of the workmen—who begin to swing to and fro with the rhythm of the song. They swing the articles of furniture as though they were dancing partners, and finally the men pair off, and puffing away at their cob pipes, they arouse the ire of the pianist, who orders them out of the room in high dudgeon.

"The musician's fingers stray back to the keys, and the melody descends to a milliner's [played by Mathilde Baring] establishment directly beneath. There the pretty assistants begin to decorate the hats in ragtime, until they pair off and dance up the stairs to the musician's room. The magic strains filter then to the office below, where a dignified banker [Alec B. Francis], his secretary and his stenographer [Muriel Ostriche] are all enthralled, while a jolly darky porter is captured in the same way at the telephone in the hall. The cook [Julia Stuart] in the kitchen and the grocer's little boy both drop dishes and vegetables to scramble upstairs to join the other tenants, who are all dancing about the enrapt pianist, under a hypnotic spell from the music. The furniture movers and a messenger boy perform mighty feats of daring to get to the pianist's room from the pavement below.

"At the end of an hour the dancers are exhausted, and yielding to weakness, sink to the floor in a stupor. The pianist finally notices the catastrophe he has caused. In alarm he rushes down the street and appeals for help to a policeman. The officer, after checking over the trouble, advises him, 'Since the ragtime has knocked out the dancers, surely a galop will revive them.' The pianist returns to try this, and as he plays at lightning speed, the people all revive and dash away on their own business at breakneck speed. Their capers as the powerful strains drive them to frenzied work show the funniest part of the whole incident at the climax."

RELEASED TUESDAY, APRIL 2, 1912

ECLAIR DRAMA
"KID, KIT, AND KITTIE"
Series I: THE
LETTER WITH THE BLACK SEALS
BY ETIENNE ARNAUD

✠ ✠

When Uncle Bill passed away in the little cabin out west, all his old comrades and friends mourned his death, especially his little pal, "Kid," whom he loved as his own child. Before he died, the old man entrusted to "Kid" the delivery of his will to his niece, "Kittie" in New York.

This will disinherits an ungrateful nephew and leaves the old man's wealth to the girl.

The nephew, learning of his ill fortune tries to marry Kittie and when she refuses, carries her off to the rendevous of the "Silk Mask Band" where she is finally traced by "Kid" and his pal "Kit" who have reached New York with the will. By a clever ruse, the boy hero places a decoy and rescues Kittie, the Silk Mask band escaping in an auto, which, owing to a disengaged brake, plunges into the Hudson river, after a wild dash down the Palisades.

Cast In Part:

"Kid," the Boy Hero	JOHNY TROYANO
Kittie	MURIEL OSTRICHE
Uncle Bill	ALEX FRANCIS
The Nephew	JOHN ADOLFI
Kittie's Mother	JULIA STUART

Silk Mask Band and others

The first Eclair film released featuring Muriel Ostriche in the cast was *The Letter With the Black Seals,* conceived and produced by French director Etienne Arnaud, who could not speak a word of English and relayed his instructions through an interpreter. Muriel Ostriche played the part of Kittie in the first episode in the "Kid, Kit, and Kittie" drama series. (*The Eclair Bulletin*)

Another article in *Moving Picture World* noted: "This is the story of a great musician who tries out a popular ragtime classic with such telling effect that he nearly puts the entire neighborhood out of commission. Businessmen, laborers, pretty girls, domestics, tradesmen fall victims to the magic power of the melody with a droll effect which will almost take your audiences off their feet!" *The Billboard* advised readers that "the terrible result of the music's intoxicating strains, and comical lure will make this picture a great laugh."

At the time, the leading actress at Eclair was Dorothy Gibson, whom Muriel numbered among her friends at the studio. As fate would have it, Miss Gibson was aboard the *Titanic* that fateful night in April 1912 when it struck an iceberg on its maiden run from England to the United States. *Moving Picture World*, issue of April 27, 1912, printed her account:

"I was seated on one of the upper decks with several others playing bridge whist. The steward had come to us time after time telling us that it was past time for the lights to go out, but we had begged insistently to be allowed to play just one more rubber. At twenty minutes of twelve I was just at the foot of one of the magnificent staircases on my way to my stateroom, when I heard that peculiar crunching sound which proved later to be the iceberg ripping open the side of the ship. My companion and I merely noted the occurrence in a passing manner, supposing that perhaps a propeller had broken, or something of that sort, for we knew that there were icebergs around us. In fact, it was impossible not to know, for they were all about. And so we continued on our way, the gentleman who was with me suggesting a certain course around the deck which would bring me closest to my stateroom.

"As we turned to come toward the stern of the ship, we found ourselves, to our great surprise, walking uphill. We both remarked that it did not look right to us, we felt that something must be wrong. Inside we found the steward, who assured us that nothing was the matter. 'Why,' said he in most confident tones, 'you couldn't sink this ship if you wanted to—and supposing you could, she couldn't sink under ten hours, anyway.'

"Leaning over the deck rail, I explained that there was water on the deck below, at which he assured me that the bulkheads had all been shut off and that it was not anything serious. Just at that moment the designer came rushing up the stairs, his face perfectly livid. Not until this moment was I certain that there was anything serious the matter. I stood in front of him as he came along and asked him what the trouble was, but he pushed me aside and tried to continue on his way. I stepped again in front of him, asking the same question, still without receiving any reply. His face was enough, however, to make me feel real concerned—and so I went immediately below and brought my mother to the deck where we were. She put on her coatsuit and we each took a steamer rug with us. I had only a sweater on over my evening dress. When I went up to my stateroom I had light satin slippers on, and when I came up I had on these black pumps that you see on me now, but I do not know when or how I got them on. I had a pair of gloves but my mother had none.

"The passengers, becoming alarmed, came one by one from their staterooms, and I shall never forget when, as we stood together there, with only three lights burning in the immense room where we were, there came to us the cry of 'All passengers to the life preservers!' Everyone went quietly without a sign of panic and did what they were told. Mr. Bruce Ismay fastened the life preserver on me. My mother was the first woman in the second boat launched, and I followed. There were only 26 in our boat. The reason for this was that most of the people, up to this time, felt safer on the big boat than down in the open sea in the small one.

"After our boat had been let down, we found that the plug had not been put in, and then when it was put in, it did not fit, and someone had to sit on it all the time to keep it down. We looked about for a lantern but there was none. Then we hunted for matches, and not a soul could find any. I happened to put my hand in my sweater pocket and found that, by some means of which I have no knowledge, a box of matches had been placed there. I may have picked them off the card table. We had neither water nor food. One man, supposed to be a French baron, gathered all of the blankets to himself. The same man, when aboard the *Carpathia,* appropriated no less than 45 blankets to make himself a soft bed.

"We were about a mile from the *Titanic* when she sank, but I will never forget the terrible cry that rang out from people who were thrown in the sea and others who were afraid for their loved ones. No one knows just how anxiously we watched for some sign of a boat. Repeatedly, some eager passenger of the lifeboat would shout that there was a ship approaching, and we would all spring up to find that the light he had seen was only the twinkling of a distant star.

"At four o'clock in the morning, when we had ceased to take notice of the calls that a ship was near, the *Carpathia* really came. She could not come to us, however; we had to row around the icebergs to get to her. I was so tired that I slept 26 hours after getting on board the *Carpathia*. Everyone was so perfectly splendid to us. The women aboard all came and offered us their berths and clothes and, in fact, anything they had of which we could make use."

Muriel Ostriche recalled: "Jules Brulatour, who was with Eastman Kodak and who was later involved in managing Eclair and Peerless, was in love with Dorothy Gibson. After she was rescued from the *Titanic* disaster, he gave her a large diamond ring which he said cost a thousand dollars. He left his wife and two daughters, got a divorce, and married Dorothy, who at the same time got a divorce from her husband. Later, Jules Brulatour divorced Dorothy and married someone else. Around 1920 she was one of my neighbors when I lived in the Hamilton Apartment Hotel in New York."

At the time, Brulatour was involved in many activities with various studios. As an importer of film stock from Europe, he supplied many independent studios, who could not buy from Eastman, who sided with the Trust companies. It has been suggested that Brulatour also sold Eastman film to the Independents, although not openly. Muriel Ostriche's reminiscences reinforce this.

Joining Muriel Ostriche in 1912 as an attractive young newcomer to the Eclair studio in Fort Lee was Isabel Lamon, who was born in Chicago in 1898 and educated in Fort Lee. At the

Isabel Lamon joined Eclair early in 1912, about the same time Muriel Ostriche was signed as a stock player there. Following appearances in many Eclair films, Miss Lamon went to Lubin in Philadelphia, where she remained about a year. During her stay with Eclair, Isabel took the Fort Lee ferry from New York City each day with Muriel. (*Motion Picture Story Magazine,* April 1913)

time she lived in New York City. Like many other film actresses, she began her career on the legitimate stage, as a child in *East Lynne, The Fatal Wedding,* and other productions. She stayed at Eclair about a year, after which she went to Lubin in Philadelphia. In June 1912, *Moving Picture World* printed a snapshot of the two teenage actresses together. Apparently, Lamon's career faded after her stint with Lubin.

The Legend of Sleepy Hollow, featuring Lamar Johnstone, John Troyano, Edward Lawrence, John Adolfi, Alec B. Francis, George Larkin, Louis R. Grisel, and Julia Stuart from the Eclair stock company, together with ingenues Muriel Ostriche and Isabel Lamon, was released on April 23, 1912.

A review in *Moving Picture World* gave the film a barely passing grade: "A pleasing picture made from Washington Irving's famous story of the school teacher of Sleepy Hollow. There's a schoolhouse scene with little Dutch-American children that was much liked, as was the quilting bee where the older folks are having a jollification. It isn't an exciting picture, and the Headless Horseman won't fool even the children, naturally. Yet we call the release a fair feature; it represents a famous and widely popular story. The little stone church of the picture looks very much like the Sleepy Hollow church at Tarrytown. It is well photographed."

A review in the *New York Dramatic Mirror* began in a favorable vein: "Washington Irving's singular and characteristic comedy tale of early Dutch life in this country has been given a very adequate reproduction in picture form and proves a thoroughly entertaining and rather novel feature, the characters and the times being most vividly intimating. Whatever lack of spontaneity and dramatic action there may be seems to arise from the overuse of subtitles, and the tendency to explain obvious facts, which follow in after action, thus eliminating natural suspense and creating a choppy disjointed effect . . . ."

In an interview with the author, Muriel Ostriche told of this film and other things: "My mother was all for my being in the pictures and often traveled with me. My father never came. The picture my mother liked best was *The Legend of Sleepy Hollow* and her favorite scene was a shot of me in a windmill. I had a lot of Washington Irving books that I got from my father, and I also had many books by Guy de Maupassant. I always read a lot and loved those authors."

April 30th saw the release of *Revenge of the Silk Masks,* the second film in Etienne Arnaud's "Kid, Kit, and Kittie" series. The picture, featuring Dorothy Gibson, Muriel Ostriche, and others, received little advertising or publicity, although a reporter for *Moving Picture World* seemed to enjoy it: "In this offering, Ralph, head of the 'Silk Masks,' gets revenge, while it lasts, and a string of pearls, while he can keep it. His object was to make money at the same time he got Kittie into trouble. We have a pretty picture of Kittie behind the bars. Kittie is soon freed, and Kit then plays Sherlock and recovers the gems. Some excellent trick photographs add to the fun. It seemed to be liked."

The Raven, a two-reel Eclair film based on the famous poem by Edgar Allan Poe, was released on May 7, 1912. The first reel of the picture illustrated brief scenes from other Poe tales, such as *The Gold Bug, The Murders in the Rue Morgue, The Pit and the Pendulum, Buried Alive,* and *A Descent into the Maelstrom.*

Muriel's part was that of a bride, buried alive in a tightly-nailed coffin. The studio craftsmen fashioned a silk-lined box. Muriel was laid to rest, and the coffin lid was tightly sealed. For a while, Muriel in real life seemed to be trapped and on the verge of suffocation. She struggled to get out, but the carpenters on the set had done their work too well. The lid wouldn't budge! When she was finally released all breathed a sigh of relief. Her mother was very upset and critical of the way the situation was handled. Eclair's response was a five dollar a week raise in pay!

The *New York Dramatic Mirror* observed that these and other Poe episodes in the first reel of *The Raven* were part of a sequence in which "Poe is seen in his home trying to receive inspiration for some literary work which may support his sick wife. He falls asleep, and the vision of these works passes before him. At the end he awakes and condemns himself for having no work. The second and last reel is occupied with the composition of *The Raven,* and as he writes the lines, they appear before the spectator—a unique effect because of the clearness and celerity with which the writing is dispatched. The scene changes for some reason, and a dark windstorm is raging without. A raven taps at the window and later lights on the bust in the study. He questions the raven, who answers "Nevermore." When the poem is completed, he presents it to his publisher, who pays him $10, with which he buys flowers for Lenore, his wife in the film. The name of his wife in actual life was Virginia." The same review contained the following curious note: "While this film hardly coincides with Poe's version of the writing of *The Raven,* it is an excellent illustration of how the poem *might have been* written, deriving as it apparently does its ideas from the poem itself."

Another Muriel Ostriche picture of the time, *Feathertop,* first screened for the public on May 28, 1912, was reviewed by *Moving Picture World:* "The Eclair people are doing very commendable work in the representations from the masterpieces from American literature. This is an adaptation of Hawthorne's sketch, *Feathertop,* and gives the adventures of a scarecrow to whom a witch gave life for as long as he should continue smoking. It is a satirical comedy in the costume of Puritan days. Its meaning is quite clear and will be popular. The acting, sets, costumes, and camera work are all good. We think it a very worthy release. It is so distinctly fresh and so clever that it will probably be welcomed heartily."

In the meantime, Carl Laemmle's Universal Film Manufacturing Company reached an agreement to buy the American Eclair. Exhibitors were advised that henceforth Eclair films would be released through the Universal program. In June 1912, Eclair stated that the deal had fallen through because Universal had not lived up to its promise to consummate the purchase quickly. However, distribution of films to the trade was continued through Universal.

Several weeks later the Universal Film Manufacturing Company noted that it would release two-reel Eclair features on Tuesday, one-reel features on Thursday, and Paris-made Eclair films on Sunday, and that Eclair productions were available through numerous exchanges throughout the country. In the meantime, the various Eclair stock players kept busy, and Muriel Ostriche routinely appeared in many productions. Increasingly, Barbara Tennant was mentioned as a prominent Eclair star. Born in

The Eclair Studio in Fort Lee, New Jersey, sometime during the teens. Within the glass-walled building various sets were erected. Muriel Ostriche made many films here in 1912 and 1913. (Eileen Bowser, Museum of Modern Art)

London in 1892, Tennant, like so many others, began her acting career on the stage, then went into the movies.

Around this time, a representative of the Lubin Manufacturing Company, a Philadelphia film maker headed by Siegmund Lubin, invited Muriel Ostriche to join the firm. The offer was declined. A subsequent notice in a trade publication identified Muriel Ostriche in a picture caption under a group of Lubin players, but this was a typographical error. Muriel *Turner* was intended. In a later instance of mistaken identity, the February 1914 issue of *Motion Picture Story Magazine* noted that Muriel Ostriche played the part of Mary in *The Profits of the Business*, a Lubin film.

In the meantime, things were busy at Fort Lee, as a notice in *Moving Picture World*, August 17, 1912, indicated: "Eclair has completed a new wing to their studio, which now makes it possible for three directors to work at the same time. Also their factory is completed to handle outside work such as developing and printing. In view of Eclair's consistently perfect photography, the new department should prove a boon to the small or freelance producer, most especially if he is inclined to be finicky as to quality. Saw there Mr. E. Arnaud, he who directed *Holy City* and *Robin Hood*, directing a forthcoming release. He was working on the scenario. He had found an engraving in a New York art store and it furnished an inspiration. On the back of it was a score of words in French. This was the working scenario—hard on the poor scenario writer who has scripts to sell. We marveled at this, whereupon Mr. Grisel, his right-hand man, told us Mr. Arnaud had done all of *Daddy*, an August 13 release, without a working script or a single word of notes. The idea of the synopsis was read to him, and that was sufficient."

The same issue reported that "Mr. Richard Sterling has been appointed manager of the Eclair Studio proper. Hereafter he will be in full charge of engaging actors, costuming, and the general details of negative production. A good man, too. Little Clara Horton has been engaged for the Eclair stock company. Little Miss Horton is one of the best child actresses, besides possessing a face of unusual childish beauty."

Horton, eight years of age, earlier did work on the stage in *Jack and the Beanstalk* and a pantomime of *Cinderella*. After staying four years with Eclair, she went to Universal, Triangle, and other studios. By 1919 she was known as Baby Clara Marie Horton and was living in Los Angeles.

During the summer of 1912, Muriel Ostriche played minor parts in a number of Eclair films staged in Fort Lee, including Etienne Arnaud's productions of *The Holy City* and *Robin Hood*. The latter was a pretentious three-reel effort which was publicly screened on August 22nd. Directed by Etienne Arnaud and Herbert Blaché, the film sported a long list of credits, including Robert Frazer, Barbara Tennant, Alec Francis, Julia Stuart, and Mathilde Baring.

A lengthy review in *Moving Picture World* reiterated the story of Robin Hood, then gave the cast of characters, with "Mabel Ostrich" as Christabel, a companion of Maid Marian. "The Eclair production, *Robin Hood*, under the masterly direction of Monsieur Arnaud, is the exquisitely illustrated tale I have not read since I was a boy, which was more or less confused in my mind with the fairies, goblins, witches, giants, knights, and ladies, and all the captivating creatures, mythical or legendary, who held my youthful mind enthralled, with the added charm of sceneries such as nature alone can paint," the reviewer noted. The same issue featured a half-page advertisement by Eclair, stating the film was three reels "of love, romance, comedy, and adventure," and suggesting that "nine out of ten persons who pass your theatre know the story of Robin Hood—eight of those nine will want to see the play—and seven of those eight will make a point to see it."

Motography, a Chicago-based trade paper which over a period of time changed its policy from detailed reviews to no reviews, then back to detailed reviews, was unqualified in its praise of *Robin Hood*: "Beautiful costumes and scenery, together with the superb work of the cast, under the direction of E. Arnaud, result in a play of surpassing beauty." Similarly, the *New York Sunday Telegraph* wrote: "The Eclair Company of America has achieved a remarkable success both as to its artistic treatment as a romantic legend of medieval chivalry as well as in its photographic presentation."

Robert Frazer, who played the part of Robin Hood in the picture, was remembered by Muriel Ostriche: "Later, he was with the World Film Corporation. He was one of the leading men, and he married a girlfriend of mine who shared my dressing room, Millie Bright. I must tell you about Millie. She belonged to the company as a stunt player. Originally she was a chorus girl in a Broadway show, then she went into the movies. Once she asked if I would meet her in a certain hired hall—it was upstairs—I don't recall the location. She said she had this guy she was teaching tango lessons to, and she knew I was a good dancer. Her student was bringing a friend, and I was offered five dollars per hour to dance with him. We were surprised when we later found out that both men were married."

An Eclair social event was whimsically chronicled in the *New York Dramatic Mirror*: "The Eclair Employees Association is to give a ball on Friday, September 27, at Cella's Hall, Fort Lee. Mr. Henry Maire, technical director of the Eclair plant, is president of the association, and he promises a great big wholehearted good time to all who will journey over to attend. Mr. Maire insists that there is not a better place in this side of the world than Cella's cuisine. He argues the beauty of the village is an attraction. Miss Tennant has promised to appear, and to attempt to make her eyes behave. Isabel and Muriel and Isabel's mother, too, have signed a bond to appear. Mrs. Stuart consents to chaperone the entire party if necessary. Little Clara Horton has secured her mother's consent to stay up until 11:00. George Larkin will start a buck and wing contest. Mr. Johnstone promises to dance with every young lady who will condescend. Mr. Francis threatens to prove he is not as old as he acts, and Mr. Frazer will put his bells on. Director Sterling declares he will give every actor present a part for the next day, and last, but not least, if abduction plans do not miscarry, Etienne Arnaud will be in the midst of Eclairtown."

Making Uncle Jealous, an Eclair film released on October 24, 1912, headlined Alec Francis as Hiram Tyler, with Isabel Lamon as Judith Hughes, Muriel Ostriche as Muriel Hughes, Mrs. Davis as Salina Huntingdon, Will Sheerer as Will Huntingdon, George Larkin as George Lamon, Clara Horton as Clara Huntingdon, and Miss Knowland as Miss Osgood. The prac-

RELEASED THURSDAY, OCTOBER 24th, 1912

"MAKING UNCLE JEALOUS"

CAST

Hiram Tyler	ALEC. FRANCIS
Judith Huges	ISABEL LAMON
Muriel Huges	MURIEL OSTRICHE
Salina Huntingdon	MRS. DAVIS
Will Huntingdon	WILL SHEERER
Geo. Lamon	GEO. LARKIN
Clara Huntingdon	CLARA HORTON
Miss Osgood	MISS KNOWLAND

FOR twenty years Hiram Tyler had courted Salina Huntingdon but had lacked the courage to propose. Will Huntingdon, Salina's nephew, returns from college for his vacation, bringing his chum Geo. Lamon with him. Will is in love with Hiram's neice, Judith Huges, and George immediately falls in love with her sister Muriel. They are very anxious to bring about a match between Aunt Salina and Uncle Hiram. Will makes up his mind that the only way to do this is to make Hiram jealous. In his trunk he has two costumes which he and George wore at a college masquerade, so dressing in these they persuade Aunt Salina to go for a walk with them, meanwhile having arranged with Judith to have Hiram at the crossroads at a certain time. To do this Judith, who is busy with a dressmaker complains of a headache and asks Uncle Hiram to drive Miss Osgood to the dressmaker's home. They arrive at the crossroads just in time to see Aunt Salina in the embrace of the supposed Mexican. Hiram's jealousy is aroused, likewise Salina's when she discovers Miss Osgood riding with Hiram. To add fuel to the flames Will describes Aunt Salina's friend to Judith in the presence of Hiram.

The next day in order to get Hiram where he can see Salina with another man Judith puts Clara into a canoe and pushes it out into the river and then rushes wildly and tells him of Clara's predicament. Hiram rushes out, dives into the river, rescues Clara and as he is starting for home for dry clothing sees Salina and a minister friend ride by in an auto. The next day Hiram gets his courage in both hands and proposes to Salina to her joy and the joy of the young people.

In Making Uncle Jealous, an Eclair film released on October 24, 1912, Muriel Ostriche played the part of Muriel Huges (also spelled Hughes in other advertising). In the above illustration, she is shown third from the right, with Isabel Lamon behind her.

— 38 —

tice of giving stage names the real first names of actors and actresses was a common one and undoubtedly aided in keeping track of the various parts, with Muriel as Muriel, Will as Will, George as George, and Clara as Clara in the present instance. The surname "Lamon" is an unusual one, and the fictional person in the play was undoubtedly named after Isabel Lamon, although the character was of the opposite gender.

Making Uncle Jealous disappointed the reviewer for the *New York Dramatic Mirror*, who felt that it had but a single redeeming feature, while the *Moving Picture World* was enthusiastic. First, the critical review:

"For twenty years uncle had been courting aunt without proposing, and it is not until his two nephews step in to take a hand that he scores. In order to do this, the boys disguise themselves as Mexicans and make love to the elderly maiden in the presence of the uncle. The uncle, in the simplicity of his soul, sees himself ousted as the first suitor, becomes jealous, and immediately brings his long courtship to a termination. It is a ridiculously improbable happening, almost too improbable to supply a picture with any degree of humor, and besides one rather feels that the old aunt deserved to lose him through failing to bring him to time after twenty years of effort. Apparently, the uncle did not suffer from a chronic case of bashfulness, and why he should have kept the lady waiting is difficult to understand. Of course, there are those who will assert that it is only a critic who would raise such questions, and that the average person would never notice such slight discrepancies. Perhaps and perhaps not. Many people sit a picture out, unimpressed, yet if they were required to give a reason for this by an analysis of the piece, they would be completely at sea. They feel rather than reason in such matters. The basic conditions, which are virtually responsible for the resultant conditions, must be clearly stated in every dramatic composition, whether of a farcical or serious nature, and where there is a failure to do this, it is found to be deficient. The players in this picture carry their roles through in a breezy manner, which is the one redeeming feature."

On the other hand, it almost seems as if the *Moving Picture World* reviewer saw a different film:

"There is a great deal of the human element underlying this release, so that it all rings true through its feeling of plausibility. The action moves with a spirited gusto.

"The work of George Larkin, Will Sheerer, Isabel Lamon, and Muriel Ostriche is of the usual faithful order. Not to forget the mention of the pretty, lovable little Eclair Kid [Clara Horton] who flits into a couple of scenes.

"The story concerns the schemes and devious ruses by which two nephews of the old maid, aided by nieces of the old bachelor uncle (Alec Francis), succeed in pairing each of the concerned old bashful lovers off with a new suitor. True to their promises, this awakening of jealousy on the part of uncle causes him to hunt up his sweetheart of years and years and propose to win her gladsome 'Yes!' in answer. The photography is of the usual fascinating Eclair variety, abundant in pretty tints and artistic settings."

The part of White Wing, an Indian maid, was played by Muriel Ostriche in *Silent Jim*, "A Tale of the Great Northwest," released by Eclair on November 5, 1912. Silent Jim, played by Alec Francis, is a sullen character who lives near a remote trading post in northern Canada, and who seldom speaks to anyone. Misinterpreting the banter of some young members of the Royal Canadian Mounted Police, Jim is hurt. He then revealed that years earlier he, too, had been a member of the Mounted Police. Near death in a remote location, Jim was rescued by a notorious criminal, who then escaped. Stripped of his uniform, Jim began his years of silence. Later, he spurns an offer of reinstatement, preferring to go in silence deep into the woods.

In *The Honor of the Firm*, released by Eclair on Tuesday, November 12, 1912, Muriel Ostriche played a stenographer in a scenario in which the faithful old manager (Robert Frazer) of the Cooper Fidelity Company, after being discharged by young Cooper (Charles Truesdell), learns that the firm is in serious financial straits. He obtains information concerning speculative oil holdings and gambles the very roof over his head on the chance of striking the precious black substance, according to a publicity release.

The December 4th issue of the *New York Dramatic Mirror* contained an interview with Henry J. Maire, technical director of the Eclair factory. He told a reporter of a problem: "If we always had clear, bright days the taking of pictures would be fun. The brightness of the atmosphere is the only thing we cannot control." He then went on to say that animals could be controlled only partially, and that recently he used up 6,000 feet of film and many hours to obtain a one-reel picture involving wild beasts. Nearly 5,000 feet of film had to be discarded. He further stated that certain subjects that were acceptable in France were not acceptable in America, and that many other differences existed. Eclair announced that it was going to open a studio in the Los Angeles area, to take advantage of the favorable weather conditions during the winter months.

Around the same time, the editor of *The Eclair Bulletin* commented on one of the studio's leading personalities: "No, Muriel, I am not going to forget you. I couldn't. Besides, you deserve to have a lot of nice things told about you in spite of your eternal little modesty. Muriel Ostriche first came to the Eclair studio as a girl who wanted to go in pictures. As she stepped into the studio she was not much different from the dozens who come each day in search of work for the day or a chance to start. But something which I expect came from the inherent ability she possesses led the director to engage her in spite of the fact that she frankly admitted that she was without experience. Well, she has been with Eclair every day since. Her future looks big to me. She is a confident little miss . . . so she has the qualifications for making good."

The Vengeance of the Fakir, a two-reel feature released on December 19, 1912, saw Muriel as Lucy, with a cast that included Alec B. Francis, Will E. Sheerer, George Larkin, Mildred Bright, Lamar Johnstone, Paul Bourgeois, Julia Stuart, and Eileen Hume. The tale was set in India and involved a confrontation between Captain Sneade, of the British army, and a Hindu fakir, whom he had struck with a whip. A sacred tiger, a kidnapped baby who is stained brown by his captor, and a fierce leopard all figured in the story. Later, *The Eclair Bulletin* was to report: "More than one heart was touched when Director Vernot came in from the taking of the East scenes for the current release of *The Venge-

ance of the Fakir. As you will see in the film, the leopard is actually killed. And why? Because it was necessary. He was considered a perfectly trained beast—so trained that he was entrusted with his liberty. But I recalled once before that you cannot trust the breed—it cannot change its spots. The scene was going along nicely—that is, seemingly so—but I will wager that right along Mr. Leopard had an idea in his pointed head—well, he bolted—came toward the camera—the guns were out in an instant, and popping. The cameraman kept turning—(why, I cannot quite dope out)—so you see that incident in the picture.

"Wounded and enraged, the infuriated leopard turned his rage to his destructors. Sentiment now had to give way to self-protection—it was the life of a dangerous beast or theirs, probably—so they fired until they struck the vulnerable spot.

"Of course, all of the womenfolk said 'Cruel'—and the happening even caused some strained glances for a day or two, but the memory of a beautiful beast soon wore away. Between the masculine and feminine of the Eclair Studio, peace now reigns again."

Lions, tigers, and the aforementioned leopard added spice to various Eclair films, often at great danger to the stock players. On the subject, Muriel Ostriche reminisced:

"After doing a series of Edgar Allan Poe scenes for Eclair, I did another picture, this one in a boarding house. There was a loose tiger, her name was Princess, and the tiger jumped over me and I was very frightened. Later, after I left Eclair, I heard that the tiger killed her trainer.

"At another time while I was at Eclair, I was making a movie at the ocean, where the camera was set up on a rock along the coast. The cameraman, a Frenchman, was on the rock when a wave came and he disappeared. [This parallels a June 29, 1918 accident in which John van den Broek, a cameraman with the Maurice Tourneur Film Company, of New York City, was drowned at Schooner Head, Maine, when a wave swept him off a rock while he was filming.]

"In another movie, this one out in Long Island, one of the players in our company—his last name was Tracy—went up in a balloon. Something went wrong, and he didn't come down for two days. In another incident I was with the Eclair crew at City Island, and they had me get in a canoe. It was November, the air was freezing cold, and I had to fall out of the canoe with all of my clothes on. I fell overboard, and although the water was not freezing, as soon as I got out I shivered uncontrollably. Soaking wet, I went to a drafty cabin with open windows, where I changed my clothes. There was no towel to dry off with. I was still sniffling a year later. They used to call me a daredevil—daredevil of the movies—because I would do scenes that others wouldn't."

The first Muriel Ostriche film released in 1913 was *A Tammany Boarder*, screened on January 2nd and billed as a burlesque, featuring the aforementioned royal Bengal tiger "Princess." The owner (played by J. Gunnis Davis) of the fierce beast can't pay his rent and is evicted so quickly that he leaves his trunk behind—and that's where he has been keeping the tiger! The greedy landlady, seeking to find something of value in the trunk, opens it, and Princess escapes, to charge through the house frightening the other boarders nearly to death.

Shortly thereafter, on January 7, 1913, *An Accidental Servant* was released, with Muriel Ostriche playing the part of May and with George Larkin, Guy Hedlund, Eleanor Parker, Mildred Bright, J. G. Davis, Alec B. Francis, Will Sheerer, Julia Stuart, and other stock players. The story involved Billy Sheldon (Larkin), an artist who aims to achieve fame when his current painting, his intended masterpiece, is completed. A complicated caper ensues, and a joke is planned for Grace Ellis (Parker), but it does not come off when she falls in love with the hero.

The *New York Dramatic Mirror* had the following to say: "Sheldon, an artist on his way to a house party, is delayed by automobile trouble. The heroine, also on her way to the same affair, has an automobile breakdown, too. Crossing through the park she meets the painter beside his car and, believing him to be a chauffeur, orders Sheldon to drive her to the house party. Arriving, the artist masquerades as a butler until the girl discovers the deception. The comedy ends with the usual wedding bells about to ring. The masquerading servant-hero is another overworked theme, but the picture was fairly well presented. The story, however, moved slowly."

The Spectre Bridegroom, a two-reel feature, was released by Eclair on January 23, 1913. Named in the publicity were over two dozen Eclair stock players, with Muriel Ostriche playing the part of Rosie, a companion to Hilda Von Landshort (the female lead, played by Mildred Bright). Apparently, it was planned that editing would reduce the picture to the standard one-reel length, as an advance note in *The Eclair Bulletin* indicated: "Eclair has just about completed an adaptation of one of Washington Irving's little classics—which classic is *The Spectre Bridegroom*. Well, it is some considerable little story and it ought to make an intensely interesting film. It is a corking satire on ghosts, told with the most ingenious of imaginable plots. And done by such a cinema master of direction such as my fine fellow E. Arnaud is, it ought to be a one-reel feature. In fact, I know it will be, for I have that confidence in his ability.

"*A Tammany Boarder* is from his pen. And believe me, it is about as hilarious a comedy as yours truly has cast his blinders on in many a pay-day. . . . Now, when a film makes me laugh, it is 'going some.' I am satiated with them, so they must belong to the features class to feaze my laughing sensibilities. But *A Tammany Boarder* did. So I proclaim it to be a comedy feature."

Toward the end of Muriel's association with the studio, *The Eclair Bulletin* carried an interesting news item: "Every single day for the past three weeks, Muriel Ostriche has been receiving a box of flowers which are shipped from Buffalo, but without a single clue to the sender other than the fact that he declares, in many ways of phrasing it, that he is very much in love with her. He is not to be unduly criticized for imagining he cares for her, but he certainly pursues a foolish or rather bashful manner of courtship. Now, if he belonged in Pittsburgh, we could recognize his type—but for a Buffalonian to grow so johnnified [a reference to "stage door johnnies"—or hangers-on]—well, comment is beyond me. This much I know of her part of it—and that is that she treats everyone to a boutonniere every day but Sunday. So much for the message of the flowers."

The Spectre Bridegroom, an Eclair film released on January 23, 1913, was adapted from Washington Irving's story of the same name. Featured were many attractive girls, Muriel Ostriche included. (*The Eclair Bulletin*)

GALLERY OF PICTURE PLAYERS

MURIEL OSTRICHE
(Eclair)

At the beginning of each issue, *Motion Picture Story Magazine* featured its Gallery of Picture Players. Muriel Ostriche, who at the time was with Eclair, was one of several shown in the March 1913 issue. More than any other periodical of its era, *Motion Picture Story Magazine* did much to popularize the movie industry. Interviews with players, quizzes, poetry, and other features did much to increase public interest in screen players. Unquestionably, *Motion Picture Story Magazine* was a strong influence in the development of the "star system."

Eclair offered theatre owners and others the opportunity to purchase matted photographs of players. Spelling in Eclair advertising was apt to be erratic, and this announcement is no exception. "Helene Marten" should be Helen Marten, "Lucile Young" should have been Lucille Younge, J.W. Johnston has a superfluous "e" at the end of his name, and Fred Truesdell appears as "Fred Truesdale."

Readers of *The Eclair Bulletin*, primarily motion picture exhibitors, were advised that for twenty five cents each, mounted photographs measuring eight by ten inches could be purchased of the following Eclair stock company players: Barbara Tennant, Helen Marten, Julia Stuart, Mildred Bright, Muriel Ostriche, Mae Wells, Eleanor Parker, Lucille Younge, Clara Horton (the Eclair Kid), Alec Francis, Lamar Johnstone, Guy Hedlund, Will E. Sheerer, Lindsay Hall, J. W. Johnston, Hal Wilson, Fred Truesdell, and George Larkin.

With a background of Niagara Falls, and with yet another appearance by a wild tiger, *The Love Chase*, a two-reel Eclair feature, was released on February 6, 1913. The cast was a familiar one and included Barbara Tennant, Julia Stuart, Muriel Ostriche (as Milly), Mildred Bright, Miss Davis, Lamar Johnstone, George Larkin, J. Gunnis Davis and Louis R. Grisel. *Moving Picture World* noted that the film "is a scenic picture with a plot similar in nature to the one Edison did some years ago titled *A Honeymoon at Niagara*. Pictures like this seldom fail to please, because they have a double interest." *Moving Picture News* (a trade paper which later changed its name to *Motion Picture News*) said the picture had "an original touch" and agreed that it "incorporated some very beautiful views of the Falls of Niagara, which alone should ensure the success of the picture." In a detailed review, the *New York Morning Telegraph* noted, among other things, that "the ball game scenes are very good, although they lose their force because they are titled 'At the Polo Grounds,' when they were taken at the Brooklyn National League Grounds."

The Crimson Cross, earlier titled *The Mysteries of the Rosary*, was released by Eclair on March 5, 1913. Muriel played the part of an angel in this religious drama combining scenes from Puritan times in America and the ancient Biblican era.

The clause, "for better or worse, till death do us part," in the marriage contract, and its implications when the husband, a writer faced with a lack of new ideas, becomes an opium addict, furnished the theme and title of *For Better or Worse*, a multiple-reel Eclair feature released on March 19, 1913. Muriel played the part of a maid in a large cast headed by Julia Stuart and Alec B. Francis.

Muriel Ostriche recalled when her relationship with the studio ended: "I left Eclair because I was let go. They never gave me a reason, and I never asked, for the same day I started working for Reliance immediately and was making $15 a week more. I think Eclair was paying me $35 per week. I remember Eclair gave each player an envelope. When you opened your envelope, if it had a green slip in it, you were out, so I was shocked. I didn't think any more about it, and right away I applied to Reliance and was signed up for $50 per week. Later, Reliance offered me $75 to stay when I went with Thanhouser, but I went to Thanhouser for $65 because I said I would."

It later turned out that Muriel Ostriche worked with Eclair during its finest year. Problems involving film distribution, the outbreak of the World War in Europe in the summer of 1914, and the difficulty of effectively managing the American operation from Paris headquarters combined to take a toll on American Eclair's fortunes. In 1915, the firm name was changed from Eclair to Ideal, after which time it was no longer a significant factor in the motion picture industry.

Unlike the earlier policy at Biograph, the Eclair studio was generous in its recognition of its stock players. Lobby cards, one-sheet posters, and photographs depicting or mentioning the stars were distributed to theatres showing Eclair films.

The April 1913 issue of *The Motion Picture Story Magazine* contained an interview, although by the time it appeared in print Muriel had departed Eclair:

"MISS MURIEL OSTRICHE, OF THE ECLAIR COMPANY. No wonder I hesitated. Surely this slip of a girl, in the homelike little sitting room on West 144th Street, could not be the whimsical Feathertop, the debonair Robin Hood, the stately Christabel that I had ventured up into the wilds of Harlem to interview—probably a younger sister—but no!

" 'I really am sixteen whole years and half another,' she laughed, 'And I haven't played dolls for a long while.'

"I can truthfully say that she does not show her advanced age. A trifle over five feet high—or low—a wee bit over one hundred pounds on charitable scales, with unruly, light brown hair and surely very recently grown up into a young lady psyche on top of her small head from a fat ribbon-tied braid, and round, interested-in-life blue eyes—do you wonder that I failed to recognize Miss Muriel Ostriche, of the Eclair players, and late of Biograph, Powers and Pathé—creator of 150 parts in her single year of motion picture work? An amazing young lady, truly! But no!

" 'I really am just a very commonplace person,' confessed Muriel, plaintfully. 'I haven't the singlest bit of a remarkable thing to tell about myself. I am not even a suffragette! And I have never been a popular actress in John Drew's company, nor a beautiful chorus girl, nor on the stage at all, though I adore the theatre. I never was nearly killed in an auto accident, and never rescued a millionaire from drowning in Atlantic City—so you can see I am most remarkably unremarkable!'

"It is not polite to contradict a lady. The etiquette books all say so. However, I venture to differ with Miss Muriel on this point. One hundred-odd pounds of vital energy and enthusiasm is not commonplace. When she is not working every day, six days a week, she is playing just as energetically, dancing her slippers—number twos—to rags, entertaining her not-to-be enumerated friends in merry parties in the wee-bit apartment, going to the theatre, skating in the cold part of the calendar, rowing in the warm. She is fond of poetry and George Barr McCutcheon, automobiles, chocolate caramels, farming, and her work, and she is charmingly, satisfyingly, remarkably alive.

" 'Is life worth living?' I asked her. The big, round, blue eyes grew bigger, rounder, bluer.

" 'To me it is!'

"The little past life that Muriel Ostriche has lived so far has been in New York. She was educated there within sound of Broadway, and the skyscrapers, noise and bluster of the big city spell *home* to her, although she is fond of traveling.

" 'What do I like to do in the way of athletics? Oh, just swimming, walking, boating, automobiling, driving, baseball, gardening, farming, skating,' she smiled. 'I am interested in Christian Science and Theosophy—or would be if I had the time. My work is really my fad. Do I believe in the future of the photoplay? Indeed I do! I think it will more and more crowd out the regular drama. No, I don't study my parts before rehearsal, but afterwards I do. I like to see the pictures after they are finished. Mistakes do look awful in black and white, but they help.'

"As I was leaving, she called me back.

" 'Oh, by the way, they call me the Turkey-Trot Girl at the studio,' she laughed. 'That's a bit unusual. And, I forgot to tell you how much I enjoy *The Motion Picture Story Magazine*—but, dear me, that's not unusual at all!' "

CHAPTER THREE

The Road to Thanhouser

Reliance, Muriel's new employer, was founded in 1910 by Adam Kessel and Charles O. Baumann, who had their fingers in many motion picture production pies. The firm was headquartered in New York City and was an independent company which later distributed films through the Mutual service—whose trademark was a winged clock inscribed with "Mutual Movies Make Time Fly."

Reporting to her new $50 per week job at Reliance, Muriel was given an important part in *The Bawlerout*, a three-reel film under the direction of Oscar C. Apfel.

"I made a couple of pictures at Reliance," Muriel reminisced. "The studio was over on the West Side of Manhattan, on a downtown street. The place was run by Mr. J. V. Ritchey, a wonderful man, who became quite devoted to me. My first film was with Irving Cummings. With him I went to the Motion Picture Ball, and we led the parade—the grand march. In another film, *The Big Boss*, George Siegmann was one of the players. He was a big, strapping man and he would overcome me. I remember I had battles with him in the scenes. Offstage he was a delightful person.

"Gertrude Robinson was a good friend of mine at Reliance. Later, she went to California to marry James Kirkwood, the director. Before long, she found out that her husband was having an affair with young Mary Miles Minter, and she divorced him and returned to New York City. She was a darling, wonderful actress, and was very famous in the movies in the silent days. I remember visiting with Mary Miles Minter at the wedding of my friend, Mollie King. Mollie, like me, went to Wadleigh High in New York. After a stage career, she was with World and Pathé. Her brother, Charles, was in *The Whirlwind Melody*."

Moving Picture World ran two articles on Muriel's first film with Reliance, *The Bawlerout*, which was released on April 30, 1913. The first was a review:

"A strong three-reel film story by Forrest Halsey. It contains a large number of well-defined characters, including a bank president who also conducts a loan shark business on the side. The 'bawler-out' is a girl employed as a collector, the part being well played by Edgena de Lespine. Other members in the large cast are Irving Cummings, Muriel Ostriche, Sue Balfour, and E. P. Sullivan. The story is rather involved, and the interest of the observer jumps from one plot thread to another, which renders the situation somewhat confusing at times, but it has a good, live theme and gives insight into loan shark manipulations, as well as showing the danger of getting into the clutches of such men. There are two love stories running through the film."

The second *Moving Picture World* article synopsized the plot:

"Miss Sullivan, the bawlerout for Charker & Co., loan bankers to the poor, is the terror of every unfortunate who has to borrow money on his salary. If they do not pay up promptly she is the one who goes to their place of employment and 'bawls them out.'

"Young Dick Lewis, a bank clerk, to help his fellow clerk, Jack Gray, borrows $200 of Charker & Co. The bawlerout is sent to his home to find out all about him. She pretends to be a book agent and talks with his mother—a kindly old gentlewoman. Satisfied that the boy is all he said, Charker & Co. advances him the money.

"Dick is engaged to Edith Downs, the pretty daughter of a bank cashier. She is a selfish, heartless girl, caring more for dress than she does for anything else. When Dick—owing to the fact that he has no evening clothes—finds himself unable to go to a ball with her, she calls his rival on the phone and makes an appointment to go with him. Dick's friend refuses to help Dick pay back the money he borrowed for his sake; so the bawlerout is sent to the bank to disgrace the boy. But as she begins she sees his mother entering with the bank president. The sight of the gentle old lady softens the girl and she goes away without accomplishing her purpose.

"John Howard—a reformer—disguises as a workman to find out the truth about the loan shark establishment. He interests the bawlerout and together they find out that President Bendis of the bank in which Dick is employed is the real head of Charker & Co. Edith's father, to keep up with his daughter's extravagance, borrows money from the bank which he is unable

— 49 —

to repay. The girl, learning of this and dreading to see her father disgraced, suggests that as Dick loves her—he take the blame. The boy agrees.

"Miss Sullivan, who has become friendly with Dick's mother, is a constant visitor at the house. But she has never permitted herself to soften toward Dick, who, despite this and the fact of his engagement to Edith, falls in love with the bawlerout.

"Howard and Miss Sullivan secure the necessary evidence against Charker's. In the bank the money is missed, and Dick accused. He says nothing and is about to be arrested when Howard enters with the bawlerout. Bendis is told that he is wanted by the police, and Miss Sullivan, seeing Dick handcuffed, asks the reason and is told. One glance from the boy to the shrinking cashier convinces her as to just who the thief is. She 'bawls out' Downs and breaks him so that he readily confesses. As he and Bendis are taken away, Edith turns to Dick and informs him that she is done with him—she has become engaged to the other man.

"With a great sigh of relief, Dick holds out his arms to Miss Sullivan, and she, despite her past coldness, enters his embrace. And it is thus that Dick's mother finds him a little later."

The Big Boss, Muriel's second film with Reliance, was released on May 14, 1913. *Moving Picture World* reviewed it: "This big two-reel feature deals with the political graft prevalent in most large cities. The 'Big Boss' will award the aqueduct contract to Bascom, who is badly in need of it, providing Bascom's daughter becomes his wife. But Muriel is already engaged to Dick, a young reporter, who has been detailed to go after the graft scandals that are alarming the city. Dick overhears a conversation between the boss and one of his men in an East Side saloon. The boss is arranging to open all of the bids submitted for the contract that night at 9:00, so that they may make his man's lower than any of the others.

"Dick, with Muriel's help, plants a dictograph, gets the information, and is nearly beaten to death by the boss, who discovers the little machine. Bascom saves the boy and gives the boss to understand what honest men think of him. Pondering the matter over, the boss experiences a change of heart and is content to let the contract go where it honestly belongs—to Bascom.

"George Siegmann plays the 'Big Boss' with telling effect. Irving Cummings as Dick, and Muriel Ostriche as Bascom's daughter, do some clever work. A. Balfour played Bascom. Frederick Sullivan directed this picture."

Muriel's stay with the Reliance studio was brief. "I had to leave because I had an opportunity with Thanhouser," Muriel Ostriche later recalled. "At Thanhouser I was hired by Lloyd Lonergan, one of two brothers who worked there, Philip and Lloyd. My first Thanhouser picture was *Miss Mischief,* which Lloyd wrote especially for me. Lloyd Lonergan was married to Edwin Thanhouser's sister. Thanhouser had sold out, retired, and moved to Sands Point, which was to be my later home."

At the time of Muriel's leaving, Reliance was a relatively minor factor in the motion picture industry. Later in the same year, revised incorporation papers were filed for the Reliance Motion Picture Company, with a capital stock of one million dollars, to produce great dramas by great authors for the Mutual Film Corporation. Henry E. Aitken, president of Mutual, organized and headed the new concern, with financing provided by New York and Chicago bankers. D. W. Griffith was set to direct the new film efforts.

"The man who got me into Thanhouser, and set up my interview with Lloyd Lonergan, was named Lyle. He was quite in love with me, and that's why he wanted me to join the company. I didn't know he was a married man at the time, for he didn't say so, but I later found out he was. When I was in the movies, I had quite a few guys in love with me," Muriel recalled. "I don't remember much about that Lyle fellow, except I know that he was a pest. He was involved in a movie. He took me out to dinner one evening, had a nice time, and told Thanhouser about me—what a beautiful girl I was, and how they should get me.

"What color was my hair back then? I was on a train once, and I was going from one car to the diner, and someone encountered me—it was such a funny thing. My hair was sort of golden—it wasn't blonde and it wasn't brown—it was lighter than brown, and some woman came through the door and she said, 'You have the most beautiful colored hair I have ever seen in my life.' It was natural, and it wasn't colored or bleached. I have gray eyes, but sometimes articles would state they were blue.

"I started with Thanhouser at $65 per week, less than the $75 I was offered to stay at Reliance, but as I told you, I agreed to go to Thanhouser before Reliance offered me more, and when I went to Thanhouser I didn't want to change the agreement.

"Thanhouser had a beautiful spot in New Rochelle. You could go out the back door of the studio and be right on the water. My mother would often go up and spend the day with me there. Soon, I met Florence LaBadie, the Thanhouser star, and each day we would take the train together from New York City to New Rochelle. Of course, I also saw her a lot in the studio. She was a wonderful girl, a great actress, and my dearest friend at Thanhouser. Later, when she died, all of us grieved.

"Mignon Anderson was another close friend of mine. She was a young leading lady and very attractive. I think she was a couple of years older than I, but she was still very young. Then there was another actress at Thanhouser who had a brother come and visit her all the time; he was constantly around the studio. All of us were surprised when it turned out that he was really her husband, for no one suspected. Irving Cummings, who was quite famous at the time, was a fine friend and lived on the same street I did. Mignon Anderson was stuck on Irving Cummings, whose real name was Caminsky—not that that was anything against him, but he didn't want the name used in the movies. They were quite intensely involved, but later she married Morris Foster.

"Charles Hite, who directed the studio after he bought it from Edwin Thanhouser, liked me very much and named a daughter after me. My experiences at Thanhouser were wonderful, and I dearly remember Florence LaBadie and all of my friends there."

The true story of Muriel's actress acquaintance and her secret husband later came to light in an incident reported in the August 15, 1914 edition of the *New Rochelle Pioneer*:

"After being married in Los Angeles, California, seven years ago, and since that time posing as brother and sister, done at the request of the latter, who, thinking that if it became known

The main plant of the Thanhouser company, New Rochelle, New York. This wooden structure was destroyed in a conflagration on January 13, 1913. A film dramatizing the incident, *When the Studio Burned,* was subsequently made to capitalize on the unfortunate situation. Damages amounted to about $80,000. By operating in garages and other premises in New Rochelle, Thanhouser kept up its production schedule, although not without difficulty. Within a year, new and larger facilities were erected. (American Museum of the Moving Image, Lawrence Williams Collection)

it might hinder her career on the stage, the wedding of Miss Lila Hayward Chester, a young and pretty woman of about twenty-five years, who is featured in one of the leading roles of the 'Million Dollar Mystery' motion picture, which is being produced by the Thanhouser Film Corporation, of this city, to Bayard Johnson, a construction engineer employed by the Canadian-Pacific Railroad, was announced to the public on Tuesday.

"When Mr. Johnson returned, last Thursday noon, from a western business trip, and being presumably 'tipped off' by friends, he found that his wife was receiving the attentions paid to her by a young society man, living in this city, whereupon, it is said, he accused her of being unfaithful and taking advantage of the deception in which he was a martyred participant to permit his girl wife to continue her success as a 'movie' star.

"It is alleged that a scene followed on the second floor of the house at 9 Rhodes Street, Stephenson Park, where Mrs. Johnson was rooming, in which the wife was the aggressor. When friends of Mr. Johnson, who is known to be a man of good moral character, were interviewed by a *Pioneer* representative at the Thanhouser studio, Tuesday afternoon, it is said that he thoroughly forgave his wife, but that she had refused to have anything to do with him. Then, it is said, that she rushed to the first floor and in an endeavor to play upon the sympathies of her husband, she fired a revolver, not aiming at herself, but with the intention of misleading her husband as to her purpose.

"Panic stricken by the report and believing that his wife had committed suicide, Mr. Johnson, it is said, rushed to the first floor and found that such was not the case, and that he then pleaded with his wife to give up the young man and return to him, but in vain, although now it is predicted that a reconciliation is soon to take place.

"Provided that it is necessary, Mr. Johnson has retained Acting City Judge Gregory Dillon to look after his interests, while Mrs. Johnson has placed her interests in the hands of John Holden.

"When the above case became known at the Thanhouser studio, it was currently rumored that the management would release the star, but such is not believed will take place.

"It was only recently that Mrs. Johnson became prominently known throughout the country as the individual who captured "Poison Fang," the snake of the Mutual Film Corporation, secured to frighten Miss Florence LaBadie, the heroine of the photoplay serial, after it had disappeared to disturb the residents of New Rochelle."

The Thanhouser Company was founded by Edwin Thanhouser in 1908. Thanhouser was born in Baltimore on November 11, 1869, educated in Ft. Wayne, Indiana, and first appeared on stage at the age of eight. He traveled extensively, going to Kansas, New Mexico, then to Georgia, where he formed a stock company, having been inspired by an orator named Alexander Salvini. Afterward, he went to Milwaukee and organized the Thanhouser Stock Company. It was there that he married Gertrude Homan, earlier a famous child star, who became an active partner in his ventures. Following his success in Milwaukee and in a related theatrical venture in Atlanta, he set up a business in Chicago. This failed, and he decided to try a new venture.

Intrigued by the burgeoning film industry, he went to the center of activity, New York City, and finally settled in nearby New Rochelle in 1908, where he opened a studio in an old roller skating rink.

Gathering a number of players about him, mostly actors and actresses with stage but not motion picture experience (a recruiting preference Thanhouser was to maintain throughout his career), from the outset he produced films based upon famous literary works, particularly those of Dickens and other English authors. His first film, *The Actor's Children*, was released in March 1910. He eschewed slapstick and superficiality, treating motion pictures as a serious form of dramatic art. In an era in which the rights of authors had not been firmly established, he often dramatized books without seeking permission, with the result that he was embroiled in a series of lengthy and expensive lawsuits.

A popularity contest conducted by *The Motion Picture Story Magazine*, with a closing date of July 23, 1913, drew upon readers to name their favorite players. When the votes were tallied, the most popular male actor was Romaine Fielding, a Lubin player, who garnered 1,311,018 votes. Coming in second was Earle Williams (Vitagraph) with 739,985. The most popular woman actress in the nation was Alice Joyce (Kalem) with 462,380 votes, followed by Thanhouser's Muriel Ostriche with 212,276 votes. No other Thanhouser player, male or female, came even close. Runner-up among Thanhouser personalities was Florence LaBadie with 108,641 votes.

Muriel Ostriche's close friend, Florence LaBadie, born in Canada in 1894, lived in 1913 with her parents in an apartment on West 124th Street, New York City. An article in *The Motion Picture Story Magazine*, January 1913, noted that she had light brown hair, golden in the sun, with bluish-gray eyes, and was a daring girl who was afraid of nothing—and was a horseback rider, swimmer, an airplane passenger, and a motorcyclist "until a recent terrible accident to a friend, who was racing with her, spoiled her enjoyment of the sport."

After studying in a convent and public schools, with her interests concentrated on art, painting, and sculpture, she went on the stage where she played two seasons with Chauncey Olcott, later appearing in *The Bluebird* at the New Theatre. During this time she posed for illustrator Penryhn Stanlaws on many occasions. In 1911, her friend Mary Pickford introduced her to the Biograph management. She was signed as an extra for a small part in a Biograph production. Subsequently, she appeared in a dozen or so films. Not sure of her future with that studio, she went to New Rochelle and visited the Thanhouser premises, but scant notice was paid to her. Later, Edwin Thanhouser saw her on the screen in a Biograph film, and remembered that he had met her when she sought employment. He wasted no time and sent for her immediately. In August 1911 she signed up. Her first Thanhouser picture was *In the Chorus*, released a few weeks later.

A 1913 interview revealed that her favorite authors included Dickens, Thackeray, and Bulwer-Lytton and that she had two tiny white toy spaniel dogs, Beauty and Teddy. A year later it was reported that she had turned down hundreds of proposals of marriage by mail from her admirers and that she received about five hundred letters a month on various subjects.

The first panel of a two-page spread in *Motion Picture Story Magazine,* October 1913, showing the winners in the annual contest to determine the most popular screen players. Among actresses, Muriel Ostriche was second in a field of dozens, with Alice Joyce capturing first prize.

Her favorite place to spend a day was Coney Island, where she earned the reputation of being indifferent to danger. When a new amusement ride was installed, Florence LaBadie would be among the first to try it. An April 4, 1914 article in the *New Rochelle Pioneer* called her "the heroine of Coney Island." City life suited her best, and unlike many of her fellow players, she preferred New York City to the open country. The main advantage of New Rochelle was that it was but a short ride back to the heart of Manhattan, she told a reporter.

Like her friend Muriel, the ever modest Florence LaBadie often minimized her accomplishments, preferring to leave publicity to others. Still, during her long stint with Thanhouser, she rose to become the most popular personality of the firm and was featured in numerous films, including the highly acclaimed serial, *The Million Dollar Mystery*, and its unsuccessful and much-changed sequel, *Zudora*, not to overlook *The Five Faults of Flo*, *Master Shakespeare*, *The Fugitive*, and over one hundred others. While numerous Thanhouserites rose to stardom and then departed for greener fields, Florence LaBadie remained.

She played every film with enthusiasm, freshness, and vitality. Not taking anything for granted, in 1916 she told a reporter that she was taking typing lessons in her spare time so that she could be a private secretary should the bottom ever fall out of the motion picture business.

A little more than a year before Muriel Ostriche went to Thanhouser, *Moving Picture World* in its April 20, 1912 issue, told of a new owner of the New Rochelle company:

"Mr. H. E. Aitken, who is interested in a number of picture concerns, and who is supposed to have conducted the details of the deal, authorizes the following announcement: 'Mr. C. J. Hite, of Chicago, is at the head of a syndicate which has just consummated the purchase of the entire plant and the assets of the Thanhouser Company. Edwin Thanhouser still remains connected with the company as its general manager. Mr. Hite has been very active in the film business in the past, and is at the present largely interested in the American, Reliance, and Majestic companies, and also has large interests in the H. & H. and Majestic Film exchanges in Chicago. He is now the second vice president and director of the Mutual Film Corporation, and is a member of its executive committee.'"

Charles J. Hite had an eye for publicity, and from the moment he took over, news of the doings at Thanhouser reached readers of all of the trade magazines and fan publications. At the same time, Hite was a benevolent employer, and the Thanhouser players enjoyed many privileges not found elsewhere in the industry. He engendered in many of his employees a fierce loyalty, and numerous stories were told of actors and actesses who spurned higher offers elsewhere in order to continue working under his direction.

Among Hite's first benevolences was what was billed as the First Annual Entertainment and Ball for Thanhouser employees, held in New Rochelle at the Germania Hall in April 1912. Mr. and Mrs. Edwin Thanhouser hosted the event, for the new management headed by Hite had not yet arrived. Hite was still in Chicago, nearly a thousand miles away, but he encouraged the gala affair, which 1,200 people attended. A comedy film with negatives and positives coming out on the screen in "terrific combinations, some upside down and some topsy-turvy," called *The Crazy Quilt*, was shown. It was stated that this film would never be released publicly. Other entertainment included skits by various Thanhouser players.

A few weeks later, a reporter stopped by and learned that carpenters were busy constructing a new office for Hite, who was still in Chicago, and who was expected in New Rochelle early in May. "Mr. Hite will engage mostly in the business end of the enterprise, giving Mr. Thanhouser more time to devote to the producing department, thus enabling him to realize an old ambition. Mr. Thanhouser has always been in very active touch with his producing force, but business details have taken up a lot of time he would like to have spent in the 'making' department. Under the present arrangement he will be able to give pretty nearly his undivided attention to the actual work of making the films, and an advanced product is necessarily looked for— if better Thanhouser pictures are really possible."

As the last sentence implies, Thanhouser films were widely acclaimed at the time, and the entire industry looked at Thanhouser as a model of production quality. Edwin Thanhouser was viewed as leader and innovator, and his peers treated him with respect bordering on reverence. Once, when the subject of nudity in "art" type films came up in a trade paper article, it was suggested that Thanhouser probably could get away with it, but nobody else could.

On several occasions, trade and fan magazines advised inquirers that the "h" in Thanhouser was indeed pronounced, not silent, and the name of the firm was not "Tanhouser," but there must have been some confusion when Thanhouser elected to produce a cinematic version of the famous opera, *Tannhäuser*. Apparently, there was little consistency in the pronunciation, for Muriel Ostriche recalled that she always called the firm "Thanhouser," as it was spelled, while in later years both Mignon Anderson and a grandson of Edwin Thanhouser told historian Anthony Slide that "Fanhouser" was preferred.

Around the same time, the Comet Film Company, an independent producer formed in November 1911 by a former Thanhouser employee, ran an advertisement promoting its products, stating: "The man with the A-1 pictures is a winner in this film game every time. THANHOUSER, for example," a fine tribute.

In the summer of 1912 the Thanhouser Twins (Marion and Madeline Fairbanks) made their debut in an appropriately-named movie, *The Twins*, and were added to the Thanhouser Kid (Marie Eline) and the Thanhouser Poodle on the roster, keeping company in the film industry with the Eclair Kid (Clara Horton) and the Vitagraph Dog (Jean).

While carpenters were building his office, Hite was building the capital structure of the company, and it was announced that the firm had been recently incorporated in the state of New York with a capitalization of $40,000, by Charles J. Hite, Crawford Livingston, and Dr. Wilbert Shallenberger.

Early in 1913, the year of Muriel Ostriche's arrival at Thanhouser, the firm made headlines all over America, but not in the manner Charles J. Hite liked. *The Billboard* noted: "New Rochelle, January 13th. The Thanhouser motion picture plant burned to the ground this morning. Several buildings adjoining

A Thanhouser outdoor set in the early teens, believed to have been in New Rochelle, production title unknown. (American Museum of the Moving Image, Lawrence Williams Collection)

caught fire but are under control. All the negatives were saved. Two stock companies are working in California. The New York company goes to California at once. There will be no interruption in the release of films."

The same magazine followed up with more details the next week: "The first reports of the disastrous fire at the plant of the Thanhouser Company in New Rochelle, as made in *Billboard* last week, seemed to differ only a little from the facts as they have come to light after the rubbish was cleared away. Starting in one of the darkrooms of the laboratory, the fire was first discovered by a small explosion. It grew rapidly and scarcely gave C. J. Hite, manager, and his assistants time to get out valuable apparatus and films. All negatives for coming releases were saved, however. . . . None of the acting staff was in the building when the fire started. Many workmen and girls were, however, but all escaped with ease except those who remained to remove films and apparatus, but these got out safely, if not easily. The loss is estimated at about $80,000. The building was insured."

The *New York Clipper* gave additional details, noting that the fire took place at 1:30 on Monday afternoon, January 13th, and that: "The flames started in the perforating room and spread to every part of the big two-story building within five minutes. Fifteen employees, mostly women, remained in the offices on the second floor with C. J. Hite, the owner, and got out just in time. . . . Mr. Hite was the last to leave the building, but even in his excitement did not overlook his cane, a recent gift from Mrs. Hite. The fire was a spectacular one, as the chemical contents of the building burned like powder, and there were several loud explosions. Fire Chief James Ross was on the scene two minutes after the alarm was sounded. The Chief placed the damages at not more than $75,000, but Mr. Hite's estimate of his loss slightly exceeded this sum. There was no insurance on the building or any of its contents. None of the actors or actresses employed by the film company were in the building at the time of the fire. Six or eight of them, including Marguerite Snow, the leading woman, and James Cruze, the leading man, were at dinner at their hotels when the alarm was sounded." Hite told a reporter that he would immediately begin construction on a new plant and would take care of paying wages to the actors and actresses in the meantime. Thanhouser produced a short film, *When the Studio Burned*, to exploit the event.

Despite Edwin Thanhouser's avowed interest in remaining with the company as its directing and artistic manager, he soon turned his attention elsewhere and decided that he would see the world. In the meantime, a new and finer factory was erected at New Rochelle, complete with many embellishments and artistic trappings. Thanhouser films, under Hite's management, continued to be a great success with exhibitors and were released as part of the Mutual program, along with Kay-Bee, Broncho, Majestic, Reliance, American, Keystone, Mutual Educational, and Mutual Weekly films. A weekly magazine, *Reel Life*, claimed a circulation in the 20,000 range and was sent to various theatre owners and operators to acquaint them with the latest news of the Mutual-affiliated companies, including Thanhouser.

By this time, the "war" between the Trust companies and the Independents was largely history, although the matter of patents was to be dragged out in the courts for years. The theory that the greatest profits go to innovators is nowhere more true than in the field of motion pictures, and any firm resting on its laurels was apt to be overtaken by its competitors and forced into merger or bankruptcy. One by one, the "old guard" members of the Trust fell by the wayside. By May 1913, when Muriel Ostriche went to work for Thanhouser, Biograph was on its way to being a has-been (the momentum in this direction was accelerated when Griffith left a few months later). Edison and Lubin films, so admired during the early years of the century when almost anything moving on a screen was a novelty to the public, were scorned by many exhibitors, and other Trust companies were mostly in a state of decline. Only Vitagraph, of the original Patents Company members, seemed to have a lot of new ideas, many of which were credited to J. Stuart Blackton, one of the Vitagraph founders, a colorful individual who styled himself as "commodore."

In the summer of 1913, Charles J. Hite was primarily involved with Thanhouser, but he kept a management hand in Majestic. Often Thanhouser staff members and players would go from an assignment with one firm to a film being produced by the other. For example, in May, *Moving Picture World* told of a temporary switch: "Photographer Carl Gregory, who made a 9,500-mile trip through the western states for scenic subjects for the Majestic Company, is back at New Rochelle in his position as senior cameraman of the Thanhouser Film Corporation. Due to his success in commissions of a similar nature, Gregory was named for the trip, which brought his camera into action in the states of Montana, Wyoming, Oregon, California [and elsewhere]. His views of 'Life Among the Navajos,' said to be intimate and unusual, were issued May 27th by Majestic." At the time, Majestic announced its intention of turning out three films a week. In contradiction to his actions, Hite issued a news release that he would not "raid" Thanhouser to get personnel for Majestic.

Following her departure from the Reliance studio, Muriel Ostriche's Thanhouser debut was heralded in an advertisement which proclaimed: "Coming! Sunday, June 8th, MISS MISCHIEF, featuring the most flirtatious of flirts." Other advertisements billed it as "a corking comedy of the countryside, featuring Muriel Ostriche. Watch her play side-splitting tricks on EVERYBODY."

Moving Picture World told of Muriel's capers: "Who was it that turned the mouse loose in the dormitory? Who put mucilage on Miss Galgreen's false teeth? Who flirted with the French dancing teacher? Who put snuff in the school books? The answer was 'Miss Mischief.' The girl remained at the seminary exactly one month. The principal finally expelled her.

"Farm life is usually very monotonous, and the section where Miss Mischief's parents lived was no exception to the rule. But the girl soon made the little rural community as lively as Main Street on Saturday night. Her father always had to hunt for his spectacles, tacks seemed to find their way into his cowhide boots, the dog frequently raced wildly about the yard with a tin can tied to his tail, and the minister passed the doorway with a hostile glare. The boys all liked her and neglected work so frequently that their irate fathers had to threaten them with horse whips in order to induce them to work. The girls, robbed of sweethearts, prayed for some awful fate to befall the siren.

"Latest addition to the Thanhouser stock company" was the original caption on this June 1913 publicity photograph, probably showing Muriel Ostriche in *Miss Mischief*. (Wisconsin Center for Film and Theatre Research)

"Two young men, to whom the girl showed the most favor, had decided to fight a duel, but the girl laughed them out of the idea and persuaded them to settle the affair by a battle between their pet roosters. The affair was shrouded with mystery, and even Miss Mischief's mother did not know about it. But when various masculine and feminine figures came hurtling down the grain chute and landed on the ground with resounding thumps, she made inquiries. They excitedly told her that the constable was after them, and limped and hobbled away as fast as they could.

"When it became known that the constable had been nowhere around, and that it was another of Miss Mischief's pranks, the rage of her dupes was great. So the girl was bundled off to another school, whose principal had a reputation as a great disciplinarian, and the little community once more enjoyed peace."

The same publication noted that "the girl is attractive and the picture is good," but that it lacked a plot, such deficiency being compensated by "a good deal of amusement."

"I remember well this, my first Thanhouser film," Muriel Ostriche told the author. "I had a great time. There was a cock fight, and I remember sliding down into a cellar with lots of hay over everything. I remember that it was staged out on a farm, and for some reason I had to climb a tree while wearing high heels, and I almost broke my leg when I fell off. No matter what I did, I always was getting into mischief, but everybody liked me.

"The other Thanhouser players were very nice to me from the very moment I joined the company. I remember Marguerite Snow, who at one time was married to James Cruze. Then there was another fellow who did stunts for Thanhouser—like jumping off of towers and getting into all sorts of trouble—but he also had a job with the Metropolitan Opera. I guess he just wanted to pick up some extra money at Thanhouser to do his studying. I believe his name was Bruce Wyman, or something like that—he was a baritone, and he had a wonderful voice. Marguerite Snow fell in love with him, and she and Jim Cruze split up.

"Florence LaBadie was my friend, as you know, and we were very close. I remember her telling me about someone who wanted to go steady with her, but she was engaged to someone else—to a man who worked for a Cadillac distributor at Broadway and 59th Street. Later, she became engaged to Daniel Carson Goodman. She always had lots of suitors. I guess we all did."

At the time, the activities of Edwin Thanhouser were being chronicled by the trade papers, and on June 21st *Moving Picture World* noted: "Edwin Thanhouser, founder of the Thanhouser Company, is here from Europe on a short trip. He left his family in Rome and is stopping in New York City. Mr. Thanhouser arrived on the *La Provence* Saturday, and that evening celebrated his homecoming with a dinner at the Players' Club, which was attended by C. J. Hite, president of the Thanhouser Film Corporation, Lloyd S. Lonergan, Bert Adler, and Elmer Harris. He spent Sunday inspecting the new Thanhouser plant at New Rochelle. His business here is in connection with his real estate, and he states that he is out of the picture game for good. Mr. Thanhouser expects to come over again next spring."

Meanwhile, production of films was accelerated at New Rochelle, and numerous two- and three-reel features, described as "a staggering list," portrayed such stars as Maude Fealy, Marguerite Snow, James Cruze, Florence LaBadie, Mignon Anderson, William Russell, Harry Benham, the Thanhouser Kid and the Thanhouser Kidlet. Muriel Ostriche, new to Thanhouser, was soon added to the list, and by August she was designated in Thanhouser advertisements as a "star."

Frazzled Finance, a Thanhouser film released on August 31, 1913, portrayed Muriel Ostriche as a distractingly beautiful milliner, who opened a shop in a small town, to the delight of all the men and the despair of the women. Thanhouser advertising billed the film as having "the best comedy boat upset you've ever seen in a picture!"

September 19, 1913 saw the release of *Flood Tide*, in which "Muriel Ostriche and the Thanhouser Kid have marvelous parts," according to an advertisement, "and Eugene Moore is even better than in a *Spartan Father*—see for yourself." *Moving Picture World* described the film as "a story which gets hold of the heartstrings.... A simple plot, but nicely pictured and acted with true feeling."

The same periodical gave a plot synopsis:

"On a lonely lighthouse lived the keeper and his wife. They were devoted to each other, and when the wife was dying her sorest grief was that she would be leaving her loved one alone. Just before she died, however, she had a dream and, upon awakening, told her husband with a smile that God would send someone to comfort him.

"A few days later, while the stricken man was praying at her grave, his attention was attracted by a bundle which had been brought in by the sea. He found it to be a little girl, senseless, who had apparently been swept ashore from some wreck. She was wrapped in a life preserver bearing the name of a yacht. A few days later he learned that the owner of the boat, a banker involved in difficulties with the law, had been lost with his child and crew while trying to escape on the vessel. There was no one to claim the child, and the pious keeper accepted her as the gift from God which he had been promised.

"Years later, when the child has grown to be a handsome young woman, her aunt, a wealthy society woman, found and claimed her. The girl at first did not want to go, but the keeper persuaded her, believing that her relatives had the first claim. Then, sorrowfully, he took up his lonely life again. One afternoon, while thinking of her, he fell into a troubled sleep. He awoke to find her beside him. She showed him a letter which she meant to send to her aunt, telling her that fashionable life had no charms for her and that she had decided to devote herself to the old man who had been a father to her for many years. So, *The Gift of God*, as he always called her, came back to him, never more to leave."

Muriel's work was enthusiastically acclaimed by Charles Hite and other Thanhouser executives, and plans were set to feature her in more films. At the same time, her popularity with the public brought her stacks of letters, each one of which received a personal reply. The "star system" was in its infancy, and although popular players were sometimes overwhelmed by the

Front of the main Thanhouser studio building, circa 1914. In its day this structure, with a glass studio at the back, was referred to as the Glass Palace. The office at the left front is believed to have been that of Charles J. Hite. (American Museum of the Moving Image, Lawrence Williams Collection)

Rear view of the Thanhouser building, also circa 1914. This structure was still standing in 1987, although with the front part considerably altered.

Muriel Ostriche (front row, far left) and other Thanhouser actresses in front of the Thanhouser Building, New Rochelle, circa 1913-1914. Standing to the right is Charles J. Hite, president of the firm. (American Museum of the Moving Image, Lawrence Williams Collection)

A Thanhouser parade float, circa 1913-1914. Muriel Ostriche is the highest figure in the rear, behind the driver. (American Museum of the Moving Image, Lawrence Williams Collection)

Charles J. Hite in his office in the Thanhouser building, New Rochelle, August 1913 (the date on the wall calendar). By this time, Muriel Ostriche had been part of the Thanhouser players for several months. She quickly became one of Hite's favorites, and he named a daughter after her. (American Museum of the Moving Image, Lawrence Williams Collection)

An unidentified interior set in the Glass Palace, at the rear of the main Thanhouser studio in New Rochelle, New York, circa 1913. (American Museum of the Moving Image, Lawrence Williams Collection)

attention of fans, most actors and actresses were just "regular people" in their personal lives. Trade publications of the time listed the home addresses of various personalities, something that in a later era security arrangements would preclude.

The September 27th issue of *Moving Picture World* showed a picture of a glacier with the caption: "Edwin Thanhouser, Mrs. Thanhouser, and their son Lloyd ascending the Jungfrau in Switzerland in the very center of the Eiger Glacier. What is the famous producer thinking about? Here are his own words on a postal card sent to a member of our staff: 'Below I saw the green foothills; above and about us the towering drifts of snow and ice. Fine to contemplate on a hot August day. Amid such scenery I am acquiring too much moving picture inspiration for an idle man.' How long can a man with dynamic energy added to inspiration keep idle?"

Featuring Muriel Ostriche as Mary, Jean Darnell as Grace, and with Billy Noel and Nolan Gane as their suitors, *The Farmer's Daughters*, released September 28th, was reviewed by *Moving Picture World* as: "One of the brightest and most original comedies shown by this company in some time. A neat, well-acted and cleverly photographed film story."

A plot synopsis described the action:

"Every year, it seems, the poor old farmer has more trouble to secure 'hands.' The Nebraska agriculturist, who came east looking for workers, found his errand fruitless. In despair he offered that men who work for him would be given a chance to court the farmer's two pretty daughters, and there would be no objection to a match on the father's part if the girls were willing. It was dull season for news, and the papers made much of the happening.

"The notice was seen by two college boys who were wondering how they would be able to get through the season until classes resumed without any money or food. They saw a chance to secure romance together with three square meals a day, and when they called upon the farmer and he showed them the pictures of his two beautiful daughters they gladly accepted his offer. The youths traveled west together, and the farmer remained behind hoping to land other 'hands.' Unfortunately for the boys, the farmer's daughters had seen the notices in the papers, and so objected to being made matrimonial prizes. They rigged up in strange clothing and made themselves as homely and unattractive as possible. The new farm hands thought them frights and tried to run away. The girls were true to father, however, and held them prisoners. Of course, all ended happily, but not until the boys had some mighty unpleasant experiences."

CHAPTER FOUR

The Little Princess

Muriel Ostriche's comedy capers in *Miss Mischief* and *The Farmer's Daughters* created a sensation. Her antics became a popular topic of conversation, and theatre patrons demanded more. Charles J. Hite realized that she had great potential. Accordingly, he set up a new branch specifically to feature her talents. It was called the Princess Department, and its pictures were known as Princess Films.

A trade paper reported: "The Mutual Program will soon release the Princess photoplays made at New Rochelle. Titles of the Mutual releases are *Looking for Trouble, Lobster Salad and Milk,* and *The Campaign Manageress*, farces, as the names would indicate. In these, Muriel Ostriche, a very attractive and petite actress, and Marie Eline, popularly known as the Thanhouser Kid, are the featured leads. This new company has the distinction of having a director who is also the cameraman. Carl Gregory fills this combined position."

Of one-reel length, Princess films were intended as a comic segment of a regular program. Although they were scarcely advertised (except in *Reel Life*, the Mutual house organ), and thus in later years were nearly completely overlooked by film historians, in their day Princess pictures attracted a wide following. The first release, *Lobster Salad and Milk*, reached the screen on October 24, 1913. *Moving Picture World* called it "a good little story of a bad little girl. Good entertainment of the kind, and nicely pictured."

A trade magazine printed the plot synopsis: "The little girl [Marie Eline] made free with her elder sister's [Muriel's] rouge, perfume and peroxide, and was punished by being sent to bed without any supper. This had little effect on the child. As soon as the house was quiet she wandered down to the icebox and had an excellent snack, consisting of lobster salad and milk; then she returned to bed and returned to sleep the dream of the just. Somehow she had a frightful dream. She could never explain it afterwards. The family doctor, when he heard about the lobster salad and milk, shook his head wisely and said that science could solve all things. She woke up finally, and was mighty glad to do so, and readily promised in the future she would keep away from her sister's bureau and the family icebox, so that in the future she might not have such thrilling experiences."

This initial Princess film was followed a week later by *Algy's Awful Auto*, released on October 31st. The character name Algy, like Rube, was a popular one with film makers at the time, and such movies as *Algy Forfeits His Claim* (Nestor, September 1913), *Algy On the Force* (Keystone, May 1913), and *Algy the Watchman* (Biograph, June 1912) are typical of the genre.

Algy's Awful Auto, the Princess release, told of an adventure on wheels: "Algy had always been contented to ride in streetcars and never dreamed of the day that he would own an auto which his neighbors would dub 'The Yellow Devil.' His sweetheart was to blame for it, however, for she induced Algy to take a number of chances in a raffle gotten up by charity and, unfortunately for Algy, he won the auto.

"His first difficulty came when he tried to use the street in front of his house as a garage, but this was one case where the auto filled the bill, for it was small and humble and he could take it into his bedroom. This gave Algy an idea, and being afraid of facing traffic conditions, he learned to be a chauffeur indoors and succeeded fairly well, although he did considerable damage to furniture.

"Later, he took his sweetheart for a ride and had all of the troubles of a real automobilist. By this time Algy was pretty well cleaned out of money, and when his 'Yellow Devil' broke down again he was glad to trade it to a rural station agent for two tickets to his home town."

A trade magazine characterized the film as "a fairly amusing number." While working on this picture, Muriel was interviewed by a reporter, who under the title "A Picture Play Ingenue," wrote the following:

"Her name is Muriel Ostriche—pronounced just like that of the big plume-bearing bird. She is an *ingenue*, and a bright particular star in a line of dramatic portrayal that five years ago practically did not exist. Brief as is the time indicated, this young lady's professional career is briefer by half. Three years ago Muriel was a schoolgirl, and today she is barely eighteen; yet she has

| WARREN KERRIGAN | RUTH ROLAND | EARLE WILLIAMS | BLANCHE SWEET | MURIEL OSTRICHE | CRANE WILBUR |

THESE SIX PICTURES IN COLORS
FREE

We are now offering free with a one-year subscription to THE MOTION PICTURE STORY MAGAZINE this set of beautiful, large-size portraits. These pictures are 8 x 10½ inches in size, printed in many colors on heavy coated paper, suitable for framing, and their equal in beauty and artistic effect cannot be obtained elsewhere at any price.

They are not for sale and can be obtained only by subscribing to THE MOTION PICTURE STORY MAGAZINE

Motion Picture enthusiasts will find them very appropriate for home or room decoration.

Take advantage of this exceptional offer now. Just fill out coupon below, mail with remittance, and these pictures will be sent you at once.

THE MOTION PICTURE STORY MAGAZINE
175 DUFFIELD STREET, BROOKLYN, N. Y.

COUPON

GENTLEMEN: Enclosed find $1.50 ($2.00 Canada, $2.50 Foreign) for which kindly send me THE MOTION PICTURE STORY MAGAZINE for 1 year beginning with............ issue and including the 6 large-size portraits of Motion Picture Players mentioned above.

Name...

Address..

In September 1913, *The Motion Picture Story Magazine,* enticed subscribers by offering six free color pictures of stars. Muriel Ostriche's image was featured along with five of her prominent contemporaries.

already created and played a greater number of parts than many a mature actress in a fully rounded-out career.

"In a recent voting contest to establish the relative popularity of motion picture favorites, the name of Muriel Ostriche stood second only to that of Alice Joyce. Beauty, of both face and figure, is undoubtedly the chief factor thus far of Miss Ostriche's phenomenal success. Yet this does not imply any disprase of her intelligence and artistic ability, since personal beauty is only the raw material upon which talent builds in acting for the photoplay film.

"She is petite, rather blonde than dark, with hair hanging in luxuriant curls, the large eager eyes of a child, a certain vivid vivacity of facial expression that people somewhat vaguely call 'French.'

" 'But I am neither French nor Austrian,' Miss Ostriche declares, 'just a New York girl, who is finishing her high school course in the motion picture studios because she has a natural liking for the work. It is exciting and pleasant and profitable, besides being a wonderful education.'

"She is right about the excitement, anyway. The interviewer arrived at the Thanhouser film-foundry in New Rochelle, just in time to see the little heroine wheel her way down the Pelham Pike in a crazy, cavorting automobile that made even the heaviest motor trucks steer out of their course. It transpired that *Algy's Awful Auto* was the picture-farce in course of visualization. Giving chase in another machine, we finally caught the eloping party at a country railway station, half a dozen miles distant. They already had the camera in position, and the 'stage' director was saying to Miss Ostriche:

" 'Now, while Algy is trying to get the magneto to work, you exclaim, "I have an idea!" and run to the station and call the ticket-seller out. Algy says to him, "Gimme two tickets for this automobile?" The guy looks it over, and says, "Taint worth it, but I'll give you the tickets." Then, when the next train comes along, you both get aboard. You can go through the car, and jump off at the rear end before the train starts.'

"This scene having been duly enacted and registered on 500 feet or so of film, Miss Ostriche was at liberty for a chat.

" 'This is nothing compared to some things I have had to do,' she tells. 'For instance, I have had to be put in a coffin and buried alive, in the picture version of one of the Edgar Allan Poe tales. In another, there was a real, live tiger prowling under my bed. But I think only of the development of the play—and my pictures come out all right.' "

Friday, the Thirteenth, the next film in the Princess sequence, was released on November 14, 1913, and was enjoyed by a *Moving Picture World* reviewer: "Quite a pleasing little comedy, with good characterizations and attractive scenes. The young husband dreams that all sorts of unpleasantness occurs on the fatal day, but when he awakes his experiences are exactly to the contrary. Slight, but well pictured and entertaining." The film provided the motion picture debut for an actor who subsequently was to appear in many Princess releases. *Moving Picture World*, informed its readers: "The handsome dark-haired, dark-eyed leading man who plays opposite Muriel Ostriche in the Princess films is playing his first 'picture' engagement. He is Boyd Marshall, from the musical comedy stage and long a favorite in Frisco and at the New York Hippodrome. He makes his film bow in a Princess reel titled *Friday, the Thirteenth*, as Miss Ostriche's superstitious husband. Several well-known picture actors went to Mr. Hite for the leading man job in the new brand, but he decided on the 'new face,' because in Miss Ostriche and Marie Eline he had old favorites. The latter is the leading lady who was famous for many years as 'The Thanhouser Kid.' "

Muriel remembered her new leading man: "We played together in many films, one a week after he started. Lots of times we made the picture but didn't know what the name was. The title wasn't given until after the picture was finished, and we were working on another one. People would say they saw me in such-and-such picture, and I had to ask them what the picture was about, for I could not connect the names. Boyd was attractive, taller than I was, and had a good voice, although the voice didn't make much difference, for the films were silent. We made a good team. He was a singer, and at Thanhouser parties he would entertain the guests. Boyd liked me a lot, and would have developed a romantic interest had I let him. He eventually married someone named Mitzi Hagos, a Hungarian who just went by her first name—few people knew what her last name was—and told me that as I wouldn't marry him, he would marry someone who was just like me."

In its July 18, 1914 issue, the *New Rochelle Pioneer* related that by that time Marshall was married to a singer "known in other circles as Dixie Crane," and that the couple had entertained the Thanhouser players at a company clambake.

Next on the Princess bill was *Looking for Trouble*, released on November 9, 1913. A trade review noted: "The little girl looks very happy because she owned more dolls than any of her playmates did. It was therefore a source of sorrow to her when she came home one afternoon and found that the pet dog had eaten the most charming doll in her collection. While bowed down with maternal grief, she did not neglect to look about for a successor to her lost one, and while passing a store she saw the very doll she wanted. The price was prohibitive, however, and she found that her balance in the toy bank was much lower than she had anticipated. Still, an inspiration came to her—an advertisement calling her attention to the value of accident insurance policies. With fifty cents she bought one, and after looking over the provisions, she decided that the easiest way to make money was to break her arm, which carried with it a cash bonus of $200.

"No one can deny that the girl tried hard to earn the money. She had all sorts of marvelous adventures, but seemed to be indestructible, for do what she would, she could not break. Finally, in despair, she went home, tore up the policy, threw the pieces away, and, tripping over a rug, fell and broke her arm. Of course, she did not get the $200, for she did not have the policy, but it taught her a lesson, and one which she remembered in later years, which is, that it does not pay to hunt for trouble because it is liable to come when one least expects it."

Moving Picture World found the plot improbable: "Some of the attempts to get hurt were well pictured, but the idea did not seem particularly humorous as a whole. It was not the sort of a scheme a child would attempt, it seems."

Boyd Marshall, a singer and stage personality, joined Thanhouser in the autumn of 1913. His first film was made under the Princess label with Muriel Ostriche. Soon, he was identified as her leading man, a position he kept, with some interruptions, for more than a year.

A mirror image of Muriel Ostriche appeared in the Gallery of Picture Players in the November 1913 issue of *Motion Picture Story Magazine*.

Not released as a Princess film, despite an earlier news item to the contrary, *A Campaign Manageress* came out on November 9th as a regular Thanhouser feature. Again, a reviewer found the plot awkward: "One of those very romantic film stories in which the pretty young heroine performs a lot of improbable acts.... The story is not very convincing, but it has action and moves along pleasantly enough. The photography is good."

Muriel played the part of a bright young girl, whose father edited a large newspaper. It happened that in a rural district there were two candidates for sheriff, one put up by the "ring," and the other a political reform candidate who happened to be in love with Muriel. Her father did not oppose the match, but he did not agree with Muriel that the newspaper should endorse his son-in-law to be. Campaigning without editorial support, Muriel's sweetheart told her that his chances of winning were nil.

The father suddenly became ill, a blessing in disguise, for someone had to produce the paper, and the task fell to Muriel. Her first course of action was to support her sweetheart in an enthusiastic article which so aroused the "ring" nominee that he came to the newspaper office, with a whip in one hand and a revolver in his pocket, to take care of the unnamed editorial writer. A crowd assembled outside, and soon the scoundrel candidate came out with his hands in the air, with Muriel behind him with the whip and revolver. Believing that he had tried to attack Muriel, and that by some miracle the girl had snatched his weapons away, the crowd shouted at him and threw stones. Muriel's sweetheart won at the polls, after which she admitted that the "ring" candidate hadn't attacked her at all, but that she had fooled him into staging the event, explaining: "All is fair in politics, especially for a campaign manageress who loves her candidate."

Next in the Princess lineup was *Bread Upon the Waters*, released on November 14, 1913, and reviewed by *Moving Picture World*: "A pleasing film story in which a broken-hearted young man goes away to forget his first sweetheart. Later he falls in love with his landlady's pretty daughter, although he does not realize it for the time being. But when the first sweetheart sends for him, he then learns that his heart belongs to the second. Boyd Marshall and Muriel Ostriche make a very pleasing couple in this."

This was followed shortly by *A Shot Gun Cupid*, a Princess one-reeler released on November 21, 1913 utilizing a story by Bud Duncan. A publicity blurb noted: "Jack loved Mabel, but Pa tells him he has no money to support a wife, and that when he can show him $500 he can marry Mabel. Chicken thieves bother the old man, and he resolves to lay for them, buys a new shot gun, and draws $500 from the bank to buy some property. He hides the money in the old shot gun and hangs it up. Mabel sees him, has an idea, tells Jack to pad his clothes and get shot and show the old man his own money. He agrees. A tramp is shot by mistake. Jack recovers the money and gets the girl with Papa's blessing."

Muriel Ostriche's next film, *The House in the Tree*, was released under the Majestic label. Controlled by Charles J. Hite and his partners, Majestic had been founded in 1910 by Harry Aitken and began business in the first month of 1911. In 1913, Majestic became affiliated with Reliance. Reliance-Majestic films were distributed through the Mutual program.

Released on November 23rd, *The House in the Tree* featured Muriel Ostriche and William Garwood in the leads. The story revolved about a playhouse built in the branches of a giant oak tree and given to a little girl on her birthday. She and Bob, her little playmate, spent many happy hours there. "The years passed, Helen became a pretty girl, and Bob a sturdy young man," a trade notice related. "Mistaking friendship for love, they became engaged, but the romance is soon shattered because of a petty quarrel. The girl went abroad, and the man plunged into business, each determined to forget the other. The house in the tree saw them no more, but stood deserted and desolate. Helen became engaged to an aristocratic foreigner and Bob to a pretty girl who claimed to care for him alone, but disillusionment came to them. Helen learned that the aristocrat cared more for her money, and Bob's fiancé cast him aside for a wealthier man. Bob, bitter and despondent, thought of his boyish romance and the tree which had played so strong a part in his early life. He returned to the little house, and the sight of the possessions of childhood awoke longings for the girl whom he had never quite forgotten. The girl had returned from Europe, and the same impulse drew her to the house in the tree. There she found the man, and the realization that both cherished the past was a tie which drew them together and awakened the love which had never died."

Moving Picture World was enthusiastic and described the film as "a pleasing offering from the very start.... An attractive cast of people and good photography helped make this a very desirable reel."

Muriel and Boyd Marshall had the leads in *Her Right to Happiness*, a Princess film released on November 28, 1913, which told of a stenographer and her boss, who were attracted to each other during office hours, fell in love, and married, only to find that in a non-business setting it was difficult for each to live up to the expectations the other had developed. To get away from it all, Boyd goes on a hunting trip. Muriel follows him, enjoys the experience, and learns that there are indeed other happinesses to share.

The Little Church Around the Corner, a Princess film first publicly screened on December 5, 1913, featured the same two players. A publicity release described the picture: "Do you believe in love at first sight? Well, Boyd Marshall, who is a bachelor in comfortable quarters and circumstances, would have told you that it is impossible until it happened to him, and then it was only a photograph of the girl which he received through the mail. The photo should have gone to the girl's brother-in-law but on account of the similarity in names, it was delivered, through the mischievous machination of Dan Cupid, into the hands of the man who was to come to be the only man in the world for the girl. She was on her way to school by way of New York and expected her brother-in-law to show her some of the showplaces of the great city before she went on to put the finishing touches to her education. Under the circumstances, can you blame Boyd for assuming the role of brother-in-law and piloting a charming companion about the city? And then when he was compelled to confess and ask forgiveness and took the girl to the brother-in-law's house, and found him out, how do you suppose he avoided the horns of the dilemma? Why, the only logical way out was 'the little church around the corner.'" The film provided some

Florence LaBadie, who worked with Thanhouser from 1911 until her death in 1917, was one of the most prominent stars of the era. She and Muriel Ostriche were close friends and took the train together each day from New York City to New Rochelle and return. At the time of her death, she was engaged to Daniel Carson Goodman, a medical doctor turned scenario writer, who produced many scripts for Thanhouser and other companies. (*Motion Picture Magazine* October 1915)

entertaining views of New York City and was "an agreeable picture," noted a reviewer.

Rick's Redemption, released by Majestic on December 7, 1913, had "unusually pleasing photography and cast of characters," according to *Moving Picture World*, "but the plot is very absurd. William Garwood and Muriel Ostriche have the leading roles. Rick never succeeded in looking like a villain, and the casting of her crutches into the sea because the girl would not kiss him was very improbable." A writer for the *New York Dramatic Mirror* had similar thoughts, and, concerning Muriel and William Garwood, stated that "no fault is to be found," but the plot was something else entirely: "The idea of a young man of good quality wantonly throwing the crutches of the crippled young woman into the sea and leaving her on the rocks at the mercy of an incoming tide just because she refused to kiss him, a stranger, is too absurd. Later, having fallen from a cliff, he entered a large hospital. Eventually he was brought again face to face with the girl whose death he believed he caused, after having given himself up to the police. The girl forgives him, and all is well."

His Imaginary Family, The Law of Humanity, and *Cupid's Lieutenant,* all Princess films, were released on December 13, 19, and 26, 1913. The first was described by a reviewer as "an amplification of an old theme in which the nephew borrows a wife and child in order to deceive his uncle, with Muriel Ostriche and Boyd Marshall. The story is a pretty one, in spite of its absurdity. The fireside scene was attractive and, of course, a genuine love affair results from the deception. A pleasing number."

The Law of Humanity, the second Princess film of the month, was noticed by *Moving Picture World*: "The Princess brand of Mutual pictures is springing an innovation. On Friday, December 19th, they released *The Law of Humanity*. The innovation lies in the nature of the picture—dramatic. Hitherto, Princess films have been farces without exception, indeed the 'leads,' Muriel Ostriche, Boyd Marshall, and Marie Eline, were recruited because of their abilities in the line of farce. Hence, it will be interesting to note their work in *The Law of Humanity* which is an emotional drama of pronounced type."

The film, a classic tale of the gulf between haves and have-nots, involves a wealthy employer who refuses to help one of his workers who is injured by a delayed blast. The employer's daughter, straying, arrives at the worker's home, where she is taken in and put to bed. Left alone, she and another girl eat many headache pills and become seriously ill. The wealthy employer, told that his daughter is dying, spends a desperate night in the impoverished home surroundings of his employee, forgets the differences that wealth and social position make, and recognizes "the law of humanity." "An appealing little story," a reviewer called it, while another article stated: "The Princess brand and the Mutual list has a way of garnering bright children. Now it's a two-year-old. Marie Eline, a featured Princess girl, is only eleven, and even Muriel Ostriche, the leading woman, hasn't passed seventeen. The two-year-old is Dorothy Benham, and she has a specialty already. It is a 'cry' and the most natural you ever saw. At a given signal by her mother, Dorothy will simply cry her eyes out. There is nothing 'fakey' or forced about it. See for yourself when Princess' *Law of Humanity* is released."

Cupid's Lieutenant, released the day after Christmas, returned to the farce category. Muriel played the part of a village school teacher in love with a college student, so much so that her scholars tell her she is neglecting them. Sensitive to her first duty, she returns Billy's ring and begins to forget about romance, when her children notice that her usual happiness has turned to gloom. That won't do, and after many comic capers the students dispatch a messenger to bring her lover back.

While Muriel Ostriche and Boyd Marshall were busy turning out Princess films at the rate of about one per week, Charles Hite was expanding Thanhouser's horizons. In November, it was announced that another glass-enclosed stage would be built at New Rochelle, and a new line of pictures, each "of many reels, containing tremendous casts, and stage as well as film stars," would be known as Thanhouser Big Productions. It was planned that these films, which did not involve Muriel Ostriche, would be released on the first day of each month.

In December, Hite announced the establishment of Thanhouser Films, Limited, in London, managed by Paul Kimberly, a step toward expanding European coverage to replace the former distribution handled by Pathé. One of the first tasks awaiting the London staff was the production of *The Thanhouser News*, a weekly house organ patterned after one issued in New Rochelle. More on Thanhouser Big Productions was announced to the trade at the end of December, when it was revealed that Carroll Fleming, a famous producer with the New York Hippodrome, had been signed to help make productions, as had Howell Hansell, who "comes from twenty years experience in the legitimate theatre." Among the Thanhouser players, "Marguerite Snow and James Cruze have joined Maude Fealy as stars in the pictures. Clarence Dull has been appointed property master of the big stuff, while Michael Schliesser is the wild animal manager."

As if activities in London and New Rochelle were not keeping Charles J. Hite busy, it was announced that the New Majestic Film Company, managed by him, was being set up in Los Angeles and hoped eventually to have one of the biggest picture producing companies on the West Coast. In the western studio were Lucille Younge, "well known in western pictures, who liked the idea of returning to her old director, Lucius Henderson," and Jessalyn Van Trump, "famous in American films."

Around the same time, Princess stars attracted the attention of a reporter: "Marie Eline, known since the inception of the Thanhouser Company as 'The Thanhouser Kid,' is grown out of the freak-name class. C. J. Hite has transferred her to his Princess films and requested that she use her real name like a regular grown-up. So, it's Marie Eline now for the first of the 'kids.' The little lady was about six when she joined the Thanhouser forces and is nearly eleven now, an age wherein she feels the dignity of her years. She is a featured player in the Princess, with Muriel Ostriche and Boyd Marshall. Miss Ostriche was likewise a 'child wonder' in her time, but Mr. Marshall never acted in his youth, having been an office boy, which is real work."

Near year's end, on December 28, 1913, *Helen's Stratagem*, a Majestic film with Muriel Ostriche and a cast of players including Lamar Johnstone (a familiar face from Eclair days), Ernest Joy, Vera Sisson, Demetrio Mitzoras, and Howard Davies was released. "A political story of quite a pleasing sort," noted

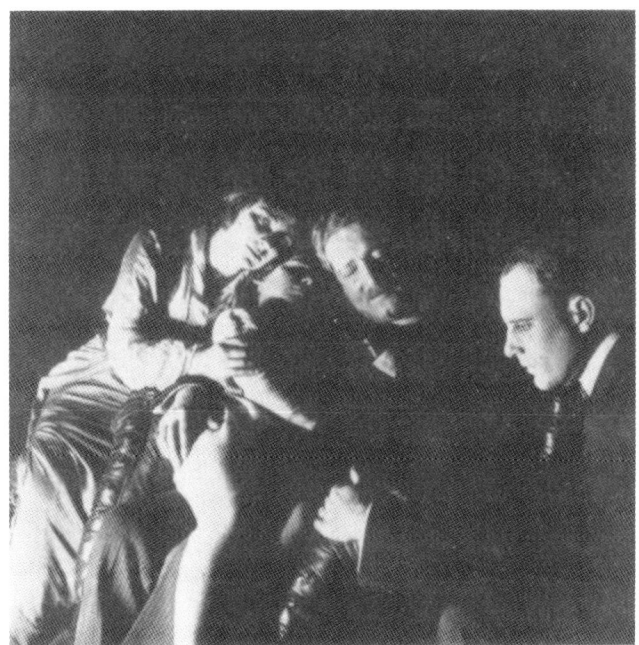

Princess Films

PRODUCED IN A PERFECT STUDIO AT NEW ROCHELLE, N. Y., THE HOME OF PERFECT PICTURES

Release of FRIDAY, December 12th, 1913

"His Imaginary Family"

FEATURING

MARIE ELINE
(The most Famous of Child Actresses)

MURIEL OSTRICHE
(The Youngest of Leading Women)

BOYD MARSHALL
(The Handsomest of Leading Men)

AND A
STRONG SUPPORTING CAST

Princess
MURIEL OSTRICHE, MARIE ELINE
ARTHUR BAUER AND BOYD MARSHALL
IN "HIS IMAGINARY FAMILY"

PRINCESS FILMS
New Rochelle, N. Y.

FEATURING
AVORITES
WITH
FOLLOWINGS

Above: Advertisement in *Reel Life* for *His Imaginary Family*, a Princess release of December 12, 1913, featuring Muriel Ostriche, Marie Eline, Arthur Bauer, and Boyd Marshall (shown in that order in the illustration).

A schoolyard scene from *Cupid's Lieutenant,* featuring Muriel Ostriche, young Marie Eline, Boyd Marshall and "50 bright children."

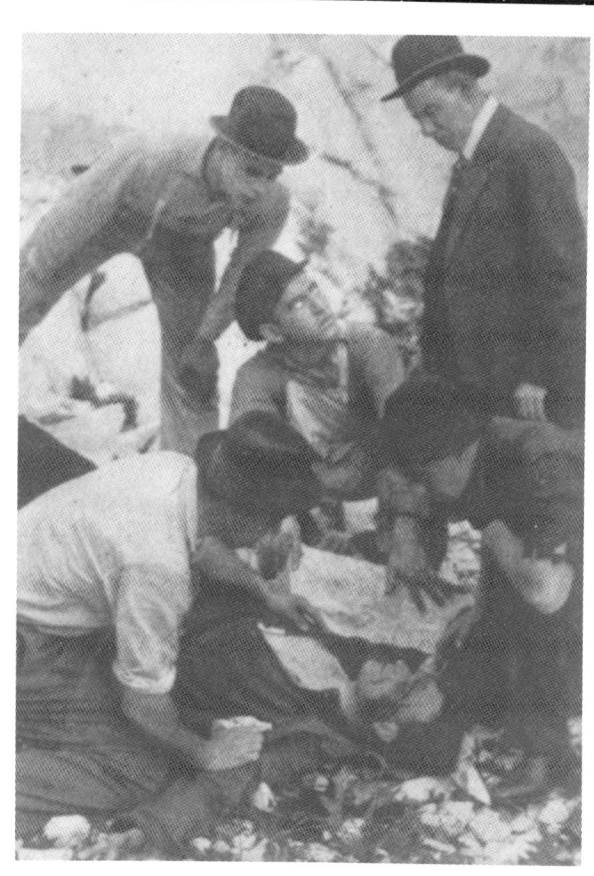

Princess Films

PRODUCED IN A PERFECT STUDIO AT NEW ROCHELLE, N. Y., THE HOME OF PERFECT PICTURES

Release of FRIDAY, December 19th, 1913

"The Law of Humanity"

The Most Powerful One Reel Drama of the Year

WITH

MURIEL OSTRICHE
MARIE ELINE
BOYD MARSHALL
CLAUDE SEIXAS
LITTLE DOROTHY BENHAM

PRINCESS FILMS
New Rochelle, N. Y.

FEATURING **F**AVORITES WITH **F**OLLOWINGS

Princess Films

PRODUCED IN A PERFECT STUDIO AT NEW ROCHELLE, N. Y., THE HOME OF PERFECT PICTURES

Release of FRIDAY, January 2nd, 1914

"A Romance of the Rural Route"

One of Those Pretty Love Stories that Have Made PRINCESS Famous

WITH

MURIEL OSTRICHE
(The Youngest of Leading Women)
BOYD MARSHALL
(The Handsomest of Leading Men)
AND A
STRONG SUPPORTING CAST

PRINCESS FILMS
New Rochelle, N. Y.

FEATURING **F**AVORITES WITH **F**OLLOWINGS

Muriel Ostriche and Catherine Webb in *The Law of Humanity,* a Princess film released on December 19, 1913. Other cast members included Marie Eline, Boyd Marshall, Claude Seixas, Dorothy Benham, Arthur Bauer, Mrs. Hool, and Morgan Jones. Until now, all Princess films had been comedies. After this picture, a drama, films of varied character were made—including comedies, dramas, and scenic features.

Marie Eline, Boyd Marshall, and Muriel Ostriche in *Cupid's Lieutenant,* a Princess film released on December 26, 1913. This still was used in advertising at the time. (American Museum of the Moving Image, Lawrence Williams Collection)

Moving Picture World. "The young candidate weakly yields to the dictation of the bosses, but the invalid sister changes his letter and makes him refuse to comply with their wishes. The story has a pleasing close."

On the last day of the year, the *New York Dramatic Mirror* printed a brief biography of Thanhouser's leader:

"That fame and fortune have been won practically overnight in the motion picture business is well illustrated by the interesting career of C. J. Hite, prominently identified with the Mutual Film Corporation, the Film Supply Company of America, the American Film Manufacturing Company, the Carlton Motion Picture Laboratories, the Majestic Motion Picture Company, the Thanhouser Company, and the Thanhouser Film Company, Ltd. of London.

"In spite of the long list of successful film companies in which he is an important figure, it is only necessary to go back to 1906 to find his first important move in the business. Only eight years ago his first venture was launched in Chicago under the name C. J. Hite Moving Picture Company. The main object of this concern was to furnish motion pictures to lyceum bureaus and private entertainments. Most of his pictures were fairy tales, scenic and religious subjects, which were the best that could be had at the time.

"He gradually found his collection of pictures assuming large proportions, which led him naturally into the film renting business. His first 'exchange' was a small office with a rickety desk in the Monadnock Building, Chicago, but he was compelled to spend so many hours a day at his work that his health began to suffer. The calling in of a doctor proved to be an important incident in his business career, for when the physician discovered that the reason for his patient's condition was the close attention he was compelled to spend in his remarkably successful office, a deal was made that led to renewed activities on a larger scale with the doctor as a financially interested associate. [This tale, involving Dr. Wilbert Shallenberger, a Thanhouser official, was repeatedly denied by the principals, but, nevertheless, it appeared in print many times.]

"In an incredibly short length of time, C. J. Hite's film exchange occupied an enormous suite of offices and had important branches in several other cities. From the renting of films to their manufacture was the next step in Mr. Hite's career. His many interests make him one of the leading factors in the moving picture world."

The year 1913 was busy for *Motion Picture Story Magazine.* Embellished scenarios were published for dozens of different motion pictures, not only for those of Patents Company films, as might be expected from the ownership interest of J. Stuart Blackton, a Vitagraph principal, but of numerous Independents as well, an unbiased spread across the producing spectrum. Muriel Ostriche was a frequent visitor to the editorial office of the magazine and would often pitch in to help the staffers during busy periods. When the publication set up exhibits at motion picture trade shows, Muriel was often on hand to greet visitors.

The Question and Answer Man, the most popular feature in *Motion Picture Story Magazine,* answered hundreds of questions during the year, some seriously, others with a touch of whimsy. Samples:

"I decline to name the best company and poorest. Anyway, sometimes you see a poor play, and a fine one next time, so how can we say that that company is best or worst? Every company has poor ones. Even the sun has its spots, and the diamond is flawed."

"What do they do with the earth that they dig from the Panama Canal? They probably bury it."

"Yes, I have been to Niagara, but I would not want to live there all the time; who wants a cataract always in his eye?"

"Pigs is pigs, and wolfs is wolfs; Mary Fuller has a pet pig, and Phillips Smalley has a pet wolf. There is no accounting for taste, especially when there are so many human animals around that want to be petted."

"It was not a mistake. I said that Christmas and New Year's came on different days of the week *this* year. The New Year's you refer to is *next* year. Now, go to the foot of the class."

"I don't know of any players who are getting rich. Money easily made is easily spent."

"I cannot advise you to adopt literature for a profession. While a few of our great writers have prospered, the large majority have lived and died in poverty. There is a compensation in writing, aside from the gratification it gives. That which is written lives, writers are immortal, but that does not buy bread."

"You have about as much chance to get into a picture company as you have to get to the moon. Don't you know that every company has a waiting list of one hundred or more? And most of them are experienced players from the stage. Nobody wants a green player in it nowadays. Acting is not as easy as it looks. There is not one in one hundred who can do the simple thing of walking in and sitting down, correctly."

"You asked, 'kindly inform me in a way of being a poser, if only for the summer.' It is just as hard to be an actress in the summer as it is in the winter. Afraid I can't help you. You remind me of the man who said he had a few moments to spare and guessed he would sit down and write a book."

Among other news of the year was the note that, effective March 24, 1913, *Motion Picture Story Magazine* would be able to answer Biograph questions and publish pictures of their artists. Further, "Yes, Biograph is a great company in which to get a reputation. Some players seem to think if they can once get with Biograph their future is secure. [However], Vitagraph seems to have the most well-known players."

In the summer of 1913, a printed notice told of Muriel's help: "We might mention a few of the pertinent things that happened at *The Motion Picture Story Magazine's* booth at the International Picture Exposition, held at the Grand Central Palace July 7th to 12th. The average daily attendance was 12,000 people, from all parts of the globe, and this magazine's headquarters was one of the centers of attraction. On the opening night many of our guests talked to the heads of the magazine and expressed disappointment that they could not see and meet some of the popular picture players. We kept a record of the stars in demand, and

Muriel Ostriche in an unattributed Thanhouser scene. (American Museum of the Moving Image, Lawrence Williams Collection)

found that the honor roll of the Popular Player Contest, without a single exception, contained the much sought for names. The following morning our telephone wires were surcharged with conversation, with the result that John Bunny, Muriel Ostriche, Maurice Costello, Arthur Johnson, and Jack Clark volunteered to help receive our guests of Tuesday evening. The following evening such well-known friends as Earle Williams, Lillian Walker, Ethel Grandin, Paul Panzer, Tefft Johnson, E. K. Lincoln, Gene Gauntier, James Young, Clara Kimball Young, Barney Oldfield, Pearl Sindelar, Rosemary Theby, and Flora Finch responded to our calls . . . ." In 1913, and for a number of years thereafter, the same magazine carried many notices of Muriel's activities.

In apparent contradiction to the title of its own magazine, *The Moving Picture News*, an up and coming challenger to the earlier-established *Moving Picture World*, ran the following notice in its September 30, 1913 issue:

"While this publication has been in existence we have endeavored to familiarize the public with the correct nomenclature of the subject—'motion' pictures, not 'moving' pictures. The latter term is clearly a misnomer, notwithstanding its almost general use both in the technical as well as the general press. They are not, cannot be moving pictures because the pictures as such do not move. They are pictures of motion and, therefore, may be correctly described as motion pictures . . . ." Following its own advice, a few issues later, on October 13, 1913, *The Moving Picture News* became *The Motion Picture News*.

By the end of 1913 the dispute between the Patents Company firms and the Independents was moot, and in November *The New York Clipper* announced that "the open market so often spoken of as a remote possibility of the future seems to have arrived in earnest. Licensed houses are showing all sorts of Independent features in conjunction with Patents Company releases, not only in New York City but throughout the country." The immutable laws of economics prevailed, and theatres devoted to Patents Company releases added the popular films of Thanhouser, Universal, and numerous other studios, while the quality of the old-line Patents Company output declined.

The first Muriel Ostriche film released in 1914 was *A Rural Free Delivery Romance*, also called *A Romance of the Rural Route*, which was screened on January 2nd. The plot was a simple one, a "light subject of about average interest" according to a reviewer, and was synopsized in a trade paper as follows:

"Ruth acts as housekeeper for her miserly Uncle Herman. Fearing the loss of her services, Herman opposed the love affair between Ruth and Fred, the rural mail carrier. A letter from the grocer threatens Herman with a lawsuit for the nonpayment of the bill. Herman then conceives a contemptible scheme to avoid payment by placing Fred under suspicion of theft and thereby also prevents his marriage to Ruth. Herman writes two letters, exact duplicates, and addresses both to the grocer. In the one letter, examined by two witnesses, he places a sum of money, but prior to the arrival of the mail carrier the crafty Herman, by distracting the attention of his witnesses, substitutes the duplicate letter which he submits for registration upon the arrival of the carrier.

"Upon receipt of the registered letter containing no money, the grocer enters a complaint at the post office. The case is put in the hands of a post office inspector, and Fred is called to account. The evidence is against the carrier. Herman holds the receipt for the letter. Two witnesses swear the letter contained money. The grocer and his clerk declare no money was received. It is proven that Fred has recently purchased an expensive ring. He is believed guilty and is about to be removed from service.

"In the meantime Ruth finds an empty envelope, addressed to the grocer, in Herman's wastebasket, and learning of Fred's trouble from the substitute carrier, her suspicions are aroused. She hastens to the post office with the new evidence. One of Herman's witnesses discovers upon the second envelope a tobacco stain imprint of his thumb. This fact, proven by the inspector's microscope, identifies the empty envelope, which has never been registered, as the one which contained the money, when examined by the witnesses. Fred is vindicated and free to seek happiness with the girl whose keen wit and quick action saves his reputation."

This little Sherlock Holmesian episode appeared a scant twelve minutes or so on the screen, and was just the sort of thing that audiences eagerly sought, a "filler" featuring a well-known actor or actress, in this instance Muriel Ostriche and Boyd Marshall, in a screenplay that was intended to amuse. If not, within a few minutes another short subject, or perhaps a main feature, would be shown. Increasingly, one-reelers were becoming a scarce commodity, as studios opted for longer features which permitted more dramatic content and an expansion of the plot, although many were the reviews suggesting that what might have been a good one-reel subject was a failure when expanded to two or three. Numerous trade paper editorials discussed whether or not the one-reel film was doomed.

Princess films were quite profitable for Thanhouser, but in the scheme of larger things, such as the Thanhouser Big Productions, the Princess Department was simply a sideline, albeit one which nearly ran itself. Muriel Ostriche recalled that Lloyd and Philip Lonergan wrote most of the scripts, although from time to time she tried her hand at crafting a plot. A contemporary article credited her with the production of many Princess and Thanhouser scenarios. Scripts for most of the early Princess films were the work of Lloyd Lonergan. By early 1914, John W. Kellette was doing most of the work, followed by Philip Lonergan in May 1914. Princess films were extensively promoted in *Reel Life*, the Mutual publication, but few notices were sent out to the general press. As a result, relatively few comments, critical or otherwise, appeared in trade publications, *Moving Picture World* excepted, and fewer yet reached the general newspapers and magazines. Muriel's energy and sparkling personality overcame the lack of studio-generated publicity, and she was regularly interviewed by newspaper and magazine reporters, who could always count on obtaining material for an interesting story.

Moving Picture World, which covered just about anything and everything under its purview, including Princess films, printed an article on January 14, 1914 which told of Carl Gregory and a new script writer for Princess:

"With the Princess brand, Carl Louis Gregory, former chief photographer for Thanhouser Film Corporation, is making pictures that are making good. Aided by clever heart-interest stories with human appeal, and by Miss Muriel Ostriche, Boyd

Studio portrait of Muriel Ostriche, one of several made for the purpose of posting in theatre lobbies and distribution to fans. (Wisconsin Center for Film and Theatre Research)

Marshall, Miss Marie Eline, Arthur Bauer, Morgan Jones, Miss Fanny Bourke, Miss Fanny Gregory, Carey Hastings, and other excellent portrayers of the silent drama, Mr. Gregory's entrance into the directing end is meeting excellent results. Mr. Gregory is doing his own camera work, scenario revision and directing and is aided by Claude Seixas as assistant. Mr. Gregory's knowledge of tone and color harmony is perhaps responsible for the wonderful effects he gains in creations like *His Imaginary Family* and excellent nature studies with outside locations. He has gone from the farce production to drama with the release on December 19 of *The Law of Humanity* . . . balancing his program with polite comedy dramas. John W. Kellette, of New Rochelle, New York, is writing the majority of the scripts."

Most of the Thanhouser-generated publicity went to Marguerite Snow, Mignon Anderson, Florence LaBadie, and James Cruze. The last was the subject of a brief biography in the January issue of *Motion Picture Story Magazine*, which noted that, devoted to his employer, he lived in an apartment house right next door to the Thanhouser studio. His favorite authors were de Maupassant, Rabelais, and Scott. (At the time, it was considered desirable for actors and actresses to appear "cultured," and numerous interviews told of the admiration of Shakespeare, Bacon, and other classic writers by various screen personalities.) Omitted was the fact that his first paying job as a teenager was huckstering on the road with the Billy Banks Medicine Show. "He is a Mormon and is also interested in Christian Science. He has been in the East since 1906. Earlier he appeared in western stock companies for a number of years. He has been in movies for four years, beginning with Pathé, then Thanhouser. He will never leave Thanhouser, he said, 'Unless it be to go into the producing end of motion pictures.' He believes there is big money in the field—also big monopoly." His favorite portrayal was a character in *Letters of a Lifetime*, and his ambition was to have a beautiful home and beautiful children. Only one thing could ever get him away from the motion picture trade, he said, and that was prize fighting. Politically, he supported women's suffrage and believed in the desirability of William Jennings Bryan (the "silver-tongued orator of the Platte," perennial Democratic candidate for president, who lost in the elections of 1896, 1900, and 1908).

The following year, in its June 1915 issue, *Motion Picture Magazine* (the name having been shortened from *Motion Picture Story Magazine* by that time) carried a full page advertisement titled: "JIM CRUZE, HERO OF 'THE MILLION DOLLAR MYSTERY,' WILL TELL YOU HOW TO BE A MOVIE ACTOR." Readers were told: "20,000,000 American picture theatre patrons want new talent, new names, new faces! How to be a movie actor or actress: Your ambition has told you time and time again that you could win in the movies! You have as much right to fame, wealth, and success as any of those you see upon the screen!"

Fortified with a still-sufficient supply of exclamation points, the copy writer continued:

"Jim Cruze points the way! You know Jim Cruze. You held your breath at his easy daring in *The Million Dollar Mystery*. You marveled at his cunning in *Zudora*. . . . You have read about him in the magazines and newspapers. You have seen his portrait before the picture houses. And now—he points the way!

"He says, 'acting is not all.' Which of these things can you do best? Swim, run, jump, drive a team, motorcar, or ride a bicycle or motorcycle, play ball, tennis, billiards? Pose, mimic, typewrite, dance, do acrobatic work? Laugh heartily, wear good clothes easily or 'look pretty'? Many movie stars never appeared on the dramatic stage. The movies call of money—call always: The beautiful, the graceful, magnetic—the tall, the short, thin, fat, ugly, dwarfed, and pay them liberally . . . . It needs THOUSANDS—needs them more and more—pays them from $50 to HUNDREDS OF DOLLARS WEEKLY, and are you not entitled to part of this? Travel! Advance socially and in business. No limitations in the movies . . . ."

Readers were invited to send for a book which promised: "Facts about the movies and every phase and feature! Dozens of beautiful pictures! Talks on make-up, studio terms, film tricks and illusions. Jim Cruze tells you how it seems to be a movie star. Marguerite Snow, Florence LaBadie, Muriel Ostriche, Pearl White, Frank Farrington, Sidney Bracy, and many others tell you what they think of the chances of the beginner in the films."

How many faithful readers of *Motion Picture Magazine* responded to the lure of this catchpenny advertisement is not known, but undoubtedly many paused before pursuing the elusive dream of a film career, for time and time again the same magazine in its editorial features had advised that the chances of a beginner breaking into the field were less than one in a thousand, or even worse. Then, as in later days, many were interested, but few were chosen, and of those who did find work before the motion picture cameras, relatively few achieved notable success.

A case in point was John Bunny, one of the screen's best-loved comedians. At the time of his death (from Bright's disease) in 1915, so revered was he that across the nation more than fifty picture houses changed their names to "Bunny Theatre." After spending most of his adult life on the stage, Bunny, a well-known figure at the time, endeavored to break into films. Again and again he was turned down, until he offered his services free of charge to a major studio, which at last signed him on at a minimum wage. He was an instant success, and within a year he was a favorite of moviegoers everywhere. Still, a writer in *Motion Picture Magazine* noted that he "died poor."

Those who did achieve success often accelerated their personal expenditures and elevated their lifestyles to the point at which outgo exceeded income. Most of the bankable profits in the industry went to producers, distributors, and exhibitors, not to actors and actresses. More realistic than Jim Cruze's inviting advertisement was an article as part of a series, "The Fakes and Frauds in Motion Pictures," by Horace A. Fuld, in the same magazine a few months later. Excerpts:

"The country-wide expression, 'pose for the movies,' is scarcely more general than the desire to do so. Next to the sincere belief of each and every citizen of these United States that he and she is qualified to write a photoplay—whose rejection, of course, means favoritism—is the secret purpose of idly ambitious boyhood and girlhood to act for the film camera. There is no doubt in his mind, or her mind, that histrionic success will mark their movie debut. But the rub is this: How to get started.

This scene from a Thanhouser film, possibly *Flood Tide* (released September 19, 1913), taken by Lawrence Williams, depicts Muriel Ostriche against a lighthouse backdrop. (Courtesy of the American Museum of the Moving Image, Lawrence Williams Collection)

"A gentleman, whom we will call 'Jiggins,' who gives his business address in a midwestern state that may, for the purposes of this warning, be called Wisota, proposes a way. It is a very profitable way, for there are hundreds of 'Jigginses' and tens of thousands of heartaches and misspent wages contributing to them. Jiggins' advertisement may be read in any number of magazines, newspapers, and periodicals. He conducts what he is pleased to style a 'directory' of amateurs who are sincere in their wish to become moving picture actors and actresses. What he wants is their full description of themselves, which he will add to his 'directory' at the modest sum of three cents a word. In the printed matter he will send you, should you be curious enough to write him for information, you will read that he promises to send his list, to which he greatly desires to add your name, to a number of the leading film companies.

"The description that Mr. Jiggins wants is to read something like this: 'Amy Simp, 16 Bow Street, Indianapolis, Indiana. Height, 5 feet 6 inches. Weight, 134 pounds; color of eyes, blue; hair, black. I can ride, drive an auto and play croquet. I look well in fine clothes. I prefer comedy. My friends all say that I imitate Anita Stewart very well. I have no bad habits.'

"The more foolish you make it, the better he likes it. At three cents a word this description would total $1.59. You are strongly urged not to be too modest concerning your fine points, and if you follow his advice you will use over $3 of your money on an aimless description of what you imagine a picture company wants to know about you. You will place a money order for this amount in an envelope along with the description and mail it to Wisota. And this act will elect you as a full-fledged member of the Order of Hopeless Boobs.

"With your money safe in his keeping, presumably there is nothing to prevent this self-styled employment agent from sending the list, every once in a while, to some of the big film makers, which he may mention by name—Vitagraph, Essanay, Thanhouser, etc. Also, provided he comply with Uncle Sam's postage requirements, there is nothing to prevent his list from traveling in the same bag with the rest of the mail and arriving at its destination. But at the Vitagraph, Essanay, Thanhouser, and other studios there is no rule to prohibit this list, after an amused perusal by those to whom it is addressed, from being thrown into the wastebasket. That is invariably what happens."

Muriel and most of her fellow players had a wry attitude about such pretentious claims of so-called movie stardom. Nearly all of them had earned their way by hard work. There was no easy way, and few if any stars of the era were "discovered" through come-on advertisements such as those placed by James Cruze.

Muriel's next film, *The Ten of Spades*, was released by Majestic on January 6, 1914, and garnered the following notice in *Moving Picture World*: "Muriel Ostriche here appears as Jess, a young girl left alone in the world in a western mining camp. She is trained up for the dancing halls. The scenes carry a certain convincing atmosphere, and the girl's sad end, after reading her fortune in the cards, brings the story to an appropriate close. Just a sketchy bit, handled pleasingly."

A detailed scenario synopsis in the same publication noted that Muriel played the part of a young girl in a mining camp, who is unlike the other "dancehall girls" and who is unwilling to engage in certain activities with the miners. She falls in love and has her fortune told. The prediction is not favorable, and she warns her sweetheart, Ralph West, of impending disaster, but he scoffs at her. An enemy attempts to shoot her lover, but Jess receives the bullet by mistake. In the last scene, which probably brought tears to the audience, "she asks Ralph to kiss her, points upward, smiles, and is gone."

Next in the Princess series was *A Circumstantial Nurse*, released on January 9, 1914. In Princess films, Muriel played in a number of scenarios which reviewers characterized as unconvincing, including this one, of which *Moving Picture World* said: "This picture is based on several old and improbable situations.... Yet with the aid of good photography and capable acting this gets hold of the interest and proves acceptable." In the story, Tom, jailed for the crime of another, is discharged from work because of his conviction. Discouraged, he plans to rob his employer's home to get money for medicine for his sick daughter. Arriving at the intended destination he finds the house empty, save for a sick baby, for the maid in charge of the infant had sneaked away on a date with her beau. Seeing the infant's distress, Tom stays to nurse her, at which time his employer returns unexpectedly to realize that Tom is indeed a fine man after all.

Around the same time, early in 1914, the Onyx Club, a nationwide group of movie fans, announced that its members had selected Muriel Ostriche as their favorite film star. Ethel Clayton was the runner-up.

Muriel Ostriche and Boyd Marshall appeared in *When the Cat Came Back* and *The Vacant Chair*, Princess releases of January 16th and 23rd. The first film, a skit involving newlyweds in a boarding house quarrel, was characterized by *Moving Picture World* as "a pretty offering that won't attract much special attention, but will please." The second production was found displeasing: "Full sympathy cannot be given by the normal spectator to anything morbid. In this picture, the old grandmother who makes memories of the dead tyrannize over the living will not be wholly popular. The story deals with her cure through her love for her grandson, but until this begins to come out, it has an unpleasant taste, and the whole picture suffers from her keeping the dead daughter's place always set at the table and her not allowing any other to occupy it. It is well acted, but the director might have made entrance and exits in a few scenes less awkward. The photography is clear and it is, as a whole, fair."

On the evening of January 13, 1914, with the outside temperature below zero, the Thanhouser Company commemorated the first anniversary of the studio fire by a gathering which drew over 500 people. "Many came from New York, all of the metropolitan studios being represented. There were also in attendance many of the prominent townspeople, who indicated in various ways the pride they feel in the success of the growing institution. The members of the company provided entertainment in the form of a cabaret show," according to a notice in *Moving Picture World*. "Refreshments were served during the evening. There were many calls for a speech from President Charles J. Hite, but he preferred to let his past year's industry speak for itself. The New Yorkers returned home on a special train which left New Rochelle at 2:06 a.m., and their departure from the studio marked the closing of a most enjoyable evening."

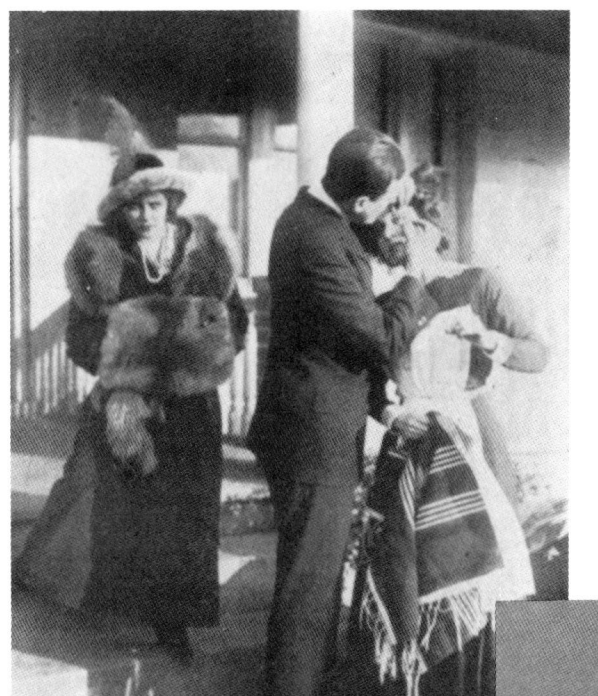

Muriel Ostriche (with fur muff) and Boyd Marshall had the leads in *When the Cat Came Back,* a Princess film released on January 16, 1914. (All illustrations on this page are from *Reel Life,* publication of the Mutual Program)

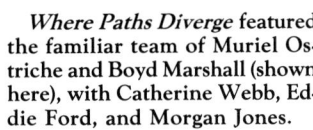

Where Paths Diverge featured the familiar team of Muriel Ostriche and Boyd Marshall (shown here), with Catherine Webb, Eddie Ford, and Morgan Jones.

All's Well That Ends Well, a Princess film released on February 20, 1914, featured Muriel Ostriche (billed as "the youngest of leading women"), Boyd Marshall ("the handsomest of leading men"), and Catherine Webb ("the newest Princess favorite"). Boyd Marshall and Catherine Webb are shown in the scene to the left.

A related story noted that a writer, George Blaisdell, had visited New Rochelle on a business day and had interviewed Hite. It was disclosed that, following the year-earlier fire, the company had moved into a garage adjoining the ruins of the studio and was able to maintain its program of three releases a week. Before long, new facilities, including a glass-covered studio of 6,500 square feet, with adjoining property and work rooms of 4,800 additional square feet, were constructed. Separately, executive offices were built.

Blaisdell wrote: "Charles J. Hite began life on a farm in Lancaster, Ohio. Then for a period he taught school—an occupation from which many men have started a successful business career. Mr. Hite's first commercial venture was in a lyceum. There he supplied films to the Redpath Lecture Bureau. Then, with S. S. Hutchinson, he opened a small film exchange in Chicago, known as the H. & H. The capital was only $1,200, but in the first year Mr. Hite cleared $5,000. This was in 1909. Harry Aitken at this time was conducting the Western Film Exchange in Milwaukee. He joined Messrs. Hite and Hutchinson and formed the American Film Manufacturing Company. Mr. Hite and Mr. Hutchinson then became interested in the Majestic Company. It will be remembered that opposition on the part of the management of the old Motion Picture Sales Company prevented the Majestic from securing a market through that group. It was this action that suggested to the two film men the idea of acquiring a number of exchanges of their own. The idea matured, and from this beginning the present Mutual Film Corporation has grown. Mr. Hite is president of the Thanhouser Company, vice president and treasurer of the Mutual, and with Crawford Livingston and Mr. Aitken is a member of the executive committee of the Mutual. He is also treasurer of the New York Motion Picture Corporation.

"The writer found Mr. Hite in his office on Monday morning. He said that business from his viewpoint was most satisfactory.... The Thanhouser Company is now turning out 325,000 feet of film each week from its New Rochelle establishment. This does not touch the foreign market, all the printing for which is done abroad. Asked as to how he viewed conditions on the other side as regards his product, Mr. Hite said that matters were in fine shape.... Mr. Hite said that he did not think that the influx of feature companies would affect the product of established brands. He said that he was interested in the theatre business and patronage, which were closely watched from an experimental viewpoint. It was his experience that picture-going is a habit. The factor that causes a man to continue going to a picture theatre may be one face or several faces he sees on the screen. Asked as to his belief in the theory expounded by one manufacturer that patrons of the theatre like to see new faces, Mr. Hite said that he thought it absurd. Old members of a stock company become to the public old friends and they are looked for. He said that when permanently engaging a new player it is important to note the impression created by the actor among picturegoers. 'An empty head and good looks mean nothing in pictures,' said Mr. Hite, 'for the public is on to the combination immediately. But given brains, looks and skill, then we have a good subject for the screen.'

" 'What about the future of the single reel?' said Mr. Hite in response to a question. 'Why, I don't think the single reel is going to disappear, but I think we've got to make them mighty good. They are to picturegoers what short stories are to magazine readers. We all like to read books, but we like to read magazines too. So, also people like to see big productions, but they like to see single reels, too. In the theatre of which I was speaking we charged for our regular program five and ten cents admission, and for features ten and fifteen cents. Did you know that on our feature nights we do three times the business that comes to the box office on our everday stuff? But we know that we cannot run the big stuff every night—it would hurt the business....

" 'We are now ready to make big pictures, and we are going to make them. As a matter of fact, we have turned out five big subjects since our fire a year ago. I think there is one thing the manufacturers have to fear, and that is the amalgamation of theatres. If that ever takes place, you can be sure that I will be one of the amalgamators.' Mr. Hite admitted, however, that it would be a practical impossibility to put in effect any plan of this sort by reason of the many conflicting interests involved." Little did the interviewer or his subject realize that a few years hence Fox, Paramount, and a few other studios would control motion picture exhibition in nearly all of America's larger cities, a situation which would vastly change the industry.

A notice in *Moving Picture World*, issue of January 30, 1914, inaccurately advised readers that Muriel Ostriche was no longer with the Princess Department of Thanhouser. Perhaps this was because *The Home of Silence*, a Princess film released on January 29th, featured Boyd Marshall not with the familiar Muriel, but with Reenie Farrington, whose first name caused lots of problems with typographers, some of whom preferred "Rene" or "Renee." Probably, "Reenie," as given out in early news releases, was what her friends called her, although her given name was Irene. Muriel continued to be involved with Princess films, but not on an exclusive basis. Occasional releases featured the work of others.

In addition to the inconsistent spelling of Miss Farrington's first name, other erratic spellings were common in the publicity notices generated by Thanhouser. Fan Bourke appeared in print as Fana and Fanny, and in one news release her last name was transmogrified to Burks. Catherine Webb also appeared as Katharine Webb, and readers sometimes wondered if Arthur Bauer also spelled his last name as Baur or Bower. Actors and actresses in other studios didn't fare any better. Ethel Grandin often had her name misspelled as Grandon, and many were the typographers who changed King Baggot's last name to Baggott.

The Purse and the Girl, some prints of which were distributed under the title *The Loser Wins*, released on January 30th, told of a misplaced billfold, the mishaps of its finder, and the inevitable love affair involving Muriel Ostriche. "The plot without novelty has sufficiently the sense of newness, and with business it is not convincing," stated a somewhat contradictory review in *Moving Picture World*, which continued: "The characters are lively and excite interest. Produced in a simple, forthright way, it makes a pleasing release."

Closing out January 1914 was the Screen Club Ball, held at the Grand Central Palace on Saturday evening, the 31st. Tickets were $2 each, admitting a lady and a gentleman, with the enticement: "Dance with your favorite player: King Baggot, Mary

Princess Films

PRODUCED IN A PERFECT STUDIO AT NEW ROCHELLE, N. Y., THE HOME OF PERFECT PICTURES

Release of FRIDAY, January 23rd, 1914

"The Vacant Chair"

One of Those Pretty Human Interest Stories that Have Made PRINCESS Famous

WITH

MURIEL OSTRICHE
(The Youngest of Leading Women)

BOYD MARSHALL
(The Handsomest of Leading Men)

AND A
STRONG SUPPORTING CAST
INCLUDING MORGAN JONES

PRINCESS FILMS
New Rochelle, N. Y.

FEATURING AVORITES WITH OLLOWINGS

Muriel Ostriche and Boyd Marshall in "The Vacant Chair" *Princess*

Princess Films

PRODUCED IN A PERFECT STUDIO AT NEW ROCHELLE, N. Y., THE HOME OF PERFECT PICTURES

Release of FRIDAY, January 30th, 1914

"The Purse and the Girl"

One of Those Pretty Love Stories that Have Made PRINCESS Famous

WITH

MURIEL OSTRICHE
(The Youngest of Leading Women)

BOYD MARSHALL
(The Handsomest of Leading Men)

MARIE ELINE
(The Most Famous of the Kids)

FAN BURKE AND A STRONG SUPPORTING CAST

PRINCESS FILMS
New Rochelle, N. Y.

FEATURING AVORITES WITH OLLOWINGS

Muriel Ostriche, Marie Eline, and Boyd Marshall stand before Arthur Bauer in *The Purse and the Girl,* a Princess film released on January 30, 1914. (*Reel Life*)

Fuller, John Bunny, Lillian Walker, Arthur Johnson, Ormi Hawley, Maurice Costello, Florence Lawrence, Billy Quirk, Helen Gardner, Irving Cummings, The Mutual Girl, Francis X. Bushman, Marion Leonard, Warren Kerrigan, Lottie Briscoe, Crane Wilbur, Edgena de Lespine, Tefft Johnson, Alice Joyce, Owen Moore, Mary Pickford, G. M. Anderson, Fritzi Brunette, Dave Wall, Muriel Ostriche, and many other notables."

A poll taken by *Motion Picture Story Magazine* noted that 5,381 people preferred multiple-reel films and 5,062 opted for single-reel pictures. Asked what topics people preferred, 5,908 named dramas, 1,600 liked educationals, 6,804 enjoyed war pictures, 1,018 were fans of westerns, and 1,446 named comedies.

Boyd Marshall made the news in a February issue of *Moving Picture World*: "The other week the Princess Company sent out a story, which some of the papers fell for, on the speech of Boyd Marshall, their leading man, in favor of Sunday closing of picture shows, before the Woman's Club of New Rochelle. It seems that the press department of the Princess Company was in error about the speech ascribed to Mr. Marshall. That player is *now* quoted as saying: 'It would have been a novelty for a man who gets his living from the movies, to address a public body on behalf of an ordinance that would forbid their exhibition at any time, but I wouldn't be novel that way! I merely advocated an editing of Sunday programs that would result in exhibitions that were more or less educational in nature. If the ministers are against the showing of red-blooded dramas on this day, we can give them light drama of an emotional character or straight educational pictures, for there certainly are enough films of that kind to go around.' "

Where Paths Diverge, a Princess film released on February 6, 1914, featured Muriel and Boyd. "Billy weds Muriel secretly, and the antagonism of mother prevents him announcing it," a trade notice stated. "Muriel secretly works on garments for her expected child, when Mrs. Greg discovers the clothes and marriage certificate. She destroys evidence of the alliance and drives Muriel out. She warns Billy if he continues the alliance that she will cast him adrift. Muriel loses her position and finds work with Boyd, keeping her past a secret. Boyd learns to love her and proposes marriage, but Muriel refuses. She requests a month's vacation, ostensibly to visit her mother, but goes to the hospital, where her child is born dead. She returns to Boyd's employment, and he insists upon at least an engagement. She is heartbroken, but then a letter permits the diverging path to converge towards happiness." A review noted: "The pretty leading lady [Muriel] acts well in the romantic scenes, but shows lack of experience in tragedy."

Released on February 8th under the Thanhouser name, rather than Princess, *Percy's First Holiday*, written by the indefatigable Lloyd F. Lonergan, saw Muriel playing the part of May, a movie actress. Percy, an Australian film actor, was played by W. S. Percy. Fan Bourke, an up and coming Thanhouser actress, took the part of Jane, while other roles fell to Justus D. Barnes and Boyd Marshall.

The Tangled Cat, a Princess release of February 13, 1914, inspired one of the best notices *Moving Picture World* ever gave to a Princess film: "This is really a neat little comedy and caused great laughter among the reviewers. The actors seemed to catch the spirit of the situation and succeeded in bringing out all the points artistically. There is a funny direction that is all too good to reveal, but it is worth seeing. It is finely directed, and the scenes well photographed. It is a picture anyone will enjoy. Muriel Ostriche, Boyd Marshall, Fan Bourke, Eddie Ford, and a strong cast of supporters foist this little offering upon the public. Do it again Mr. Director."

The plot synopsis: "Fanny, a rural old maid, lives with her niece, May [Muriel Ostriche], and has a primitive fear of tramps, burglars, and the male sex in general. She has, according to traditions of her kind, a cat, and as the cat wandered at night it brought trouble to Fanny. Silas, a neighbor, entertaining homefolk at a reunion, needed Ford's bed for the company, and sent him to Fanny's house to seek shelter for the night. Fanny and May had just spread fly paper to catch a pesky fly, and the cat got into it after Ford had retired, and Fanny and May got beneath the coverlets. Fanny was sure it was Ford prowling around. Ford imagined it was the old maid with designs on his freedom, and he escaped before she had a chance to drag him to the marriage market. Fanny and May get out to go to Silas,' and after a brave party returns to Fanny's house, they discover that Fanny's fear of burglars is unnecessary, and Boyd, a city fellow captivated with the rosy-cheeked May, made known his intention of protecting her until death did them part."

Muriel and Boyd next appeared in *All's Well That Ends Well*, a Princess film released on February 20th, set in a Japanese tea room.

Another Princess film, *The Hold-Up*, with Muriel Ostriche, James Ayres, and Catherine Webb, appeared on February 27, 1914 to an indifferent review: "This picture has a plot too old to amount to much as entertainment, although it is true that to many spectators even this trite story will be interesting. In order to cure two romantic myths, her parents conspire with the man who loves her and let her elope with her music teacher, whom they know is a bigamist and forger, then hold up the two, bringing them home to show the girl the forger's picture as a man 'wanted' by the police. The setting and photography are of high quality, but the acting is not strong."

Her Way, again featuring Muriel in a character part as May, was screened on March 6, 1914. The episode was "another version of the prodigal son," according to the *New York Dramatic Mirror*, while *Moving Picture World* noted that the plot "uses the same idea as *She Stoops to Conquer*." Synopsis: "Ford and Gale are great friends. Gale desires that Ford's son shall marry his daughter, May, but Jim won't listen to such an arrangement, because he likes the 'white lights' and the gay cabaret life too well to lie down to any one woman. Ford plans that if Gale can induce May to enter his household as a maid and study Jim, she might find out whether the spendthrift was worth marrying. After some coaxing, the humorous situation appeals to May and she goes, swapping positions with Ford's maid. Being beautiful, she appeals to Jim's idea of women, and the cabaret loses its charm, but when Jim proposes and offers an engagement ring, she refuses him, and plots with Ford. Jim the next morning is disconsolate when he finds she has left his life. It is not until Ford asks him to go to Gale's, as 'she came from Gale's town,' that Jim thinks he might run across her. He goes. Much as he dislikes to meet Gale's daughter, he feels he must on account

Muriel Ostriche and Boyd Marshall in a scene from *Where Paths Diverge,* a Princess film released by Thanhouser on February 6, 1914. The cast also included Catherine Webb, Eddie Ford, and Morgan Jones. The action took place in the Thanhouser studio in New Rochelle, New York. (American Museum of the Moving Image, Lawrence Williams Collection)

Muriel Ostriche, Justus D. Barnes, and W.S. Percy are shown in a scene from *Percy's First Holiday,* a Thanhouser film released on February 8, 1914. Also in the cast were Fan Bourke, Babe Wallace, Charles Van Hout, Boyd Marshall, Ed Ford, Arthur Bauer, Grace Eline, and Lydia Mead. The story told of the travels of an Australian film actor.

of association, and when he turns to find the maid he made love to none other than the girl they wanted him to marry, well, they don't have to work at all after the introduction."

March 1914 was the month when *Motion Picture Story Magazine* dropped *Story* from its title. In the meantime, its circulation was growing, and several competing periodicals had sprung up.

Mutual, with its familiar "Mutual Movies Make Time Fly" motto superimposed on a winged clock, distributed frosted white electric light globes with the trademark to theatres, ideal for placing out front to draw patrons. The Mutual program at the time consisted of films made under the American, Reliance, Keystone, Royal, Thanhouser, Majestic, Beauty, Broncho, Comic, Domino, Mutual Weekly, Kay Bee, Princess, and Apollo brand names.

The subject of whether movies should be shown on Sundays was of nationwide concern, with the continuing debate in New Rochelle, Thanhouser's home town, making the trade papers. On March 17, *Moving Picture World* carried the following notice:

"Muriel Ostriche, Princess films, will follow her leading man, Boyd Marshall, as a speaker before the Woman's Club of New Rochelle in the public discussion of Sunday opening of picture shows that is taking up most of the club's time right now. Marshall, in his talk of some weeks ago, advised the women to work for Sunday picture programs that were carefully edited in advance and of an educational nature. 'The youngest leading woman in pictures—Miss Ostriche is 17—will take issue with Mr. Marshall. It is her idea that an all-educational show bores, that it would keep people out of the picture theatres and in that way would have the same effect as the Sabbath closing law that the exhibitors are fighting. In the talk, which is scheduled for this coming Sunday, she will counsel the women to work for either 'bright' programs or flat closing down inasmuch as the educational program will not 'draw' the people. Miss Ostriche does not advocate the showing of sensational photoplays on the Sabbath, nor the total elimination of educational pictures, but she does think that the showing of comedies and farces that people would enjoy constitutes no disrespect for the Sabbath. The 'closing' measure comes up to the New Rochelle Common Council for final decision within ten days."

Conscious of their image with the public, motion picture companies of the time made much of the scattered educational films they released, although they were not good drawing cards. Often, ministers and public officials would be called upon to endorse such features. In the meantime, as Muriel Ostriche was well aware, the public, although stating in surveys that educational films were high on the list of popularity, put down their nickels and dimes to see as many comedies and farces as possible.

Among Muriel's co-workers in the New Rochelle studio in March 1914 were Morris Foster, Arthur Bauer, and Fan Bourke, the last playing comedy leads. All were busy at work in their new jobs, it being the first time in pictures for two of the three, Arthur Bauer having briefly acted a few years earlier at the Great Northern studio in Denmark. Whenever the name of D.W. Griffith could be mentioned in a biography, no matter how slight the connection, advantage was taken of it. In telling of his life, Morris Foster noted that his career started in 1903 on the stage at the Central Theatre, San Francisco, distinguished as being a place where Griffith once played.

"Boyd has never skated, but he will try anything for Muriel's sake, and Billy professes to be a champion fancy skating artist," noted a plot synopsis of *Billy's Ruse*, a Princess film released on March 13, 1914. "Billy has a 'chewing match' with Fanny, his wife, and while she entertains a neighbor, Billy looks through a window and listens to the call of the ice. He sees what a terrible time Muriel is having in trying to teach Boyd to skate. She looks good to him, so he offers to teach Boyd to skate and offers himself as an escort. Muriel, not knowing he is married, has a delightful time. Fanny, in the meantime, parts with her caller and discovers Billy's absence. She sees him from the house displaying his ability to Muriel. She goes after him, and after exciting mixups and eccentric comedy, Billy gets chased, and finding Fanny some skater, realizes his only means of escape is through a fisherman's hole in the ice, and he goes into it. It is only after apparently being given up as lost that Billy appears, but he enjoys the scene from another hole. When he makes his appearance, Fanny promises to let bygones be bygones."

Moving Picture World noted of the film: "An ice pond farce with some novices on skates furnishing fun. It is very laughable, for the author has kept his situation cleverly developing into freshly astonishing forms, and it is brightly acted. Good number for fun."

The Grand Passion, a Princess film released on March 20, 1914, featured Muriel Ostriche, Morris Foster (playing the part of a character named Boyd), and Nolan Gane. One reviewer thought that Muriel "had too much makeup on and was dressed too flashily for a businesswoman" in her role, "but she is a pretty little thing always." A trade release noted:

"Boyd secretly loves Muriel, whose preference is Joe, and upon her birthday the office force presents her with a lavalliere, while Boyd's gift is a flower. Enthused at the gift she wants to kiss everybody but Boyd, knowing that a kiss from her would mean a lot to him. She changes her mind to please the onlookers, but he refrains from taking a kiss so lightly given. The crowd looks on his action as an insult to Muriel and bind him, while Muriel kisses him thrice, and with the last kiss goes the hate of a woman's scorn. His flower gift to her is used to slap her face after the third kiss. Enraged, the crowd starts to assault Boyd, taking their cue from Muriel's treatment, but she prevents it. Later, with hope and spirit crushed, Boyd takes to drink and, leaving the barroom, falls and his head is injured. When he recovers his mind is blank, and it is only when Muriel insists that the scene of the birthday kissing be re-enacted that his memory is restored."

Such plot synopses, printed in the trade papers, were often disjointed, and in lieu of seeing a print of the film itself, the only way to piece the story together is to read multiple reviews, and even then the descriptions of the action sometimes differ. Another review of *The Grand Passion* gives the impression that Muriel was in love with Boyd, which the preceeding synopsis does not indicate.

The policy of not featuring Muriel Ostriche in each and every Princess film was continued, and the publicity for the March 27th release, *Beautiful Snow*, and the April 3rd picture, *Her First Lesson*, did not mention her. The latter picture featured "dancing introduced by Nellie Williams" and was panned by *Moving Picture World*: "What excuse the producers of this picture will have for releasing it will be welcomed; if it ever gets by. There is nothing in it to cause the censors to condemn, nor is there anything of merit to recommend it."

Too Much Turkey, an April 13, 1914 Princess release featuring Muriel Ostriche, was reviewed by *Moving Picture World*: "An appealing comedy that concerns a newly married couple that are hard up on Thanksgiving Day. Each determines that they must have a turkey, and secretly they determine to make a sacrifice to surprise the other. How they come out in the end is laughable; just for the minute it is almost tragic. The finale is highly satisfactory. This is a clean little comedy."

The same publication subsequently described *Her Awakening*, a Princess film released on April 17, 1914: "This is an entertaining picture which carries with it a lesson to girls who are forced by circumstances to hold positions in offices where they are the mercy of unprincipled employers. Muriel Ostriche plays the part of the little stenographer, in a natural and artistic manner. She is the oldest of three children, whom a loving and widowed father is attempting to the best of his abilities to provide for. A well-made worthy offering on any program."

Throughout April, other news pertaining to Muriel Ostriche and Thanhouser reached print, including an article in the *New York Dramatic Mirror*, which observed her March 24th birthday. "Lloyd Lonergan, the scenario editor, is now writing a feature dancing picture for Miss Ostriche, in which she will exhibit the many prizes she has won at the new dances, and show her many admirers the various steps," the same account noted.

David Thompson was appointed as cast director for the Thanhouser plant, apparently a position involving risk, for the *New York Dramatic Mirror* stated: "He has engaged the services of a valet, the same being a huge Ethiopian nicknamed 'Jasbo,' who also acts as his personal bodyguard." Irving Cummings, who like many of his fellow actors practiced studio-hopping, was back on deck with Thanhouser, and was again making pictures for the Mutual Program. "When I left the Mutual last year I felt ill at ease over the change and I have not been contented ever since then," he noted in an interview. He had been with Reliance, a Mutual Company, then had gone to Pathé, then to Thanhouser.

At the Thanhouser studio, dozens of employees were kept busy in as many different directions. A new department devoted to Apollo brand films was trying to establish a reputation, several different Thanhouser Big Productions were in the works, and, most important, it was announced that a serial feature, *The Million Dollar Mystery*, was being readied for release on June 29th, to be preceded by related stories in newspapers on a weekly installment basis beginning on June 28th, the day before. By that time, motion picture production companies had discovered that serials were a powerful magnet, and that movie attendance could be increased dramatically by having cooperative newspapers print the story of the film immediately before its release to theatres. In his excellent essay on the Thanhouser Company, in *Aspects of American Film History Prior to 1920*, Anthony Slide noted: "Thanhouser entered the serial field in 1914 with *The Million Dollar Mystery*, starring Florence LaBadie, James Cruze, and Marguerite Snow, and directed by a newcomer to the Thanhouser ranks, Howell Hansell. Produced at a cost of $80,000 [another account placed the amount at $125,000], it was claimed that the serial grossed $1,600,000. Interestingly, the financing and distribution of *The Million Dollar Mystery* was handled by W. Ray Johnston, who had been C. J. Hite's secretary."

In other news concerning the industry, it was noted that Dr. Leonard Keene Hirshberg, of The Johns Hopkins University in Baltimore, not only felt that movies were not injurious to the eyes, contrary to what numerous colleagues in the medical profession had stated, but "I go even further and assert that two hours a day in the dark auditorium of a picture playhouse, spent before the motion-photo screen, is actually a tonic to the tired eyes."

It is not certain who counted them, but *The Morning Tribune*, of Tampa, Florida, stated that during the previous year 6,380,000,000 nickels were spent at moving picture theatres in America, an amount equal to $319,000,000. Meanwhile, on the Thanhouser lot, Irving Cummings and Mignon Anderson were paying increasing attention to each other. The following month they announced their engagement and stated they would marry in June. Soon, Mignon Anderson did a turnabout and married Morris Foster instead.

While others were taking her place in Princess films, Muriel was working on a Thanhouser production, *The Strike*, which was released on April 21st and which featured her and Morris Foster in the lead roles, with George Walsh and Fan Bourke also playing important parts. The picture pleased reviewers, and *Moving Picture World* noted: "This superior two-reel picture illustrates the influence a strike agitator holds over unionism and how he can induce employees to inaugurate a strike against their own interests. This is a strong picture and of much interest to labor organizations. Superior explosion and fire scenes are involved in the plot."

The *New York Dramatic Mirror* advised its readers: "Staging is satisfactory throughout, and the actors are successful in suggesting the contrasting types found in a factory town. Muriel Ostriche is particularly winning in her portrayal of Mary. Photography is clear." The same review noted concerning the plot: "The one error seems to be the placing of labor unions in a too unfavorable light, even granting the dangerous character of professional agitators such as Black, the trouble-maker in this story. We are shown the worst elements of organized labor, and none of the better; whereas capital is the virtuous, innocent part, save for a persistent obstinancy in refusing to compromise."

Muriel was again seen in a Princess film when *Politeness Pays* reached the theatres on May 1st. "This is a very meritorious offering; one that might be used by clerks and salesmen as a wholesome lesson," noted *Moving Picture World*. "Nolan Gane plays the part of the polite young clerk, to the disgust of the store associates. Muriel Ostriche is his sweetheart. They are waiting and saving for the wedding day, but politeness on the lover's part to a crusty old maiden lady unexpectedly brings a check which enables them to marry at once. An interesting, well-played and produced number."

In Her Sleep, a Princess one-reeler screened on May 15, 1914, starred Muriel Ostriche in the company of Morgan Jones, Madeline Fairbanks (or was it Marion, the other Thanhouser twin?—trade accounts differ), Charlie Horan, and Mrs. Arthur Ellery

PRINCESS FILMS

PRODUCED IN A PERFECT STUDIO AT NEW ROCHELLE, N. Y.,
THE HOME OF PERFECT PICTURES

Release of FRIDAY, FEBRUARY 27th, 1914

"THE HOLD-UP"

One of Those Pretty Human Interest Stories that Have Made
PRINCESS Famous

WITH

MURIEL OSTRICHE
(The Youngest of Leading Women)

BOYD MARSHALL
(The Handsomest of Leading Men)

CATHERINE WEBB

AND A

STRONG SUPPORTING CAST INCLUDING

JAMES AYRES and JOE SPARKS

PRINCESS FILMS
NEW ROCHELLE, N. Y.

FEATURING
AVORITES
WITH
FOLLOWINGS

Muriel Ostriche in "The Hold-up"—Princess

The Hold Up, a "pretty human interest story," was released on February 27, 1914 as part of the Mutual Program. (*Reel Life*)

Muriel Ostriche and Boyd Marshall in a bedtime scene. From *The Tangled Cat*, a Princess release of February 13, 1914.

Boyd Marshall and Muriel Ostriche in a scene from *Billy's Ruse,* released on March 13, 1914 and billed as, "A drama of deception." Also in the cast were Billy Noel, Fan Bourke, Catherine Webb, Charles Emerson, and Eugene Redding.

A REAL INNOVATION

The PRINCESS Company
New Rochelle, N. Y.

Continues the

"Traveling Star" System

(Presenting the Princess Players in association with leading Players from other companies)

THF FIRST TIME OF THIS SYSTEM IN MOTION PICTURES!

FRIDAY, APRIL 3RD,

MURIEL OSTRICHE
(The youngest of leading women)

NELLIE WILLIAMS, DOROTHY BENHAM, MADELINE THOMPSON and Princess Players Players offer

"Her First Lesson"

In Association with

MORRIS FOSTER and NOLAN GANE

See the Princess Favorites as they "line up" with your other New Rochelle favorites! Show your approval of this innovation by insisting on PRINCESS FILMS at your exchange!

Boyd Marshall and Muriel Ostriche in *Her First Lesson,* a Princess release of Friday, April 3, 1914. Each Friday, a one-reel Princess film was part of the Mutual Program. (*Reel Life*)

Muriel Ostriche, third from the left, in a circa 1914 Thanhouser scene. To her right is Janet Clendenning-Henry, a New Rochelle girl who by 1914 claimed to have had parts in "about 300 photoplays." To Muriel's left is Nolan Gane, whose real surname was Gagne, and who considered *The Grand Passion* (Princess, March 20, 1914) to be his best film. He died of pneumonia in September 1914.

The doings of Thanhouserites, as they were called, occupied many pages of *Motion Picture Magazine* over the years. The cartoons shown here were published in April 1914. Had Muriel not followed an acting career, she probably would have become a teacher, a sentiment often expressed in interviews—hence the reference in the lower right panel. James Cruze, Florence LaBadie, Mignon Anderson, Muriel Ostriche, Marguerite Snow, Maud Fealy, Harry Benham, and Marie Eline were all well known in their time, and their screen activities were followed by millions of theatre patrons.

Morris Foster and Muriel Ostriche in a scene from *The Strike*, a Thanhouser film released April 21, 1914. A review in *Moving Picture World* noted: "This superior two-reel picture illustrates the influence a strike agitator holds over unionism and how he can induce employees to inaugurate a strike against their own interests. This is a strong picture and of much interest to labor organizations. Superior explosion and fire scenes are involved in the plot."

(otherwise known as Marie Rainford). "The acting is all that could be desired," *Moving Picture World* commented.

Muriel Ostriche remembered the Thanhouser Twins: "They attracted a lot of attention. Marion and Madeline were identical, and the only way the Thanhouser players could tell them apart was to look at their elbows. There was a mark on one. We all had to remember that. Both were beautiful girls."

Motion picture scripts could be copyrighted, but titles could not, and this led to numerous instances of different films bearing the same name. An example is provided by *A Circus Romance*, a Princess film with Muriel Ostriche, which was released on May 22nd, which may have inspired an identically-titled movie issued by Méliès a few months later, not to overlook still another *A Circus Romance* film in which Muriel Ostriche played, this one by Vitagraph, released on February 5, 1916. Concerning the 1914 Princess effort, *Motion Picture News* noted: "Muriel Ostriche is featured in this drama, which is too ordinary to be good. Pepita, the circus rider, is injured in the ring. Her admirer, a doctor, cares for her and later marries her." *Moving Picture World*, still the dominant trade paper, observed: "New Rochelle companies seem fond of circus pictures and usually make good ones; this is a good one though the story is slight. It has the usual circus parade, which we commend. The melodrama seems new enough and will interest and please. The photography is good."

Muriel Ostriche played the part of Ruth (or Beth, accounts differ) Alden, operator of a telephone exchange, in *A Telephone Strategy*, a Princess film released on May 29th, with Boyd Marshall playing the opposite role. It was a "pleasing little melodrama, lively, exciting, and free from anything objectionable. It is romance that makes such pictures go, and they are popular just now. Well photographed, it has good scenes," observed *Moving Picture World*. The story involved a young telephone girl who was in love with the son of a rich man, the town banker, who pursued the romance over the strong objections of his father. Not wishing to start a family feud, Muriel refuses to marry her suitor without his father's consent and, to avoid complications, requests to be transferred to night duty so she will not see her lover again. "One evening, when Ralph [her lover] is alone after hours at the bank, robbers break in. He is seized and bound, and they plan to imprison him in the vault, but the young man, by a clever ruse, manages to get in communication with Ruth Alden at the telephone exchange. She arrives with help in time to release Ralph from the vault and to save his life. When Colonel Parker hears the whole story from his son, he says, 'I guess you need someone to take care of you,' and gives his consent to the marriage."

Motography, the Chicago-based trade magazine which often expressed the hope that the moving picture industry would eventually be centered in Chicago, carried a detailed article on Muriel Ostriche in its May 30, 1914 issue. Written by Mabel Condon, it was part of the "Sans Grease Paint and Wig" series of interviews with players. A popular feature writer for *Motography* and other publications, the interviewer later moved to Los Angeles where she opened the Mabel Condon Exchange, which handled scripts and acted as an intermediary between authors and film companies. By two years later, in August 1916, she announced that "over 800 photodramas were handled in the play department and 48 sold," and noted that she was opening branches in New York City and Chicago. In 1914, Condon journeyed to New Rochelle to check on Muriel:

"At three-forty-five o'clock on a recent warm afternoon Muriel—there is only *one* Muriel!—danced herself out of a studio setting and into her dressing room with the remark, 'We'll get that 4:15 train yet.' But would we? Anyway, Muriel said so and I was ready to run for it whenever she would be, and the rate at which she doffed makeup and clothes promised well for the fulfillment of her word. So I sat back in a most out-of-the-way corner of the little room to give her as much room as possible, and guessed we had better both play sphinx until the 4:15 out of New Rochelle had been captured. But Muriel had no such kindred thought.

" 'It's been a wonderful day,' she began with the letting of her long, naturally blonde and naturally curly hair out of a tight psyche. 'It's been a rush from one scene to another and from the studio to the dressing room and back again. And that's what I love—lots of rush.'

"With her monogrammed white comb she deftly pulled a blonde ripple over the top of each ear, then drew it up away from the ears so that they—the ears—were in plain sight. For they are wearing ears this season. . . .

" 'We are very, very busy, and when we are not—well, when we are not I wish we were.' Again she paused; this time to insert a large amber pin behind her left ear in a completed coiffure.

"Were it almost anybody else but Muriel I would have asked, 'Tired?' but one would never think of asking such a thing of Muriel, for she always looks the pink of fresh restfulness. And she is a joy to look at. Also, she is a rapid dresser, and was even then slipping into a lavender-striped frock with lacy throat and sleeves. 'You know, if I don't get away when I say I do, there is always somebody sure to say, 'Maybe we will use you in another scene.' But it's always so late that there's never another scene, so I manage to be ready when I say I will be.'

"She reached up for the top button of her dress, stood on tiptoe and got the wrong one.

" 'Allow me,' and she did.

" 'Thank you; most times I could do it myself, but when I am in a hurry I miss, sometimes.'

" 'Miss Ostriche! Muriel!' came a heavy voice from somewhere. It approached, it hesitated outside the door.

" 'Well? asked Muriel, stooping to the glass to better direct the service of her powder-puff.

" 'Want you for another scene—hope you haven't taken your makeup off yet?'

" 'Yes I have, and I am hurrying for the 4:15. But if you *really* want me!'

"There was a sweetness in Muriel's voice; there was plaintiveness in its tone and, clearly, there is evident self-sacrifice in this sentence that she purposefully, or otherwise, left incomplete. Meanwhile she pinned on her hat and looked for her gloves.

" 'No! That's all right. Go right ahead. We'll do it the first thing in the morning,' came the voice from the other side of the door and, then, as it wandered down the halls:

" 'Better hurry.'

" 'The director—he's the dearest thing,' was Muriel's explanation of the voice as she came out of the shirt-waist box with the gloves. 'Now, my commutation ticket—and I am ready!'

"She snapped off the light, we closed the door after us and got as far as the end of the hall.

" 'That hat won't do at all, not at all,' a big man in shirtsleeves was saying to a big woman in a semitailored frock. 'You must have one bigger than that—wider and kind of—' he made wonderful movements with his hands by way of illustrating just what kind of a hat it was he desired her to have.

" 'There, that's the kind of hat I want for this scene.' The unfortunate 'kind' reposed upon my head.

" 'Come on—let's hurry,' Muriel whispered, pretending to neither see nor hear the shirt-sleeved one. 'He'll make you stop and give it to him, if he wants it badly enough, but we haven't the time.'

" 'The scene will take only fifteen minutes—and then you can have your hat back,' promised the man blocking our path.

" 'But we haven't time, really we haven't. And, besides, this lady's company,' defended Muriel.

" 'But I have to have the hat,' insisted the shirt-sleeved director.

" 'Wait—I have just the thing for you,' offered Muriel in a bright-idea tone. She ran back to her dressing room and emerged in less than a minute with a shapeless straw hat that could be pinned up or down, that could be be-feathered or be-flowered but, that, just that minute, was entirely trimmingless. Thrusting it into the director's hands, she declared triumphantly—

" 'There—just the thing!' And before he could recover we were gone. But, wait, not entirely! From a window, Bert Adler signaled a message of importance.

" 'Don't be a minute—I'll signal the car when it comes,' and I hurried into the Adler sanctum. At the end of this prescribed minute there were calls from the street. A motorman's bell clanged five-second intervals. At the end of another stolen minute Muriel appeared at the door.

" 'We're waiting,' she said and was gone. I was with her. The street-car was standing at attention in front of the studio, and when we were seated and Muriel had said 'Thank you' to the motorman in her very sweetest voice, she exclaimed, 'He waited a whole minute.'

"Yes, we got the 4:15, and Muriel picked out the shady side of the almost empty coach and tucked her feet under her and smoothed the lavender stripes of her dress. And she smiled.

" 'Nice New Rochelle,' she said soothingly, as the train purred out of the station. 'It doesn't seem possible that I have been going to the Thanhouser Studio for a whole year. I wonder where I would be now if I had taken the stage offer I had a year ago, instead of staying in pictures and shifting to New Rochelle?' There was a little pause to extend her commutation book to the conductor, and she smiled a 'thank you' to him and resumed:

" 'I am eighteen and I started when I was fifteen. Just playing as an extra, though, at the Biograph Studio. I was going to high school then. A little later, I played in a Pathé picture and several Reliance stories, and then I joined the Eclair stock company at Fort Lee. Then I came to the Thanhouser studio—and for the last several months I have played all of their Princess brand leads. Mr. Hite is the grandest man to work for! Everybody at the studio likes him so well! And the directors and everybody else there are so nice, that it is a pleasure to be with them.'

"And it was a decided pleasure to watch Muriel as she talked. Every expression finds its outlet so surely in her wide blue eyes, and she has a little trick of making a question, that is yet not supposed to be a question, out of her statements every minute or two, until you begin to listen for it.

"For instance, she said, 'It is a positive pleasure to be with them—see?' And you are under no obligation whatsoever to say either yes or no. Watch for it if you ever talk with Muriel. The first time, though, you are apt to be so interested in thinking to yourself, 'Isn't she pretty?' that you won't notice, but the second time, you will, surely.

" 'Here is my station—125th Street. I just have to ride fifteen more minutes on the El and then I'm home—see?'

"She waved a good-bye from the platform and I entertained myself with my first thought, 'Isn't she pretty!' "

Another article, "Praise Doesn't Turn the Head of Muriel Ostriche," in the *New Rochelle Pioneer*, June 6, 1914, told of the actress, her modesty, and certain of her fans:

"To be a leading lady and the head of your own company at just eighteen would be enough to turn the heads of many girls, but it has no such effect on Muriel Ostriche.

"Muriel is as charming and unaffected as if she had never heard a word of praise in her life, although that is as far as possible from her actual experience. Of course, any pretty girl of eighteen has her admirers, but not many can number them by thousands. We realized that popular motion picture actresses have a tremendously wide and extended influence, but a call at Miss Ostriche's home convinced us that, in her case at least, we had greatly underestimated the interest which the public takes in her.

"By way of starting a conversation, we asked her whether she had many letters from picture fans.

" 'Just a few,' she replied. 'I'll get some and let you look at them.'

"Business of waiting a few minutes, when there suddenly appeared approaching a huge pile of letters, behind which Muriel was barely discernible. We hastened to her aid, and the stack was soon heaped upon the table and the adjacent floor. It made the parlor look like the interior of a railway car just after the clerks have broached the sacks.

"Any attempt to read the heap would have been useless, but fortunately Muriel could sport some of the best by the color of the paper. A brief but full experience has taught her that the silliest and strangest letters are always written on some of that weirdly tinted notepaper that the corner drug store sells as the latest importation.

This photograph of Muriel Ostriche in a fur-brimmed hat appeared in the May 1914 issue of *Motion Picture Magazine*. The image, distributed by Thanhouser, was a popular one and saw service in numerous Thanhouser and Princess advertisements as well as news stories in trade magazines and popular periodicals.

One of these letters purported to come from a thirteen-year-old cripple, whose only pleasure in life was when he was wheeled to the movie theatre. He begged Miss Ostriche to send him a picture, as he regarded her as his ideal. Naturally, such a pathetic appeal resulted in the immediate sending of a photograph, but imagine the little lady's disgust when a second letter from the same person told her that he was not what he had said at all, but a healthy young broker of twenty-five, and that his first letter had been a test of her kind-heartedness. Probably her picture and note of sympathy convinced him that Miss Muriel was worthy of what he fondly but mistakenly imagines himself to be, and he supposed that she would at once be captivated by his cunning ways.

" 'I didn't even write him to return my picture. I was so annoyed by his cheap lying,' remarked Miss Ostriche.

"A whole set of letters from a well-known preparatory school offers a diverting sidelight on schoolboy nature. It seems that one boy in the school had in some way obtained a photograph of Miss Ostriche, and had proudly exhibited it to some of his classmates. A number of them at once wrote to the screen star, and the tenor of all the letters is the same, namely, that the writer is grieved to see her picture in the hands of the boy who has it, as he does not have a proper regard for her, but that if she will send him one, then she can be sure that a real admirer has it and that it will be cherished.

"Another cycle of letters is from a member of the West Point football team, who also sent a nearly life-size photograph of himself. These are good, manly epistles largely devoted to bemoaning the confining nature of life at the Military Academy and expressing respectful admiration.

"But the communications are by no means confined to foolish youths. There are scores of them from women of all ages and positions, and they are crowded with human interest. Perhaps more than any others, come from working girls and women into whose colorless lives she carries inspiration and encouragement through motion pictures.

" 'I am only a poor little stenographer in a big law office,' one such letter from an Iowa city begins, 'but I hope you won't mind my writing to tell you how much I adore you and enjoy seeing you in the pictures.' And there are many more in the same vein, which makes it seem small wonder that Miss Ostriche likes her work.

"The sudden rise and, in all probability, her appearance in any way in motion pictures are really due to the unerring eye of a French director, formerly at the Eclair studios, in Fort Lee.

" 'My mother,' explained Muriel, 'said I was a silly little girl when I asked to be allowed to try for some extra parts in pictures. She told me I ought to stick to my high school work and become a school teacher, as I was expecting to do. Imagine me, a school teacher,' she added with a ripple of laughter.

" 'It takes too much imagination,' we returned.

" 'Mother finally saw I was so keen for it that when the Pathé company called up one day, having had my name on file for a long time, she let me go over to Jersey City. I had a lot of fun there, but the very next day the Eclair studio called, and, of course, I got mother to let me go.'

" 'I thought I was foolish to do it,' commented Mrs. Ostriche [sic, actually Oestrich], who was present, 'but it looks as if mothers may sometimes be mistaken, after all.'

" 'Over at Fort Lee they were getting ready for a picture which had to do with a girls' boarding school, and they had a lot of extras there. The director lined us all up, and went down the row looking us over as if we were animals on exhibition. It made me sort of wish I hadn't come, but all of a sudden he took my arm and led me out in front. 'It is you I want, mam'selle,' he said. 'It is you who shall play the lead; only, first, there are many things that we must teach you, but we will do it quickly.'

" 'In other words, you became a leading lady in your first picture?' we inquired.

" 'Well, not exactly; as I had done a couple of extra parts before; but, believe me it was not so easy. There certainly were many things that they had to teach me, and they wanted them learned very quickly, as the director had said. But I was so happy that I didn't mind the hard work, and even mother had to admit that it was sort of nice.'

"After a short time across the river Miss Ostriche went to the Majestic and then to Thanhouser. In the latter studio her charm was fully recognized and a special brand was created for her benefit. They were appropriately called 'Princess' films, and Muriel was made the leading lady, with Boyd Marshall as the masculine principal. Her very first picture was hardly three years ago, but she has been a favorite from the start. However, as we remarked at the beginning, popularity has not turned her head. She lives in New York with her parents, but comes up to New Rochelle every day. She is a typical American girl of eighteen, full of life, sensible and wholehearted and altogether delightful. It is fortunate that the public can see her sort on the motion picture screen."

Muriel's next screen effort was *His Enemy*, a Princess film released on June 5, 1914, synopsized as follows:

"John Baird, an old counterfeiter, is released from prison and resolves to lead a better life. Jameson, a detective, desires information concerning the movements of Baird's former associates, and when Baird refuses to aid him, he systematically hounds the old man, forcing him to be discharged from position after position.

"Baird finally secures employment in a quarry many miles away from the nearest city and for a time is happy. The young superintendent falls in love with Muriel, Baird's daughter, and the future seems very bright. Again the sinister shadow of Baird's enemy falls across her father, and the detective appears with orders from the general offices of the company to discharge the ex-convict. The daughter casts her lot with the father and refuses to marry the superintendent. The day that Baird and his daughter are to start once more on their wanderings presents an opportunity to the old man to rid himself from his enemy, for the detective falls from a steep cliff into the quarry just as a blast is about to be set off. Baird, however, goes to his rescue and saves his life, but at the cost of his own. He passes away, happy in the knowledge that his daughter has found a husband and protector in the young superintendent, while 'his enemy' remorsefully goes away."

Although Lloyd and Philip Lonergan were widely acclaimed in the trade press for their great output of film scripts, review after review of Princess films found the acting to be of acceptable or even excellent quality, but the Lonergans' stories to be deficient. One wonders why they were allowed to continue writing scripts, in the face of continuing condemnation of their film plots. In particular, Philip Lonergan's scripts seemed to be substandard.

The Toy Shop, released on June 12th and subsequently reviewed by *Moving Picture World*, is typical: "The situation which starts this love story is unconvincing, but it develops into a pretty romance with good 'pipe dream' quality. It is not very significant, but will be acceptable, for the staging, acting and photography are all of excellent quality. The author is Philip Lonergan."

Featuring Muriel Ostriche and Boyd Marshall, together with James Dunne and Maurice Stewart, the film involved the lonely proprietor of a toy shop, who befriended the children in town but who secretly longed for a wife and family of his own. Ruth, a poor factory girl out of a job, was hired as an assistant, and soon the shopkeeper found himself loving her with all of his heart, the plot synopsis noted. The shop owner worked hard, hoping to amass sufficient money so he could buy a modest home and then reveal his secret love to the young assistant. One day news came that she had inherited a fortune from a rich uncle. Her uncle's lawyer beckoned her to another location, and she became involved in high society. The novelty wore thin, and she longed for the cozy days back at the toy shop. Returning to the scene, she found the shop locked, and her employer ill in the hospital. She visited him the first day, then the next day, then the next. Their love ripened, and soon he was well again.

In the meantime, publicity for the forthcoming *Million Dollar Mystery* serial continued apace, with a publicity statement noting that the release date had been advanced to June 22nd, that nine miles of film had been shot to create 46 reels of a drama "involving love, romance and adventure, of startling surprises and new thrills," and that $10,000 would be paid to the movie patron submitting the best 100-word solution to the mystery.

A writer for *Motion Picture News* visited Thanhouser in June and wrote of his experience:

"A short walk down Main Street in New Rochelle brings one to a distinctive group of concrete buildings, the home of Thanhouser films. A step further down Thanhouser Lane took the reporter to the offices of C. J. Hite, president of the Thanhouser Film Corporation. Mr. Hite was busy signing a stack of checks, and outside of his door a swarm of players chatted in pleasant anticipation of receiving the checks.

"Mr. Hite is decidedly a busy man. While he signed checks, his directors, one after another, came in to report the progress of their work; once in a while a player edged in to obtain official consideration of his woes or his dreams, as the case happened to be. With hardly a glance upward from his desk, Mr. Hite disposed of the plaints and complaints, and it was noticeable from the way the visitors walked on air as they left his magnificently furnished office, that Mr. Hite believes in the motto 'always leave them smiling when you say good-bye.'

"Then Roy McCardell, author of the 'Mr. and Mrs. Jarr' series in the New York *World*, and father of a large and growing number of photoplays, walked in with his wife and a party of 'studio tourists.' It was Saturday afternoon, and Mr. Hite felt free to escort the party through his plant.

"A first visit was paid to Thanhouser Lane, where some interior sets of *The Million Dollar Mystery* are in position. With pardonable pride, Mr. Thanhouser pointed to rare tapestries, statuary of classic design, a Tudor staircase which was recently taken intact from a country house in England, and the library lined with shelves filled with real books—not the customary array of faked bindings.

"Mr. Hite then led the way to a new fireproof concrete and hollow tile property room, where in a few weeks all scenery and properties not in actual use will be stored. Luncheon time was about over, but Mr. Hite took his guests to the dining room, where Thanhouser employers may obtain well-cooked food for half the price they would have to pay elsewhere. The next person the party met after leaving the dainty waitresses of the lunchroom was Al J. Jennings, an ex-bandit, two-handed gunman, survivor of six years in a federal prison for robbing the mail, who was finally pardoned and returned to citizenship by President Roosevelt. The life of Al Jennings was written by himself and Will Irwin in *The Saturday Evening Post*. It is now being put into a six-reel picture under the title of *Beating Back*."

The tour went on to the developing and mechanical departments. Hite then led his visitors by a long corridor of drying drums, where thousands of feet of film were under electric fans. The tour next stopped to see a $200,000 mansion which Hite said was the most expensive "prop" ever acquired by a motion picture company. Complete with a great lawn, fountains, flower beds, and furnished with antiques and fine carpeting, it was a major setting for *The Million Dollar Mystery*. "They do things on a big scale at the Thanhouser plant," the article continued. "If a certain effect is to be achieved, cost is no consideration. Month by month the plant continues to grow. Recently, carpenters and masons worked day and night erecting a new stage. This month a new fireproof 'prop' room will be furnished. Meanwhile, a baker's dozen of directors keep shoals of people on the run, and the cameras click merrily on."

Toward the end of June, the Second International Exposition of the Motion Picture Arts, held in Grand Central Palace, New York City, "was the Mecca for all visitors and delegates, besides attracting thousands of picture fans from all over the country," reported *Motography*. "From the boxoffice standpoint the Exposition was an overwhelming success, while those who exhibited there were delighted with the flood of orders they received as a result of their displays and the publicity the products were given. Jeannette Cohan and Muriel Ostriche were the winners of the cups on the New York roof on Lasky Night, and Anita Stewart won the weekly prize on Saturday night."

The Little Senorita, a Princess film released on June 19, 1914, was reviewed by *Motion Picture News*: "The plot is vague. Muriel Ostriche plays the leading role. The young American wins the Mexican girl by saving her father from bandits. The scenes are

This studio portrait of Muriel Ostriche was widely distributed circa 1914-1915. Later, an oil painting copied from this image was created for the World Film Corporation and was reproduced for exhibit in theatre lobbies. (Georgetown University Library)

beautiful and the numerous encounters that appear are realistic to the extreme." Boyd Marshall played her lover, in a plot set on a mysterious island.

Professor Snaith, featuring Muriel Ostriche, was released on June 26th. Trade papers had great difficulty with the "Snaith" name, and in numerous listings it appeared incorrectly as "Smith." *Motion Picture News* commented: "The athlete wins the girl from her lover. He enlists the services of a husky bartender, who proves the athlete is no pugilist. The other wins back the girl. Muriel Ostriche and Boyd Marshall play the leads in this highly amusing comedy." *Moving Picture World*, calling it *Professor Smith*, printed a review: "A farce with Muriel Ostriche. Its best asset is photography and pretty scenes. The situation was once fairly comic and will still please such as have seen few pictures, but it is quite artificial." Again, it was a Philip Lonergan script.

The Decoy, a Princess film released on July 3, 1914, featured Muriel in the part of a young girl sent by her parents to stay with a respectable family in the city. Arriving there, Muriel is provided with beautiful clothes, not knowing that her hosts plan to use her to lure victims to lose money at the card table. Muriel attracts many men, including a millionaire, but she herself is innocent of the swindle being perpetrated by her keepers. Boyd Marshall, as a young businessman, falls in love with Muriel, but her dishonest sponsors steal money from him. At the same time Muriel responds with her love, she discovers the deception and threatens to expose the cardsharps, then hesitates to do so when they convince her that she would not be able to prove her innocence in the matter. Finally, she faces up to the situation and exposes them. Then, as the crooks are led to justice, Muriel and Boyd head to the altar.

Muriel must have enjoyed making *The Girl of the Seasons*, a Princess film released on July 10th. A synopsis noted: "A picture of Muriel in winter, spring, summer and autumn. At each season she gets a new lover, and they come the same night to propose, so she introduces them all at the same time to her elderly husband." *Moving Picture World* described the film as "too slight to be really effective, but it has pretty scenes and makes a fair offering."

"Reporting" an event which did not happen, *Moving Picture World*, in its July 4th issue, noted: "The Broadway Rose Gardens and Danse de Pierrette, Broadway and 52nd Street, were formally opened Sunday evening, June 27th. Moving pictures, dancing and dining are offered in the novel place of music. *The Million Dollar Mystery*, the new Thanhouser serial, is to be the feature of the picture show for months to come. Another feature on the opening photoplay program was *The Terrors of the Deep*, also a Thanhouser project. Charles J. Hite, president of Thanhouser Film Corporation, is also president of the Delta Theatre Corporation, which has built and will operate the new place. George F. Kerr has been named as general manager, and Ben H. Atwell as director of publicity." It fell to a competing magazine, the *New York Dramatic Mirror*, to point out that the Broadway Rose Gardens did not open as scheduled and the attraction would make its debut at a future date.

Charles Hite had his fingers in other pies, one of which was a venture launched by the Williamson brothers, who constructed a tubular device which made it possible for an underwater cameraman, connected to a ship above, to take moving pictures in the briny deep. Bids for the rights were tendered by various studios, and Thanhouser won. After showings at the Smithsonian Institution and the National Press Club in Washington, the first public exhibition was staged a few weeks later in New Rochelle, where more than 300 people came to the North Avenue Theatre to see "the thrilling underwater scene—man battling the sharks, and the sharks battling among themselves—bringing rounds of applause from those privileged to be present at this first public exhibition. These pictures will be shown at the Broadway Rose Gardens." In the meantime, on various securities exchanges, several companies in which Charles Hite had an interest were actively traded, including Mutual Film, New York Motion Picture Corporation, Reliance, Thanhouser, and Universal Film Manufacturing Company.

While Princess films were doing well as fillers on the Mutual program, the industry was focused on a landmark event, the film *Cabiria*, which created a sensation unequaled by any other motion picture of its time, a film which numerous reviewers designated as the greatest ever. *Motography* noted:

"Mr. Webster's well-known dictionary is pitifully inadequate when it comes to supplying the adjectives with which to describe *Cabiria*, now playing at the Illinois Theatre, Chicago, the stupendous film offering of the Itala Film Company of Torino, Italy, the story of which is from the pen of Gabriele D'Annunzio. One sits spellbound through the entire three acts and five episodes necessary for the telling of the story, and when the curtain falls at the end feels speechless with awe, for never before have film patrons been offered such a tremendous triumph of motion picture art, never have they beheld such awe-inspiring panoramas outspread before their eyes, never have they seen such spectacular battles or witnessed more massively staged productions. *Cabiria* is the last word in motion pictures—it is the great element beyond which it seems impossible for any manufacturer to go." A record was established in New York City at the Knickerbocker Theatre during the week of June 8, 1914, when over 21,000 persons paid from twenty-five cents to one dollar each to see the exhibition.

Typical admission prices in America, particularly in small towns, were still a nickel to a dime, with a quarter or more being reserved for the larger cities. However, in August 1914, *Motion Picture News* noted that "Rochester (New York) has a three-cent picture house, the Bijou, on State Street. The venture is comparatively new as yet, and it is not known how the house will make out under this policy. The location is in a tenement-house section, and it is figured that the extremely low price will draw much trade."

Nomenclature occupied many columns of print at the time, and countless debates raged over whether "movies" and "motion pictures" were one and the same, whether either should be *moving* or *motion* pictures, whether the art of capturing scenes on film was cinematography, kinematography, motography, or something else, and what was the definition of a "feature" film.

Hite was at the apex of his career. The lavish Broadway Rose Gardens was being readied for opening. A block in depth, the spa was to offer dining, music, dancing, and motion picture entertainment. On July 7th, another attraction, Thanhouser Park, surrounding the Thanhouser studios, was dedicated. An observer related that "Charles J. Hite, president of the Thanhouser Company, ordered open house on that day, and every man, woman, and child in New Rochelle was welcomed to the studio. The broad acres to the east of the main building in the Thanhouser group have been converted into a park, with driveways, rustic bridges, bungalows, and, most wonderful of all, a fall over which water rushes and tumbles, just as though nature had planned what Joseph Turner, Thanhouser's scenic artist, has built." In theatres across the country, *The Million Dollar Mystery* was received with enthusiasm. Although most episodes were yet to come, Hite was already planning for a sequel.

An awe-struck reporter for *Motography* told of Hite in an article which reached print early in August:

"I have discovered two things that I have been suspecting for quite some time, and these will be set down right away. The first seems to be the more significant: The film game is a bonanza rather than a business. Ingalls Kimball and I agreed on that after two hours of palaver over a delightful luncheon at the Lafayette.

"The other thing we will charge up directly to Harry Aitken, for he is the responsible agent. He advertises the 'movies,' and the movies are here. 'Movies' is the other discovery. Movies has drawn the line through the film offerings. It is as sharply defined as the wake of an ocean liner. Movies is program stuff—short lengths intended for the common people. It has sunk the whole gamut of single reels to a lower level, and there is no hope of bringing back 'motion pictures' to the everyday fan. And I am sincerely mournful. The long lengths survived the term 'movie.' They will be known in polite circles as motion pictures, now and henceforth. Now and henceforth it will be necessary to manufacture both movies and motion pictures. Either can be features. It is the film that gets the business that is entitled to the rank of feature.

"Bonanza rather than business can best be proven when one jogs about a bit. I am thinking of Charlie Hite. When I was first in Hite's town—it was actually that—he was comparatively new as a resident. It was shortly after the fire at the Thanhouser studio and 'the works' was merely a makeshift, the friendly maw of an idle garage substituting for general offices and a factory. The studio was a platform on a leased lot conveniently nearby. I recall an elaborate set of blueprints contemplating a splendid, ornate building with Corinthian columns and mosaic floors and a swimming pool for the help and general stores and a gold knob for the lofty flagstaff. It would be the home of Thanhouser by the time I came back, judging time by my previous visit.

"It didn't turn out that way. Film men are irrational. Charlie Hite meant to build that great monumental pile right away, but he discovered that the immediate thing was more necessary, so he started his 'little studio' back of the garage—he owned that lot. The little studio didn't have that name right away. It was wonderfully big when it was built, with a lunch room downstairs and dressing rooms nearly everywhere, and great sides, ends and roof of glass. It was built snug up to the garage, which gave up a lot of things when the buildings became one. No, the 'little studio' got its name after the big one across the street had been finished.

"You see, that leased lot and open-air platform had become so vital a part of Thanhouser that the little studio was merely incidental. So there was still time to shut down the works for the elaborate blueprint scheme. So Hite dickered for and bought the platform lot and then the next and then the next and took options on the whole block and kept right on spending the money he was making all the while, and building the things he had to have in a hurry. And now he has a big, homey, efficient studio and business offices on one side of his street, the little studio and factory on the other. There are 140 on the payroll, not counting extras. The Thanhouser plant always changes between my visits. It is one of those things that grows. I have never been there when the nail beaters weren't busy.

"I went with Charlie Hite and his new Cole roadster over to see the missus and the kiddies. You may recall that Hite started in the films from very unpretentious beginnings. Even in my brief day he might have loaded all of his physical film assets in a wheelbarrow and made away with them single handed. That was six years ago. We motored down Meadow Lane to *The Million Dollar Mystery* house, which was built by Francis Wilson in his heyday. That is C. J. Hite's home—that truly imposing and magnificent mansion snugged into the trees and shrubbery of its lofty three acres. Mrs. Hite apologized for some of the missing furniture, which had been whisked out of place to the studio. *The Million Dollar Mystery* centers about the Hite home. Exteriors are made there. Interiors at the studio are replicas of the home itself, so you get on the screen just what I got at close range. The garage at the Hite home was being enlarged to take care of more cars.

"This new Cole roadster is Hite's very latest pet. He has turned the big limousine and the chauffeur over to Mrs. Hite. Hite won't be arrested for breaking speed laws, for he is a sworn-in deputy sheriff or something. For my own protection I carry Bert Adler's badge, which declared that I was 'Special Deputy Sheriff No. 355, Bronx County, New York.' It covered the period from 1914 to 1918. In addition to his present mania for speed, Hite has added a new speedboat to his ocean fleet and wears a lifebelt when he drives it. All of these little incidents work back to my admonition of a few years ago when I warned the New Yorkers to be aware of Hite, Aitken and Freuler—those western speeders who are now in their midst.

"Then you will remember that Pop Rock [of Vitagraph] and his crowd, George Kleine and his, and some others were forming the habit of building or acquiring Broadway theatres. It is quite a costly diversion, but not to be outdone, Charlie Hite thought that he would uphold the dignity of Thanhouser by building a little place of his own. When I was taking my leave at New Rochelle, W. Ray Johnston, treasurer of Hite's Broadway Rose Gardens, volunteered to go along and show me the rest of it.

"Hite's Broadway Rose Gardens are at 53rd and Broadway and extend right through 7th Avenue. You will recall that the wedge is pretty thick that far up. It is a block north of the Winter Garden, and I was so flabbergasted when I saw it that I forgot to ask for dimensions. But it is very generous in width. The Broadway side represents a beautiful, modern motion picture theatre and a lavish expenditure of money in all of its appointments. The 7th Avenue side represents all that New York craves—a place to spend money on the Great White Way. It is

MISS MURIEL OSTRICHE
(Princess)

THE youngest leading lady on the motion-picture screen is Muriel Ostriche, for whom Thanhouser created the Princess films. She is just seventeen years old—and she doesn't care who knows it. At fifteen, she was with the Eclair Stock Company, and, even then, played leads occasionally. Now, scarcely two years later, she plays nothing but leads. Also, she is the only leading lady in the Princess productions. Few stars in filmdom have risen so quickly, or attained such brilliancy and distinction in so short a time.

From her early experience in the Eclair Company—where, from her first appearance, her acting gave exceptional promise—Miss Ostriche went to the Reliance, where she played opposite Irving Cummings. In Forrest Halsey's famous loan-shark drama, "The Bawlerout," Miss Ostriche was cast for "Edith Downs," the ingenue lead; and the youthful actress held her own with such practiced photoplayers as E. P. Sullivan, Sue Balfour, George Siegmann and Ralph Lewis.

Her engagement with the Thanhouser was in the nature of a transfer from one Mutual company to another, as the Thanhouser at that time appeared to offer greater opportunities for an actress of her peculiar talents. C. J. Hite, President of the Thanhouser company, created in the Fall of 1913 the brand of pictures in which Miss Ostriche was to score new triumphs for herself and for the New Rochelle studios.

The girlish beauty of the youthful star, her petiteness, the exceeding daintiness of her performance, inspired the title of Princess for her own playlets. Her productions are the purest of romances. She carries a wide variety of emotional and lightsome serio-comedy parts, in which she is irresistible. Her pathos is delicate, never overdrawn. In the love scenes she is all charm and simplicity. Her personality is always fresh and appealing, and essentially spontaneous.

Miss Ostriche is one of the few leading women in pictures who comes to the screen without stage experience. Before she became a photoplayer, she was never behind the scenes in her life. Yet, she brought to her work, natural dramatic technique. She is a born actress. Her simplicity and naturalness are the expression of a vivid, romantic temperament, combined with an artist's sense of what is effective and pleasing, and an intense eagerness to share her feelings with her audience.

As she has a delightful singing voice with possibilities, Miss Ostriche is besieged by managers of musical comedy who continue to hope that she will some day forsake motion pictures for the legitimate stage. But, although, she is ambitious, the little leading lady of the Princess is not dazzled by promises of a brilliant career in musical comedy. She sees a future on the screen even more alluring than before the footlights.

To star in a new play every week—to create fifty-two different roles, appearing in each, two hundred and fifty times, in a twelve month—that is to say, to make thirteen thousand appearances on the screen in a single year—is a record Miss Ostriche far from scorns. She is devoted to motion pictures as the great popular theatre, with the broadest emotional appeal of any art in the world to-day. To hold a high rank among photoplayers, and a still higher place in the love and enthusiasm of the seven or eight million persons who fill the motion-picture theatres daily, is the height of this youthful star's ambition.

It is remarkable how children invariably adopt Miss Ostriche, both on the screen and off, for, as a rule, the little ones pick for their favorite, either a child player or an older woman. Wherever the Princess film is billed with Miss Ostriche's name on the paper, the theatre is sure to be thronged with little ones, who worship at her shrine. At the Thanhouser studios, in New Rochelle, there are many children employed in the various companies and they all cluster around the door of Miss Ostriche's dressing-room to receive her cheery greeting, for she loves the youngsters as much as they love her. She is little more than a child herself and it is no unusual occurrence for her to stop a few minutes after her work to play with her youthful admirers.

The Biographer.

"The Biographer," a writer for *Reel Life,* gave a character sketch of Muriel Ostriche. Her way with children was famous and was mentioned in numerous stories, including this one.

the Jardin de Danse brought down to a street level for a better class of people. There is a liberal dancing floor and promenades and loges and places to dine on balconies and on the main floor. I never saw anything quite like it, and neither did you, for it is alone in its class. There are sumptuous quarters for the employees and all of the conveniences for the guests. It's a quarter to get in on one side, and a dollar to get out on the other—or vice-versa—providing you require no refreshment en route. When you are in New York, Hite has a plan to get you coming and going, remember that.

"At the Hite Gardens I met many of the executive staff—all fine people. Hite has maintained that program all the way. But I miss Doc Shallenberger. Dr. Wilbert Shallenberger, be it known, also of Chicago, is the lucky guy who grabbed Hite's coattails a few years ago and never let go. Where goes Charlie Hite you will find the genial Doc.

"So, I tell you here is proof positive that the film game is a bonanza instead of a business. I wouldn't have it leak out that any dub might get away with it a la Charles Jackson Hite. That would be discounting all of the care, the knowhow, the shrewdness, the hard, incessant work that he has put into it. But other men in other lines have failed while Hite has his behind and the tide is coming in. Put her into high, Steve. I've got a sheriff's medal!"

The Veteran's Sword, a Princess film released on July 17, 1914, again starred Muriel Ostriche and Boyd Marshall. The acting of the two leads was fine, while the other characters were "below standard," noted *Motion Picture News*, while, once again, *Moving Picture World* criticized the scenario while praising the acting: "The story is weak to the point of being at least, at times, foolish. Yet there is something in the atmosphere of the thing that makes a spectator wish they were better, one would like to see something convincing of such interesting people as these characters. That what is shown could have happened is more than doubtful, and we dare not call it a good offering. The camera work and staging are, like the acting, excellent." A reading of several versions of the plot reveals what seems to be a rather insipid story involving a Civil War veteran who gives his coveted sword to the employer of a young man who then consents to drop the false charges which led to the young man's imprisonment. The soldier's veteran buddies believe that the sword has been sold for money and are very upset, a situation which is remedied when the innocence of the prisoner is proved, the sword is returned, and a full explanation is given.

A new genre of scenic and documentary Princess films appeared around this time, with such titles as *Harvesting Ice* and *The Cavalry at Fort Meyer, Virginia*. These and several other pictures were produced without Muriel's participation.

The Target of Destiny, a Princess production, released on July 31st, again earned encomiums for the acting but acid comments about the weak script. Muriel, a simple country girl, falls in love with Boyd, whose wealthy parents summer near her village. Boyd proposes, but Muriel, knowing she would not be accepted in his social class, declines. Later, Muriel rescues Boyd's little sister from a hazardous situation, earns the acclaim of his parents, and is married to Boyd. The same "forlorn girl falls in love with a rich boy against his parent's wishes, and finally wins them over" plot was used countless times.

Her Duty, a Princess film released on August 7th, was not appreciated by *Motion Picture News*: "An inferior offering that has not much to recommend it, and rather poorly played. Due to the plotting of her employer's daughter, the stenographer is dismissed. The other woman then persuades her to give up her sweetheart to her, with the promise that she will aid her invalid mother. This she does. Muriel Ostriche and Boyd Marshall play the leads. Both have done better."

An article in the *New Rochelle Pioneer*, August 8, 1914, told of plans for local newsreels and gave an overview of the Thanhouser facilities at the time:

"Westchester County is soon to have a weekly news moving picture devoted exclusively to events that occur in the county if a plan now under consideration by the Thanhouser Film Corporation materializes. Every event of interest will be taken and then will be shown in the moving picture houses throughout Westchester.

"This film will be truly a Westchester film made in Westchester, for the Thanhouser plant is located within our own city limits. There the company owns 10 acres of ground on which stand two buildings and a number of 'sets' of outdoor scenery. Several hundred people are employed in the factory where the motion pictures are not only acted, but manufactured ready for the use of the 'movie' houses.

"One building, known as the Administration Building, contains the business offices and a large studio. The latter part of the building is constructed entirely of glass and steel in order to admit all the daylight possible. Here it is possible to take 10 different pictures at one time, which makes the building one of the largest studios in the United States.

"Despite the abundance of daylight, it is often necessary to use arc lights to get the proper effects in order that the moving picture film will not appear dim. The Thanhouser Company has nearly a hundred of these which may be moved about the floor to any position.

"The second building of the plant is known as the factory. Here is located all the machinery necessary for the manufacture of the films and a small studio in which pictures that do not require much space may be taken. The factory part is separated from the studio by means of a fire wall for the films are made of celluloid and are very inflammable. Fire extinguishers are located at frequent intervals along the wall, and every precaution is taken to prevent any fire from reaching the inflammable materials used.

"After a film has been exposed in the camera it is brought into a darkroom in this building. It is removed from the machine and wound on a large wooden rack. This frame is then dipped into a large wooden tank which contains the various developing and fixing solutions. This process is the same as in ordinary photography, but necessarily it is carried on in a much larger scale.

"After the films have been developed they are wound on a large wheel which revolves at a high rate of speed in a draught. This

Fur-clad Muriel in a winter scene for a Thanhouser film, circa 1914. (Courtesy of the American Museum of the Moving Image, Lawrence Williams Collection)

thoroughly dries the films. They are then placed in a duplicating machine. This device contains a reel of undeveloped film and one that has been exposed. The two are unwound and pass together through a small slot in front of a red light. As each picture on the finished film passes in front of the slot the light flashes. This practically makes a duplicate of the unexposed film. The latter is then developed, the same as the original, and two complete pictures are available. Several duplicate pictures of each picture are made in this way.

"The next process is the inserting of strips of film that contain the name of the picture and the short 'flashes' here and there throughout the film which tell what is to happen in the division to follow. These 'cut-ins' are made in a most unusual manner. A board with small grooves running lengthwise is used. Small letters with clips on the back are placed in these grooves. They are set up, much like ordinary type, to spell out whatever words are required. Then they are photographed with a regular moving picture camera, so much time being allowed for each line. A board with three lines will be photographed just three times as long as one with one line.

"These 'cut-ins' are then pasted into the films in their proper places and the entire picture is ready for the theatres. It is sent to an exchange in New York City which rents it out to the various picture houses all over the country.

"The outside scenery of the company consists of a number of 'wild West' layouts, among which is a series of imitation mountains.

"As the visiting newspaperman was being shown through the ground one of the directors of the company pointed to a small frame house and said, 'A few days ago we had a battle around that place in which 100 men took part. We have no further use for the building and have got to take it down. I guess we'll write a play and burn it down.'

"The reporter pointed to two tanks about 200 feet from the little house that were labeled 'Standard Oil Company' and asked, 'What will the oil trust say about that?'

" 'Oh, I suppose they will raise a big howl, like they do every time we have a fire. People around here have no sense of humor, anyway,' was the reply. 'Once we blew up a house at Pelham at midnight to get the proper effects and all the volunteer firemen for about 100 miles around came running up to get into our way something awful.'

"The last thing shown the visitor was the equipment owned by the company. They have six beautiful saddle horses, seven up-to-date automobiles and a marine flotilla consisting of one 60-mile-an-hour speed boat, two 40-mile-an-hour launches, two sail boats and a steam yacht, 165 feet in length. All these are used from time to time, especially the horses and automobiles. . . ."

A Rural Romance, Muriel's next film, was a Princess release of August 14, 1914, and was synopsized by *Motion Picture News*: "The son doesn't marry the daughter of his father's selection, but he marries her sister, which suits the father just as well. This comedy-drama is worked out in a clever way, with Muriel Ostriche and Boyd Marshall leading the cast."

CHAPTER FIVE

Thanhouser in Decline

The Belle of the School, a Princess film screened on August 21, 1914, pleased a reviewer for *The Motion Picture News:* "A well-produced story and one of the best of the Princess offerings. Muriel Ostriche, Boyd Marshall, and Rene Farrington are the principals. The belle of the school assumes the blame for the thefts of a poor girl, whose thefts were instigated by her lack of smart clothes. But her lover discovers the truth and the story ends well for all concerned." *Moving Picture World* described it as a "bright, well-pictured offering."

Around the same time an event happened which forever changed the fortunes of Thanhouser and probably of the motion picture industry itself. *Motion Picture News* told the story:

"Charles J. Hite, president of Thanhouser Film Corporation and first vice president and treasurer of Mutual Film Corporation, died at 4:30 Saturday morning, August 22, in the Harlem Hospital from injuries sustained in an automobile accident Friday night a few hours before.

"Mr. Hite was returning from superintending the opening of the new Rose Gardens at 53rd Street and Broadway, New York City, and directing the finishing touches of *The Million Dollar Mystery* and was driving alone in his roadster when the car plunged over the 155th Street viaduct, about 60 feet from Macomb's Dam Road, landing 50 feet below on the grounds of the Manhattan Casino. He sustained a compound fracture of the jaw and severe intestinal injuries. In falling, the car turned turtle and pinned Mr. Hite to the ground. The force of the plunge drove the automobile through the fence of the amusement grounds.

"Mr. Hite was still conscious when patrons of the casino and several pedestrians raced to his rescue. Efforts were made to release the imprisoned man, but they were unavailing until jacks were brought from the elevated railroad shops nearby. Mr. Hite relapsed into unconsciousness the moment the car was lifted from his body. Before he became conscious, however, Mr. Hite managed to tell his name and give directions for communicating with his wife.

"Mr. Hite was driving east, intending to cross the bridge to the Bronx, on the way to his home in New Rochelle, the old estate of Francis Wilson in Meadow Lane. It is supposed that the machine skidded on the pavement, wet from a previous thunderstorm. According to the account of one eyewitness, the unfortunate man tried to jump from the car at the first sign of an accident, but wasn't able to extricate himself from the steering gear in time to make the leap. The machine crashed into the iron railing of the viaduct, carrying away nearly fifteen feet of the iron work.

"Another account relates that Mr. Hite drove his auto upon the sidewalk to avoid running into a child which had stepped from a Bronx car and was crossing the tracks in a direct line with the machine. Mr. Hite was only 39 years old at the time of his death. . . . The funeral was held at the Hite residence on July 25th. The ceremony was simple but impressive, and attended by many prominent in the industry. He is survived by a widow and two children, Marjorie, age four, and Muriel [named after Miss Ostriche], a baby only one year old, and by his parents, who live in Lancaster, Ohio, as well as three sisters, two unmarried, who live in Lancaster, and Mrs. W. Ray Johnston."

Bert Adler wrote a tribute to Hite, which noted in part: "Unfavorable criticism of his products in the press hurt him more than most people thought. He was wounded by the criticism of our pictures right after the Thanhouser fire, at a time when he thought reviewers should have been lenient. And I never saw a big man who was so sincerely thankful for the smallest paragraph of praise. Mr. Hite was the best man to his family that I have ever seen. They were ever in his thoughts. He would bring his little daughter Marjorie to his office on his busiest days, if it was her wish to be with him. Of his associates, he had known Dr. Shallenberger the longest, by quite a margin; as young men they had taught school together in the Midwest. This must kill the oft-published yarn about Mr. Hite, overworked in his Chicago exchange, going to see a strange doctor [Shallenberger] for treatment and receiving instead a check—to invest any old way! Of course, the story was inspired by the faith that men had in C. J. Hite."

Muriel Ostriche recalled the incident: "The Thanhouser players had gathered at a restaurant in Westchester County, where a big affair was being put on by a soda water company called Clysmic Waters. Charles Hite had an interest in that, and at one time I was going to buy some stock, but I didn't. Things could not start until Mr. Hite arrived, and we kept waiting and waiting. Finally, we learned that he had been in an accident, and I went with James Cruze and my mother in an automobile down to the hospital. He was dead by the time we got there. We were very close to Mr. Hite, and the tragedy was devastating. After Hite's death, things were not the same at Thanhouser, and most of the players left."

After several false starts, but with enthusiasm expressed by visitors who attended several private functions, the Broadway Rose Gardens finally opened to the public on Monday, September 14th. A bright electric sign on the facade of the establishment attracted the attention of a *Motography* writer: "Electric roses dropped in showers from the extended hands of the gay pierrette topping the perpendicular sign which beckons to Broadway for blocks on either side of the theatre, and when the baskets at the base of this sign are flowing over with roses—lo!—the baskets empty themselves and the shower starts all over again."

After Hite's death Dr. Wilbert Shallenberger took charge of the Broadway Rose Gardens and also was named president of the Thanhouser Film Corporation. On opening day, music was provided by a pipe organ and two orchestras. Visitors were treated to *Thirty Leagues Under the Sea*, a Williamson brothers movie of undersea life. Alas, in Charles Hite's absence, the Broadway Rose Gardens went into bankruptcy the following month.

Other dreams ended as well. "I was going to star as Alice in *Alice in Wonderland*, Muriel Ostriche remembered. "After Charles Hite died, and the management changed, most of Charles Hite's plans were changed or scrapped. The Thanhouser enthusiasm was gone, and it was a different place."

The order of things in the Princess Department changed, and Muriel appeared in relatively few Princess subjects after Hite's death.

In *The Keeper of the Light*, a Princess story filmed on City Island, released on August 28th, Muriel Ostriche played a lighthouse keeper's daughter. *Motion Picture News* reviewed the one-reel film: "Muriel Ostriche and Boyd Marshall lead the cast of this drama. The rich man is in love with the daughter of the lighthouse keeper, but his mother objects to the marriage. When thieves attempt to put out the light to wreck a ship she, with the man's aid, prevents them, but due to a bullet wound she dies." *Moving Picture World* informed its readers that "the picture is very good."

Most of the Princess films beyond this point involved others. *His Winning Way*, a comedy released on September 4th, starred Boyd Marshall with Mayre Hall and Riley Chamberlin, while in *Sis*, released September 11th, Reenie Farrington had the lead. Indeed, Muriel Ostriche was officially replaced as the leading figure in the Princess Department, as a notice in *Moving Picture World*, September 12, 1914 related:

"Reenie Farrington, daughter of Frank Farrington, the 'brain' of *The Million Dollar Mystery*, has suddenly jumped into the spotlight in the delightful character acting as lead of Princess. A short time ago she appeared as a slavey in one of Arthur Ellery's comedy scripts, and her work was so good that she was retained. Her latest work is the ingenue lead in *Sis*, by Phil Lonergan." From another article: "Boyd Marshall and Mayre Hall, in *His Winning Way*, booked for release under Princess, September 4, took the leads in a most spritely manner, showing these juveniles at their best."

The executives at Thanhouser decided that Muriel Ostriche could be used to better advantage in the regular Thanhouser multiple-reel releases. An opportunity came for a major part when she played the ingenue lead in *The Varsity Race*, a two-reel feature released on September 22nd, directed by Carroll Fleming using a script by Philip Lonergan. Irving Cummings, Arthur Bauer, Carey L. Hastings, Nolan Gane, Ethel Jewett, Bill Noel, Edward Hoyt, and Walter Cameron were also in the cast. For once, *Moving Picture World* liked Lonergan's work, for it noted that he and the director "are to be congratulated on this story which they have built around events connected with the races of the National Amateur Rowing Regatta, which took place recently near Philadelphia. The pictures of the actual races that were obtained would, if issued by themselves as an educational, have made a remarkably noteworthy release of historic and athletic value, but the author and director have so skillfully interwoven these with such a simple, natural, clean story of university life that they may well be proud of the combination of heart interest, suspense, and thrill that they have achieved. It is really a big three-reel story, and the cutting of it down to two reels has marred the effect somewhat by jamming the actions in the early scenes and necessitating the employment of one or two otherwise needless leaders.

"But in one respect, the picture is most decidedly refreshing and unique. Not only are the actors entered into the idea and spirit of the author and director with marked intelligent capability, but they have actually reproduced the university atmosphere and look like genuine personages of real university life. . . . Even the actors' 'varsity team,' when it is lined up, as it is in a couple of pictures, alongside of the genuine teams, looks natural, an effect made possible by the fact that Thanhouser had a real crew of its own, composed of members of the studio force, that went down to Philadelphia and put in a couple of weeks of good hard work, training with the regatta entries."

The *New York Dramatic Mirror* was laudatory concerning the lead performer: "Muriel Ostriche is her usual pretty self and adds to her good graces the capabilities of a first-class actress."

Mabel Condon, who interviewed Muriel Ostriche earlier as she was leaving for a train from New Rochelle, wrote a story about Boyd Marshall, which appeared in the October 3rd issue of *Motography*. Marshall was interviewed while waiting under a sheltering oak tree—or maybe it was a maple tree, Mabel Condon noted in her casual manner—at the entrance to the private road that ran by the Thanhouser-Princess studio overlooking Thanhouser Park, Thanhouser Road, and the streetcar tracks. He was waiting for an automobile to come along and take him to a stone quarry, where the Princess crew was set to work on another of Phil Lonergan's scripts.

Muriel Ostriche, studio portrait. (Georgetown University Library)

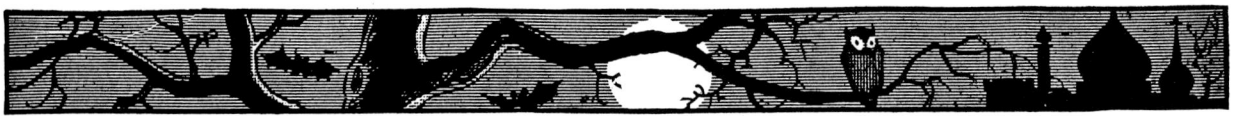

THE MILLION DOLLAR MYSTERY

Story by Harold MacGrath
Scenario by Lloyd Lonergan

Thanhouser's Million Dollar Motion Picture Production

The Million Dollar
Mystery has been a greater drawing-card for exhibitors than any motion picture production ever brought out. *Mark that!* This production positively has played to bigger audiences than have ever attended the movies.

Twenty episodes are now
appearing everywhere. The entire story will take 23 episodes. Episode No. 23 will be written from the best solution of the mystery. 300 leading newspapers are running this story.

Exhibitors who are seeking
a real attraction—*one that is bound to pack houses*—must make arrangements *at once*. This is an independent release and may be obtained regardless of the regular program being used. Apply to

SYNDICATE FILM CORPORATION
71 West 23rd Street, New York
Room 411, 5 S. Wabash Avenue, Chicago

or Syndicate Film Corporation Representative at any Mutual Exchange in the United States and Canada

The Thanhouser Three-a-Week

Following are the Thanhouser releases for the current week. These releases are distributed exclusively in the United States and Canada by the Mutual Film Corporation.

Tuesday, November 3rd, "The Turning of the Road" (two reels). This is a powerful drama of society life. It portrays the actions of a band of thieves who work among the best society. A member of the band— Della Fletcher — is the character around which the plot revolves. Her stealing of the gems and her ultimate reformation and marriage to a handsome rector form a basis for many tense scenes. She is led by love out of the shadows into the light and the turning of a new road. The cast includes Muriel Ostriche, Frank Woods, John Reinhard, Ethyle Cook, Ernest Ward, Carey Hastings, Arthur Bauer, Perry Horton.

Sunday, November 8th, "Keeping a Husband" (one reel). A decidedly clever drama of home life, showing how a wife's strategy makes it possible for her to retain her husband's love in spite of severe temptations. This photoplay is very capably enacted by Muriel Ostriche, Carey L. Hastings and Ernest C. Ward.

Thanhouser Film Corporation
New Rochelle, N. Y.

Head European Office, Thanhouser Films, Ltd., London, W. C., England

The Thanhouser Film Corporation and the related Syndicate Film Corporation were prolific advertisers in industry periodicals. Shown here are announcements published in the November 7, 1914 issue of *Moving Picture World*. Muriel Ostriche had the lead in two productions, *The Turning of the Road* and *Keeping a Husband*.

Boyd Marshall told that he came from Port Clinton, Ohio, where there were "lots of goods times and homey folks, but not much opportunity, in this line anyway . . . . The stage was not my aim as I left Port Clinton. My ambition was to be a professor of Latin or Greek. I probably would have become one eventually if, in my second year at Ann Arbor, they hadn't elected me a member of the Glee Club." He went on to note that because this presented a conflict with his classical studies, he dropped the ancient languages. "The folks at home very nearly gave me up. It took some time before they would consent to my attending the Michigan Conservatory of Music; their consent was quite necessary as it meant assuming the expense. Well, I vocalized through a course that seemed to satisfy everybody, then I decided to try for the stage. I did and attained it through a Lasky act. Then there were other Lasky vaudeville engagements, and then I obtained a singing and dancing partner and toured in an act of my own titled 'The Wall Between,' then I went to the Coast and played in stock. My next ventures were with Della Fox in *Delightful Dolly*, and with Fritzi Scheff in *Mlle. Modiste*. After that I played musical stock in Elmira (New York). Elmira is a perfectly good place to rest; but I didn't care about resting indefinitely, so I came to New York, and because I had been in the habit of patronizing the picture theatres all my spare time while on tour, the thought of applying for a position in a picture company fascinated me, so I came to the Thanhouser studio. The Princess Company was just being formed, and I seemed to fill the requirement of the youthful lead, so here I have been ever since."

Mabel Condon added her own recollection: "I remember that Mr. Marshall, with his sleek black hair, his brown eyes and well-rounded frame that wears well the newest mandates of fashion, had been rushed into a *Friday the Thirteenth* film as his tryout (in the first Princess release) and as a result there was a flood of inquiry as to the identity of the nice-looking young lead. Remember that program and dance last January out at the Thanhouser studios? Then you remember hearing Boyd's singing voice, for it was a feature of the program. It is a baritone, and Boyd seems to enjoy using it as much as his audience enjoys hearing it."

Among other Thanhouser events, Philip Lonergan, editor of scenarios and scripts at Thanhouser, was put in charge of the entire production of the studio when his older brother, Lloyd, went to California to investigate exhibits and film making possibilities for the 1915 Panama-Pacific International Exposition. Lloyd's absence meant increased duties for Philip: "In addition to writing scripts to take care of the Thanhouser 'three a week,' and the Princess weekly release, he has to devote the rest of his hours to the factory and studios. . . . But it is all in a day's work to genial Phil, and he feels that his big brother deserves a vacation away from the plant after writing eight hundred or more scripts in the past five years," according to *Moving Picture World*. The same publication reported the departure of Thanhouser's long-term publicity agent: "After almost five years of service at Thanhouser, starting as the concern's first publicity manager and winding up as special representative of the late C. J. Hite, Bert Adler has gone to Universal." A few weeks later, it was announced that Maude Fealy, earlier a star with Thanhouser and Majestic, had gone to work for the Holland Film Manufacturing Company, a new Boston organization, and was also going to play a part in a stage performance.

Mayre Hall, Muriel's replacement as the leading lady in the Princess Department, apparently planned to stay for a while, for she told a reporter her work was very enjoyable. Around the same time, an article in *Moving Picture World* noted that she was born on a farm in Ohio and moved to Cincinnati when she was a small child. At the age of eight she was playing in stock companies and remained there until she was fifteen years old, when she went to vaudeville. Working alone, she made her greatest hit while doing Italian impersonations. In April 1913 she came to New York to join Carl Laemmle's Independent Moving Pictures Company. "Miss Hall is nineteen years old and very pretty," the article noted. "She lives in New Rochelle near the Thanhouser studio."

On October 13th *The Diamond of Disaster*, a two-reel Thanhouser film, was released. Like *The Varsity Race*, it was written by Philip Lonergan and directed by Carroll Fleming. *Moving Picture World* noted that "the acting throughout was of a high order, and especially noticeable was J. S. Murray as the Hindu merchant; Justus D. Barnes as the bandit; Ernest Ward as the fakir; Morgan Jones as the rajah; John Richards as Hassan, the rajah's captain; Muriel Ostriche as Zelda, the dancing girl; Irving Cummings as the Englishman, Carey L. Hastings as his wife, and David Thompson as their servant."

Motion Picture News gave a synopsis: "Quite a mystifying atmosphere is uppermost throughout this picture, which materially heightens the interest. A young American is warned not to accept a priceless diamond from an Indian as a token of gratitude. The dire results that it visited upon others are shown in fadeouts. The American takes it anyway, and while he is away from his home an outlaw attacks his house to gain possession of it. In his struggle with the confederate the house is blown up, and it is thought that the wife and child of the man are dead, but they live to see the gem hurled into the water."

The theme of *The Diamond of Disaster*, set in India, apparently had something in common with Thanhouser's most ambitious post-Hite project, a sequel to *The Million Dollar Mystery*, which was titled *Zudora*.

Motion Picture News announced that *Zudora*, billed as Thanhouser's greatest photoplay, "will be a revelation of Hindu mysticism and science. *Zudora* is the masterful creation of Daniel Carson Goodman and has been novelized by Harold McGrath for the newspapers. The story will be complete in twenty episodes. A two-reel episode will be released each week starting November 23rd."

Marguerite Snow was to play Zudora, while James Cruze was to play Hassam Ali, "a weird Oriental character around whose mysticism revolves much of the story."

The trade papers, grateful for Thanhouser's massive advertising, did their best to present *Zudora* with enthusiasm. *Motion Picture News* noted: "The first chapter contains all the effects which go to make a strong picture. The situation of the characters is quickly and clearly outlined, and the first adventure of *Zudora* is then presented. The settings are unusually fine. . . . The photography is flawless, and the interest is heightened by a number of remarkably good dissolves and fadeaway effects showing other scenes imagined or described by the characters in the foreground. When it is discovered that the first chapter of the serial film is necessarily the least interesting [apparently a glimpse of the reviewer's true feelings!] it is safe to predict that *Zudora* will meet with a brilliant success."

The same writer later viewed the second episode, hopeful that the interest would improve, and he gamely wrote: "Even if the witness of the second episode of *The Adventures of Zudora* finds it slightly unfathomable until the termination of the first thousand feet, his interest will be so well sustained by the remarkable atmosphere of mysticism and secludedness which pervades the film that the little complexities in the plot itself will pass unnoticed. In the class of mystery stories, this episode of *Zudora* was certainly one of the best in every degree." The third episode was called "quite complicated" in a subsequent review. By the seventh and eighth episodes, Thanhouser realized it was in water over its head, and an abrupt change was made to the plot. *Motion Picture News* reported: "The producers of this serial have seen fit to divert from the original line of events. Perhaps they were figuring on changing from the start, but at any rate, with a dual personality proposition in sway, *Zudora* bids fair to become even more engrossing than it has been heretofore."

Thanhouser executives realized that more surgery had to be performed, and by the ninth episode the title *Zudora* was dropped, despite publicity releases that exhibitors were clamoring for more episodes. Up went signs for *The Twenty Million Dollar Mystery*, a takeoff on the earlier and quite successful *Million Dollar Mystery*. As a transition, one advertisement was titled "Zudora in the Twenty Million Dollar Mystery." Throughout its life *Zudora*, later *The Twenty Million Dollar Mystery*, was heavily advertised in *Motion Picture News*, so what the reviewer really wanted to say probably could not get past the management! Historian Anthony Slide, in *Aspects of American Film History Prior to 1920*, puts it succinctly:

"*The Million Dollar Mystery* was followed by *Zudora*, which was not a success. The Loew theatre circuit cancelled the serial after the first five episodes because of the poor quality of the production. A sophisticated audience of today viewing a chapter of *Zudora* is completely confused by the incomprehensible plot, and one is hard pressed to understand how Thanhouser would dare to produce, let alone release, such a monstrosity."

One has to read between the lines in early trade publications to learn the truth. From all outward indications and announcements, *Zudora* was riding a crest. A more realistic indication was given by the price of the stock of the related firm which distributed the film, the Thanhouser Syndicate Corporation, which at first rose and then fell precipitately.

Thanhouser players continued to leave for greener pastures. In November, director Lucius Henderson joined the Independent Moving Pictures Company. A trade release noted: "Mr. Henderson worked under Mr. Thanhouser at the New Rochelle studios until the company was taken over by the present regime."

Adrift from Princess, Muriel Ostriche continued her work in Thanhouser multiple-reel productions, which were considered to be higher up the ladder than the Princess "fillers." Still, Princess fans clamored for her, and many letters requesting her return were received at the New Rochelle offices.

On October 27, *A Madonna of the Poor*, a two-reel Thanhouser feature, made its debut with Muriel Ostriche in the leading role. *Moving Picture World* called the film "an exceptionally interesting drama" and noted that the director, Carroll Fleming, was a "man with 10,000,000 friends—his popularity as a writer and director is due to his wonderful ability." The same publication gave a plot synopsis:

"John Allerdyce, artist, accepts a commission to paint religious subjects for a new church. His automobile wrecks the plaster casts in an Italian's shop, and, carried away with the beauty of a statue, he learns where the model lives, goes there, and persuades Margarita [Muriel] to pose for him. She is married to Pedro, and they have a child, but the artist knows nothing of her husband. When Allerdyce attempts to make love to her, the Italian girl repels him, and tells Pedro. Pedro, however, being out of work, has only one reply: 'You are a little fool not to accept this man's money.' Gradually, Margarita comes to realize that she has been virtually sold to the artist. One day, however, in Pedro's presence, secure in his possession of her, Allerdyce tries to kiss her. The man in Pedro is aroused by her pleadings. He turns in rage against the artist, and Margarita goes home with her husband."

The next two-reel Thanhouser picture with Muriel Ostriche was *The Turning of the Road*, released on November 3, 1914. Thanhouser's publicity notice described it as "a powerful drama of society life. It portrays the action of a band of thieves who work among the best society. A member of the band—Della Fletcher—is the character around which the plot revolves. Her stealing of the gems and her ultimate reformation and marriage to a handsome rector form a basis for many tense scenes. She is led by love out of the shadows into the light and the turning of a new road. The cast includes Muriel Ostriche, Frank Woods, John Reinhard, Ethyle Cooke, Ernest Ward, Carey Hastings, Arthur Bouer, and Perry Horton." Reviews in *Motion Picture News* and *Moving Picture World* were indifferent, although the photography was praised.

Muriel's next Thanhouser picture was a one-reel film released on November 8th, *Keeping a Husband*. The story involved Mrs. Strong, who wrote in her diary "Married twenty-five years today—I still love my husband." Muriel, as the beautiful daughter of an old friend, arrives to visit the happy couple and, before long, she and Mr. Strong become attached to each other. Tension builds, but before the family is split apart, the husband and young visitor each come to their senses, and Muriel departs by the first train in the morning. "A decidedly clever drama of home life, showing how a wife's strategy makes it possible for her to retain her husband's love in spite of severe temptations," noted a Thanhouser advertisement. "This photoplay is very capably enacted by Muriel Ostriche, Carey L. Hastings, and Ernest C. Ward."

Princess films without Muriel were spewed out at the rate of one a week, but demand for them by exhibitors was falling, and the Princess Department realized it was in trouble. In the middle of November Thanhouser announced that Arthur Ellery, Mayre Hall, and several other Princess employees had been laid off—"a retrenchment because of the war—until the market adjusts itself." In the meantime, Muriel continued with mainstream Thanhouser films. On November 24, 1914, the two-reel *Mrs. Van Ruyter's Stratagem* was released. Written by Philip Lonergan and

Muriel Ostriche, studio portrait. (Georgetown University Library)

directed by Carroll Fleming, a familiar team, the film featured a cast which included Carey L. Hastings, Ethyle Cooke, Harry Benham, Helen Badgley, Fan Bourke, and Ed Hoyt in addition to Muriel Ostriche. A review appeared in *Motion Picture News*: "Although we have seen the same idea that is the basis of this drama picturized before, it is so different from the general run of dramas that it has an air of originality. The rich widow is in a quandary as to which of her relatives shall receive her fortune. At the suggestion of her lawyer she changes places with her housekeeper and invites them all to stay at her home for some length of time. They are all imposing, haughty, or artifically friendly, except for one [Muriel Ostriche] who happens to be serving the widow in the capacity of a maid. She wins the fortune and also the young lawyer's heart." *Moving Picture World* noted that the film was "carefully constructed and carries the interest of the observer in a pleasing way; it makes a comedy drama somewhat above the average."

The Amateur Detective, a Thanhouser film released on December 6, 1914, featured Muriel Ostriche as a young girl and Carey L. Hastings as a cook. *Motion Picture News* reported: "Burdened with a conventional plot, the players of this offering make the most of their opportunities and afford a number of laughs. Father refuses his daughter's suitor, until he procures $500, which he does by threatening the gentleman with secret signs and then charging him the required sum to fathom the mystery." *Moving Picture World* found the cast "pleasing" and the photography "good."

The following day, December 7th, the Motion Picture Exhibitors' Association of Greater New York staged its fifth annual ball. A large crowd attended to see Clara Kimball Young, King Baggot, Mary Pickford, James Cruze, Muriel Ostriche, Marguerite Snow, and others introduced from the platform.

Philip Lonergan and Carroll Fleming teamed up to produce *The Reader of Minds*, a two-reel Thanhouser picture released on December 8, 1914. The film, with Muriel Ostriche as the switchboard girl, Harris Gordon as Lieutenant Esmold, and Carey L. Hastings as the lieutenant's mother, received good reviews from *Motion Picture News* and *Moving Picture World*. The *New York Dramatic Mirror* gave a plot synopsis which contrasted Lonergan's efforts with those of Muriel:

"Mr. Lonergan drifts to sea this time and remains for the length of the offering over the unfathomable mysteries of a marvelous invention. This is nothing else than a machine that reads men's minds and projects a hidden thought on a screen by means of a moving picture film. Mr. Lonergan seems not to believe in working out little homely facts of life. Our imaginations are to be startled by the incredible, coupled in some measure with the melodramatic. If these be slots for pictures, then the entrance of inventors who have propelled aeroplanes by transmitting power from the earth, or a myriad of similar improbable theories into the film field, would seem imminent.

"Nor is the very unusual subject borne out by a similar treatment in the staging of it. A foreign spy seems to drag the offering back into known channels; recognize his dark looks. The cast is one of well-known names, who are undoubtedly hampered by the nature of the subject. Muriel Ostriche is the one pleasant spot in the picture.

"The story tells of the invention by the lieutenant of a machine that destroys ships at a distance, the theft of his invention by a foreign spy with his mind reader—'the machine photographs the plans as the inventor thinks of his invention.' The telephone girl, overhearing a conversation, is able to solve the mystery of how the lieutenant managed to lose the secret of his plans."

A December article in *Motography* concerned Philip Lonergan: "His coming to the Thanhouser studio last spring did not mark his beginning in the script world. That occurred in May 1912, and the New Rochelle studio provided the start. For twenty weeks earlier he had been gathering experience by helping his brother Lloyd when the latter was confined to his home with a broken leg and at the same time was providing the Thanhouser directors with working material. So Phil, as people best know the younger of the two Lonergans, gleaned valuable knowledge in exchange for valuable help and was at home in the position of assistant script editor when the opportunity was offered. In July 1913, the late C. J. Hite chose Phil Lonergan to go to the Majestic coast studio where he wrote and selected scripts until last May, when Mr. Hite summoned him back to New Rochelle and gave him the entire charge of the Princess script department. But a great part of the work attendant upon Thanhouser productions devolved upon Phil, and with the bestowal of the title of manager of production upon Lloyd, that of Thanhouser editor became Phil's."

A biographical feature in the September 5, 1914 issue of the *New Rochelle Pioneer* noted that Philip Lonergan was born in Hackensack, New Jersey, May 18, 1885, and was known as a story writer for Munsey publications. *The Little Girl Next Door* [with the Thanhouser Twins] was his first film scenario. By September 1914 he had written about 250 stories for the screen. It was stated that his brother Lloyd had married Edwin Thanhouser's sister.

In the various trade papers in December 1914, Thanhouser boasted that it had more leading personalities than any other production company: "Stars such as Florence LaBadie, Sidney Bracy, James Cruze, Marguerite Snow, Harry Benham, Muriel Ostriche, Morris Foster, Mignon Anderson, Arthur Ashley, Helen Badgley, The Thanhouser Twins—and a score of others—are found in Thanhouser casts. No other motion picture producer can boast of such a group of stars! Thanhouser is FIRST in stars!"

Separately, a news article revealed that Mrs. Grover Baluser, of North Baltimore, Ohio, a sister of the late Charles J. Hite, "has a new smiling face in her home, and she has given the baby the name of Zudora."

The *New York Dramatic Mirror*, issue of November 23, 1914, printed a portent of the future: "Edwin Thanhouser's period of absence from the picture game, following his sale of control of the Thanhouser Corporation to the late Charles J. Hite and associates, is apparently nearing its end. The founder of the Thanhouser Corporation, who was a leader in the ranks of the Independents until his retirement two years ago, is now looking around for a studio and factory site, and from all indications will probably settle down near his old stamping ground, New Rochelle.

"Mr. Thanhouser returned from Europe at the outbreak of war, but no intimation was given then of his intention to return to the game. On last Thursday he is said to have had a conference with Mayor Fiske, of Mount Vernon, over the possibilities of finding a suitable site in that city. That the plans have been maturing for some time is evident from the fact that propositions have been made to Mr. Thanhouser to locate in Pelham, Eastchester, and Tuckahoe."

The worsening situation at Princess Films was corrected in December. The *New York Dramatic Mirror* undoubtedly pleased many with this brief notice: "Muriel Ostriche, forsaking the Thanhouser brand, has resumed playing leading roles in the Princess productions, a change brought about by insistent demands of the fans."

A better Christmas present for Muriel's many admirers could not be imagined than the release on December 25th of a Princess feature, *The White Rose*, with Muriel Ostriche and Boyd Marshall back as the leads. No matter that the story was not particularly exciting, it was still received with enthusiasm. The synopsis, from *Moving Picture World*, follows:

"George Bolton [Boyd Marshall] is the foolishly wild son of a country baker. He quarrels with his father, and neglects his sweetheart, Nell Morrison [Muriel], posing before the cheaper element in the place as the town sport. At last he decides that Elmwood is too slow for him, and taking what money he has and his banjo, he goes to New York. Nell meets him on the way to the depot and gives him a white rose that she is wearing. As he climbs the train's steps he laughingly tosses it from him.

"In the city Bolton seeks theatrical work in vain, and finally gets a job playing and singing ragtime in a rathskeller. Here he sinks from bad to worse, with little pay and much drinking. One night, a white rose, bought from a flower peddler by a habitue of the place, finds its way into Bolton's hand. With it come rushing back memories of Nell. Smashing his banjo against the table, he bursts out of the café—and sets his face toward his home village. He makes the journey on foot, arriving at his father's office, dirty, footsore and haggard-eyed. To complete his humiliation, Nell enters and sees him. But with the boy's earnest entreaties for another chance at honest work, his father receives him back. And when he pulls from his pocket the faded counterpart of Nell's last gift, she throws her arms about him, kissing her forgiveness."

When Fate Rebelled, a Princess film, was released on January 1, 1915. *Motion Picture News* reviewed it: "When a girl's sweetheart is robbed of money which he is taking to pay off the men at a quarry, the job is done so cleverly that there seems to be little for the thieves to fear. Not only does the girl discover that her lover's rival is guilty, but she recovers all of the funds by a daring act. A picture with considerable action. Muriel Ostriche and Boyd Marshall are seen as the lovers, and Frank Wood as the chief." The *New York Dramatic Mirror* noted that "Muriel Ostriche makes an attractive heroine, and she is given adequate support by Boyd Marshall and Frank Wood," while *Moving Picture World* noted that the feature contained "a great deal that is interesting."

Advertised as "a dramatic story of love and business powerfully portrayed," *Check No. 130*, a Princess film, was released on January 8th, 1915. *Motion Picture News* had good news and bad news: "The old Muriel Ostriche-Boyd Marshall combination comes into action again in this reel, and perhaps their return will so overjoy the people that they will overlook the poor story they appear in, but this is hardly likely, as it is so confusing that not many will enjoy it. It concerns a girl coming between a loving husband and hatefully suspicious wife, but all ends well." A reviewer for *Moving Picture World* reacted differently: "A good screen story, worked out in a creditable manner. Muriel Ostriche and Boyd Marshall play the lovers. The businessman's wife sees the check for funds loaned to his stenographer and becomes jealous. The development is natural and convincing and leads up to a dramatic close."

Reviewing *The Speed King*, a Thanhouser film released on January 12th, the *New York Dramatic Mirror* noted: "Perhaps the most interesting incident in this two-part drama, written by Philip Lonergan and featuring Arthur Ashley and Muriel Ostriche, shows the manner in which a perfectly honorable young man is suspected of cheating of cards. Alfred's valet, bribed by his enemy, Ranston, has secreted a number of aces and kings in the lining of Alfred's vest and, at the psychological moment, he is caught with the goods. His father disowns him, he is ostracized by his friends, his fiancé proves faithless, but the fiancé's younger sister retains confidence in his innocence. Several years later Muriel's trust is rewarded by proof of Alfred's honesty, and she, of course, becomes his sweetheart. The picture gets its title from the automobile race in which the hero drives the car to victory. These scenes, photographed at an actual race at Brighton Beach, add some excitement to the second reel."

Of *Pleasing Uncle*, a Muriel Ostriche-Boyd Marshall Princess film released on January 15, 1915, *Moving Picture World* wrote: "Another variation of the old comedy, 'Jane,' in which the nephew borrows a wife and child to deceive his trusting uncle. In this case a whole bedful of babies adds to the amusement of the story. An old theme well handled."

On January 22nd, *An Innocent Burglar*, a Princess film, was released, subsequently to be reviewed by *Motion Picture News*: "An old story acted by a company headed by Muriel Ostriche and Boyd Marshall. The wayward son is disowned by his father and is obliged to seek a position. He lives with his employer, whose wife takes a kindly interest in him. Later he is accused of stealing, but the real culprit is an organ grinder's monkey. The wife discovers this after the man has been imprisoned. He is released, and his honesty is well established. This will afford good entertainment, and the followers of the two leads will find it more than interesting."

On a scale of 1 being excellent, 2 good, 3 fair, and 4 bad, *Variety* rated the story, acting, and production each as 2.

By the time *An Innocent Burglar* was released, Muriel Ostriche had left Thanhouser, disillusioned with the new management. Perhaps because of this, a full-page advertisement in *Moving Picture World*, January 23, 1915, for the Thanhouser Film Corporation noted that for Princess films *An Innocent Burglar* is "a one-reel drama of exceptional merit featuring Boyd Marshall and Reenie Farrington." Muriel was not mentioned!

Motion Picture Magazine, in its February 1915 issue, ran an article written early in January:

When Fate Rebelled, a Princess film released on January 1, 1915, featured Muriel Ostriche and Boyd Marshall in the lead roles. Other cast members included Frank Wood and the Thanhouser Twins, although the twins are not illustrated here. The center and bottom pictures show the familiar team of Muriel and Boyd.

Scenes from *Pleasing Uncle,* a Thanhouser film released on January 15, 1915, toward the end of Muriel Ostriche's tenure with Thanhouser. Above and to the right: Muriel Ostriche is seen with Boyd Marshall, while in the image below, John Reinhard stands directly behind her.

"Only seventeen, looks fifteen, and can make up to fool you into believing her half that age—this is Muriel Ostriche. And she is leading woman—a photoplay star—for the Princess Department of the Thanhouser Company.

"Muriel Ostriche was born in New York and danced her way through school. She has been dancing ever since with great success when she is not being embodied in film. The smart hotels and winter gardens in New York say that she is a clever tangoist and has captured prizes galore.

"She started in at fifteen, playing extra at the Biograph studio after high school hours. After that she played through a whole Pathé picture, then joined the Eclair Company as a stock member. But when Princess wanted an ingenue lead, a pirouetting one with russet-brown hair, they captured Muriel Ostriche."

During the month Muriel left, the *Zudora* disaster continued to chip away at the market price of Thanhouser stock, although the problems with the serial were not acknowledged in print. "Most of the stockholders are awaiting some rather unusual developments promised with later episodes," a financial note in *Motography* observed. In the meantime, Daniel Carson Goodman, who was to be engaged to Florence LaBadie two years later, departed, and a number of other Thanhouser regulars used the exit door. Reenie Farrington appeared in an increasing number of Princess productions as the successor to Muriel, often opposite Boyd Marshall.

Perhaps emulating what Charles J. Hite might have done had he been alive, the Thanhouser directors decided to go into motion picture exhibition, their first attempt at theatre ownership since the failure of the Broadway Rose Gardens. The North Avenue Theatre in New Rochelle was purchased, and its name was changed to the Thanhouser Players Theatre, under the ownership of a new firm, Thanhouser Players Photoplays. Seating 500, the building was placed under the direction of W. Ray Johnston, Hite's brother-in-law. "Each night a Thanhouser player appears. Monday is *Zudora* day, Wednesday is Thanhouser feature day, and on Friday nights there are provided souvenirs for the women," an announcement proclaimed.

Without regard for veracity, Thanhouser Film Corporation executives informed securities analysts that all was well, and that *Zudora* was a top performer. However, the truth was that just 115 prints were being made of current episodes, enough for the exchanges to distribute over a period of time to a thousand or two picture houses, a trivial number compared to the approximately 15,000 theatres in the United States at the time. By contrast, an early account stated that Thanhouser's first successful serial, *The Million Dollar Mystery*, cost $125,000 to produce but earned a whopping $1,500,000 or so during its run in over 6,000 theatres.

In March 1915 the trade papers noted that Edwin Thanhouser would resume the management of the company bearing his name. Wilbert Shallenberger had since disposed of his stock, but his brother Edgar bid to assume a more active directorship and management role, together with Crawford Livingston. "An entirely new policy will be inaugurated in this company at once," according to a release in *Motography*. "Mr. Thanhouser will undoubtedly arrange to produce some more of those sterling films which have made the name of Thanhouser one to reckon with in the independent field."

In the same month, *Moving Picture World* gave a brief biographical sketch of Edwin Thanhouser, noting that it was in November 1912 that he left the men and women who had been associated with him since 1908 in making films (although, the first Thanhouser picture did not make its debut until 1910). With his wife and children he went abroad, returning when the European war broke out. "On Monday, February 22, general manager of the Thanhouser Corporation, Mr. Thanhouser, was back at his old desk in the New Rochelle studio. When two days later a *Moving Picture World* man called on him he very suddenly discovered that Mr. Thanhouser was not a talkative man. To a somewhat thinly veiled reference to this outstanding fact, the founder of the institution of which New Rochelle is so proud said that he much preferred to be judged by results than to be estimated by his promises. He readily admitted, however, that he was full of ambition and that he was anxious to make good films. He said it would take some little while for him to find himself."

Thanhouser noted that when he left the studio in 1912 he felt that European films were markedly superior to American products, but since his return the situation had changed, and that American films and European efforts were on a par with each other. He went on to say that he was the first to advocate the "natural length story," so that if a film plot fit properly into 1,500 feet there was no reason either to extend it to 2,000 feet or to cut it to 1,000 feet. He stressed his oft-expressed interest in adapting novels and poems to movies, stating that there were many more of these than the limited field of plays afforded.

"Asked if his re-entry into the affairs of the Thanhouser Company portended any change in policy, the new general manager said that it would not. 'We will make the regular program as strong as possible,' he added. 'You may be sure that the film that bears my name will be as good as anything I can do will make it. Our output is now six and a quarter reels a week, of which all but two go into the regular program. We plan soon to increase the amount. In spite of the fact that our facilities here are capable of material expansion over present requirements, it is our intention soon to erect an additional studio on adjacent property. We may begin construction during the summer.' "

Motography took note of Thanhouser's return to the profession he loved: "It is said that Thanhouser stock jumped six points the day Wall Street received information of Edwin Thanhouser's resuming general charge of the Thanhouser Company. Time turned back three pages, took the Thanhouser president of 1912 and earlier, and placed him in the 1915 setting afforded by the New Rochelle studio and offices. Time then mounted to the top of the Thanhouser mahogany roll-top desk, and Mr. Thanhouser states that it alone is to be judged of whatever the Thanhouser plants and management will mean to the company now under his jurisdiction.

"Other things happened, in addition to the rise of the stock market. The studio scintillated in the bright sunshine which ushered in the return of the general manager, and three scenes were underway in the filming in record time. Gertrude Thanhouser—who is Mrs. Edwin Thanhouser and whose dramatic perception was greatly responsible for earlier Thanhouser successes—said a cheery 'good morning' to everybody and slipped out of her motor coat and into a swivel chair to the pleasurable task of writing dramatic moments in the film plot. Lloyd Lonergan, after two months' absence, walked around the corner from his apartment and resumed the desk of scenario chief. . . . The Thanhousers, who have been married 'fifteen short years,' as Mr. Thanhouser puts it, have an apartment-home on Riverside Drive. They will motor out to New Rochelle every morning in a Winton Six which Mr. Thanhouser drives."

Advertising signed by Edwin Thanhouser and aimed at exhibitors expressed optimism: "I am back where you knew me for years—at the head of the Thanhouser Film Corporation of New Rochelle, New York, which I founded in 1908. After three years of travel and study abroad, the men who bought out my interest in the studio I started persuaded me to return. Naturally, it will be some little time before the pictures bearing my personal endorsement will be released. In the meantime, I request that my friends recall the reputation which the Thanhouser productions enjoyed during the period from 1908 until 1912, when I was personally in charge. I am a showman and I know your needs; I am a producer and I will meet your needs; I am the guarantee against unrest of your patrons. . . . Watch for the date of the first Edwin Thanhouser releases."

There were some contrary notes, however. A paragraph in *Variety* stated: "With the return of Edwin Thanhouser to active control of the New Rochelle plant, several changes have been made in the company. Last week fourteen players were laid off. It is reported that Sidney Bracy and Frank Farrington [father of Reenie], two of Thanhouser's leads, severed their connection with the concern this week. With Thanhouser taking hold, a policy of single- and double-reel subjects is in effect, with nothing in the way of a feature being attempted."

Princess films continued to be advertised in the trade papers, more so than when Muriel Ostriche was involved, when notices were primarily limited to *Reel Life*, the house organ of the Mutual Program. Reenie Farrington and Boyd Marshall were the stars. Before long, however, the Princess name disappeared, and it was announced that in its place the Falstaff Department had been set up to produce comedies. The Falstaff debut occurred on April 16, 1915, with *The Actor and the Rube*. Edwin Thanhouser noted that all Falstaff productions had his personal endorsement. Unfortunately, his personal endorsement notwithstanding, early releases fared poorly with reviewers. For example, in *Motion Picture News*, *Ferdie Fink's Flirtations* was described as follows: "This won't give much amusement as it is poorly introduced and largely padded," while *The House That Jack Moved* was thus evaluated: "This contains a good idea, but it is hardly well enough produced to create much laughter." *The Refugee*, a Thanhouser film, was described as: "This reel gives an utterly meaningless appearance. . . . This is neither funny nor entertaining in a dramatic sense." Still, Thanhouser gamely sent out news release after news release, reminding readers of the great tradition that his studio had built in the early years. Thanhouser, no advocate of the "star system," stated on numerous occasions that he would draw his new players from the legitimate stage, not from other motion picture companies, for motion picture stars were apt to have an inflated value of their worth. Replacing Bert Adler, Leon J. Rubenstein was hired as publicity director. Lloyd Lonergan was given complete charge of motion picture scenarios.

Leon J. Rubenstein set about his new advertising job with gusto, and in a limousine he brought to New Rochelle representatives from *Motography*, *The Morning Telegraph*, *The Evening Mail*, *The Dramatic New York Mirror*, *Motion Picture News*, *The Billboard*, and *Moving Picture World*. The scribes were regaled with impressive plans for the future: "Deals for property near the present buildings are pending, and unless all signs fail the early summer months will find New Rochelle carpenters hammering on the framework of several new structures. There is going to be plenty of room for all of the seven or eight companies that will have been organized by that time. At present there are six, with the prospect of another within a few weeks. In addition to the regular Thanhouser release and the new Falstaff brand—the great pet of Mr. Thanhouser, by the way—four-reel Mutual Masterpieces are being made at the rate of two every five weeks. . . ."

Following the hiring of several Broadway stage personalities, Thanhouser told a writer for *Motion Picture News*: "I feel that eventually the production of films will be in the hands of the masters of the speaking stage; of course, there will be exceptions, but the legitimate experience of these gentlemen brings an appreciation of possibilities which will mold the destiny of the silent drama."

Amidst this publicity, two leading Thanhouser personalities, Mignon Anderson, who had been with the company for a number of years, and Morris Foster, "who has been in pictures about two years," were married in one of the gala events of the social season. The Thanhouserites presented the couple with a set of colonial silver.

Misleading Thanhouser financial reports were issued, with Edgar Shallenberger advising Wall Street: "The popularity [of *The Twenty Million Dollar Mystery*] not only shows no sign of abating, but constantly increases." He fooled very few, for the company's securities, after a spurt of interest caused by Edwin Thanhouser's return, drifted downward. In mid-June a financial reporter wrote: "That the ask price is higher than the earning power the company would warrant seems to be the opinion of most of the stockholders."

Old-time Thanhouser employees continued their exodus, to be replaced by stage figures, with accompanying fanfare as new directors, actors, and actresses climbed aboard the Thanhouser wagon. Florence LaBadie, who had weathered several Thanhouser storms, was the most prominent New Rochelle film personality of the period.

An article in *Moving Picture World*, July 30, 1915, featured W. Edgar Shallenberger, brother of Wilbert, who at that time was involved with the Thanhouser Syndicate Corporation, the Thanhouser Film Corporation, and the American, Mutual, and other motion picture organizations. It was stated that Edgar had been a silent partner in various Hite enterprises, and upon the latter's death he was summoned to New Rochelle to take charge of various projects, including *Zudora*.

In the same article, Edgar Shallenberger was quoted on the subject of scenarios, noting that the film dramatization of popu-

Thanhouser's Jacksonville, Florida studio facility. During the teens Jacksonville saw several production companies locate there. (Courtesy of the American Museum of the Moving Image, Lawrence Williams Collection)

lar books "will not serve the film industry much longer," a contradiction to Edwin Thanhouser's view of the subject.

Edwin Thanhouser's grandiose plans continued, and in August 1915 he announced that the production of Falstaff comedies would be doubled, to be followed a month later by the introduction of a series of three-reel features, known as Than-O-Play films (the first of which featured reliable Florence LaBadie). Plans nearly came to a premature conclusion—shades of Charles J. Hite—when in his touring car Thanhouser swerved to miss another vehicle and was saved by a thin wire cable from plunging over a steep embankment.

In October, more plans were announced. A large studio building was to be set up in Jacksonville, Florida, from which location companies would depart for Cuba, the Bahamas, and Bermuda. As if that were not enough, two more companies were to be sent from New Rochelle to Labrador, to permit extended filming in the land of snow and ice. From the Arctic to the equator, at any given moment Thanhouser crews would be busy. The price of Thanhouser stock went up slightly, then back down again, the decline precipitated in June 1916 by unofficial news of Thanhouser's withdrawal from the Mutual organization. Apparently, Mutual threw Thanhouser out, for a news item in *Motography* observed: "It probably takes some courage to put into execution a radical move of this kind, but, if the product of this particular company is not earning according to requirements, the Mutual management is to be commended upon its action."

Thanhouser's fortunes didn't improve, and many trains from New Rochelle carried actors and their belongings. It was announced that the New Rochelle laboratories were available to process films of other companies. Things went from bad to worse, and production continued to diminish. Thanhouser began releasing through Pathé under the "Gold Rooster" label. Florence LaBadie held to her post, and in June 1917 various advertisements for the six-reel Gold Rooster Play, *The Woman in White*, appeared in the trade papers. In September, *War and the Woman*, featuring the same actress, received modest publicity.

In the autumn of 1917, *Moving Picture World* carried this story:

"It is with sorrow that the moving picture industry and its patrons learn of the untimely death at the age of 23 years of Florence LaBadie, who has for the past five years been one of the leading stars of the Thanhouser studios and was featured recently in the Pathé Gold Rooster plays. About two months ago Miss LaBadie, accompanied by a friend [her fiance, Daniel Carson Goodman, a scriptwriter who lived in New York City, who had a medical background, who at one time did scenario work for D. W. Griffith, and who eventually married Alma Rubens] was driving down a hill near Ossining (New York), when, due to failure of the brakes to operate, the car plunged down the hill at a rate of speed which caused it to overturn at the bottom. The occupants of the car were thrown out, Miss LaBadie sustaining injuries with which the best of specialists were unable to cope. Much loved by all who knew her, she passed away on Saturday, October 13, leaving her mother and many friends to mourn her. Miss LaBadie was born in Montreal, Canada, but for the past few years had been a resident of New York City, and at the time of the accident lived with her mother at the St. Andrew Hotel at Broadway and 72nd Street. The funeral took place from the Campbell Funeral Church, 66th Street and Broadway, at 11:00 on Wednesday morning, October 17th, to the Greenwood Cemetery, where interment was made."

Early in 1918, an article appeared in *Moving Picture World*:
"Edwin Thanhouser retires. Sometime between February 20 and March 1, directors of the Thanhouser Film Corporation will elect a new president, and Edwin Thanhouser will be at Bayville, Long Island, putting the finishing touches to Shorewood, a beautiful estate on Long Island Sound. . . . At the present day, as a result of Mr. Thanhouser's management, the corporation's financial condition is unique. With studios and laboratories in New Rochelle and another glass studio in Jacksonville, both in up-to-date condition and free from debt, and a large capital accumulated in banks, financial worries will not be among the problems that face the new management of the Thanhouser Film Corporation. Several flattering propositions have been made to him by certain film interests, but Mr. Thanhouser is not inclined to remain in the motion picture field. There is a rumor, however, that he might consider one or two 'big productions.'"

By early 1918, Thanhouser films were unwanted in the marketplace. In spite of this, the following optimistic notice appeared in *Motography* in May 1918:

"The Thanhouser Film Corporation, it is reported, will shortly resume active production in its studios in New Rochelle. Plans have been perfected, it is said, for the filming of six big superfeatures a year, which will be released through the Arrow Film Corporation as well as a number of propaganda and program pictures.

"W. E. Shallenberger, president of the Arrow Film Corporation, also the treasurer and active manager of the Thanhouser Film Corporation, was noncommittal when asked about Thanhouser's plans. He admitted it was probable that the company would soon resume making pictures, but he said he could not announce any definite plans at the present time. Thanhouser has been out of the production field for some time. For several years it was one of the best-known producing organizations in the world and some of the most noteworthy pictures ever seen on the screen were filmed in its studios. In the old days Thanhouser set a pace for most of the other producers. It was perfectly capable of doing this, for on the Thanhouser payroll were some of the keenest and best equipped mentalities in the entire industry, and many of the devices and inventions that have been facilitated and so greatly improved the making and showing of motion pictures were thought out and perfected in the New Rochelle studios.

"Unlike many other motion picture organizations, Thanhouser temporarily discontinued producing with plenty of money in the bank and a high financial rating on Wall Street. The officials of the company determined to quit making pictures for a while; 'Let the wheels spin, and then enter the actual production game again with a lot of new, practical ideas.' When the company stopped filming in its own name it had, according to reports, a bank balance of more than $275,000. This has never been withdrawn and probably will remain intact until the company launches its new activities. The Thanhouser studios in New Rochelle are among the best equipped of their kind in the country. They have been leased at various times to different producers, and only recently the Clara Kimball Young Company completed its eastern work here and left for California. Many eastern producers have tried to buy the studios, but the Thanhouser Company has always retained them. A few weeks ago the Thanhouser Company held its annual meeting and elected Crawford Livingston as president, Wilbert Shallenberger, vice president, A. E. Jones, secretary, W. E. Shallenberger, vice president and treasurer."

The studio facilities were subsequently sold to the officers of the company, who then resold them to A. A. Fischer, whose Fischer Studios were involved with B. A. Rolfe Productions. The Thanhouser name, so brilliant in years past, faded from the scene.

Edwin Thanhouser remained at his home in Sands Point, Long Island, until 1945, when he sold his home and art collection and moved into a New York City apartment. "The best advice I can give to people getting on in years is to rid themselves of most of the things they have collected during their lives and live simply," he told a reporter for the New Rochelle *Standard-Star* in a December 1949 interview. "It makes life much easier as you get older, and, besides, those are the things of the young. I have done with my life exactly what I wanted. I was in the theatre and made enough money, but, most of all, I retired young enough to enjoy it. I wish I could give it all away just to be again the visionary 16-year-old I once was. The years have flown so." Edwin Thanhouser passed away at the age of 90 in March 1956, survived by a son, a daughter, five grandchildren, and two great-grandchildren.

Thanhouser Today

The views on this and the next several pages were taken in January 1987 by Doug Duijan, with assistance provided by Rick Moody. Shown are a number of structures which existed in Muriel Ostriche's time and were used by Thanhouser and its players.

The front of the Thanhouser building. This structure was built after the 1913 fire demolished the earlier facilities. (Photographed by Doug Duijan)

The back of the Thanhouser Film Company building shows the extensive area of glass panels used to let sunlight into the studio for indoor scenes. (Photographed by Doug Duijan)

Beacon Hall with the Thanhouser building visible to the left. From time to time various Thanhouser players lived in this apartment complex. (Photographed by Doug Duijan)

This lot on Evans Street was used by Thanhouser for outdoor sets. (Photographed by Doug Duijan)

Evans Street, with the side of the Thanhouser building at the left. (Photographed by Doug Duijan)

Two buildings, which in the Thanhouser days formed a part of the Pepperday Inn complex, a high-class lodging facility and restaurant in its day. Numerous Thanhouser functions were held here. Mrs. Mary Pepperday was also a part owner of the Beacon Hall, where several Thanhouser players lived. (Photographed by Doug Duijan)

The estate of Francis Wilson, known as "The Orchard," at 3 Meadow Lane. Charles J. Hite lived here in 1914, and the grounds were used in several Thanhouser films. (Photographed by Doug Duijan)

CHAPTER SIX

Moxie and More Movies

In 1914, Moxie, a popular soft drink with bottling facilities in Boston and New York, launched a nationwide contest to find the Moxie Girl. Fifteen hundred entrants competed for the honor. The winner was Muriel Ostriche, who later recalled:

"The Moxie Company sent a photographer who must have taken hundreds of pictures. While he was in New York City, he met my father's sister, my aunt Cora Oestrich, and became quite attracted to her, but no romance developed. Before long, my picture was everywhere. Every drugstore in the United States, it seemed, had a life-size cardboard figure of me, and I remember a lot of posters, thermometers, and other things with my image."

Moxie, first called Moxie Nerve Food, was the brainchild of Dr. Augustin Thompson, a distinguished veteran of the Civil War who studied homeopathic medicine and in 1867 set up practice in Lowell, Massachusetts. Two decades later he claimed to be New England's most successful physician.

In 1884, Thompson formulated Moxie Nerve Food, a carbonated beverage which supposedly cured numerous ailments. Soon, the story of "Lieutenant Moxie" reached print. One account stated that while on military maneuvers near the equator, the fortunate lieutenant happened upon a miraculous plant which enabled natives to work long periods of time without other sustenance and which cured many ailments. Another advertisement placed the discovery near the Strait of Magellan, thousands of miles to the south of the equator.

On July 16, 1885, Thompson filed a trademark registration for Moxie Nerve Food, which by that time was enjoying remarkable sales in the Lowell area. The beverage label accompanying the trademark application to the Patent Office noted, in part:

"MOXIE NERVE FOOD has not a drop of medicine, poison, stimulant or alcohol in its composition, but is a simple starchy plant grown in South America and the only positive nerve food known that can recover brain and nervous exhaustion, and loss of manhood, at once, unaided. It has cured paralysis, softening of the brain, and mental imbecility. It gives a durable, solid strength, and makes you eat voraciously. The tired, sleepy, lifeless feeling disappears like magic. Will not interfere with the action of vegetable medicines. Dose: a wineglassful four times a day."

Moxie prospered, and soon bottling was transferred from Lowell to Boston, with an additional facility in New York City. In 1896, Frank M. Archer, seemingly born with a gift for publicity and advertising, was hired. Soon, Moxie's advertising became the most innovative in the beverage trade. When automobiles started to become popular shortly after the turn of the century, the Moxie Company bought a fleet of them, using them to deliver the beverage while, at the same time, garnering reams of publicity. In 1903 Augustin Thompson died, and Archer, while maintaining but a minor ownership stock position, managed the company, guiding it down a road marked with many successes.

In 1911 the Moxie Boy appeared, an artist's rendering of a young man dressed in a soda fountain attendant's jacket, with his index finger pointing toward the viewer, commanding him to "drink Moxie!" The Moxie Boy was an instant success, and within a matter of months hundreds of thousands of signs, posters, and other representations of him appeared everywhere from window displays to billboards. Finding a partner for the Moxie Boy was undoubtedly the reason for the subsequent search, this time for a real person, for the Moxie Girl.

Not long after Muriel Ostriche won the Moxie contest, her likeness appeared on the first of several varieties of hand-held cardboard fans, on cardboard cut-out advertising signs, baseball score cards, thermometers, and numerous other novelties, including large sets of china dinnerware.

In May 1915, the month that the first Muriel Ostriche Moxie advertising cardboard fan was copyrighted, Frank Archer pasted a photograph of her in his personal scrapbook, putting "Moxie Girl" as the caption in pencil above her portrait, and noting in the margin that her home address was 565 West 144th Street, New York City. Separately, a brief biography was attached to the page:

"MURIEL OSTRICHE has risked her life more than once to add realism to moving pictures, and has been christened the

Souvenir china dishes, circa 1916, featuring Muriel Ostriche. Distributed by the Moxie Company, New England's best known soft drink manufacturer, such items were used as premiums and prizes in theatre contests, state and local fairs, and other events.

The first of several varieties of hand-held fans featuring Muriel Ostriche was released in May 1915.

Another Moxie fan featuring Muriel Ostriche, this one first issued in 1916. Such fans were given away by the thousands to promote Moxie, a beverage which was first marketed in the 1880s under the Moxie Nerve Food name.

A third variety of hand-held cardboard fan featuring Muriel Ostriche, issued by the Moxie Company.

'daredevil of the movies.' She was born in New York City. . . .While in Wadleigh High she began posing for pictures as an extra. Her success was so great that during her second year she left to become a stock member in one of the larger moving picture companies. She had more than usual success, not only as an actress, but as a writer of scenarios, having written original stories in which she played the lead."

Moxie china, with Muriel's portrait, which was in distribution by 1916, was often given as prizes in various exhibitions, fairs, and contests. To Frank Archer's scrapbook were added many clippings of such events. One notice announced that in Rutland, Vermont, August 1916, at the Shrine Theatre, on Monday, Wednesday, and Saturday nights, the Moxie Company would present a beautiful set of dishes to the young lady who most resembled Muriel Ostriche.

Concurrent with Muriel Ostriche, Fred H. Wilson, known as the Moxie Stilt Man, garnered much newspaper publicity. Garbed in coat and pants printed with reproductions of Moxie advertisements, Fred on his wooden stilts stood more than twice the height of a normal person. An article in the *Boston American*, August 16, 1916, was illustrated by a cartoonist who depicted Muriel Ostriche at a second story window, with the Moxie Stilt Man at ground level. A fanciful dialogue between Fred Wilson and Muriel Ostriche was related:

" 'Oh, see the Custom House Tower,' exclaimed Muriel Ostriche, the celebrated star . . . looking out her second-story window right into the eyes of the curious Mr. Wilson.

" 'I am not the Custom House Tower. That has a clock for a face,' retorted Mr. Wilson, who wasn't at all abashed at looking into second-story windows.

" 'Then what are you?' demanded Muriel, as perplexed as Alice in Wonderland. 'You must be something.'

" 'Perhaps I'm a wireless station,' replied the tall person.

" 'Do you hear anything from the *Bremen?*'

" 'No, but I can hear the wind blowing through huge whiskers.'

" 'I refuse to talk politics,' responded the dainty Muriel. 'I must go now and be thrown over a cliff to be rescued by the hero. Would you like to be a movie actor?'

" 'I tried,' sadly answered Mr. Wilson, 'but they couldn't get all of me in the camera.'

"Golden-haired Muriel, who is known all over the country as the Moxie Girl, left her window and trotted off to the picture studio."

The second day of the Barnstable, Massachusetts Fair, held at the end of August 1916, was officially designated as Governor's Day, but the *Boston Herald* noted that history would forever remember it as "Moxie Day," for:

"In every part of the spacious grounds one encountered the word Moxie. Invariably a gift went with the name. Hundreds of Moxie bells were distributed. Moxie canes of special design were seized eagerly by a youthful attendance. They were even more popular than the 'Charlie Chaplin' canes of a year ago. For the fairer sex there were thousands of Moxie fans, with pictures of such famous motion picture stars as Mary Pickford [an inaccurate account; Pickford's image was never used] and Muriel Ostriche imprinted on them."

On later occasions, when Muriel visited New England, the Moxie Company picked up the tab and escorted her through a series of theatre appearances. In a memorable 1919 swing through Massachusetts and New Hampshire, Muriel was trailed by more newspaper reporters and photographers than she could easily count. After 1915, other actresses, including Laura Walker, Frances Pritchard, Lillian MacKenzie, Eileen Percy, and Ann Pennington, were featured by name in Moxie advertising, although none came close to achieving the acclaim or widespread use in Moxie publicity accorded to Muriel Ostriche. *The Moxie Girl* was Muriel Ostriche, and Muriel reigned until about 1920.

In January 1915, just before her appearance in Moxie advertising, Muriel said good-bye to Thanhouser and checked in at the studio of the Independent Moving Pictures Company of America, familiarly known as "IMP," a part of the Universal organization headed by Carl Laemmle. In its February 6, 1915 issue, *Motion Picture News* reported:

"MURIEL OSTRICHE IN LEADS AT IMP STUDIO. Muriel Ostriche, who has been featured in Thanhouser and Princess productions for more than a year, and who was with Eclair before that, is now playing leading roles at the IMP Studio. Miss Ostriche is one of the youngest of screen stars, being not more than nineteen years old. Earle Foxe, who has been seen in Kalem, Ryno, and Reliance pictures, has left the Winter Garden show to play opposite her."

Under the Universal banner, IMP was grouped with many other divisions and trademarks, including Frontier, Bison, Rex, Joker, Nestor, Majestic, Victor, Crystal, Solax, Lux, Gem, and Powers. Universal also distributed the films of others, including the rapidly-waning Eclair, which was involved at the time in an ownership fight between American and French interests. Facilities were maintained in Fort Lee, New Jersey, utilizing the studios of companies taken under the Universal wing, but Laemmle's eye was on the West, and the Los Angeles area provided the prime focus for the firm. By the mid-teens eighty directors were kept busy producing films, primarily at the Universal City Studios, a Los Angeles facility which had its formal opening on March 15, 1915. Laemmle, who delighted in various advertising stunts, was as close to P. T. Barnum as anyone in the movie business ever came at the time. Whereas the Thanhouser studio had a family-like atmosphere, Universal was regarded as a "film factory."

Muriel's stay with Universal was unpleasant. The transition from Thanhouser was not smooth. After a brief stay, she departed, but not before making at least two films, *The Heart Breaker* (released April 8, 1915) and *Celeste* (released May 20). In Muriel's own words:

"Carl Laemmle was the owner, but he had his brother-in-law, Julius Stern, manage the studio. Many people thought he was a nice fellow, but I had a run-in with him when he made a play for me and I resisted. It got rather rough. He wanted me to sleep with him. No chance! I made up my mind to get out of there.

"While I was at Universal, in one of my pictures, *The Heart Breaker*, I was dressed in pajamas. It was about a girl's school and dormitory. Raymond Schrock wrote it."

Earlier (in the April 27, 1912 issue) *Moving Picture World*, described Julius Stern, Muriel's would-be seducer: "A man of great endurance, persistence, and efficiency. He is positive in his opinion, but logical in his reason, and open to correction whenever a man opposed him in views can command his interest and respect."

Motion Picture News reviewed *The Heart Breaker*: "Two reels. A comedy showing the havoc which a carefree girl (Muriel Ostriche) brought on her own head and those of a good many others while passing the time in boarding school. The scenes in which the girl is enticing the old man by a shameless display of her nether limbs will in all probability be cut out; if they are not, they ought to be. The photography is poor in several scenes, but aside from this the picture is good. Lorimer Johnston directed the work, while Charles Ogle is seen as the professor." *Moving Picture World* noted: "A girl's school story, featuring Muriel Ostriche as a mischievous miss who wins the love of the professor and keeps the students in an uproar. This is very much like the other offerings with the same locale; some observers will find it a little drawn out. Those who have not seen similar stories in this setting will no doubt enjoy it very much. The girl students are attractive and the atmosphere of the production is accurate. The photography is also pleasing."

Phyllis (Muriel Ostriche), in a script somewhat reminiscent of Muriel's early *Miss Mischief* film with Thanhouser, was brought to the Bleeding Heart Seminary by her aunt, who told the matron that "Phyllis is almost incorrigible and needs correction." Muriel went from one caper to another, upsetting the whole institution, and eventually involved everyone in a free-for-all.

An idea of the mischief perpetrated can be gained by a few sentences from the scenario: "That day in class Sniffles [the old professor] discovers that Phyllis is reading Robert W. Chambers' *The Common Law* behind her regular manual of instruction and takes it away from her, ordering her to remain after class. After the students are dismissed, Sniffles, alone with Phyllis, urges her to be good. Phyllis pats him on the head and entices him with girlish fervor which drives the old codger nearly wild. Just as he tries to kiss her, the door opens and in steps Mrs. Saxe [who runs the place]. Noting the expression of innocence that Phyllis adopts, she suspects Sniffles of improper conduct."

Celeste, released under the Big U emblem by Universal, was screened on May 20, 1915, and featured Muriel Ostriche as the girl lead, supported by Earle Foxe and Charles Ogle. Foxe, born in Oxford, Ohio in 1888, was educated at the Ohio State University, and embarked on a lengthy stage career, followed by many film productions, according to a biography in the 1919 edition of the *Motion Picture Studio Directory*. He was described as being six feet, one inch high, weighing 178 pounds, of light complexion, light brown hair, blue eyes, and as liking riding, swimming, and racing automobiles.

Moving Picture World reviewed *Celeste*: "A story of the present war, with numerous actual scenes in it, which are fitted into the plot very well. Muriel Ostriche plays the part of a refugee with two children in her charge. All reach a neutral country and find a good home. The number is one of fair strength." *Motion Picture News* stated: "The story will please although there is not a great deal to it."

In the meantime, such questions as censorship, Sunday showings, the admission of blacks to theatres, and the like, kept tradepaper writers busy. Not the least of the articles was one in *Motion Picture News*, February 20, 1915, which brought up the seemingly important matter, raised by members of the Los Angeles Board of Motion Picture Censors, as to "how long a film kiss should be." It was learned that the Chicago Board of Censors requested that no kiss should occupy more than two feet of film. Some members of the Los Angeles Board were perplexed, so they put the question to three actresses. Mary Alden declared that a prolonged kiss was unnecessary, while Fay Tincher said that one foot should be sufficient (but the article noted that she was currently playing in a comedy, not a romance), and a third actress, perhaps wanting to keep her options open, refused to give a definite length.

These were heady times in the motion picture industry, and scarcely a business day went by without several production companies being incorporated. Typical is the listing in *Variety*, February 27, 1915, which posted the names of dozens of new firms recently incorporated in New York state, including the Terriss Feature Film Company, the Century Motion Picture Corporation, the Polychrolatin Film Corporation, the S & O Feature Film Company, the Drako Film Company, the Kinetic Films Company (established "to operate motion pictures on railroad trains, etc."), Preferred Picture Corporation (a modest New York City corporation capitalized at just $1,000), Frederick McKay Productions, American Film (capitalized at an impressive $150,000), Hesser Motion Picture Corporation, Knowlton Feature Films, Empress Picture Corporation, Alice in Wonderland Picture Company, Essemar Film Company, War Film Corporation (at $200,000), S. & A. Feature Film Company, Epoch Producing Company (a D.W. Griffith venture capitalized at $125,000), Pre-Eminent Films, and Prohibition Film Corporation.

Around the same time, *Variety*, earlier devoted to vaudeville and legitimate stage acts, began to increase its coverage of the film industry. A late starter, *Variety* virtually ignored the new medium as late as 1912. By 1915, issues typically carried reviews of a half dozen or more films, a listing of new releases, and "Film Flashes," a series of short paragraphs on various aspects of production companies, players, and films. Emphasis was on the production and distribution aspects of the business. Little was said concerning theatre buildings or exhibition. Dominating the advertising pages of *Variety* at the time was Eva Tanguay, a vaudeville dancer who splashed her name in capital letters across numerous one- and two-page advertisements which noted her as being "cyclonic" (apparently her favorite adjective, for she used it often), exuberant, magnetic, and even "a pretty good businessman." Her sign-off vocal number, *I Don't Care*, became famous. Later, she made several films, while at the same time trying to suppress an earlier film which she claimed was made under primitive conditions and should not be allowed to reach distribution channels, for it would show her in an unfavorable light.

The March 12th issue of *Variety* was heralded by an editorial feature noting "Griffith's $2 Feature Film Sensation of Picture Trade," predicting that *The Birth of a Nation*, playing at the Liberty

Theatre, New York City, "will do $14,000 at box office this week—the theatre seats 1,200, capacity crowds thronging house twice daily. Griffith Company renting theatre—first week's advertising bill $12,000."

After her unhappy experience with Universal, Muriel Ostriche signed up with Charles K. Harris, best known as the composer of the song, *After the Ball*, who had great plans to succeed in the motion picture business and who set up a company known as the Charles K. Harris Feature Film Corporation. It was announced that Perry N. Vekroff would direct the films. Verkoff, a Bulgarian, during the Balkan War served for seventeen months as secretary on the staff of Bulgaria's King Ferdinand, according to a biographical note in the *New York Dramatic Mirror*. The scripts, based on "a song written by himself or based on a theme that contains all of the material necessary for a proper song," were to be the work of Harris himself.

Muriel Ostriche became part of the cast of *When It Strikes Home*. Harris' background was given in *Motography* by Mabel Condon:

"While you will always know him best as the man who wrote *After the Ball*, it will be but a short number of weeks before his name will connect itself in your memory with a feature film company that has for its working foundation several things which it will *not* do.

"The Charles K. Harris Feature Film Company is the name of the new organization which has Albert E. Lowe as its president and Mr. Harris as its writer of scenarios and its generally useful man. It was Mr. Harris who vouched for the fulfillment of the promise that the Harris Feature Film Company intends to give the public 'something new.' This particular vouching was done in Mr. Harris' private office on the fifth floor of the Columbia Theatre Building one afternoon last week. Mr. Lowe was present and nodded in support to all the Harris statements. 'There are to be no betrayed women in the films we are going to make,' announced Mr. Harris with determination. . . . The children will not have the blight of illegitimacy upon them. They will all be honorably born. We are not going to take our stories from plays and books; they are all to be original. There will be a picturization of some of my old and best-known songs, which I shall scenarioize, and I shall also supply the other original stories to be filmed. . . . We are not going to give an advance synopsis of any of our pictures. The public likes to be surprised, and there is a lack of this element when it knows exactly what is coming next. . . ."

Harris also stated that he would not make the type of film that was fit to be shown only to those over twenty-one years of age. He related that two companies were at work making his films, one in the South and the other close by in Yonkers. He told of work being done in New York City: "In Yonkers, Perry N. Vekroff is producing *When it Strikes Home*. Both will be ready for release early in May, and the World Film Corporation has arranged to exploit them."

Mabel Condon continued the interview, describing Harris' commentary: " '*When it Strikes Home*,' Mr. Harris went on, 'I wrote at this desk. Wait—I will show you the story as I wrote it out first.' From under a number of papers he took huge saffron-tinted sheets of paper, pencil-written. The top one began–'On this day, February 1, 1915, while looking through my office window onto Broadway toward 47th Street, I saw a crowd gather about a policeman and a baby carriage. A touring car drew up and a beautiful woman stepped out and made her way to the center of the crowd. I called one of the office boys and said, 'Quick, go down there and see what it's all about!' He returned with the information that a baby had been abandoned and that the beautiful woman wanted to take it. The policeman said she would have to accompany him to the station and make her request there. So the woman got back into her car and followed in the wake of the policeman and baby carriage.'

" 'That,' said Mr. Harris, replacing the saffron sheets, 'was my inspiration for the film *When it Strikes Home*.' And because he knew there wouldn't be space for the printing of the synopsis, he related its story.

"He was then asked what he would do after the film *When it Strikes Home* and said that 'the next will surpass anything I have written, for heart interest. It will cost $50,000 to produce, and it will be a natural colored picture.' He said that the process was one that Kinemacolor had been working on for the past year."

Muriel Ostriche remembered: "I worked with Charles K. Harris in a film. I kept thinking of *After the Ball*, but the title was something different. When it was finished it opened at the Hippodrome in New York City, and I saw my name in lights. It was quite a big story about a newborn baby boy and a newborn baby girl, but the thing I remember most was a near tragedy:

"I was doing a crying scene, but I don't know what I was crying about. The particular scene opened with another couple. They had a boy, and my parents had me, a girl, and they made a marriage compact at that time. As babies, we didn't know anything about it. They wanted the families to get together and merge, and we did. As I was crying, I was illuminated with a floodlight diffuser. They made close-ups, and something must have happened, but I didn't feel it at the time. I became dizzy, and they had a car take me home, and when I was in the car I started to feel pain. I thought it was the light, and the lamps were still on, and it was still daylight—the light seemed so intense that I knocked on the dividing window and had the chauffeur pull down the shades. Then I couldn't see a thing. I remember that Raymond Schrock—he was a writer—came to my apartment to see me. I was going around with a fellow named Charlie Gerhardt at the time, and he came up as well. I asked them both to leave, for the pain was so intense. I was blind for a couple of days. I didn't care if I ever saw again. It was so sharp—just like blades going in my eyes. I was lucky to get my sight back. Then, when I got better, I returned to the studio and finished the film. It turned out very nice, and *After the Ball* was one of the melodies they used when it was played."

The same incident was related in *Moving Picture World*:

"Muriel Ostriche, who was featured in the Charles K. Harris photoplay *When it Strikes Home*, of which Grace Washburn is the star, is still under twenty (and a nice and pretty girl at that), but she has condensed into her few hundred days of work before the camera a great deal of hard and perilous venturing. . . .

"Muriel's beauty and popularity are proverbial. She is a clever and versatile actress, and easy to direct. Her tractability before the camera is one of her valuable assets, and her intrepidity constitutes her a veritable picture heroine.

"Muriel Ostriche's devotion to duty recently temporarily struck her blind. This pretty girl, who is famous for her fearlessness, whom nothing daunts, who has risked her life time and time again under the edicts of her directors and in order to entertain and amuse the public, ran yet another serious risk recently.

"Working on the picture *When it Strikes Home*, Miss Ostriche had to pose in the immensely powerful light of the studio for a close-up. The fierce rays instantly paralyzed her power of vision, and she was totally blind for twelve hours. Miss Ostriche, however, has recovered and has gone back to work. She is the object of mingled sympathy and congratulations, for Miss Ostriche is popular and everybody wishes her continued success in her motion picture work.

"The dangers that pretty actresses are compelled to encounter strike home, don't they?"

After recalling the unfortunate blindness incident, Muriel went on to relate: "I was always doing crazy things. Another daredevil stunt I remember involved a train. In the film I was trying to commit suicide, but instead of running over me the speeding train quickly turned right before it reached me and went down a side track. It didn't hit me, but I certainly was taking quite a chance. After it was all over, I was a bit frightened. Often, the directors would call on me to do things that other actresses would refuse to do."

When it Strikes Home was released on May 17, 1915. A synopsis of the plot appeared in the *New York Dramatic Mirror*: "The story deals with a sudden infatuation and the multiplicity of complications resulting from it. Dick Hartley [played by Edwin August], the son of a millionaire, though in love with a girl in his own set, while at a studio party becomes intoxicated and marries a dancing girl. In the cold gray dawn of the morning after he repents and, as he is still a minor, his father is successful in having the marriage annulled. In due course, the dancing girl has a son, and Hartley, after a sojourn in Europe, marries the girl of his choice. While happy, the marriage is childless, and the young couple adopt the dancing girl's baby in ignorance of its true identity. The time jumps twenty-two years, and the young boy, now a rising young physician, is about to be admitted to an exclusive club when a rival for the hand of the girl to whom he is engaged digs up his mysterious past. His mother, in order to be near her son, has taken a position as a nurse in the same hospital, and at the last moment she appears before the board of governors of the club and discloses her son's parentage. The senior Hartley's wife has died several years before, and his old infatuation and love for the dancer returns, and as a reward for her devotion to her son, he marries her."

The film received excellent reviews from the trade magazines. The *New York Dramatic Mirror* noted: "The Dresden doll-like beauty of Muriel Ostriche aided her greatly in her work and served to make the parts of the picture in which she appeared bright, vivacious, and pleasing." The work of Grace Washburn and Edwin August likewise received favorable comment. The scriptwriter fell short of the mark, however: "Mr. Harris has shown a keen knowledge of life but has failed to depict it in a strong dramatic manner." *Moving Picture World* credited the film with "plenty of melodramatic excitement" and noted that "Muriel Ostriche, appearing in the last two reels, is charming as usual and, of course, becomes a real asset to the picture." Impresario Lee Shubert said the picture was "one of the best features we have run at the New York Hippodrome."

Muriel's stay with Harris Feature Films was short-lived, and she was gone before *When It Strikes Home* was released. An article in *Moving Picture World*, issue of April 10, 1915, told of a change:

"The newest addition to the forces of the Vitagraph Company is Miss Muriel Ostriche, who began work on Monday, March 22nd. Miss Ostriche will be seen in a number of roles that are distinctly different from any work she has done previously. Her first appearance for the Vitagraph Company will be in a three-reel feature.

"Miss Ostriche was recently stricken blind while at work on a film, and for a time it was feared that she would never recover her sight, but now she is prepared for active work. She has made quite a reputation for daring, among her feats of bravery before the camera being a climb across a 25-foot chasm 300 feet in the air on a narrow strip of board. Miss Ostriche has also spent twenty minutes in a cage with a tiger for a picture, and she describes it as one of her most harrowing experiences. The young lady has been before the public for three years."

The Vitagraph Company was an early entry into the American motion picture business. By 1897 a one-minute subject, *The Burglar on the Roof*, had been filmed high atop a New York City building. The Spanish-American War of 1898 furnished other opportunities, including action faked by filming a toy flotilla. The principals of the company were J. Stuart Blackton, William T. ("Pop") Rock, and Albert E. Smith. The most visible member of the Vitagraph camp was J. Stuart Blackton, a colorful individual who voiced his opinions on many subjects. A member of the Patents Trust, Vitagraph had a healthy share of business and was one of the best-known companies from its inception through the teens. In 1925 it died with a whimper when it was unceremoniously merged into Warner Bros. In Muriel Ostriche's time, large studio facilities were maintained in Brooklyn.

Shortly after Muriel Ostriche drew her first Vitagraph paycheck, the firm announced that its products would henceforth be distributed through the Vitagraph-Lubin-Selig-Essanay Motion Picture Company, familiarly known as V-L-S-E, incorporated in New York, April 5, 1915, for $500,000, which commenced operation immediately afterward. Among other things happening in the Vitagraph world, a 200-acre estate in Bayside, Long Island had been leased recently and comprised 30 greenhouses, a mansion, and access to Long Island Sound.

Apart from film production and the personal activities of J. Stuart Blackton, especially his private yachts, the most notable Vitagraph news of the time was the operation of the Vitagraph Theatre, which boasted a large electric Vitagraph eagle sign in electric lights on the front, and which opened in February 1914, following a remodeling of the old Criterion Theatre. It was announced that the theatre would be a showcase and testing ground for Vitagraph productions, but the immediate reaction from other theatre owners who showed Vitagraph films was that it was a form of competition. An attraction was the Wurlitzer Hope-Jones

THE VITAGRAPH COMPANY OF AMERICA. 45

"What's Ours"

Love is Blind, Marriage is a Leap in the Dark. Another Instance of Two Loving Hearts
Who Are Willing to Take a Chance.
Released Thursday, June 24th.

Produced by S. Rankin Drew.   Author—Winona Godfrey.

CAST:

*SYLVIA CHASE	MURIEL OSTRICHE
BURTON TREMPER	RAYMOND BLOOMER
*FREDERICK TREMPER, HIS FATHER	ANDERS RANDOLF
MRS. TREMPER	LOUISE BEAUDET
MRS. BURKE	BILLY BILLINGS
WIRT, FLOOR WALKER	DONALD MACBRIDE

Stars indicate Portraits shown on this Page.

At Hathaway & Eaton's, a big department store, Sylvia Chase applies for and secures a position at the glove counter. Mrs. Burke, wife of a millionaire, and a lady of philanthropic tendencies, who had once been a salesgirl herself, becomes interested in Sylvia, and the two become great friends. Burton Tremper, a young man with very wealthy parents living in Philadelphia, comes to New York to learn the meaning of the word, "work," and falls in love with Sylvia. Arthur Meadows, Tremper's friend, feeling the affair is only an infatuation, very kindly writes his aristocratic mother that she is in danger of losing her son to a salesgirl. Mother starts for New York at once to put a stop to the affair, but Sylvia has something to say about the matter herself, and politely but firmly announces she will reserve decision. After vainly trying to solve the matter to her own satisfaction, Sylvia goes to her friend, Mrs. Burke, and asks her advice. That wise lady sums up her wisdom in the simple words: "If he loves you, leave the decision to him, but don't let the world's foolish little barriers keep you from your own!" Cheered by the words and strengthened in her resolution to refuse to give up Burton, Sylvia goes back to her work with a light heart, feeling certain that her lover will make a true decision. Meanwhile, Mrs. Tremper and her son argue and argue, but all in vain; both are equally obstinate, and finally, after Burton states emphatically that he intends to marry the girl he loves and the money can go hang, Mrs. Tremper angrily disinherits him. He takes it bravely, however, for he has learned what it is to work, and with a determination to succeed in his chosen profession, that of law, he goes to Sylvia, tells her all, and secures the momentous "Yes" to his ardent proposal and the happiness which is theirs.

Vitagraph One and Three-Sheet Posters of this Release.

What's Ours, a Vitagraph film released on June 24, 1915, featured Muriel Ostriche in the lead role. (From *The Vitagraph Bulletin;* the Academy of Motion Picture Arts and Sciences)

Unit Orchestra, a pipe organ which furnished musical accompaniment to the action on the screen. Not to be outdone, George Kleine, a major motion picture distributor, announced that he was going to buy a theatre. Before many years had passed, theatre ownership was to go hand in hand with the operation of motion picture studios and the distribution of films. Trade paper accounts of the time gave glowing reports of the success of the Vitagraph Theatre, but such stories belied the truth. In actuality, the operation was run at a loss, and when the lease ran out two years later, Vitagraph put the Wurlitzer pipe organ up for sale, took down its landmark electric sign, and the old Criterion Theatre name was restored.

Muriel Ostriche's first role at Vitagraph was in *What's Ours*, released on June 24, 1915, directed by S. Rankin Drew. The son of Sidney Drew (who was one of America's best-loved comedians and a member of the popular "Mr. & Mrs. Drew" duo), S. Rankin Drew was popular with Vitagraph players and became one of Muriel Ostriche's friends. Later, the motion picture community was saddened when he was killed in action in World War I.

The story of *What's Ours* was billed as: "A comedy drama. Love is blind, marriage is a leap in the dark. Another instance of two loving hearts who are willing to take a chance. Presenting Muriel Ostriche, Anders Randolf, Louise Beaudet and Donald MacBride." *Motion Picture News* reviewed it: "The plot of this picture, said to be written by Winona Godfrey, is strongly reminiscent of a magazine story written by a widely-known author and published last summer. It tells of a young man of wealth who marries a department store clerk in spite of family opposition, which leads to disinheritance. Raymond Bloomer and Muriel Ostriche are the lovers."

Muriel's performance was praised by the *New York Dramatic Mirror*: "Muriel Ostriche has a feature role, and handles it in a manner consistent with her fresh, young beauty and innate ability." *Moving Picture World* informed its readers that: "Muriel Ostriche is a sufficient excuse for the infatuation of her prince, and uniformly capable portrayals are given by Raymond Bloomer, Anders Randolf and Louise Baudet."

During much of the summer, Muriel was occupied with her role in *Mortmain*, a five-reel Vitagraph picture released with tremendous publicity on September 6, 1915. In the meantime, Vitagraph continued to make the news. A review of the firm's history published in July noted that by that time the firm had completed 3,000 subjects since it began business, while another report related that Vitagraph had twenty-two directors in its regular employ.

Muriel Ostriche was a very small cog in the very big Vitagraph wheel, and announcements concerning her activities were few and far between, simply because there were so many people at Vitagraph, she was new there, and other players were more prominent.

Motion Picture Magazine surveyed its readers to compile a ranking of the great classics of the screen. Completed by the end of the year, the poll showed that the leaders, in decreasing order of popularity, were: *The Christian* (Vitagraph), *Tess of the Storm Country* (Famous Players), *A Million Bid* (Vitagraph), *Hearts Adrift* (Famous Players), *My Official Wife* (Vitagraph), *Quo Vadis?* (Kleine), *Birth of a Nation* (Griffith), *Love's Sunset* (Vitagraph), *The Spoilers* (Selig), *Cabiria* (Itala), *Judith of Bethulia* (Biograph; Griffith-directed), *The Juggernaut* (Vitagraph), *The Eternal City* (Famous Players), *Island of Regeneration* (Vitagraph), *The Last Days of Pompeii* (Kleine), *The Escape* (Mutual), *The Stoning* (Edison), *Wildflower* (Famous Players), *The Avenging Conscience* (Griffith), *Neptune's Daughter* (Universal), *The Captive* (Famous Players), *Hearts in Exile* (World), *From the Manger to the Cross* (Kalem), *Graustark* (Essanay), and *The Dawn of a Tomorrow* (Famous Players).

Vitagraph must have been pleased with its first-place showing as well as the number of its films in the top twenty-five, greater than any of its competitors. It probably didn't hurt that *Motion Picture Magazine* was partially owned by J. Stuart Blackton.

Vast publicity was given to Vitagraph's production of *Mortmain*, and within a month or two of its appearance, anyone reading movie notices in magazines and newspapers knew the plot by heart, not to overlook the thousands who flocked to see the film itself. The star of the film was Robert Edeson, a well-known stage actor. *Moving Picture World* reviewed the picture:

"Conventional appreciation is likely to fall short of giving a correct impression of this five-part Vitagraph production to be released on the V-L-S-E program. In its particular sphere, that of mystery drama with a scientific background, it comes pretty close to being a model of motion picture craftsmanship. Theodore Marston directed the picture from an adaptation of a story by Arthur Train, and Robert Edeson acted the title role so exceedingly well that it seems safe to call it his best screen performance, without inviting contradiction. But the photoplay is so good in its entirety, such a thorough work of art, that there is no need to place emphasis on the contribution of any particular player."

Variety noted that Muriel was "a little youthful to play opposite Mr. Edeson, both in the matter of years and experience, but she does quite well, all things considered. *Mortmain* is like a story that one picks up indifferently, scans casually for a few paragraphs, and then reads with active interest to the end. Before the first reel has been run, there is enough to arouse hope of something exceptional, and the hope is justified in a picture that is original in idea, and replete with weird suggestions and developed with extraordinary plausibility.

"The basis for the strange experience in *Mortmain* is established in a clinic where it is shown that modern surgery makes possible the grafting of the limb of one animal onto the body of another. A cat with a paw seemingly grafted into place is used for illustration. Then, step by step, we are led into an engrossing story, too involved for a brief summary, but presented so clearly and logically and there is no excuse for an audience missing any of the points. The significance of this surgical operation with which the picture opens is readily appreciated when Mortmain's left hand is crushed under a falling piece of furniture. He is told that the hand must be amputated, and that $10,000 will buy the hand of another man. As Mortmain loses consciousness under an anesthetic, the screen shows floating visions of faces as they appear in his mind, a novel idea handled with marked success.

"The hand grafted onto Mortmain's arm belonged to his sweetheart's brother, who died under the operation. Had Poe or de Maupassant written scenarios they would not have been ashamed of a plot with such haunting possibilities. Worthy of Poe is the pleasant fancy of a lover placing the alien fingers on his fiancé's arm, not knowing their origin, and wondering why she instinctively recoils from his touch. By ghostly light effects and atmospheric settings, and expressive acting that conveys the meaning without spoiling the illusion by disclosing too much, the hidden horror that everyone feels but cannot explain is worked up with consummate skill. And then we are told that it was all a dream. This is the one artistic mistake in the picture, due, of course, to the prevalent belief that the public must have a happy ending. It seems, however, as if the concession might have been avoided in a story of this caliber.

"Edward Elkas makes a truly Dickensian character of Flaggs; James Morrison is convincing as the unfortunate brother; and Muriel Ostriche is adequate as the girl, although an actress suggesting more spiritual sensitiveness might have been preferable."

Muriel fared better in the pages of *Motography*: "Gripping action and unique developments characterized the five-part Vitagraph release for September titled *Mortmain*, which features Robert Edeson in the title role.... His portrayal of the suspense and terror in which the character lives is remarkably fine. Pleasing indeed is Donald Hall's performance as Russell, he has a commanding presence and his acting is finished. Edward Elkas makes Flaggs an appropriately weird figure. Herbert Frank as Dr. Crisp, and Muriel Ostriche as Bella, and James Morrison as Forsythe enact the other important parts in an entirely satisfactory manner...."

The *New York Dramatic Mirror* commented: "Muriel Ostriche, in the leading feminine role, was thoroughly pleasing, rising to meet her infrequent opportunities with an ability that was charming to witness. Her Dresden doll-like beauty [a phrase which recurs in various reviews] is very much in evidence, but there is real ability lying underneath it."

The movie opened at the Vitagraph Theatre and shared billing with the first of a new series of Sunny Jim comedies by Elaine Sterne, featuring Bobby Connelly, called *Sunny Jim and the Amusement Co., Ltd.*, the comical adventures of a tramp titled *Willie Stayed Single*, and a Mr. and Mrs. Sidney Drew comedy, *The Professional Diner*.

Muriel Ostriche remembered the film: "We did most of the picture in the residence of one of the owners of the Vitagraph Company—on 57th Street in New York City—an apartment owned by Stuart Blackton. He was a charming person, and all of the cast members liked him. He was, of course, very famous.

"Robert Edeson was also a charming man, who was years and years older than I—he seemed to be at least three times my age. He was a Broadway star, and he had very little motion picture experience before this film. All of the newspaper writers knew him well, and they wanted to see how he would do in the film.

"There was a scene in the picture in which we had to ride on horseback through a city park in Brooklyn, and before we started the film he asked me if I would ride with him. I appreciated the opportunity as I wanted to get the practice. Every day we would ride through the park for an hour or two, with Vitagraph furnishing the horses. Once I was on this horse, and it was standing still, then all of a sudden it took off like a shot. I couldn't control it. I didn't even know the horse, so I couldn't call it by name, so I called him everything else I could think of—darling, please sweetheart, dear—there were two young men on horses on the trail ahead of me, and then my horse went shooting by them. One of the guys—I later found out that his family owned a very large department store—came over and got me by the collar. I was already down, but he picked me up and told me I had to get back on my horse right away or I would never ride again. So, I did, and on my second try I was knocked over the horse—I went right over the horse's head—but at least after he threw me he stopped."

By the time that *Mortmain* made its appearance, Muriel Ostriche had departed involuntarily, as part of a staff reduction announced by Vitagraph in July. In the meantime, another of her Vitagraph movies, *For the Honor of the Crew*, was being prepared for release. Unlike Thanhouser, Vitagraph required a long time for film production, editing, and other work, and it was often many months from the inception of a picture until it reached the screen. Issued on November 9, 1915, *For the Honor of the Crew* had been announced the preceding summer.

Muriel Ostriche recalled: "Each day the Vitagraph players would take the Hudson River Day Line up the river, then change for a train to Poughkeepsie, where intercollegiate races were held. We would do our shooting and then return. There were many exciting racing scenes using real college crews."

The *New York Dramatic Mirror* noted: "A three-part story of college life featuring Muriel Ostriche. Produced by the Vitagraph Company under the direction of P. S. Earle for release as a Broadway Star Feature on the General Film Company program. Dick Morgan was played by James Morrison; Robert Brent by William B. Davidson; Viola Scott by Muriel Ostriche; her mother, by Hattie Delaro; and Rosenberg by Edward Elkas.

"With the exception of two or three little inconsistencies, this feature has been well done, showing as it does some of the most excellent scenes of the intercollegiate regatta at Poughkeepsie....

"For some unknown reason Muriel Ostriche did not photograph as well in this picture as is usually the case. Whether there was something wrong with her makeup or whether the cameraman was at fault it is hard to determine, but the fact remains that the well-known beauty of this young star was not given a fair chance to show itself. James Morrison, as the stroke of the varsity crew, gave a good portrayal of a young bronze giant, and the supporting cast was good.

"The story deals with two young men both in love with the same girl. Both are trying for the crew, although one is already the manager. The manager gambles with the crew money and loses, and then in order to recoup and save himself from disgrace enters into a nefarious plot with a crooked gambler. The night before the race he weakens one of the oars by sawing it part way through under the leather. At the most exciting part of the race, just as the crews have entered on the last mile, the weakened oar, in the hands of the stroke, by the way, breaks. It looks like a certain disaster, but the stroke, with rare presence of mind, jumps overboard and the crew with the remaining seven

Muriel Ostriche and Robert Edeson in *Mortmain,* a Vitagraph feature released on September 6, 1915, with the intial showing at the Vitagraph Theatre, New York City. (*Motion Picture Magazine,* September 1915)

A scene from the 1915 Vitagraph Blue Ribbon Feature, *Mortmain,* showing Robert Edeson, Edward Elkas, and Muriel Ostriche. Others in the cast included Donald Hall, Joseph Weber, James Morrison, Karin Norman, J. Herbert Frank, Claude James, Roland Osborne, and Helen Pillsbury. Certain scenes were filmed in the New York City apartment of Vitagraph's Chief Executive Officer, J. Stuart Blackton. (Geraldine Duclow, Free Library of Philadelphia Theatre Collection)

A scene from *Mortmain*, showing Donald Hall, Robert Edeson, and Muriel Ostriche. *Mortmain* was released on September 16, 1915, by which time Muriel Ostriche had left Vitagraph. Although Edeson had been in films before, he was primarily known as a stage actor. Reviewers and others paid close attention to his *Mortmain* starring role. The story, from a novel by Arthur Train, involves eerie circumstances surrounding a hand from one person grafted onto the arm of another, a plot worthy of Poe according to one observer. (Geraldine Duclow, Free Library of Philadelphia Theatre Collection)

men pulling their hearts out wins by a nose. The crooked manager confesses to his roommate, the stroke, and the latter gives him the necessary money to make good his peculations. The stroke, of course, wins the girl."

When the film was released, Vitagraph dropped mention of Muriel from much of its advertising, presumably because she was no longer with the company at that time.

Muriel Ostriche worked on another Vitagraph feature in the early summer of 1915, but it was not released until February 21, 1916. In keeping with Vitagraph policy, numerous releases were sent out as the film progressed. On May 29, 1915, *Motion Picture News* noted: "Baltimore in 1850 furnishes the background for F. Hopkinson Smith's drama, *Kennedy Square*, that S. Rankin Drew is producing from his first big scenario as a full-fledged director for the Vitagraph Company. *Kennedy Square*, with its delightful southern atmosphere, lovable characters typical of the period in which the scenes are laid, and beautiful scenery, will be made doubly attractive by a heart-interest element in a love story that is refreshingly sincere, and the enactment of its characters by a cast that includes Charles Kent as St. George Temple, Antonio Moreno as Harry Rutter, Muriel Ostriche as Kate Seymour, and Raymond Bloomer as Langdon Willetts. *Kennedy Square* will be a five-part Vitagraph Blue Ribbon feature that will have its initial showing at the Vitagraph Theatre, New York City."

A synopsis of the plot appeared in *Moving Picture World*: "St. George Temple, a typical Maryland gentleman of the old school, lives in an aristocratic home on Kennedy Square, liked and respected by everyone. Harry Rutter, a warmblooded young southerner, tells him of his falling out with Grace Seymour, with whom he is in love, and her father, the Honorable Douglas Seymour, on account of his having been intoxicated. The old southerner gives him a good scolding, then promises to act as a peacemaker. He does so very effectively, and some time later, in a reception in the Rutter home, the engagement is about to be announced when he gets into a quarrel with Willetts, who is also in love with Kate. Words come to blows, and the two men fight a duel in one of the outbuildings by torchlight. Willetts is severely wounded. Colonel Rutter, the boy's father, disowns him, angrily exclaiming that he has disgraced himself and his family and has broken every law of hospitality. Kate refuses to see him, and Rutter turns to his friend, St. George, who takes the boy to live with him. Kate remains firm, and the colonel cuts both his son and St. George at the club.

"The Patapsco Bank fails, and St. George mortgages his home to pay Harry's debts. He learns this, and goes to South America. There, after many exciting adventures, he is given half interest in a valuable ruby mine by Senor Ortiz, a wealthy South American, and Harry's fortune is made. Shortly after, Harry returns to his old Maryland home to find St. George living in extreme poverty. He buys back the home and restores the old gentleman to his proper position; then a reconciliation is affected by Colonel Rutter asking his son's pardon. The meeting between Kate and Harry is brought about, and Kate, with a cry of joy, comes into Harry's arms."

One reviewer in *Moving Picture World* noted that "Little Muriel Ostriche was dainty as Kate," but another writer in the same publication looked at her differently: "Muriel Ostriche had by far the best opportunities for dramatic work, but she did not rise to them. She has a very handsome face and an agreeable stage presence, but her acting lacks fire." *Variety* considered the film to be "rather prettily screened, and if it hadn't been padded out it would have made a dainty three-reeler."

Muriel Ostriche recalled some of the principals in the film: "In *Kennedy Square*, S. Rankin Drew, who later was killed in the war, was in his early twenties, and he was a wonderful, patient person. I really enjoyed working with him. After the filming of the picture was over, he went and punched Antonio Moreno in the nose, and they had a big fight. I don't know the reason for it, but evidently Moreno was giving him trouble during the entire time in the picture, and Rankin didn't want to do anything to disturb the filming until it was over, then he practically knocked him out. My mother and I used to pick up Tony Moreno quite often and drive him to the studio with us—for he would wait for us on the sidewalk between where we lived and Vitagraph. I understand that he later married a very rich woman. I considered him to be a very nice fellow, I didn't mind working with him, and he didn't give me any trouble at all. He played every scene right along with me."

CHAPTER SEVEN

The World Years

Muriel departed from Vitagraph toward the end of the summer, without any specific idea of where she would go next. Before long, she found an opportunity, as related in *Motography*, September 11, 1915:

"Muriel Ostriche, a famous star, has been secured by Equitable. Muriel Ostriche, formerly a star of the Thanhouser Princess brand, and recently star of numerous Vitagraph films in which she appeared jointly with Robert Edeson in big features, has been engaged by Equitable Motion Pictures Corporation for appearance in that concern's productions.

"After a brief vacation in Atlantic City, she will begin work at the Equitable Flushing Studio in a series of serious and important dramatic vehicles now being selected for her by the directors of the Equitable concern . . . and which are adaptable to Miss Ostriche's peculiar talent and youthful beauty." At the same time, Equitable announced that a number of other players had been signed with the firm, including Margarita Fischer, Harry A. Pollard (a director), Charles J. Ross, and Robert Edeson. Equitable released its productions through the World Film Corporation.

An article in the *New York Dramatic Mirror*, August 21, 1915, noted that the Equitable Motion Picture Company had been in business for just seven weeks and intended to have ten complete pictures on the shelves before the first one was issued. The complete list of Equitable directors included Isadore Bernstein, John Ince, Charles Seay, Webster Cullison, Joseph Golden, and Walter McNamara. The executive staff consisted of Felix Feist as general manager, Arthur H. Spiegel, and Harry Reichenbach.

The World Film Corporation, distributor of Equitable pictures, was founded on February 14, 1914 and was to play an important part in the motion picture scene during the next several years. The financial manipulations of World and its various divisions, including Equitable and Peerless, occupied many columns of print in the trade publications. The hiring of numerous actors, actresses, and directors likewise commanded attention, as did numerous statements concerning World's policies and philosophies.

Toward the end of the year, Russell E. Smith, of Equitable's scenario department, sent out a form letter seeking stories suitable for production as five-reel features, desiring them either in synopsis form or as completed scripts. "We want only stories that are big, really big in theme and purpose; in drama and situation, rather than big in masses of men and exploding steamships and such melodramatic plots, which usually pass for big stories. The bigness of the price we will pay will be commensurate with the bigness of the story, and our lowest price will be $100 per reel, but we want stories that are worth a great deal more than that from authors of great reputation, from novelists and playwrights, and from strictly photo-playwrights. . . ."

Equitable claimed to be equally particular about the quality of its players: "Expensive errors have no place in the Equitable policy of production. Every legitimate star engaged for an Equitable production has proven his or her worth for the camera in a big and successful venture." A list of Equitable players together with the film companies they were with before they came to Equitable was presented, noting, for example, that Muriel Ostriche had been with Vitagraph, Katharine Kaelred had been with Triangle, and that William H. Tooker had been with Life. Nor were inexperienced directors wanted, as an October advertisement noted: "Each tried and proven star works under the direction of a director who has accomplished big things. Each director is under the indirect supervision of men who have earned their laurels in competition with other men. There can be no mistake. The possibility of inferior results is eliminated through the policy of using only tried and proven material." Then followed a listing of stars, eighteen in number, Muriel Ostriche among them.

Lewis J. Selznick managed World Film Corporation and the Equitable division from offices at 130 West 46th Street, New York City. From its founding in 1915 until early in 1916, Equitable was a separate corporate entity. In the latter year the two combined, with Arthur H. Spiegel, whose family was connected with a large Chicago mail order merchandising firm, as the directing head. Around the same time, Lewis J. Selznick was ousted and went to set up a new company featuring actress Clara Kimball

Director and Actor

Why My Latest Picture Proves My Contentions for Harmony Between Them.

By Muriel Ostriche.

HOW many times I have sat in a darkened theater while around me sat friends and strangers, commenting on my lack of dramatic ability, my apparent ignoring of certain stage tricks employed by other artists and my

Chas. Seay Instructing Muriel Ostriche in the Art of Crying

seeming indifference in big dramatic moments, I will not attempt to enumerate.

I have sat within earshot of dear friends, unaware of my presence and heard them "roast" my work to a frazzle. They were dear friends, for they prefaced their remarks with apologetic statements of how much they thought of me, personally, but how little they liked me on the screen.

"She is a lovely girl," they would say, "but my, how little she is fitted to that role."

Oh, how I would have liked to go up on the stage and enlighten them. How I would have sacrificed everything if only I could have told them how, while the big scene was being taken, Mr. Blank, the director, was frothing at some trivial incident. How I would have loved to tell them how, that very afternoon, the director had flung his coat upon the floor and in primeval anger wiped his shoes on the coat. But this was impossible. This, the unseen side of film acting, was not for the public, Not for the ears of my friends. Not meant to dispel the magic illusion screen work builds up in the spectator. All must be rosy in the minds of the motion picture audience, else the hallucination is gone.

True, all directors have not been unsatisfactory. There have been moments in my work when I imagined myself in paradise. When the end of my day's work found me tired unto being ill, yet wanting to continue. But this type of director seems to lack virility. The courteous, smiling producing genius, whatever else may be his virtues, fails to bring forth what lies latent in his subject.

My latest effort, and my first for the Equitable Motion Pictures Corporation, proves every contention I have made. The contentions are:

1. Absolute harmony must exist between director and actor.
2. Courtesy and a bond of good fellowship must characterize the two important elements, director and cast.
3. Equal intelligence of actor and director.
4. Favoritism in the studio must disappear.
5. Absolute knowledge of the theme and subject by both director and cast.

When the actor and director meet on a plane of absolute equality, aggressiveness and hostility disappear and the bonds of co-operation and friendship seal the work with harmony, then will the every picture result in fifty per cent. better acting and one hundred per cent. greater effectiveness.

In "A Daughter of the Seas," in which I was placed under the direction of Charles Seay and for the first time I found four of my contentions personified—the fifth developing.

We had a hard story to visualize. It is a sea story and required many technical touches, which were they to be screened in any manner at all in keeping with sea tradition, would need the touch of a seasoned mariner.

I was introduced to Mr. Seay by General Manager Feist of the Equitable. Russell Edgar Smith, author of the story, read the script to us in Mr. Feist's office. We all liked the story and it was decided that my personality would fit the principal role.

To take the picture, then, with maritime atmosphere, and yet retain the effete contrast, called for by the author, was of prime importance.

Several days later, Mr. Seay called me on the phone. "I am going to Block Island for a few days," he said. "Do you think you would like to go along?"

We went to Block Island, to New London and thence to Cape Cod and there, for nine days, this able man studied fisher folk and their ways and I studied the female life. Result, I consider my work in that picture one hundred per cent. better than anything I have ever done.

At Block Island we engaged forty fishermen and their families to play small parts. It was a most satisfying sight to see the way Mr. Seay handled these crude, childish people. He deftly measured every word, he blended his theatrical knowledge and the local atmosphere and before the week had passed there was not a fisherman, or any one of his family who would not have gone out into the worst kind of a storm if Mr. Seay had requested it of them.

"Thank you, Miss Ostriche," he would say if something went well. "That's not exactly right, what do you say to trying it over again?" was his strongest epithet when he was not pleased with a bit of business. And the humblest supernumerary received the same courteous treatment.

Miss Ethel Langtry, playing a very small part, was taken ill with ptomaine poisoning during the taking of the last scenes at Block Island. Miss Langtry worked the last three days in perfect misery and a much weakened condition.

"Do you think for an instant," she said upon returning to New York, "that I would inconvenience Mr. Seay. I'd rather have died than delay his work for a minute." Thus spoke an ordinary extra woman. Imagine then, how far we, who are considered of more importance, would go for the proper director, who is ever proper.

Harmony, co-operation, courtesy, consideration, all work to a successful picture, as much as oodles and oodles of money. One without the other is not sufficient.

A director must build the illusions for his actor. He must make our imaginations leap out through the invisibility to the realization of things that are to happen—beyond—in the distant future of the story in hand.

He must be our constant inspiration, our companion, our cause, for we are a common cause indeed.

After completing *A Daughter of the Sea*, Muriel Ostriche wrote an article for *Moving Picture World* on the subject of harmony between players and directors. Years later, Miss Ostriche stated that *A Daughter of the Sea* was her favorite film among the more than 200 she played in between 1911 and 1921. (*Moving Picture World*, October 30, 1915)

Young, a situation which caused many problems. Young was under contract to World Film Corporation, from which Selznick had just departed, and the contract didn't expire until several months later, on August 31st. During the period of change and controversy, the price of World stock dropped to just $1 bid per share, less than half of its price a few weeks earlier.

Enamored with the ability of Clara Kimball Young, Lewis J. Selznick issued a flood of announcements concerning his great plans featuring her talents. At least one person was less than happy with the situation, as a notice in the February 9, 1916 issue of *Moving Picture World* revealed:

"James Young, husband of Clara Kimball Young, has commenced an action in the Supreme Court against Lewis J. Selznick for alienation of the affections of his wife. He claims damages to the amount of $100,000. Mr. Selznick, in his answer, denies all the allegations of Mr. Young's complaint and said that the trouble of the Youngs commenced long before he became interested in the artistic success of Mrs. Young."

Despite the fact that Selznick boasted that his Clara Kimball Young Film Corporation was capitalized at one million dollars, not all went as planned, and eventually he faced Mrs. Young in court. She stated that he had misrepresented himself, and had cheated her in a number of ways.

Following the ouster of Selznick, no sooner was Arthur Spiegel installed as president of World than he died, leaving a vacuum which was filled by William A. Brady, a long-time figure in the stage and film world. His daughter, Alice, was an accomplished actress.

Muriel Ostriche's first Equitable-World release was *A Daughter of the Sea*, which was first publicly screened on November 22, 1915. Charles W. Seay directed a script adapted by Russell E. Smith from Frances Marion's story, *The Fisher Girl*. In keeping with World Film policy at the time, the finished name of the picture was not announced until the release date approached, so in trade papers *A Fisher Girl* was the working title. The film opened to excellent reviews, and Muriel Ostriche's work was highly praised. *Motography* noted:

"In *A Daughter of the Sea*, the fascinating romance of a young fisher girl, Muriel Ostriche makes her Equitable debut. This story is treated with wonderful effect by Charles Seay through all the technicalities that comprise good directing, including excellent choice of locations. For the purpose the director had at his disposal the whole of Block Island, Rhode Island. To anyone who loves the ocean beach some of these sets will fairly convey the salt air itself.

"Muriel Ostriche is all that can be wished for as the bewitching 'Daughter of the Sea,' which, by the way, is an unusually appropriate title. The part calls for a portrayal of the extremely girlish Margot, tattered and disheveled, but happy, notwithstanding. Into the part Miss Ostriche instills many subtle mannerisms and sincere acting. Mr. W. H. Tooker makes a typical characterization of the fisherman, Margot's father, while Clifford Grey is a very satisfactory juvenile lead. There is an indefinabe charm and finish to the whole production which makes for thorough enjoyment.

"Margot, the carefree and rollicking daughter of an old fisherman, has grown up without a mother's care. During the long hours of the day she loves to read about and imitate the doings of the society folk. One day she gets hold of a magazine, reads about Mrs. Rutland's family living across the cove, and falls in love with the picture of Jack Rutland. Sometime after, Mrs. Rutland, subsequent to the burning of her launch, is rescued by Margot and her father. During the convalescence of the wealthy lady at the fisherman's home, Margot meets and falls in love with Jack. The latter is also captivated by the charms of the unsophisticated fisher girl.

"The grateful mother takes Margot to her home to educate her. Margot proves such an apt pupil in the ways of society that she arouses the jealousy of Adele, Jack's sister. The sister is in love with a married man, but Margot's efforts to warn her only result in further inflaming Adele's jealousy. When Mrs. Rutland tells Margot that her son cannot marry below his social standing, the girl, downcast, decides to return to her father. But Mrs. Rutland retracts somewhat when she is told by the fisherman that Margot's mother was one of her old school friends, and has blood every bit as good as the Rutland family.

"Adele learns of her lover's deceit, and their quarrel leads to an accidental shooting. Margot shoulders the blame in order to shield Jack's sister, but, at last, in the courtroom, Adele confesses. The court's decision is that the man was killed by accident. Margot is about to return with her father when the son appears, declares his love, and the two fall into each other's arms."

"We cannot speak too highly of the work of pretty little Muriel Ostriche in this picture. It was undoubtedly the best thing she has ever done in all of her screen career. In the early scenes, as the uncultured and uncouth fisher-girl, she was particularly delightful, with a naiveté of spirit and manner that was most pleasing to witness, and, later, after she had been educated, refined, and become familiar with the ways of society, she still conveyed, under the polish, the naturalness of thought and action which characterized her early life," stated the *New York Dramatic Mirror*.

A reporter for *Moving Picture World* took a minority view: "Muriel Ostriche has the part of Margot, the maid, who, through reading magazines, becomes excited over the limelighted doings of persons of means and who later is given an opportunity to live with and try to be one of them. Muriel Ostriche's part is of the ingenue sort. The little player tries hard to make an impression, but it must be said that she is unsuccessful. She is handicapped on one side by a story that lacks depth—that fails to stir."

Undoubtedly, in her day Muriel Ostriche enjoyed reading in *Motion Picture Magazine* a review by Hazel Simpson Naylor: "Muriel Ostriche was a regular little will-o-the-wisp in the photoplay, *A Daughter of the Sea*. Her sweetness of expression was so appealing that just to see her brought a lump to one's throat."

Reminiscing, Muriel Ostriche spoke of the film: "*A Daughter of the Sea* was the best picture I ever made. We went to Block Island for that, and I spent a month up there. We caught lobsters in the water and brought them to the shore, cooked them, and ate them on the spot. I have always liked lobsters.

A Daughter of the Sea, an Equitable Motion Pictures Corporation feature released through World Film on November 22, 1915, featured Muriel Ostriche as a young fisher girl in a story filmed on Block Island. Other members of the cast included William H. Tooker, Clara Whipple, Catherine Calhoun, Clifford Grey, and Roy Applegate.

"In the film I was a fisherman's daughter and loved my father very much. After a shipwreck, all these magazines washed to the shore, and I picked them up, read them, and would act out what I saw—like staging a society tea party. In my fantasy I put pebbles around a little table, like cups of tea, and had imaginary guests. I was very happy and had a good time doing it. Then there was another boat accident, and some society people were washed ashore. They grew to like me and took me back to be part of their life. Of course, the son fell in love with me. I got into some false trouble and then got out of it—and married the boy.

"Block Island was very beautiful. I walked on the sand a lot. At first the pebbles nearly killed me. However, when the month was over I was glad to get back home, back to civilization.

"For the introduction to the movie I gave them an idea. They built a break-apart box, and they put me in it, way out in the ocean. The picture itself had been filmed, and now we were going to do the scene which, after cutting and editing, would be placed in the beginning. The box didn't float properly, it turned over, I was trapped inside, and the ocean water came in. I figured it was a very funny way to die, because the picture was already finished. There was nothing I could do about it—I was trapped in the box, and I expected to be drowned. The director and cameraman and everyone saw it happen, and they rushed in and pulled me out—but they didn't take the scene over again—in the film they used it just as it happened—the actual scene of me thinking I was a goner.

"Around the same time I remember that Clara Kimball Young was with the World Film Corporation. Her parents were always there when she was filming—her mother and father—Mr. and Mrs. Kimball. They were lovely people, and she was a lovely woman. After James Young divorced Clara Kimball Young, he married Clara Whipple, who then used the same name, Clara Young, that his first wife did. So, there were two Clara Youngs, but they were two different people."

The last part of 1915 and the early part of 1916 were troubled times in the film industry. At the same time that Equitable and World were seeking growth, a number of West Coast studios dismissed dozens of staff members and laid off hundreds more. The Vitagraph Company, faced with falling revenues at the Vitagraph Theatre, announced that after two years of operation the theatre lease would not be renewed when it expired in April. Trade papers in February and March noted that the total number of moving picture admissions was down, and that numerous problems beset the industry.

Reduced theatre admissions notwithstanding, the public continued to express a strong interest in motion pictures. Rare was the daily metropolitan paper without a feature column on the movies, and leading magazines found that stories about movies and their stars were sure builders of circulation. Many magazines were devoted exclusively to the motion picture industry. Some, like *Motion Picture Magazine*, *Photoplay Magazine*, *Moving Picture Stories*, and *Photoplaygoer's Review*, among a dozen or more others, appealed to audiences, while *Motion Picture News*, *Moving Picture World*, *Motography*, and film departments in entertainment magazines, including *Billboard*, *Variety*, *New York Dramatic Mirror*, and *New York Clipper*, were read by producers and exhibitors. In addition, many producing companies and film distributors issued house organs.

In *Motion Picture Magazine*'s November 1915 issue, reader Laura Jane Williams contributed a rhyming "Alphabet of Popular Players," commencing with "A is for Anderson; Oh, Gilbert's dear—Whenever he's around there is nothing to fear," and progressing a few lines later to this rather forgettable verse: "O is for Ostriche; Oh, Muriel's the girl—You cannot forget her teeth of pearl."

On December 4, 1915, *Moving Picture World* told of a new project: "Charles M. Seay, who since the finish of *A Daughter of the Sea* has been making arrangements for filming his new script, *Babette of the Ballyhoo*, in which Muriel Ostriche will play the part of a circus girl, is ready to take his principals into the southland, where they will join a road show and get 'atmosphere.' "

The *New York Dramatic Mirror*, issue of December 18, 1915, carried this story: "Charles M. Seay, the indefatigable feature director, helped gather up the pieces of the wrecked Con. Kennedy Carnival Company, and during its reorganization in Jacksonville, Florida, used it as the background for *Babette of the Ballyhoo*. Seay's company is headed by Muriel Ostriche, and includes Edwards Davis, George Larkin, Jack Hopkins, Charles Brandt, Nellie King, Catherine Calhoun, Al Hombourg, and Raymond Agnell. Being an old-time showman himself, Seay was right at home with the carnival people, except when he tried to convert the lady lion-tamer to a snake charmer. She didn't mind eating and sleeping with the big cats, but shied at snakes."

Still another blurb on the same effort appeared in *Moving Picture World* on December 11th: "Charles Seay, accompanied by Muriel Ostriche, Mollie King, and eighteen other principals, left last week for Albany, Georgia, where, in conjunction with the Con. T. Kennedy Carnival and Gala Week Company, Miss Ostriche's next picture, *Babette of the Ballyhoo*, a purely circus story, will be staged. The production of the Ostriche picture was delayed one week because of the accident suffered by the Kennedy Company, when five of their people and a number of animals were killed in a train wreck. At the Civic Ball held by the municipal authorities of Albany, director Seay procured the use of the big open-air ballroom and staged a number of essential scenes, using several thousand natives as extras." A subsequent issue continued: "For five weeks the director and his players traveled around with the carnival company touring the small towns of Georgia, and it is only natural that the results, insofar as they pertain to the experiences of a circus troupe, are realistic. We meet many oddly interesting types among these wanderers and catch something of the spirit of their restless existence—here one day, there tomorrow, facing the joys and sorrows born of their unstable life.

"There is a distinct romantic appeal to the picturing of these modern gypsies, and it is made stronger and more personal by focusing the attention on two youthful performers of the company, Babette, a dancer, and Petey, the daredevil performer of the show. Early in the production we learn something of the antecedents of Babette, how her mother, deserted and penniless, became a fortuneteller with the troupe, and how Babette

EQUITABLE

EXPENSIVE ERRORS

have no place in the EQUITABLE policy of PRODUCTION

EVERY LEGITIMATE STAR ENGAGED FOR AN EQUITABLE PRODUCTION

has proven his or her worth before the camera in a big and successful feature

They Include.

GAIL KANE (PATHE)	**HENRY KOLKER** (METRO)	**CHARLES J. ROSS** (PLAY GOERS)
KATHARINE KAELRED (TRIANGLE)	**FLORENCE REED** (DEBUT)	**CYRIL SCOTT** (DEBUT)
GEORGE SOULE SPENCER (LUBIN)	**WILLIAM COURTENAY** (DEBUT)	**ALEXANDRA CARLISLE** (DEBUT)
MURIEL OSTRICHE (VITAGRAPH)	**MARGARITA FISCHER** (MUTUAL)	**LILLIAN LORRAINE** (BALBOA)
BRANDON TYNAN (PARAMOUNT)	**EMMET CORRIGAN** (METRO)	**FRANK SHERIDAN** (PATHE)
CLARA WHIPPLE (STOCK)	**WILLIAM H. TOOKER** (LIFE)	**MARY CHARLESON** (LUBIN)
LENORE ULRICH (PARAMOUNT)		**ARTHUR ASHLEY** (METRO)

All proven material
No doubt of their screening and acting ability

This same rule applies in all
EQUITABLE
departments

EQUITABLE MOTION PICTURES CORPORATION
LEWIS J. SELZNICK, VICE PRES. AND ADVISORY DIRECTOR
RELEASING THROUGH
WORLD FILM CORPORATION

In November 1915 the Equitable Motion Pictures Corporation, associated with World Film, boasted an impressive lineup of stars, nearly all of whom had gained experience with other studios. Muriel Ostriche was noted as having "proven her worth before the camera" with Vitagraph. (*Moving Picture World*, November 27, 1915)

became a typical product of the nomad existence without, however, losing her girlish gayety of spirit.

"In developing the story, the author causes the death of the fortuneteller and permits the daughter to discover the whereabouts of her father, who has married again and who is an influential citizen in a small town, one of the towns visited by the company. The sympathy, of course, was all with the girl, and her case is strengthened by the emphasis placed on the hypocritical natures of the gossipy townsfolk. Butterworth does not acknowledge his daughter openly, but he makes a place for her in his home and immediately the deacons of the church and the deacons' wives are scandalized. The girl's one true friend is the young minister, who wants to marry her, but the hypocrisy of the village does not appeal to Babette. She breathes more freely among her easy-going companions at the circus and is relieved on returning to them and her daredevil lover, Petey.

"Muriel Ostriche, small, vivacious, and pretty, is precisely the type for the role of the dancer. In recent months she has had no part that suited her so well. George Larkin is appropriately cast as Petey, and Edwards Davis is sufficiently dignified as the father."

In keeping with World Film policy at the time, *Babette of the Ballyhoo* was the working title. It was feared—and there were ample precedents in the industry to make the fear realistic—that if World published the actual title far in advance, another firm might produce a similarly-titled movie in the meantime, or, as happened even more often, an old film would be resurrected from the vaults, retitled with a copycat name, and exhibited in competition with the real thing.

A Circus Romance was the title decided upon, and following its release on February 5, 1916, the film garnered many reviews, mostly favorable, but with a dissenting opinion in *Variety*: "The story is too simple and direct and has to be padded to string it out to five parts. Some good rural comedy. Will do nicely for program picture. Someday when Miss Ostriche learns to tone down her superabundance of gushiness and throw back her shoulders, she may shine brilliantly as a picture star." *Motography* noted that the part of Babette "demands only that the player be girlish of manner and good-looking, and Muriel Ostriche can do both of these things very well." Shortly thereafter, the same publication had more to say: "Muriel Ostriche, who created a field for herself by her work in *Mortmain*, *A Daughter of the Sea*, and *A Circus Romance*, is the Equitable ingenue piece-de-resistance. Dainty, diminutive, and attractive of face and form, productions in which she has appeared have had extremely satisfactory return engagements, wide distribution, and have more than pleased from every standpoint."

"I really enjoyed *A Circus Romance*," Muriel Ostriche stated in an interview many years later. "We went to Georgia and Florida. I traveled with the circus, I ballyhooed with them and got involved in everything they did. Each night the circus people slept in railway cars, and the moving picture players stayed in hotels. We spent a lot of time in Albany, Georgia, and also in Florida.

"All of the circus performers seemed to be intermarried. They were very interesting and friendly people. In front of the circus spectators I danced—like a tightrope dancer—on a bareback horse. I also got on a camel and fed elephants. I did all of this as I wanted to really be part of the circus, and that's what the circus is all about. It took about four or five weeks to finish everything."

The working title for *By Whose Hand?*, released on April 17, 1916, was *Who Killed Simon Baird?*, and under the latter name many trade notices appeared prior to its issue.

Upon release, the picture earned generally favorable reviews, with the *New York Clipper* noting: "Muriel Ostriche captured feminine honors in a rather well-played role."

The convoluted plot involved Simon Baird, a man of wealth, who alienated a number of people, any one of whom might have committed his murder. The following synopsis is from *Moving Picture World*:

"Dave Sterling [James Riley], the superintendent of the Maitland estate, is in love with Helen Maitland [Muriel Ostriche], his employer's daughter. The father, however, refuses to give consent until Sterling can show at least $10,000. Sterling has saved $5,000. He has invented a machine in which an agent interests a wealthy landowner, Simon Baird. Baird comes to see Sterling, finds some petty flaw in it, and flaunts the five $1,000 bills in Sterling's face, which he had come prepared to spend if the invention were satisfactory. Helen notices that one of these bills had been torn and pasted together again. Sterling persuades Baird to stay overnight—at which time he can remedy the defects in the machine—and Baird, attracted by Helen, decides to stay in the Maitland house.

"A look of hatred appears on the face of the Negro servant, Kimba, when he sees Baird. There is a hated look of recognition between Baird and Maitland. Baird's shadow, as he places his wallet on the table before retiring for the night, appears on the window shade, where it is noticed by Sterling, Mrs. Maitland and Mr. Maitland [Charles J. Ross], who pass by in the garden at intervals a few minutes apart. In the morning, just as Sterling is showing Helen ten $1,000 bills, a servant rushes in with word of Baird's murder.

"Sterling is arrested—the empty wallet and the money throwing suspicion his way. At the trial Helen testifies against the man she loves, establishing his motive for the crime. Kimba's testimony brings out the reason for his look of hatred at seeing Baird. Years before, when Maitland and Baird were mining partners, Baird had been inhuman in his treatment of their servant, Kimba. Next, John Maitland's testimony showed his reason for hating Baird, who had stolen from him his lawful profits in their mining venture. Mrs. Maitland's testimony brings out the story of how, when she was a singer in a picturesque honkytonk in South Africa, Baird had betrayed and deserted her. After Baird's departure, Maitland falls in love with the girl and marries her, ignorant of her former relations with Baird. Baird, in the evening of his murder, on meeting the woman again as Maitland's wife, threatened to tell her husband. He flaunted in her face the five $1,000 bills which he had refused to give her in years gone by and left them on the table. Sterling, coming into the room, not knowing from where the money had come, accepts it as a loan from Mrs. Maitland.

A Circus Romance, an Equitable-World film released on February 5, 1916, featured Muriel Ostriche, Edwards Davis, Jack Hopkins, Catherine Calhoun, George Larkin, and other players, and was filmed on location with the Con. T. Kennedy Circus in Albany, Georgia and elsewhere. Muriel Ostriche, shown near the right above, played the part of a circus performer. (*Motography*)

Advertisement in *Moving Picture World* for the Equitable-World picture, *By Whose Hand?* Simon Baird, a man of wealth, had alienated several of his friends and associates, any one of whom might have committed his murder. The audience is shown several possibilities, followed by a courtroom scene in which the audience is left hanging with the question, "Who killed Simon Baird?" One reviewer noted critically that though this ending might have been fine for a chapter in a serial, it would not do for a feature.

"Her testimony clears Sterling, but the question arises, 'Is she lying to save the man her daughter loves?' Mrs. Maitland says she is guilty, which is promptly denied by Sterling, who says he is the guilty one. Question on the screen: 'Is he lying to save the mother of the woman he loves?' An acquittal from the jury, and the audience is left wondering who killed Simon Baird."

This up in the air ending provoked much criticism, with *Motography* stating that it would be appropriate as an episode in a serial feature but was not satisfactory for a five-reel production. "The spectator is more or less inclined to reply to the judge's question by answering, 'Why ask me?'—which is not the effect the ending should have." Muriel Ostriche, whose performance was well reviewed, had her name in lights on Broadway when the show opened there.

Motion Picture Magazine in its June 1916 issue printed an article by Howard Reich which told of Muriel Ostriche's dancing ability, a talent which earned her many awards: "Muriel Ostriche is nineteen years of age. She is one of the youngest, if not the very youngest screen star, and whiles away her spare moments teaching the latest dancing steps at $5 per teach. Muriel maintains a studio at Carnegie Hall and boasts no less than 60 regular scholars. Miss Ostriche gives an hour's lesson for $5 and never accepts a pupil for less than 15 lessons. She has a waiting list of 40 and takes a new pupil each time one of her old ones graduates. She hires an orchestra of five pieces and has four assistants; one of them, Professor Walter Ross, receives $100 a week. Muriel's income from this sideline exceeds $5,000 a year. She is the possessor of 80 cups awarded her in various dancing contests, including that held at the Grand Central Palace in 1915 by the Motion Picture Exhibitors' League."

Muriel Ostriche and Carlyle Blackwell were on their way to an unidentified town somewhere in the Midwest according to an erroneous July 1916 trade paper notice. A scenario writer had discovered an isolated village that was an intact relic of the olden days, complete with a village blacksmith, town pump, and other trappings. The town was said to be an ideal set for *Sally in Our Alley*, with the working title of *Mollie o' Pigtail Alley*. As it turned out, the story was filmed not in the Midwest but, rather, in and about the Peerless Studios of World Films in Fort Lee. The film concerned young Sally, a poor little Irish girl who lives in a slum and who works to support her entire family. In the employ of a wealthy childless woman, Mrs. Rockwell, Sally attracts two admirers. Her social position causes problems, but in the end love overcomes all. *Variety* wrote: "Miss Ostriche is no longer the cute little ingenue of a year or two ago, having grown perceptibly plumper. She isn't pretty enough for straight leads and will have to be assigned to character leads in order to get the best results before the camera." On the other hand, *Moving Picture World* stated that Muriel played a "very winsome role" as Sally. The film did well at the box office.

With a screenplay adapted from a story by Harold Vickers, published in *Snappy Stories Magazine*, the film *The Men She Married* was produced by the Peerless Division of World and was released on November 27, 1916. *Motography* summarized the plot:

"The story deals with a society crook who marries an heiress and then deserts her. Later she marries again, this time to a wealthy man who has a grown-up daughter. She does not tell him of her first marriage, and when her first husband returns to blackmail her, he is able to force her to influence her present husband to aid in a dishonest mining scheme. Then the crook wins the love of the young daughter. The wife, in trying to save the girl, goes to the man's apartment, where she is discovered by her husband. There is a highly dramatic scene, in the course of which the woman's true motive is discovered. And then, too, the fact that the first marriage was illegal is discovered, and the power of the crook is at an end." Starring in the film was Gail Kane, who was assisted by Arthur Ashley, Muriel Ostriche, and Montagu Love. The picture opened to generally good reviews.

Many years later, Muriel Ostriche recalled the film: "Gail Kane was the star. Earlier, she was very involved with Arthur Spiegel of World Film. He was a millionaire from a Chicago mail order company and was in films only a short time. I recall that he signed me up for three years with the company, and I remember meeting his wife and two children. They had a summer place, a farm, which I visited. He became attracted to Gail Kane, and the two spent a lot of time together. Most of the players thought they were having an affair. When Spiegel died suddenly of pneumonia—he was living at a suite at the Plaza Hotel in New York City—it hit Gail Kane very hard.

"Montagu Love, an Englishman, was a close friend of mine. Later, when I was married, my husband and I would often have him over for dinner. He was an excellent actor and did well in every movie he played. He was a 'heavy'—the second lead, not the star. After working in Fort Lee he went to Hollywood and was in many big pictures."

World and its Equitable and Peerless divisions underwent a number of changes during the autumn of 1916. Advertisements primarily featured the name of William A. Brady and gave his wide-ranging personal statements of policy. His daughter, Alice, was likewise mentioned with frequency.

In 1916, writers for *Motion Picture News*, *Variety*, and other trade papers considered Griffith's *The Birth of a Nation* to be the industry's greatest accomplishment to date, although *Intolerance*, another Griffith production, was noted by *Moving Picture World* as being an even greater work.

By that time Mary Pickford was far and away the most famous and most successful of film actresses, drawing crowds whenever she appeared at conventions, motion picture expositions, and balls. Writers seemed to treat her with a special reverence such as would be accorded a reigning queen, which for the industry she certainly was. Alice Brady, Dorothy and Lillian Gish, Clara Kimball Young, Blanche Sweet, and Mary Miles Minter, among others, were also high on the popularity list at the time.

Charlie Chaplin held the publicity honors among male performers, with tales of record-breaking crowds attending his movies and his ever-increasing compensation reaching print frequently. Published comments from theatre owners indicated that when a Chaplin picture was shown, a packed house usually would result.

Lewis J. Selznick's intense campaign featuring Clara Kimball Young, which was well underway before she became free of her World contract, gained momentum, and the first film under Selznick's aegis, *The Common Law*, attracted an enthusiastic review

In the summer of 1916, World Pictures announced several forthcoming features, including *Sally in our Alley,* starring Carlyle Blackwell and Muriel Ostriche. Other World personalities illustrated include Kitty Gordon, Robert Warwick, Ethel Clayton, House Peters, Clara Kimball Young, Clara Whipple, John Hines, Doris Kenyon, Mollie King, Holbrook Blinn, Frances Nelson, Gail Kane, Arthur Ashley, and Alice Beach. (*Moving Picture World,* July 1, 1916)

Sally in our Alley, a World Film Corporation production featuring Carlyle Blackwell and Muriel Ostriche, was released on July 17, 1916. The picture was exceedingly popular and was played in many theatres for the next several years. (*Moving Picture World,* July 22, 1916)

in *Moving Picture World*. This particular publication, like most others (but less so with *Variety*), was apt to review favorably or look kindly upon the products of its leading advertisers, of which Selznick certainly was one, although numerous films, particularly smaller productions, were panned on occasion. Many "reviews" and "advance reports" of films were simply reprintings of studio-generated publicity. Infrequently did any equipment, service, or industry executive receive a negative comment. The same treatment was extended to various corporations in the film trade. Everything seemed to be wonderful, new productions were marvelous, and projected plans were the best yet. When there was a problem it was overlooked more often than not, until the inevitable notice of bankruptcy or merger appeared.

Film players and directors were pawns in an increasingly larger game in which producers and exhibitors garnered most of the profits. Universal remained the giant of the industry. Biograph, the leader of earlier years, was fading rapidly. The best it could do was to re-release earlier films, belatedly advertising the names of its players and, in particular, showcasing its former director, D.W. Griffith.

Emphasis was on the star system, and despite criticism given to Chaplin's six-figure remuneration, virtually every producing company heavily advertised its leading personalities. Sometimes the situation got confusing, and it was difficult for magazine readers to follow the players. For example, the January 13, 1917 issue of *Moving Picture World* ran one full-page featuring Gail Kane as a World actress and another page featuring her in an American-brand film. Similarly, in late 1916 and early 1917 it was difficult for the public to determine where Clara Kimball Young belonged—with her new affiliation with Selznick, or with her old affiliation with World, for riding on the Selznick publicity bandwagon concerning her, World re-released many old Clara Kimball Young features, even setting up a new branch to distribute them.

Among William A. Brady's lofty and often pretentious pronouncements to the press was the oft-repeated World Film policy of producing films far in advance, usually with working titles that would be later changed, and having on the shelf a number of features ready to go when the release time came. World was the best-managed producer in the field, he proclaimed. Unfortunately, polls often showed that World pictures were less popular with the public than were the films of certain of its less well managed competitors!

Among the films in the works was *The Parasites*, with June Elvidge, Muriel Ostriche, and Henry Hull. Released under the name of *A Square Deal* on February 19, 1917, the film was reviewed as sentimental and entertaining, if a bit superficial. Muriel played the part of Ruby Trailes, whose conniving mother maneuvers her into a society marriage, resulting in all sorts of complications.

Martin Saxe, proprietor of the Knickerbocker Theatre, sent a note to *Motography* advising that the film was "a very good production which pleased the audiences completely," while E. W. Gould, of the Dixie Theatre, Cartersville, Georgia, likewise reported enthusiasm and a good business.

In an interview printed in *Motography*, William Brady, the director-general of World Film, stated that his method was to let the different directors complete various pictures, after which he would "take the picture and supply any deficiencies that I am able to detect. After that, perhaps two months before the release date, I go over the play again, and if I find anything of a serious nature requiring time to fix up, the date of issue is postponed, and another picture is substituted. We go at our work with all of the deliberation we need. There are several reasons why I do not direct our pictures from start to finish. First, we issue a picture every week and frequently have three or four underway at the same time. Secondly, under the present system I am able to give my best attention to putting the finishing touches upon all of them."

In the meantime, the Famous Players-Lasky Corporation increased its capitalization from $12,500,000 to $20,000,000. The much-diminished American branch of the Eclair Film Company, holding forth in offices at 18 East 41st Street, New York City, announced that problems with its French parent had been complicated because Charles Jourjon, head of the French company, "has until recently been confined to the trenches on the west front, and the management of the French company was misinformed by outsiders as to real conditions in America." Hoping to regain a niche in the American market, Eclair announced that it was "prepared to manufacture immediately and will entertain any meritorious propositions."

Moving Picture World printed a notice in March: "The World Film Corporation now has fifteen Brady-made motion pictures completed and ready for release upon a few hours' notice if it were desirable—which of course it is not. In the regular line the last of these photoplays will not reach the public until June 11th, three months hence. The list includes . . . *The Wit of a Woman*, with Muriel Ostriche as the star, assisted by Arthur Ashley, Johnny Hines, and Alec Francis. . . . The names of several of these pictures will be changed before final release, in accord with Mr. Brady's frequently exercised practice of making leisurely substitution of title when he feels that such a course will be of benefit."

Released on May 14, 1917, with the title changed from *The Wit of a Woman* to *Moral Courage*, the film received mixed reviews, but Muriel Ostriche's performance in it earned several accolades. *Moving Picture World* noted that she "does one of the best pieces of acting in her career," while the harder to please *Variety* reviewer echoed the sentiment: "Muriel Ostriche is doing quite the best work in it that she has done in some time." The story involved the son of a wealthy factory owner who falls in love with Muriel, a worker. Her father, a Scotchman, contemplates what he views as an unfavorable situation, and comes up with the idea of bribing his daughter-in-law to divorce her husband by paying her $100,000. Muriel agrees to the proposition, goes to Reno and obtains a divorce, collects the reward, and immediately remarries her former husband, a clever piece of financial maneuvering which impresses the father, who then accepts his ingenious relative. *Variety* stated there were two things about the picture that stood out: One was Muriel's acting, and the other was the balance of the cast which was well suited to the roles assigned. However, the story was dismissed as unconvincing: "Moral courage in this case means that if your father-in-law doesn't like you and wants you to give his son a divorce, just turn around and trim the old man for 100,000 bucks and he will respect you and tell you that you are a good businesswoman and that you

Directed by Harley Knoles, under the general supervision of William A. Brady, *A Square Deal* was released on February 19, 1917. Carlyle Blackwell, June Elvidge, and Muriel Ostriche had the leading parts. (*Moving Picture World,* February 24, 1917)

An enlargement from a glass slide made by the Excelsior Illustrating Company mentions Muriel Ostriche as a member of the cast. The World Pictures production of *The Social Leper* was released on March 19, 1917. It is not certain whether Muriel was in the film, but if she was, her part was minor. Contemporary reviews in leading trade publications do not mention her in connection with the feature. (Courtesy of Mary Corliss, Museum of Modern Art)

ALICE BRADY
in
"Darkest Russia"

CARLYLE BLACKWELL
JUNE ELVIDGE
in "The Page Mystery" with
Arthur Ashley

MURIEL OSTRICHE
ARTHUR ASHLEY
in
"Moral Courage"

SARAH BERNHARDT
in
"Mothers of France"
Directed by Louis Mercanton

Current Specials on the Dependable Program

A World franchise guarantees dependable pictures—plus dependable service—backed by square deal policies that absolutely assure its holders the best that the industry offers.

Moral Courage, made by Peerless and released through World on May 14, 1917, was one of four films featured in this advertisement to the trade. (*Moving Picture World*, July 5, 1917)

can have the boy. So much for the story of this Peerless-World feature photoplay production." Among exhibitors, A. O. Landry, of the Victor Theatre, Abbeville, Louisiana, stated that in his theatre *Moral Courage* was "a splendid attraction; drew good business."

In June 1917, *Motion Picture Classic* printed an "impressionistic sketch" of Muriel, written by Hazel Simpson Naylor: "Finespun hair of gleaming gold, coiled into a crown of glistening curls; a winsomely molded face, whose long, almond-shaped eyes can scan you with the slightly mysterious veiling of their azure depths; all in a plump, well-rounded little personage encased in a simply constructed dancing-frock of cloth-of-silver, garnitured with richly encrusted silver lace—that was Muriel Ostriche as I saw her, dancing tirelessly to the strains of scintillating music, while all the black-coated, white-gloved dancing men buzzed about her like flies about a jam pot.

"It was during an intermission that I noticed a small, humpback lad, whose large, pathetic eyes spoke of ages of suffering. Not once did this hungry gaze leave Miss Ostriche's face. One could clearly guess his thought as he stood there, 'Who am I, to covet a dance with such as she?'

"Then suddenly I saw Miss Ostriche slip away from the five lithe-bodied men who were teasing her for the next dance. She approached the lonely hunchback with no air of condescension, but as one who asks a favor. 'Won't you dance the next with me?' she asked in a singularly soft voice. The lad turned quite pale. It was impossible for him to articulate, but he nodded vehemently.

"The music struck up a one-step, and the ill-matched couple went bobbing away, observed by all.

"But Muriel Ostriche's silver-shod feet twinkled as merrily, her golden ringlets fluttered as cheerfully as if she were dancing with the handsomest man in the hall.

"This bright little sunbeam who has danced her way through everything and into the hearts of everyone who saw her as 'Babette,' the dainty butterfly dancer of *A Circus Romance*, and have viewed the silver loving-cups, dancing trophies, which she modestly exhibits, cannot fail to understand the dancing bit of sunshiny joy that she must have infused in the heart of her chosen partner.

"When she brought the lad back to his corner of observation, his face flushed with happiness, his eyes alight with joy, something to dream about through his dreary days safe in his heart, she shook hands with him like an old comrade and thanked him prettily for the dance.

" 'Muriel Ostriche,' I said to myself, 'here's to you!' "

In the meantime, the rather plain buildings housing World Film in Fort Lee were enlarged by a new 8,000 square-foot structure. A trade paper noted that five or six separate films were being made simultaneously on a stage measuring 65 by 125 feet. Alice Brady, apple of her father's eye, demonstrated her independence and announced that she was leaving World to form Alice Brady Pictures, Inc., incorporated for $250,000.

The next Peerless-World Muriel Ostriche feature was *Youth*, produced with the working title of *The Waster* and released on July 30, 1917. *Moving Picture World* accused the photoplaywright of a "want of skill" and noted that Romaine Fielding fell short as the director. "It will please many of the less critical screen patrons" was the ambiguous conclusion, although it was noted that "the acting is generally capable." The picture starred Carlyle Blackwell and June Elvidge, with Johnny Hines, Muriel Ostriche, George Cowell, Victor Kennard, Henrietta Simpson, Robert Broderick, and Henry West taking other parts. The story involved an alcoholic worker on the Tennessee River Dam project, who reformed his ways and won back the girl of his dreams.

The Dormant Power, a Peerless-World film released on October 22, 1917, featured Ethel Clayton and Montagu Love in the leading roles, supported by Joseph Herbert, Muriel Ostriche, Edward Langford, and George Morgan. The story, set in Mexico and the United States, had enough counterplots to furnish material for six separate films, according to one reviewer.

Muriel Ostriche remembered an unusual encounter: "Ethel Clayton was the star of *The Dormant Power*, and we all went to Florida to make it. I remember being on a motorboat with her on Lake Worth and staying at the Palm Beach Hotel. When I signed in the hotel, I agreed to pay for my mother as well, because World Film didn't want anyone else along—and they wouldn't pay the bill. My father said I was too young to go such a distance alone, so at my expense I brought my mother with me. I remember we would walk up and down the street and buy grapefruit, bringing it back to the hotel for lunch.

"When I checked in, I noticed a man watching my mother and me. Soon, this guy asked to be introduced to me, and then invited my mother and me to go out to dinner. We went to meet a lady friend of his who was a wonderful cook, her name was Mrs. Winter, and I remember that he called her Mrs. Wintersnip. I found out he was the great composer, Rudolf Friml. He fell in love with me, but there was a problem, he was married. He told me that he had married his wife, who was in a play he wrote the music for, because they were taking a trip around the United States together and they couldn't go across the state lines without being married, because of the white slave laws. However, to me they both seemed to be happily married. I wasn't interested in stealing her husband, but he was in love with me and said so.

"At the hotel, people would ask me to ask Mr. Friml if he would play the piano for them, for he was wonderful to hear—a terrific concert pianist who had been playing ever since he was four years old. Later, I saw him up North. He took me to the theatre and to the opening of several of his plays. He wrote a bunch of musicals, including *High Jinks* and *Rose Marie*—there were so many plays and a lot of good music. I remember that he later wrote a song used in a movie with Nelson Eddy, a beautiful melody, and when he played it for me it was wonderful.

"In Florida, his wife didn't know he was paying so much attention to me. She was staying in a room behind the hotel, and no one saw much of her. The more Rudolph Friml saw of me, the more he told me he was in love.

"He had asked me to be his third wife. I met his children, and they adored me—his children with his first wife out in Long Island. I have forgotten her name. His second wife was Blanche, and I was to be the third if I chose, but then he married

Elsie Lawson—who was in one of the shows he wrote the music for, and they had a little boy, joining the little boy and girl he already had. She then divorced him, which caused lots of problems, for a lot of his friends became disgusted with him. Years later I saw him at a party, right after he married a Japanese lady."

Muriel's next Peerless-World film was *The Good For Nothing*, released on December 10, 1917. The working title was *The Ladder of Fame*, and for a while it was intended to be titled *Jack, the Good For Nothing*. A review in *Motography* noted:

"The situations in this play, while not out of the ordinary, are of the type which have proved popular in the past to picture fans. They are arranged in this story in a fashion which allows Carlyle Blackwell to play a pleasing role, and are effective if a little forced.

"The characters are conventional ones, well known to picture enthusiasts. There is the disinherited son who finally makes good, the worthless step-brother who goes the pace, the wronged girl, the vaudeville actress with a passion for jewels, and the cold mother who finally realizes the worth of the son she cast off. Some humor has been interpolated into the play.

"Carlyle Blackwell does as well with his role as he could be expected to do, but while his many admirers will undoubtedly enjoy his performance, the part will add no new laurels to his name. Muriel Ostriche and Evelyn Greeley, whose names are featured with Blackwell, have little to do in the picture but they do that little well.

"The story: Jack Burkshaw arrives at home after an absence of ten years to find that his mother has married again and that he is not particularly welcome in the new family, which includes a step-brother and sister. The step-brother, Jerry Alston, is a worthless young fellow who is infatuated with a vaudeville actress. Barbara Manning, Jerry's stenographer, begs him to do the honorable act, under the circumstances, and marry her, but Jerry refuses to listen to her pleading. Instead he engages himself to an heiress from whom a short time before he has stolen a necklace. Jack is accused of the theft, distrusted by his mother.

"Despairing that his mother hasn't more faith in him, Jack decides at least to make a man of his step-brother. He kidnaps Jerry on the day of his wedding to the heiress, compels him to marry Barbara, returns the necklace to its rightful owner, and wins the confidence of his mother as well as the love of his step-sister."

Moving Picture World noted that "Evelyn Greeley and Muriel Ostriche, co-stars with Carlyle Blackwell, are satisfactory as the half-sister and stenographer respectively." M. J. Weil, of the Lakeshore Theatre, Chicago, located "in a high class neighborhood," advised *Motography* that *The Good For Nothing* was "a very good picture—pleased everyone—very good business," while M. Thompson, of the White Way Theatre, Concordia, Kansas, advised that it was "a fair production—one that makes good entertainment but has no drawing power," and H. C. Johnson, proprietor of the Crystal Theatre, Stamford, Texas, wasn't sure whether he liked it or not: "Good picture, but it did not draw. Patrons pleased."

A reporter from *Moving Picture World* went to the Peerless Studio in Fort Lee and expressed astonishment at his discovery that no fewer than seven pictures were being produced simultaneously under a single roof. Director General William A. Brady showed him around and told of the growth, new efficiency, and modern methods of film making: "In place of all of this, the simple principles which have made big business in steel, leather, rubber, automobiles, harvesters, and many other branches of industry are gradually and surely making big business in the pictures."

The Volunteer, a World film released on December 24, 1917, was titled in some advertisements as *The Little Volunteer*. The star was Madge Evans, whom Muriel Ostriche later remembered: "She was a little girl, about eight years old at the time, and I played her mother. Her real mother was always with her on the set. Years later, she married Sidney Kingsley, a writer. By that time her roles as a little girl had made her famous."

Young Madge played the part of a girl actress in the picture. Her parents enlist in the war and send her off to live with her grandparents, who are strict Quakers. Her grandfather is horrified at the idea that an actress is living with him, but when the rest of the family enjoys seeing her in a picture in a local theatre, he sneaks in, the first time he has ever been in a theatre, and has a good time. The picture enjoyed favorable reviews. *Motography* observed that it was of special merit as it portrayed Madge Evans as an actress in a film-within-a-film, behind the scenes in the World Film studios. "It is quite unique to thus bring the mechanism of the studio life before the public. Picture fans who are keen about the personal side of celebrities' lives will be overjoyed. Madge Evans is seen in intimate chats with Carlyle Blackwell, June Elvidge, Kitty Gordon and others."

Around this time, Muriel was making $300 per week, not in the league of top film actresses, but comfortably above most players. World Films publicized Muriel and its other stars, setting up large pictures of them in movie lobbies and arranging for personal appearances before fans.

"I don't remember when I first talked to a movie audience," Muriel recalled, "but I was frightened when I first did it. Later, I grew quite used to it and enjoyed it very much. I would go to different movie houses which had advertised in advance that I would be there. My little speech started something like: 'You can hardly realize how much I appreciate the opportunity of appearing in person before those who have seen me on the screen.'

"I should also tell you about Rudolph Valentino. We were good friends. I used to dance with him when he worked as a waiter in Rector's restaurant in New York City. I would often go there at tea time, and we would dance together. He would often warn me: 'Don't you tango with anyone else but me!' Once, we won a big dance contest. Later, he became famous and went into vaudeville with Joan Sawyer, who also worked at Rector's. He then went into films. I never saw him again after that."

One evening in December 1917, while she was dancing in a Manhattan nightclub, a lawyer friend introduced Muriel to Frank A. Brady, who said, "I saw you today," to which she replied, "Where?" He told her that he was taking a bus ride and saw her face on a poster. A romance ensued, and seven weeks later, on January 28, 1918, they were married at City Hall. "It was a very miserable day—terrible weather," Muriel Ostriche recalled. "Frank was in the service, and after we were married I went to stay with two friends of his, Nat and Loretta, who had an extra

THE WORLD FILM HERALD

"THE GOOD FOR NOTHING"

Jack Burkshaw had been fired from his job on the ranch. He wandered into the general store in the little Western town and greeted all the people there. He was popular, though only a good-for-nothing.

"Howdy, folks," said Jack, "I've been thrown out of my job and now I'm looking for something else to do."

"I'm looking for a handy man around the store," said the proprietor. "Do you want the job?"

"I've been everything around this place except the school mistress and the barber," said Jack, "I'll take the job."

LONELINESS

That night, after completing his first day's work in his new job, Jack was overcome with loneliness. He drew a sheet of paper to him and began writing.

"Dear Mother," he wrote, "when father threw me out of home ten years ago for misbehavior, he did the right thing. I'm a no-account, a good-for-nothing. I guess its no use in me trying to make good. To-night I am lonely and have been thinking of you and dad and I've decided to come home and see you again."

Jack signed the letter and mailed it at once.

The next day he boarded a train for the East and home.

JACK FINDS HIS MOTHER

Jack's mother was not at the old home and from neighbors he learned that his father was dead and that his mother had married again, her husband being Eugene Alston, a wealthy widower. So to the Alston home Jack went.

There Jack found his mother.

"Oh, Jack, I am glad to see you again," exclaimed his mother, "but, oh, how rough you look."

At this moment Marion Alston, daughter of Mr. Alston, came out and upon finding her stepmother in the arms of a strange man, went in and reported the occurrence to her father.

"This is my son, Jack," said Mrs. Alston. "He—he has been out West a long time," she added, trying to excuse Jack's uncouth appearance.

JACK MAKES PROGRESS

Jack was not very cordially received at first by Mr. Alston, his daughter, Marion and his son, Jerry. But in time Jack's general good nature and big heart, won the family over to a certain extent.

And then Laurel Baxter, a friend of Marion's who spent a night with her, threw a bombshell into the family one morning when Jack was not there.

"My diamond pendant is gone," she declared. "Last evening Marion, Jack and I were in the music room at the piano and Jack admired it very much. I took it off and showed it to him and then placed it on the piano. And then we all went away and I forgot it. When I went back, it was gone. Jack must have taken it."

Jack was accused of the theft.

"I—I don't know what to say," stammered Jack. "This is a big surprise. I never thought I'd be accused of such a thing."

The upshot of the matter was that Jack was forbidden to come into the Alston home.

But there was one person who did not believe in his guilt. And she—

The guilty party and the experiences which later came to Jack are fascinatingly told in "The Good for Nothing" which will be shown in this theatre.

JACK IS WELCOMED BY THE ALSTON FAMILY

JACK AS A SODA CLERK

THE WORLD FILM HERALD

STUDIO GOSSIP

The cast of characters appearing in "The Good for Nothing" consists of the following:

Jack Burkshaw....Carlyle Blackwell
Marion Alston........Evelyn Greeley
Mrs. Burkshaw..........Kate Lester
Eugene Alston......Charles Duncan
Jerry Alston......William Sherwood
Barbara Manning....Muriel Ostriche
Barbara's Mother, Eugenie Woodward
Laurel Baxter....Katherine Johnston

One of the scenes in "The Good for Nothing" shows Jack, in his first dress suit, trying to capture a bunch of chickens that have escaped from their coops. He slips and slides around in his efforts and the suit becomes a mess. The scene is a hilarious one. A very interesting thing about it is that the scene is a leaf from Mr. Blackwell's own life. He has visualized on the screen one of his experiences while a store clerk in South Dakota.

Miss Evelyn Greeley wears some very stunning frocks in "The Good for Nothing," in which she portrays the role of Marion Alston, the girl with whom Jack falls in love.

Carlyle Blackwell directed "The Good for Nothing" himself and his long experience in pictures has enabled him to put punches and laughs in every scene in the picture.

JACK IS THE MOST POPULAR MAN AT THE PARTY

WILLIAM A. BRADY,
Director-General,
WORLD-PICTURES
present

CARLYLE BLACKWELL
MURIEL OSTRICHE
EVELYN GREELEY
in
"The Good For Nothing"
Story by A. Alexander-Thomas, Directed by Carlyle Blackwell

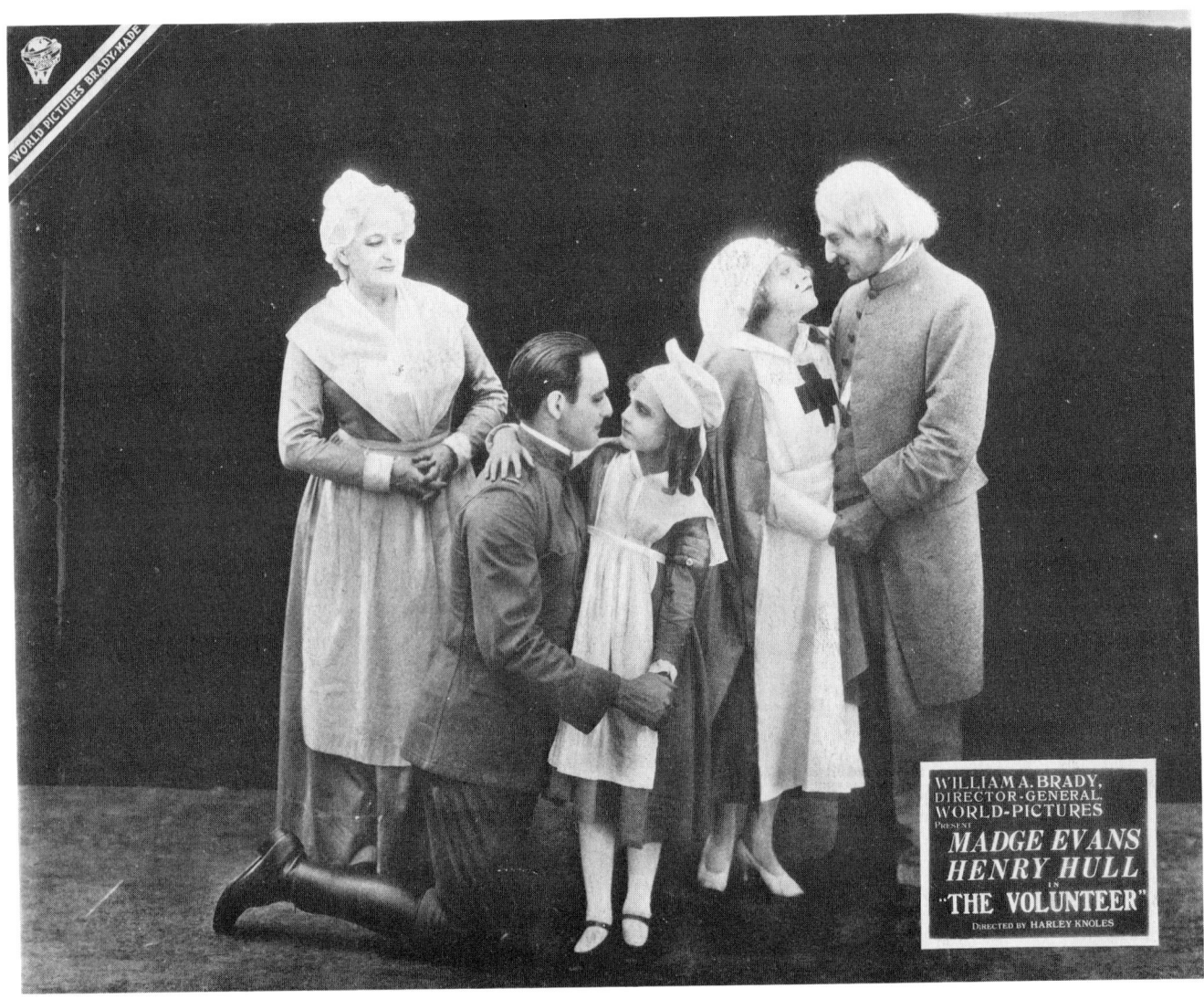

Lobby card for *The Volunteer* starring young Madge Evans (center). Muriel Ostriche, in a Red Cross uniform, played her mother. Produced by World Pictures and released on December 24, 1917, the film was enthusiastically received. (Courtesy of Sidney Kingsley, husband of Madge Evans)

Various studio portraits of Muriel Ostriche, circa 1915-1920. The image shown at the top of the page was used in the earlier year. (Wisconsin Center for Film and Theatre Research)

room in their apartment on Madison Avenue. When he came back we took an apartment at 13 Gramercy Park—a very nicely furnished place. In this apartment many pictures were taken of me by Underwood & Underwood as well as other photographers—pictures including me applying makeup, lying on pillows, and sitting at a piano. Later, we took an apartment in the Hamilton Hotel on West 73rd Street.

"Frank went to Fordham University in the Bronx. He was an architect and was involved in building and remodeling. I remember that he had a big job doing waterproofing work for the Traymore Hotel in Atlantic City. He was born on October 26, 1887 and was thirty when I met him. Frank was the first man I was serious about. I had many boyfriends and admirers earlier. I remember, for example, Frank Carroll, a cameraman from Vitagraph. We went together for six or seven months. Then, there was Lloyd Davis. He wasn't in films, but I don't remember much else about him.

"Frank did not interfere with my films. I went right ahead with my work. He never watched me perform before the camera, but he did go to personal appearances with me and sometimes would introduce me to the audience. I don't remember that he ever saw any of my movies—I don't know why—I guess he just did not want to at the time.

"I remember that he gave me a Stutz Bearcat car. Before that, I used my father's car, then a small car—an Oldsmobile or a Reo—which I bought. Later, I bought a Mitchell limousine. I had various chauffeurs over a period of time—I remember one named Harry.

"Jack Dempsey, the boxer, was a close friend of my husband, and we would go up to Luther's Farm, outside of Saratoga, and watch him train for fights. Once he was knocked out of the ring and into Frank's lap—they pulled him back, he awoke and went on to win the fight. Jack was his nickname. The real Jack Dempsey was his younger brother, but few people knew that. Many years later I was in Palm Beach with my daughter Jean, and I saw Jack Dempsey in a hotel bar. We hadn't seen each other for many years, and we exchanged reminiscences."

Frank Brady had three siblings. Thomas Joseph became a justice of the New York Supreme Court. John Casper became an engineer and entrepreneur and was the only sibling who had children. Mary never married.

Around 1918, Selma Howe and a photographer from Underwood & Underwood peeked in on Muriel during a social event. The result was an illustrated story, "When Muriel Gave a Party—The Guests' Names Were Not in the 'Blue Book,' but They Had a Wonderful Time:

"The house, which stood in the Gramercy Park section of New York City, looked entirely too 'grand' to the gang, and some of them thought for a minute they wouldn't go in, but one of the girls had been to a party there before, and she said it was all right, so in they went.

"It was much warmer indoors than any of their houses were, and they stared around in amazement, until suddenly a little, blue-eyed, yellow-haired girl appeared on the scene and hugged all the little ones, crying: 'Oh, the kiddies have come!' The girl was Muriel Ostriche.

" 'Oh, I seen *her* in the movies!' one of the boys whispered excitedly.

" 'Sure you did, one of the others announced. 'I seen her a lot of times.'

"Then one of the girls—who just had to speak up—exclaimed: 'I saw you in *Sally in Our Alley*!'

"The little hostess laughed happily. 'That was with Carlyle Blackwell. Wasn't it a nice one?' she asked. 'And now come on, everybody—refreshments!'

"You see, she had given parties like that before, and she knew that it's very important to have food the very first thing. So they gathered around the big table, and ate chicken and hot potatoes and things like that. If you hadn't known it was just an afternoon party you'd have thought it was a regular dinner! Of course, there were fancy things like cake and bananas, too; everybody was urged to take some home with them, because there were so many cakes left over.

"After the refreshments everybody played games for prizes—prizes enough that everybody got one whether they won a game or not. And later on everybody sat around the fire, and Muriel, as they all called her by that name, told them stories about how movies are made—much better than fairy tales.

"Then everybody told what they most wanted to be. Muriel confessed that she'd always longed to be a school teacher, and Tim Clancy, who was sitting on the arm of her chair, announced he was going to be a chauffeur. 'I know how to blow the horn now,' he said, and Muriel was interested right away.

" 'You have a wonderful start, and when everybody goes home in my car you can sit up in front with the driver and blow the horn all the way,' she told him. Tim was delighted, and wanted to start right then, so they did, but they didn't go right home; they took a long ride up Fifth Avenue and through Central Park and out on Riverside Drive, where they could see the battleships in the river. . . .

"Everybody was told that they were to be ready to come to more parties like that one; Muriel Ostriche often gives them, much to the amazement of the fashionable children who live in her neighborhood. She gathers her guests up off the streets, bundles them into her big car, and whisks them off to the fairyland of her home. Sometimes the janitor finds them for her, or the chauffeur picks them out, but however they happen to come to her parties they always remember the address, and they very frequently 'come again.'

"Perhaps you remember her, too. She has been in World pictures for some time, and before that she appeared in Thanhouser and Vitagraph productions."

A notice in *Moving Picture World*, issue of February 16, 1918, told of a management change: "William A. Brady quit producing for World Film—will conduct propaganda for better business conditions—also will make pictures after his own ideas."

"What my motion picture plans for the future are has not yet been decided," Brady related. "For the present I shall devote myself to the completion of my big picture—*Stolen Orders*. . . . I don't propose to stand around the studio and see a star come in at

Crane Wilbur, prototype of a famous Greek god, leading man, author and co-director of Horsley productions, was born in Athens, N.Y., February 17, 1889, and educated in the public schools in that town. At the age of fifteen Mr. Wilbur was attracted to the footlights and began his professional career in stock. For seven years he was with Mrs. Fiske's company, but deserted the legitimate stage to take up his brilliant motion picture work with Pathe in "The Perils of Pauline" series. Lubin then secured him for "Road of Strife," and from there he was lured to Horsley, for whom he has appeared successfully in "The Protest," "The Blood of Our Brothers," "Could A Man Do More," etc. He is five feet nine inches tall and a lover of all sports.

Muriel Ostriche, one of the youngest and prettiest screen stars, has played lead in over a hundred productions. She was born in New York City, March 4, 1897, and educated in the public schools. After a short experience as regular extra, she secured a position with the Eclair Film Corporation as ingenue in stock. For two years her courage and patience were tested by such feats as entering a lion's cage, plunging into water when she couldn't swim, riding horses and similar experiences. Her reward is the success and popularity she now enjoys. Miss Ostriche's special hobby is teaching the latest dancing steps in her Carnegie Hall studio. She has the distinction of having won eighty cups in dancing contests, including that awarded by the Motion Picture Exhibitors' League in 1914.

Pearl White, known as "Pathe's Pearl," is one of the most popular girls in the movies. She was born in Sedalia, Missouri, May 2, 1895, and began her theatrical career as "Little Eva" in "Uncle Tom's Cabin," and afterwards became a bareback rider. For several years she appeared in various productions on the legitimate stage and in 1911 made her debut in films, where her clever and fearless work for Pathe has made her famous. Miss White has played in more serials than any other player before the public. Her first screen hit was in "The Perils of Pauline," and this was followed by an equal success in "Exploits of Elaine." Her best work was in the "Iron Claw." Motoring and aviation are her favorite pastimes.

Carlyle Blackwell, popular leading man, was born in Troy, Pennsylvania, and spent his early life in Syracuse, New York. After several years on the road and in stock in New York, he began his motion picture career with the Vitagraph Company in "Uncle Tom's Cabin," since which he has built up an enviable reputation as a "Favorite Player." After a short time with Kalem and Famous Players, he appeared opposite Blanche Sweet and with Ina Claire in "The Puppet Crown" for Lasky. Mr. Blackwell is good looking, a good fellow, and a good actor. He is also a poet, and uses "Carl Black" as his nom de plume. He is fond of outdoor sports, but once in a while finds time to bring forth a scenario.

James Cruze, leading man for Palo Alto, was born in Ogden, Utah, March 22, 1884. His theatrical career began by touring the country with medicine shows; he afterwards founded his own company, and when this disbanded he played in stock in "The Heart of Maryland" and similar productions for several years. In 1911 Thannouser secured him for the screen, for "She," "Joseph in the Land of Egypt," "Legend of Provence," "Adventures of a Diplomatic Free Lance," and others. He played lead in "Million Dollar Mystery" and "Twenty Million Dollar Mystery." He joined his present company in 1915, where he has done exceptional work. Mr. Cruze is a big, splendid man and actor, very fond of baseball and boxing.

Clara Kimball Young, the beautiful and far-famed screen star, was born in Chicago about twenty-three years ago. When less than three years old, Miss Young made her first stage appearance at an impromptu theatrical, staging the then popular "Ta Ra Ra, Boom De-ay." She traveled West and secured a small part in a musical comedy in Seattle. In 1912, while playing in vaudeville, James Young engaged her for Vitagraph, and her brilliant work in "Lola," "Hearts in Exile," "My Official Wife," "Trilby," and "Heart of the Blue Ridge" made her a great favorite. For World Films she appeared in "Camille," "The Yellow Passport," and "The Feast of Life." Her first picture for "The Clara Kimball Young Film Corporation" is from "The Common Law."

Images and captions from a set of cigarette cards made for collectors, circa 1916. Muriel Ostriche's birthdate, which was March 24, 1896, is incorrectly given as March 4, 1897. (Courtesy of Dr. Gerald Rose)

11:00, do a couple of scenes, go out at 12:00 for lunch, stay away for a couple of hours more, come back and put in an hour or two and then have an engagement which requires immediate departure.

"I had been supposed to install an efficient system, and I got tired of trying to put up with such things as I have outlined here. If the man or woman is to be paid $500 or $1,000 a week by a company for whose expenditure I am responsible, the player must deliver the goods. I have resigned the position paying $100,000 a year, because as conditions are, I don't feel that I can earn it. . . . For these past eighteen months I have been in a studio working with my coat off, and I know what goes on in these studios. I have seen with my own eyes what some of these people do. I am going to wake them up. I know many industrious and conscientious directors, actors, and studio employees—people who really work—I am not referring to these, because their honest efforts are blocked by the incompetents and ingrates who refuse to give value for payment received. I am leaving the World Film in excellent shape. The product is provided for up to June 1st. I know of no other company in this country that is 24 pictures ahead of its schedule."

Then began a series of experimental management ideas. Articles in trade papers noted that the World Film Corporation was doing its best to promote efficiency. The hiring of the friends of actors and actresses to play parts was to be discontinued, and greater care would be taken in the future when picking people for the roles. Those with assigned duties, such as handling certain properties, were to wear specifically colored clothing in order to be readily identified while on the set. In one experiment, a group of writers on the scenario staff of World Film endeavored as a large committee to write a script—the venture being viewed with skepticism by others.

The Way Out, a Peerless-World film, was released on March 25, 1918 and featured Carlyle Blackwell and June Elvidge in the lead parts. *Moving Picture World* noted: "The acting is the best feature of the picture. June Elvidge played Alice Thornton with all of the attractiveness demanded by the character, and Carlyle Blackwell is a good-looking and earnest Robert Barr. John Bowers as the Count, Muriel Ostriche as Marcelle, Kate Lester as Mrs. Thornton, Jack Drumier as LaRoche, and Marie Pagano as Claudine are the other members of the cast." The picture, with scenes set in France and America and with the World War as a background, was generally favorably reviewed, and Muriel Ostriche's part, although not mentioned in detail, was noted as being "carefully handled" and "effective."

Then came Muriel's appearance in *The Purple Lily*, a World film released on April 22, 1918. Kitty Gordon had the lead in what *Moving Picture World* characterized as a "weak story of the Canadian wilds." In its issue of April 27th, two reviews were printed, each apparently the work of a different writer, for one noted: "Kitty Gordon and the other members seem to realize the want of merit in the story and reflect it in their acting," while the other said: "It is a strange and supremely fascinating story and will positively hold the attention of any audience from beginning to end."

Leap to Fame, a World film starring Carlyle Blackwell, with Muriel Ostriche taking the part of Tootsie Brown, opened on April 29, 1918. The action was reminiscent of years earlier: "There are chases in automobiles, on motorcycles, on horseback, and in motorboats, and the entire picture has the bustle and atmosphere of a melodramatic serial," noted *Moving Picture World*.

The management of World Film, which issued a steady stream of news releases stating how carefully crafted World features were, must not have enjoyed a comment in *Moving Picture World* which viewed the story as "rather indefinite," and must have winced at the following *Variety* notice: "Carlyle Blackwell, a World Film star, is a good screen actor, also a good director, but when, in screening a picture, he runs out of the house without a hat and is seen outside wearing it, somebody should suggest that he be a bit more careful of detail."

In *Journey's End*, a World film released on May 13, 1918, Muriel Ostriche shared top billing with Ethel Clayton and John Bowers in a story of high society. "Aline [Ethel Clayton], the young and pretty wife of Phil Marsden [John Bowers], longs for an admirer. Jessica Alden [Muriel Ostriche], Aline's sister, is shocked, but the spirit of adventure has seized Aline. Aline bets her sister that within five hours she will capture a suitor, and Jessica, although astonished beyond measure, takes the bet. In less than an hour Aline has the admirer she craved for. From this point on events happen rapidly for Aline, her admirer and her husband. Phil comes to the seashore where Aline, her sister, her guardian, and her admirer are shopping, and Phil finds it impossible to interfere with Aline's freedom, because he had signed an agreement guaranteeing Aline absolute freedom and independence for three months. But, seeing Aline admired and courted by another man, it perturbs him greatly. To add to this discomfiture, the stage woman with whom he had been infatuated comes to the seashore. It would be injuring to the effect to relate here the startling and thrilling incident that brings the offering to a most unexpected close," noted a *Moving Picture World* reviewer. The management of World Film must have been disappointed by another comment which noted: "The story never goes very far below the surface, and some of the complications are more ingenious than plausible. The big situation, where the adventuress tries to compromise the heroine and falls into her own trap, is built up none too skillfully, but the play has its entertaining moments, for which it is largely indebted to the members of the cast and the attractiveness of the Florida scene." Like several other World features, the picture was filmed in Palm Beach.

At a time when most World films were faring quite indifferently at the hands of reviewers, much to the management's consternation, the company's ruling committee instituted some new regulations—the latest in a series of internal procedures publicized in trade releases. The following appeared in *Motography*: "World adopts new rules for casting. Executives will choose players in conference instead of directors alone and all will be tried out first. . . . Hereafter, no directors will do the casting for any World pictures. All casting will be done in this manner:

"When a story is accepted by the scenario department and the continuity has been written and approved, a conference will be held by the production department managers, scenario editor, and general manager as to which stars shall be assigned to the principal roles. When this point is determined, the work of

Scene from *Tinsel,* a World film released on June 8, 1918, featuring Kitty Gordon, Muriel Ostriche (shown above), Frank Mayo, Anthony Merlo, Bradley Barker, George DeCarlton, Marie Nau, Ann Dearing, and Ralph Graves. (George Eastman House Film Archive)

Muriel Ostriche behind the scenes on a studio set, location unknown.

casting the remainder of the players will be given to the casting director, whose selections will be approved in another conference.

"Absolutely every part in the picture will be filled on proven merit only. The past record of every candidate for the position will be looked up, screen tests will be made, and the candidate will be given a trial rehearsal and several scenes before the final decision is reached. In this way it will be thoroughly determined in advance whether or not all of the players are entirely suited to their roles. The beauty of this arrangement is primarily that it assures perfect casts."

Tinsel, a World film released on July 8, 1918, featured Kitty Gordon, Muriel Ostriche, and Frank Mayo in a twisted tale of family problems and romance. Reviews were mixed, with *Moving Picture World* stating: "The effect of the whole is artistic and satisfying, and the observer feels that its lesson is a valuable one to mothers and daughters, as the press sheets advertise.... While the motive is slight, in this instance good teamwork of an agreeable cast of performers holds the interest firmly." *Motography* felt differently: "While this is not the sort of a picture calculated to make you proud you are in the motion picture business, it will go over in a way with audiences that are not too critical." *Variety* noted: "The theme is a flimsy affair, done many times before, but with little change in the angle.... Miss Gordon has a wealth of wonderful clothes, and the same applies to her daughter Ruth [Muriel Ostriche]."

On August 2, 1918, Muriel Ostriche's life was disrupted when the following newspaper article appeared: "BROKER SUES WIFE: MUST PAY ALIMONY. MISS OSTRICHE, MOVIE ACTRESS, FIGURES IN LEWIS FAMILY TROUBLES. In the suit of William J. Lewis, who is connected with a large piano house, against Hattie Lewis, for divorce on the grounds of her alleged fondness for her cousin, Henry J. Butler, the wealthy lumber merchant, Justice McAvoy today ordered the husband to pay his wife suitable alimony pending the determination of the action in which she brought a counterclaim asking for a separation. Mrs. Lewis is to have custody of her child pending a decision.

"Several of Mrs. Lewis' brothers are in the stock brokerage business. Her father left her considerable money. In her counterclaim she alleges that in their ten years of married life she has frequently been required to draw on her own resources for household expenses, while her husband expended both time and money with others. She alleged that his latest diversion was a 'Miss Ostriche,' a moving picture actress. From what Mrs. Lewis says about her husband's associations with Miss Ostriche, it is likely that if the wife and Miss Ostriche should meet, some Ostriche feathers would fly...."

Muriel Ostriche recalled her reaction: "William Lewis was my piano teacher. He was my father's age, and he came over once a week to teach me lessons. I had no romantic connection with him, for he was old enough to be my father. Mr. and Mrs. Lewis had parties, and they would invite me to come over to dance. At one of these parties Mrs. Lewis fell in love with her cousin, and William Lewis filed a divorce suit against her. I guess she felt embarrassed and wanted a counterclaim, so she mentioned me—but I certainly had no involvement in any way. In fact, I didn't even know about the situation.

"Then, on the day the article was printed, I ran into Mrs. Lewis on the street. I hadn't seen the paper yet and didn't know the scandal was in the headlines. As she approached me, she tried to look the other way—and I thought, gee, what's the matter with her? Why is she acting so strangely? When I got home I read all about it. I suppose I should have sued her for defamation of character or whatever, but I didn't have enough sense to do that—and, besides, she wouldn't have had much money anyway."

Merely Players, a World film released on August 9, 1918, drew a review in *Moving Picture World*:

"Lulu Case Russell is the author of *Merely Players*, a five-part World photoplay directed by Oscar Apfel and featuring Kitty Gordon. Irving Cummings, George MacQuarrie, Johnny Hines and Muriel Ostriche are the principal members of the supporting company. The story is light and will entertain the large number of persons who are interested in the stage. It also throws more or less light on the professional dramatic critic and the consequences of telling the truth about an aspiring young woman's first attempt at acting.

"In this case, the debut is an absolute failure, and the notices in the morning paper drive the disappointed girl to try to turn on the gas and escape from her heartache by the suicide route. The tragedy is averted just in time, and the critic is given an object lesson in the danger of not sidestepping while reviewing the efforts of well-meaning but misguided attempts to act. In spite of the warning, dramatic critics and screen reviewers will probably keep on their heartless but necessary task of telling the truth—as they understand it.

"*Merely Players* has its dramatic foundation built upon the infatuation of Hollis Foster, a married man, for Nadine Trent, a society lady who is fond of acting in amateur theatricals and who turns her talent to account when Foster's attentions become too pronounced. There are several side issues to the story that are none too well blended, and director Oscar Apfel has worked out a lot of familiar business into the comedy scenes. The acting is generally satisfactory...."

The reviewer for *Variety* enjoyed the film and wrote: "Technically and in other ways the picture is one of the best World has produced in quite a long time."

Muriel Ostriche's next vehicle was *The Road to France*, a World film released on October 14, 1918. Starring Carlyle Blackwell and Evelyn Greeley, the film had a cast which included Jack Drumier, Muriel Ostriche, George DeCarlton, and many others. The title was derived from words spoken earlier by Edward M. Hurley, chairman of the United States Shipping Board: "I want the American people to know our giant shipbuilding industry has sprung up overnight—building the road to France." A thumbnail sketch of the plot was given in *Moving Picture World*: "Tom Whitney, well-connected but a social derelict because of his weakness for drink, is released from the draft because of an old football injury, but a policeman persuades him that he can still do his bit in the shipyards. He takes a job in the yard owned by a man to whose daughter he was engaged in happier times. Three German propagandists seek to foment a strike to delay his work, and largely through Tom's efforts the plan goes amiss and the strike is called off. Rehabilitated by work, the launching of the

Liberty is a forecast of his own rebirth." The same publication noted that while the film was "headed for first honors" in the opening reels, it suffered later "from the infusion of a series of prolonged melodramatic situations of a very unconvincing sort." *Variety* didn't like the principals in the cast, but apparently liked the supporting players: "The picture could have been told in half the footage. Mr. Blackwell as the hero is painstaking but always 'acting.' Miss Greeley does her best with a role of little strength. Other members of the cast perform creditably."

The timing of *The Road to France* was poor. By the time it was released in theatres, the war in Europe had ended, and, as if this was not enough, thousands of theatres were closed because of the nationwide Spanish influenza epidemic. Little was heard of the picture in the weeks following its release.

Around the same time it was announced that Perry N. Vekroff had been added to the staff of directors employed by World. Although an earlier trade notice placed Mr. Vekroff as a Bulgarian, a 1918 statement placed his birth in Alexandria, and his education at Robert College in Constantinople. "His screen career embraces three and half years spent with the American Kinemacolor, Metro, Vitagraph, and others. His first production with the World Company will be *What Love Forgives*."

Internal procedures in the World studios were again the topic of an article in the trade press: "World actors organized to diminish wastage. The actors pledged themselves to make retakes unnecessary, whenever possible; to save time by being prompt at the studio and ready at scenes so that the greatest amount of work can be done in a day, and to have all costumes and clothes ready for scenes in advance. A system of fines was also agreed upon, the fines to go to the Red Cross. When retakes are necessary, the footage will be estimated by a committee and a fine of four cents a foot is to be assessed against the guilty party. A one-dollar fine is to be assessed on each actor who is late if he has no legitimate excuse. A dollar fine will also be levied if the actor is late because of not being made up when the director is ready to shoot a scene. The agreement has been signed by all actors and actresses who are presently employed by the World. Present at the meeting were the following: Montagu Love, Carlyle Blackwell, Evelyn Greeley, Louise Huff, Barbara Castleton, June Elvidge, Madge Evans, Johnny Hines, Frank Mayo, John Bowers, Muriel Ostriche, George MacQuarrie, and Jack Drumier."

Those in attendance apparently comprised just a small part of the staff, for another article issued around the same time noted that 300 actors were at work on four different World films.

Hitting the Trail, released by World on December 2, 1918, again starred Carlyle Blackwell and Evelyn Greeley. This melodrama of New York City's East Side was reviewed indifferently by *Moving Picture World*, which noted that "there is not a great deal of suspense at any time." Similarly, *Variety* found fault with the script and its subject, however there was a bright spot: "Muriel Ostriche is particularly good." The cast also included Joseph Smiley, George MacQuarrie, Mabel Bunyea, Edward Elkas, and Walter Green.

Photoplay in its December 1918 issue gave Muriel's horoscope, apparently not knowing she had been married since the first part of the year: "This native came to this world to be a mother of a very high order. I have never seen such a strong tendency in any nativity to be always mothering somebody, but strange as it may seem, she should not have the care of children; she would be too good to them and they in return would become unruly under her guidance. In the drama, she will do well in parts in which she has to suffer from her children's cruelty and neglect, from the loss of fortune and from the injustice of her parents who may drive her away from her home. She is musical, poetical, mystically inclined and very quick-witted. This nativity does not indicate much money earned or even saved from the earnings, but it does point out a number of legacies left her from father, mother, and husband, or someone who holds a public position. Marriage should be very pleasant. The husband will have much worldly goods and will be a leader. In 1918 and 1919 she will have several offers of marriage, two from men over fifty, which are good matches, but the *real* man whom she will marry for love will be about her own age."

What Love Forgives, a World film directed by Perry N. Vekroff, opened on January 6, 1919. Barbara Castleton and Johnny Hines were the stars, supported by John Bowers, Bobby Connelly, Florence Coventry, Muriel Ostriche, Hazel Coates, and Joe Smiley. "Situations and titles leave nothing to the imagination, and there is a lot of mawkish sentimentality," noted *Variety*, which went on to praise Muriel Ostriche's performance: "Muriel Ostriche stands out. Miss Ostriche is especially excellent in the character which has little that is likeable in it. As Dorothy Deal she is the star in a road company who is willing to go any length in the 'interest of her profession,' with the result that she becomes the mistress of a young college song writer, then later becomes the wife of the man whose daughter the collegiate marries." Barbara Castleton's performance in the same review received commendation, but the others overacted, it was said.

The Bluffer, a World film released on January 20, 1919, was directed by Travers Vale and starred June Elvidge and Irving Cummings. Muriel Ostriche, George MacQuarrie, Elizabeth Garrison, Louis Grisel, Jack Raymond, Jack Davidson, and others made up the supporting cast. "Sybil Van Norden [June Elvidge] discovers herself penniless on the death of her father. Vaughan [Irving Cummings], her father's partner, whom he cheated along with the others, advises her to bluff it through, and, innocent of the world, it is all that Sybil can do. The money lender stakes her and she makes a match with a supposed catch only to find that he is a bluffer, like herself, and he forces her to prey upon Moran [George MacQuarrie], a wealthy westerner. It is Vaughan who finally rescues her from the quicksand and leads her to happiness, but not until her adventures have been many and desperate," noted *Moving Picture World*, which also praised the film as being "well made and quite absorbing of the plot."

In February 1919, a reporter for *Moving Picture World* visited Fort Lee to observe the activity there. After finding the Universal, Paragon, and Fox studios in varying degrees of inactivity or desertion, he visited World's Peerless studio. There everything was in excellent order: "Mr. Rosenthal took us through the plant. On entering the studio we ran into Carlyle Blackwell, who had just finished a scene under the direction of Dell Henderson. We were impressed with the system and every department in the place. The properties were catalogued and kept in cases with glass doors, very much like a museum or the Smithsonian Institution.

Above: Muriel Ostriche, in her New York City apartment at 13 Gramercy Place, is shown at the keyboard of a Knabe Ampico reproducing grand piano, which she purchased for $3,000.

Right: Muriel looks small standing at the door of the passenger compartment of her Mitchell limousine. (The four illustrations on this page are from an article, "How a Star Spends Her Time," published in the *Photo-Play Journal*, May 1919)

Above: Muriel's Stutz car was a gift from her husband ("but using my money," she recalled).

Left: the actress rehearses a scene with a dummy and director Perry N. Vekroff.

It was fascinating to inspect the innumerable items—antiques, bric-a-brac, zoological specimens, tapestry, tableware, and everything else under the sun. . . . At 1:30 we were on our way to Coytesville. About a mile and a half walk and we were there. The Solax Studio presented an inviting appearance. Everything about it was in excellent shape, but no evidences of life were in sight. Approaching the entrance, we were greeted by an Italian caretaker, who told us the place was deserted and nothing was doing."

Muriel Ostriche's next World Film was *The Moral Deadline*, released on February 24, 1919. Again, Travers Vale was the director. In the starring roles were June Elvidge and Frank Mayo, supported by a large cast, including Muriel Ostriche in the part of Barbara Van Vliets.

"It is the old hackneyed scene of the shopgirl who marries the son of a financier, under an assumed name, and the latter is cut off by his father," noted a synopsis in *Variety*. "The hero goes through almost the whole list of melodramatic situations, even to being caught in a waterfront dive and shanghaied. Miss Elvidge is Evelyn Merrill, the young woman who falls in love with a millionaire's son, finally securing happiness, and making the most of her 'virtue triumphs in the end' part. It is not a particularly pleasing role, and although well done, the situations are so commonplace they fail to hold." The same publication noted that "the production is far better than the story," while *Moving Picture World* considered the plot to be "of a commonplace character, possessing little dramatic or humorous appeal—it has, at the same time, well defined narrative interests which will give it considerable entertainment value for many people." Neither review mentioned Muriel Ostriche's performance.

The Hand Invisible, released on March 17, 1919, was Muriel Ostriche's last film with World. The feature roles were played by Montagu Love and Virginia Hammond, assisted by a half dozen or more others, including Muriel Ostriche in the part of Helen Haynes. The story was of a magnate in the steel industry who wants an heir, but his wife cannot have children. He divorces her and subsequently forces his attention upon a debutante who is in love with a young miner, but who is finally coerced to the altar, a ceremony made easier when the miner is killed on the eve of the wedding. A child is born, and her husband worships it, but the debutante dies shortly thereafter. Years go on, and the son grows up and becomes a leading figure at his college. It turns out that he is really the son of the debutante's miner boyfriend and not of the steel executive. The wealthy man tries to change his will, but is paralyzed while attempting it.

By this time, Muriel Ostriche had been reduced to playing minor parts for World. When her contract came up for renewal they let her go. At the same time, the fortunes of the World Film Corporation were waning, numerous other actors and actresses were dismissed, public reception to its features was poor, and within a year the company was out of business.

Toward the end of 1918, Muriel Ostriche made an arrangement with a publicist, Regina B. Kruh, who subsequently wrote many articles concerning her. "A Little Bird-Girl," which appeared in the *Photo-Play Journal*, February 1919, is typical:

"If childish dreams came true, Muriel Ostriche would be sitting behind a desk in a schoolroom teaching kiddies 'stepping stones to literature,' instead of appearing nightly on the screen, much to the joy of thousands of movie fans.

"Miss Ostriche confided to me that her first great ambition was to be a teacher. That ambition promised to dominate her life; in fact, so keen were her desires in this direction that every opportunity which presented itself found Muriel gathering together rows of chairs, pretending they were her pupils. With the stage set in that manner, she was in the habit of studying her lessons.

" 'No, I never dreamed of being an actress,' laughed Muriel, as she made herself comfortable among the rose-colored cushions. 'If I could have looked into the future and had seen that I would not have had about 40 youngsters of different degress of raggedness under my care, I would not have thought it worthwhile growing up.

" 'Every day I assembled the chairs in my playroom and started the morning's lessons, naming each chair a child—Geraldine and Joan being my favorites. This 'intellectual' habit often proved embarrassing to my mother. I recall one instance when the president of her club called very unexpectedly. She was most anxious to make the visit a success, and when she cordially invited her to be seated, our visitor looked around, mother's glance following hers and, much to her dismay, discovered for the first time that the room was empty of chairs—Geraldine and Joan, Billy, Gladys, and Arthur had been called to school.'

"But there was more of the school girl than of the teacher about Miss Ostriche, as she entertained me in her beautiful drawing room where 'Geraldine and Joan' of the early days have given place to big, heavy Jacobean chairs. Her beautiful apartment is in one of the most exclusive sections in New York, known as Gramercy Park, where only the oldest and best families reside, and the place is most significant of Miss Ostriche's individuality. I wish I could adequately explain what a bright, sweet, happy-looking home it is. You enter a foyer, which is lined from floor to ceiling with books. This leads into her drawing room, and the first thing that captures your eyes is a long, beautifully carved table upon which is a rare peachblow vase. The walls are covered with etchings, also watercolors, pleasantly tinted in flower-like shades. Built into the wall is an open-brick fireplace which always gives such a warm glow to the room. Then there is a large divan massed with cushions, and in the far-end corner a Grande Welte-Mignon piano [actually a Knabe Ampico piano, which cost Muriel $3,000 and which was sold years later "for a song" when it stopped working] which affords this little star many happy hours.

"Miss Ostriche was born and educated in New York. While she was still a slip of a child she used to go to the Biograph studios after school to play extra parts, and it was here that she first secured a firm footing as her medium in pictures, and figured in many of this company's productions. The Biograph kept her busy until finally she left school and gave most of her time to the silver sheet. Her mother engaged a private tutor for her and thus she completed her studies, which included French and a thorough course in music. Then she was engaged in stock under the Eclair auspices, and one year later went to Thanhouser, where she played leads; in fact, she had her own company, the

Muriel Ostriche, studio portrait
(Georgetown University Library)

pictures being known and released under the name of Princess Films.

"From Thanhouser the World Film offered her an attractive contract. Her favorite picture is *A Daughter of the Sea*, and among her best-known and recent successes are *Journey's End*, *By Whose Hand?*, *A Circus Romance*, *Moral Courage*, *Tinsel*, and *Hitting the Trail*, with Carlyle Blackwell.

"Our little World star has wonderful golden hair and deep blue eyes, and if you are not a movie fan and do not know her pictures by that medium, you surely know her as the 'Moxie Girl,' for that is who she is, and it is her smiling, lovely face which gazes upon you from the Moxie sheet.

"She is fond of reading. As I saw her open book on the table I noticed it was not one of the popular novels of the day, but Sir Oliver Lodge's book on 'Spiritualism.' Almost every one of her books shows that it has been in the hands of an exhaustive reader, not the property of one who treasures books as a mere ornament.

"Miss Ostriche loves the theatre—every phase of it—and pictures most of all. She says pictures fascinate her to such a degree that if she were not a screen personage herself she thinks she would spend most of her time at the movies. She has no divided ambitions and has never attempted to go off in a tangent or follow false gods. Her career has simplified itself into an unswerving drive to overcome the obstacles encountered in the profession, and to surmount every day until she has finally attained the highest eminence known to the picture profession; and so she studies and works with the one idea of perfecting herself as much as possible in her art—an art which has already been so enriched by her presence and which has every right to expect much from her.

"But, studious and industrious as she is, Miss Ostriche still takes a keen interest in amusement and recreation, for she figures that these are a necessary respite from hard labor and a requisite to the best effort. She has two automobiles—a Mitchell and a Stutz—both of which she drives herself.

" 'I believe,' she concluded laughingly, 'that if dire necessity drove me to it, I could manage to earn an existence from my knowledge of cars and how to run them.'

"With this I made my exit, and as I came back to my little cubby-hole, I was still so enrapt with her charm that I looked around the room and it seemed to be filled with her magnetic presence."

In March 1919, Muriel Ostriche, in the company of her publicist, Regina Kruh, went to New England and was feted in several theatre appearances. Muriel remembered Regina:

"We went to Boston together. We appeared at the Park Theatre, where the manager—his first name was Tom—with an Italian last name [Sorerio]—a really wonderful fellow—treated us royally. After I finished my stage performance Regina and I went somewhere to dance and listen to music and to have a drink. Two fellows came over to ask us to dance, and I remember that both of them danced very well. Before I knew it, I fainted, and I was taken back to my hotel, where a doctor came to see me. I remember that Regina and the two fellows we danced with came up to see me as well.

"Regina was with me for just a short time, for the publicity agent idea didn't work out. Years later I met her at the Algonquin Hotel in New York City, and we had lunch together. She asked me if I remembered when the two fellows asked us to dance when we were traveling together in Boston. I said I did, and she said, 'Well, I married one of them.'

"I then went back to Boston again. I remember being driven around in a gold Cadillac."

The *Boston Post* in March 1919 carried this story: "Muriel Ostriche, who is not only beautiful in the face and figure and an accomplished actress, but is known all over the world as 'The Moxie Girl,' will assume a dual capacity this week at the Park and Franklin Park theatres. She will be seen in a photoplay and will also appear in person, giving a brief talk to the audiences on timely topics. In her honor The Moxie Company will put at her disposal a golden car driven by Brig Young, and in this gorgeous vehicle Miss Ostriche will be conveyed from one theatre to the other."

A subsequent story told more: "The star came to Lowell accompanied by General Manager Sorerio, and between the afternoon and evening performances made a run up to Nashua, New Hampshire where they were entertained as guests of the Nashua Country Club at a dinner party.

"Miss Ostriche came to town in the Moxie "gold car" and after a short sightseeing trip around the city—the real home of Moxie—reached the Strand for the first performance of the afternoon. She was introduced to the audience by manager Sorerio and her presentation was marked by a genuine welcome from all. She spoke of the motion picture business—its trials and tribulations, as well as its pleasures and comforts—and told a few amusing stories about herself and some of the other stars of filmdom. Later she held a reception in the lobby of the theatre and met personally a majority of the patrons. The same schedule was carried out at the night performance. In connection with her presence on the stage, a short film in which she appeared was shown on the screen. It gave the audiences an opportunity of seeing Miss Ostriche as a 'reel star' and in 'real life.' The comparison was interesting indeed."

In New Hampshire, the *Nashua Telegraph* took notice of Miss Ostriche's visit:

"LITTLE MOXIE GIRL GREETED BY THOUSANDS. Muriel Ostriche, the winsome little Moxie Girl, famed as a World movie star, came to Nashua, liked the city, appeared at two performances at the Park Theatre, dined at Nashua's famous Country Club, and departed having made many new friends among her myriads of screen admirers.

"When you say that Muriel is a winsome little miss she is just that. As movie queen she is certainly a stellar attraction, and Manager Thomas of the Park is to be congratulated at adding this attraction to the many excellent features he is introducing to Nashua audiences.

"Muriel has been touring New England in a gold car—a Moxie car. Of course it isn't all gold, that is the wheels are just

Boston's Park Theater welcomes Muriel Ostriche with her name in lights. Muriel, shown sitting on the running board of the Moxie Gold Car, was hosted by new England's most famous soft drink. On stage she told the audience anecdotes and experiences of her movie career. The film *Wilson or the Kaiser*, also mentioned on the marquee, is unrelated.

Muriel Ostriche, in a star-spangled dress and wearing a wreath in her hair, campaigned on behalf of the war effort.

This advertisement placed by the Strand Theatre, Chelsea, Massachusetts invites patrons to "the first appearance of a movie star in Chelsea." Two thousand hand-held cardboard fans were to be given away, each bearing Muriel Ostriche's portrait.

ordinary auto wheels and the tires are of rubber and the windshield is glass and iron, the top is leather, and so on, but the body panels are finished in gold leaf as are the tire supports, the wheel hubs, mud guards, hood cover, and various and anon features converting a big Cadillac roadster into an automobile attraction that makes everyone who sees it sit up and take notice.

"And Muriel can certainly drive that car. She has driven it over a part of New England already and she's going to run up a few more miles before she gets back to business at the New Jersey studio.

"Tuesday Muriel came from Lowell to Nashua. In the Spindle City [Lowell], she was met by a Nashua reception committee who saw her perform at the Strand Theatre. Then Muriel got into one of Howard Hartman's Franklin sedans and, taking hold of the wheel, headed for Nashua. It certainly was some ride. Muriel thought the road from Nashua to Lowell was dandy, particularly the stretch from the state line to the city. Every few moments on the auto ride to this city she would exclaim about this and that feature of the Franklin car. She says it's a great car to ride in, and a perfectly wonderful one to drive. And these were not idle words as Muriel is to have a fine new closed model Franklin of her own, all finished in the nattiest of colors and upholstery. She says that when she is behind a Franklin wheel she has no fear of traffic cops or anything. The car simply has to glide along, and Muriel certainly knows how to make it glide.

"Her appearance in film and on the stage brought forth rounds of applause from a crowded house, while the clerks in the stores and operatives in the factories could hardly wait until evening to get a real view of a real live screen favorite.

"The evening performance was greeted by a house that tested the seating capacity to the limit. Muriel's entrance upon the stage was greeted by storms of applause."

Muriel Ostriche made the news in the *Providence Bulletin* on April 19, 1919:

"MURIEL OSTRICHE AND HER $25,000 GOWN TO APPEAR. Muriel Ostriche with her $25,000 gown, and Olive Thomas, movie star, whom Harrison Fisher, the artist, has pronounced the most beautiful girl in America, are among the latest photoplay notables who have sent word to the movie ball committee that they will come to this city for the benefit to be given in the State Armory, April 24, for the Fatherless Children of France Fund. . . . One of the side features will be the taking of moving pictures of the stars as they arrive in this city and while they are at the Armory."

Around this time, Muriel Ostriche, who posed for a photographer while draped in an American flag and wearing a victory wreath in her hair, helped sell bonds and raise money for the relief of war orphans.

On July 4, 1919, it was announced that Miss Ostriche would appear in Boston again:

"PARK THEATRE PATRONS TO SEE MISS OSTRICHE. The patrons of the Park Theatre this week will have a chance to see Miss Muriel Ostriche herself, who will appear in person on Monday afternoon and evening at the Park Theatre. . . . Miss Ostriche is well known all over the country as The Moxie Girl and is one of the most beautiful stars on the screen today. Manager Thomas D. Sorerio of the Park Theatre is giving away on Monday 1,000 fancy china ice cream dishes with Miss Ostriche's picture painted on each one."

For Bonnie-B, an imported hair net, Muriel Ostriche appeared in a July 1919 advertisement in *The Motion Picture Magazine*. Muriel was shown seated at her dressing table, mirror in hand, and, in another pose, lounging on a sofa. "I appeared in their ads, but they never paid me," Muriel recalled years later.

In the meantime the *Photo-Play Journal* carried another article by Regina B. Kruh, "When A Dance Partner was a Girl's Hero," which told of Muriel's favorite pastime:

" 'I want to dance!'

"These words were uttered in the tone of one who knows what she wants when she wants it; the scene was laid in a staid New England city; the actress attracted a fair representation of the elite of the place; the lion of the occasion (or shall we say lioness) was Muriel Ostriche.

"The social leaders of the city had paid her homage; influential political lights of the city chatted with her; the great literary celebrities who had helped to make the place famous beamed upon her and told her how much they admired her. One after another the feminine element of the assembly told her how much they liked her and questioned her about New York and its fashions; one after another the male portion inquired about her work and vied with each other in paying her pretty compliments.

"The little star was charming through the whole ordeal, she smiled on everyone, answered their questions with a great show of patience and furnished them with enough information to supply them with a general knowledge of all the little details of the screen star's routine. But, when the inevitable lull came, she simply forgot all politeness—just simply cast aside all pose—stamped her little foot—and exclaimed so that the whole assembly was bound to hear:

" 'I want to dance!'

"The reception she received everywhere was quite enough to turn the head of any sane and sensible young woman, but Muriel is really very modest—and she has returned to Broadway not one bit more conceited than when she went away, and those who know her will concede that conceit was never one of her failings. It seemed almost as though every city was bent on entertaining its guest on a more lavish scale than that which had marked her reception in the other cities. A famous hero returning from 'over there' could hardly have received a more royal welcome, yet, ever and anon, from out of a clear sky, the proceedings would be interrupted with her irresistible: 'Oh, I want to dance!'

"That tour of New England will long be remembered. It will be remembered by Muriel in the quiet after-years when she goes over the pleasant chapters in Life's Book; it will be remembered by the thousands who saw her, and by many who had the privilege of meeting her personally and conversing with her. But, while many will recall Muriel for her pretty ways, her quaint sociability and her wise little sayings, there will be others who will remember her longer and think of her oftener as the girl who always wanted to dance. . . ."

CHAPTER EIGHT

Later Films

After a hiatus which spanned most of the spring and all of the summer of 1919, Muriel returned to films. An article in the September 27, 1919 issue of *Moving Picture World* noted:

"Emily Stevens and Muriel Ostriche will be seen in Schomer's latest film, *The Sacred Flame*. With many of the big dramatic scenes, in which the star and leading man are chiefly concerned, completed for the new feature *The Sacred Flame*, (Abraham S. Schomer's latest offering as author and director) announcement is made of the addition of several new members to the already big cast. Director Schomer, of Schomer-Ross Productions, Inc., has already started work with them at the Biograph Studios [which were available for rental at the time]. . . .

"Emily Stevens returns to the screen after an absence of some months to star in the picture, and Earl Schenck is the leading man. Miss Stevens is enthusiastic about the story, declaring that it gives her one of the best dramatic chances of her life.

"A notable addition to the cast is Muriel Ostriche, who needs no introduction to screen devotees. She has been seen as ingenue and leading woman in Thanhouser, World, and Vitagraph productions and is to play the ingenue role in the new feature. Like Miss Stevens this, too, is in the way of a return to the screen, for Miss Ostriche has devoted almost her entire time for two years to the Stage Woman's War Relief, having gained a special commendation for her success in obtaining re-employment for soldiers and sailors. The most appreciated of all of her commendations, Miss Ostriche confesses, is the praise she received from her brother [actually, her brother-in-law] Major Thomas J. Brady, of the old Seventh Regiment, who served abroad with the 107th Infantry.

"Muriel Ostriche has been before the public since she played child's parts with the old Biograph. Then, too, she is the 'Moxie Girl' and has been leading woman for many notable screen productions since she has 'grown up,' if one can call this 90-pound beauty grown up. Among the best known of the screen plays in which she has been leading woman are *A Daughter of the Sea*, *Journey's End*, *By Whose Hand?*, *A Circus Romance*, *Moral Courage*, *Tinsel*, and *Hitting the Trail*."

Abraham S. Schomer, a writer, announced his entry into motion pictures a year earlier, in August 1918, with the establishment of the Schomer Photoplay Producing Company, located at 1440 Broadway. The firm later evolved into the Schomer-Ross Company, which announced that it would produce four special features a year to be sold on a states' rights basis. "This concern has entered the field on a large scale, and an extensive exploitation and publicity campaign has been inaugurated," a trade release noted. In 1919, the firm maintained offices at 126 West 46th Street, New York City.

Before *The Sacred Flame* was screened, the public had a chance to see Muriel Ostriche in another role, as a dancer in the only stage production of her adult life, a musical titled *Dream Girl*. *The Billboard* told of the event:

"MURIEL OSTRICHE TO STAR IN MUSICAL COMEDY. WILL MAKE DEBUT IN *DREAM GIRL*, BRAND NEW PLAY, SPONSORED BY POPULAR PRODUCTIONS, INC. Everything is in complete readiness for the debut of Muriel Ostriche as a musical comedy star in a brand new musical play titled *Dream Girl*, which is the joint work of Walter Irving and Arthur C. King, the initial performance taking place in the Lyceum Theatre, Paterson, New Jersey, October 13.

"The Popular Productions, Inc. is sponsoring the Ostriche show which will have an attractive feminine chorus of sixty voices, with everything new, including the scenery, wardrobe and equipment. The Popular Productions, Inc. has routed *Dream Girl* through one-night stands adjacent to New York preparatory to whipping the show into perfect shape for its forthcoming New York premiere.

"Miss Ostriche has long been a motion picture star, her work with World and Thanhouser subjects being well remembered by the movie fans. A large, capable, and competent cast surrounds her with such 'names' from the big musical revues and legitimate realm as Paul E. Burns, late of *Fiddlers Three*; George Leonard, from *A Royal Vagabond*; Edward S. Forbes, recently of *Oh Boy*; Ely Dawson, late of George White's *Scandals of 1919*; Fay Tunis of Lew Fields's show, *A Lonely Romeo*; Gene Leoni, Bobbi Lorens, Barry Melton, Matty Scanlon, etc. . . .

"James Gorman has put on the dances, and among some of the big numbers Miss Ostriche will be given a chance to display her singing and dancing ability.... The Popular Productions, Inc. plans to make a picture production of *Dream Girl*, with Miss Ostriche as the picture star, the photoplay proposition to feature the New York opening of the show."

Muriel Ostriche remembered the production:

"The play had its problems. Apparently, the producers hadn't paid their bills, and after four or five performances were given, creditors came and took away the scenery and props."

The Sacred Flame, produced by Schomer-Ross, was released on November 8, 1919. Earlier, a special preview had been given for the trade. "Fred," the reviewer for *Variety*, did not like it at all:

"The cast included Emily Stevens, Muriel Ostriche, Maud Hill, Violet Axzelle, Earl Schenck, Lionel Adams, Frederick Clayton, and James P. Laffey. The Schomer-Ross Productions, Inc., gave a pre-release showing of their latest feature, *The Sacred Flame*, at Wurlitzer Hall. The feature is a six-reel production, with Emily Stevens starred. Abraham S. Schomer is the author and director of the picture.

"At present there are three facts that stand out regarding the picture. They are that it needs 1,500 feet cut out of the early part of the film, that it needs retitling, that a couple of hundred feet showing the headstone and graveyard sets at the end of the picture need to be lopped off.

"The first three reels of the picture are all devoted to a lengthy preamble to the real plot of the story. Then when the story gets started the end is in sight from the first. With a lot of preliminary deleted, and the action gotten to after about a reel of introductory, the picture will be one that will get by. The trouble with the titling is that the subtitles are virtually a calendar. It is a case of 'That Night,' 'Three Months Later,' 'The Next Day,' 'After Three Years', etc. A constant repetition of these makes the picture rather tiresome. The reading titles are stilted, suggesting that they were originally written in a foreign tongue and are literal translations.

"Tacked onto the finish of the picture there is a scene showing the setting of a headstone over the grave of the man who is loved by the heroine, but who jilted her after she had made possible his rise in the world. This is all wrong, and the story might have been chopped a short time after he dropped dead in the cabaret scene. That is the finish of the story.

"Abraham Schomer has taken for his theme the sacred flame of love, maintaining that whatever else happens in this life, it is but a contributory factor to love. In this case a high school teacher is loved by a doctor, but she in turn falls in love with a down-and-out friend of his and finances him through law school. They are engaged to be married after he has 'arrived,' but at that time he jilts her in favor of the daughter of the head of the corporation which employs him as legal advisor. The doctor again takes up his suit and is successful. The former lover becomes jealous and, finally, when he sees them both together, drops dead of heart failure.

"The direction at the hands of the author does not advance the story speedily enough, and there are repeats of bits of action that should be eliminated. Especially the bit of looking at the watch. He is also negligent of his detail. One of the glowing errors is the use of the daughter of the doctor. The girl is about four years old at the opening of the picture, and during the time that it takes to tell the story (approximately six years, judging from the calendar titles) she remains at the same age.

"Emily Stevens gives a corking performance as the heroine in the story, with Muriel Ostriche in a light bit that suited her perfectly. Earl Schenck plays the heavy lead, while Lionel Adams is the doctor. There was considerable money spent on the production, but as a six-reeler there is little in it that will get it back...."

The Sacred Flame was a failure, although trade paper advertisements for the next two or three months noted that it was "selling well."

Toward the end of 1919, Muriel Ostriche made an accounting of her earnings earlier as a child actress. She determined that her income from films had been approximately $32,400. Although her endorsement appeared in various advertisements for cosmetics and beauty aids, her remuneration from these was insignificant. In one instance, that of Sempre Giovine, her name and those of other Thanhouser players was used without permission.

Following her stint with Schomer-Ross, Muriel Ostriche signed up with Arrow Film Corporation, a firm which had been formed in the autumn of 1915 when the Shallenberger brothers (of Thanhouser connection) announced that production would begin at the old Standard Studio in Yonkers, while executive offices would be at 71 West 23rd Street, New York City. "Internationally famous stars of the stage and screen will be seen in forthcoming Arrow releases," a trade notice related. "The stories will be written especially for Arrow pictures by the best known and capable American authors and playwrights. These stories will be put in scenario form under the plan developed by W. E. Shallenberger for the perfect coordination of all units of production, collaboration by story writer, scenario writer, and director."

The firm later increased its capitalization from $30,000 to $350,000. Formerly a New York corporation, it was reorganized under the laws of Virginia, with W. E. Shallenberger as president. During the next year, John F. Shallenberger, another brother, joined Wilbert and W. Edgar in the enterprise. Albert S. LeVino was at one time secretary and treasurer and assisted the president in various ways. Extensive plans were announced to the press.

Moving Picture World, in its issue of June 5, 1920, noted: "Arrow preparing big exploitation campaign for several new subjects.... The campaign will include the Muriel Ostriche two-reel comedies, which Arvid Gillstrom is directing. Vide Dudley has written several of the stories. They are being offered for release beginning about the 15th of June."

Another article noted: "Work on the series of Muriel Ostriche two-reel comedies to be released by Arrow is already well underway at Fort Lee, New Jersey, and the tentative titles of the first of a series of twelve are *Betty Sets the Pace* and *Love Birds*.

"Arvid Gillstrom will direct the entire series. Mr. Gillstrom needs no introduction in the comedy field of motion pictures, inasmuch as he has directed this type of screen production for several years. Muriel Ostriche has had leading parts in many productions for the large producing companies...."

Mr. Shallenberger announces the sale of the rights for the series of twelve for the following territories: New York, northern New Jersey and eastern Pennsylvania, southern New Jersey. . . . The comedies are said to be of the highest quality and appeal to the old and young."

Another notice related: "Arrow expects great results from Gillstrom. President Shallenberger of Arrow is enthusiastic over the prospects for Arvid E. Gillstrom-directed comedies starring Muriel Ostriche. July 15 is the date set for the first release of the series." *Moving Picture World*, July 3, 1920, presented a full-page advertisement showing Muriel Ostriche hugging a man, captioned: "She will treat your audience the same way!—They will be 'wrapped up' in her. Garnette Sabin presents MURIEL OSTRICHE in two-reel, high-class comedies. Filling that want with comedies is as near the 'one hundred percent perfect' as human endeavor can achieve."

The same issue noted that S. Rubenstein, a special representative of the Arrow Film Corporation, "will leave for a trip through the South and East, calling on the independent exchanges in Atlanta, Philadelphia, Washington, and other cities. Mr. Rubenstein will concentrate on this trip on the Ostriche comedies which are distributed by Arrow."

The July 24, 1920 issue of the same magazine gave more information:

"REMAINING MURIEL OSTRICHE COMEDIES WILL BE FILMED ON THE PACIFIC COAST. The remainder of the series of Muriel Ostriche comedies will be produced on the West Coast, according to an announcement from the Arrow offices this week. Garnette Sabin, who is producing the comedies, expects to leave for Los Angeles on August 1. Three of the Ostriche comedies have been produced in the East. They are: *Betty Sets the Pace*, *Betty's Green-Eyed Monster*, and *Betty's Husband*.

"The Ostriche comedies have been sold in practically every important territory and have been booked in leading theatres. Arvid Gillstrom, director, will go to the Coast with the Ostriche company, as will Garnette Sabin and her little daughter Barbara. Barbara Sabin has been given a role in each of the comedies produced to date."

Another trade paper notice related: "Loew Books Ostriche Comedies: An announcement is made by the Arrow Film Corporation that Mrs. Garnette Sabin, producer of the Arrow Muriel Ostriche Comedies, has completely recovered from her illness and has resumed production of the comedies. The series has been booked over the entire Marcus Loew circuit where it is meeting with much approval it is said."

An autumn notice stated: "Word has been received at the Arrow offices from Mrs. Garnette Sabin, producer of the Arrow Muriel Ostriche Comedies, that Lucien Tainguy and Ollie Leach have been engaged to photograph the next Muriel Ostriche comedy, the production of which has begun. Both Mr. Tainguy and Mr. Leach are well-known cinematographers, who have reputations for turning out good work, it is said."

Muriel Ostriche recalled Garnette Sabin: "She and her daughter had an apartment next to me and my husband in the Hamilton Hotel on West 73rd Street, where I moved after leaving Gramercy Place. She approached me about starting an independent film company, and I agreed. As I recall, we made three movies—all comedies—one in Atlanta, Georgia, and the other two in New York City."

Around this time many advertisements were placed by Muriel Ostriche Productions, located at 141 West 73rd Street, with studios at 512-14-16 West 53rd Street, New York City, headed by Garnette Sabin.

A testimonial on behalf of *Moving Picture World*, dated September 29, 1920, was signed by Garnette Sabin: "Having been connected with the moving picture industry for some time, my interest in moving picture trade papers has been more than cursory, and since I have been producing the Muriel Ostriche Comedies for the Arrow Film Corporation, it has been a matter of careful study with me. As a result of this study I have been forced to the conclusion that the *Moving Picture World* is far and away the best publication in the field. . . ."

In November it was announced that rights to the Muriel Ostriche Comedies had been sold to the Luporini Brothers for showing in Italy and to Horsfall Productions for distribution in eastern Canada. A trade notice about a deal between Arrow Film Corporation and Ritchey Lithograph Company told of a $75,000 transaction for a complete line of posters, including those for twelve Muriel Ostriche two-reel comedies. The next month, December 1920, it was related that Muriel Ostriche Comedies had been sold for projection throughout the United Kingdom.

The Muriel Ostriche Comedies, despite the enthusiastic advertising given to them, were short-lived. It is believed that only a few of the twelve announced subjects were ever made, although a subsequent trade notice declared that ten of the films were ready for distribution.

In 1921, Muriel Ostriche signed up with another film enterprise, as announced in the April 16th issue of *Moving Picture World*: "FORWARD WILL HANDLE TEN SALIENT FILMS FEATURING MURIEL OSTRICHE. Max F. C. Goosman, president of Salient Films, Inc. announces that a series of ten productions featuring Muriel Ostriche will be distributed by Forward Film Distributors, Inc., of 110 West 40th Street, New York, of which J. Joseph Sameth is president. Involving as it does ten feature productions, this is one of the largest recent deals in the states rights market.

"The first production, *The Shadow*, written and directed by J. Charles Davis, is ready for distribution. 'Satisfied that Miss Ostriche had established a box office reputation,' said Mr. Goosman , we started to work on the series, and independent exchanges will see a new Muriel Ostriche, for she has been given a story and setting especially adapted to her ability. *The Shadow* is a production that speaks for itself, but before closing the contract with Mr. Sameth, we planned a nationwide advertising and exploitation campaign. We promised productions worthy of the Salient trademark and have kept our promise.'

"Max F. C. Goosman, directing Salient Films, Inc. is well-known in the film world. He has been with some of the largest companies and recently resigned from Robertson-Cole to assume his present position. J. Charles Davis has had seven years of experience in various branches of the industry, having been advertising manager, special writer, exchange man, assistant director,

Garnette Sabin, who formed Muriel Ostriche Productions, announced a series of two-reel "high-class comedies" in this advertisement in the July 3, 1920 issue of *Moving Picture World.* Although it was announced that 12 films were to be made, no more than four or five were ever produced. Distribution was through the Arrow Film Corporation, a firm controlled by Dr. Wilbert E. Shallenberger, who had earlier been associated with Thanhouser.

director and producer. He has been connected with Famous Players and more recently with Arrow Film Corporation. Mr. Sameth is making elaborate plans for immediate release of The Shadow." Separately, Mr. Sameth told a reporter: "I consider The Shadow a big bet, and with Muriel Ostriche in the lead, I am confident that it will go over big."

It was stated that numerous requests for the film had been received from distributors. On May 21, 1921, *Moving Picture World* noted that The Shadow was ready for distribution and that press books, accessories, and other advertising and exploitation material had been sent to independent buyers. The press book was written by Jack Reilley and Tom Monroe. On July 19th, the same publication noted that "Forward Film Distributors report a sale a day has been attained during the past ten days for three of its productions. *The Shadow*, starring Muriel Ostriche, has been purchased by Griever Productions for northern Illinois and Indiana; Boston's Photoplay Company for New England, and Exhibitors Film and Service Company for New York." In June it was announced that J. Charles Davis, who wrote and directed The Shadow, was assembling a cast and preparing to start work on the second Salient feature, tentatively titled *The Call of the Open*. No players were identified.

Early in the morning of July 3, 1922, Muriel's mother, Mrs. Miriam Oestrich, jumped or fell from an eighth floor window in the Hotel Wellington, Albany, New York. Muriel and her husband were asleep at the time in an adjoining room. Mrs. Oestrich, widowed, lived in the Hotel Gotham, New York City, and was in ill health. At the time of her death she was on her way to Saratoga with the Bradys. The group had planned to continue to the Berkshires, where Muriel, who was pregnant, intended to spend the rest of the summer with her mother.

On September 26, 1922, a daughter, Gloria, was born to Mr. and Mrs. Frank A. Brady, followed by the birth of another daughter, Mollie, on October 28, 1923. "My daughter Mollie was christened Mary Alexander Brady in the Catholic Church at 72nd Street and Broadway," recalled Muriel. "She was named after my actress friend, Mollie King Alexander, who was professionally known as Mollie King. Kenneth Alexander was her godfather. Mollie King was my best friend from the movies, and we saw each other for many years afterward."

"After Gloria was born, Frank and I were still living in New York City. Later we moved to Great Neck, Long Island. Babe Ruth, the baseball star, had an apartment near us in New York City, and he would often come over to visit and to see Gloria. One morning, when Frank was away, Babe Ruth stopped by to suggest that we should be more than platonic friends. He asked me what I thought of the idea, and I said, 'Not much.' He had quite a reputation as a ladies' man. On another occasion, for one reason or another, Babe Ruth stayed over with us one evening and was asleep on the living room sofa when our cleaning lady came in. Later, she said, 'That man on the sofa looked a lot like Babe Ruth.' 'It was Babe Ruth,' I told her.

Trouble developed between the Bradys. A fictionalized "here is what *might* have happened" article in *The American Weekly* in 1925, titled "Mrs. Brady's New Idea of Married Life," noted:

"Six years ago the Frank A. Bradys, who live down in the smart Great Neck, Long Island colony of artists, stagefolk, writers and thinkers, were married. Mr. Brady is a very clever and successful young architect. Mrs. Brady was Muriel Ostriche, the youngest grown-up motion picture actress in the world, and successful star of *Kennedy Square, Mortmain, Daughter of the Sea*, and a dozen more first-rate pictures. Now she is going back again to the screen.

"For six years the Bradys played the game of married life according to the best accepted standards. They teed off in perfect harmony, and in due course the little twosome became first a threesome and then a foursome.

"Mrs. Brady put her career in a closet and locked the door on it. During those four years she looked after the house and the babies, and her husband, in the old-fashioned way. When they went away they always went together. So just a few days ago the neighbors were much surprised to see young Mr. Brady standing on his doorstep, with two heavy suitcases in his hands, while young Mrs. Brady, holding the baby, Margot [sic], 19 months old in her arms, and three-year old Gloria at her skirts was plainly bidding him good-bye.

"But they would have been more surprised if they had heard the conversation between the two, just before the parting.

" 'Well, goodbye my dear,' said Mr. Brady, in effect. 'I will always cherish the memory of those days when you and I lived together in old-fashioned matrimony and took turns walking up and down at midnight with our mutual children. Ah, well—I suppose those days are over. You will keep your house and I will keep mine, but nothing dearest, nothing will ever change my feeling for you.'

" 'Now, be a good boy,' she had also said to him, in effect. 'Remember art is long, but anybody can get married almost any day in the week. I will be glad to see you, always, and glad to be invited to your house—when you can spare the time. Dearest, my heart is yours for evermore, even though you and I are not going to keep house together any longer.'

"What had happened was that after those six years of old-fashioned wedlock, Mrs. Brady had an entirely new idea of what married life ought to be, and she and her husband were putting the theory into practice.

"But what was wrong with the idea that made Mrs. Brady take up anew? She explains:

" 'In the first place,' she says, 'I don't think that this has anything to do with divorce. Nothing could be further from my heart and mind than that. Mr. Brady is leaving or I am simply putting him out of the house, because we have agreed to divorce our artistic and working selves. We are separating for ourselves our work in life, our art.

" 'But as for hearts, our sympathies, our love, our harmony, and our mutual children, all of these are more united than they ever have been since we were first married.

" 'We are living in separate establishments from this time forth to preserve the bloom on the butterfly wings of romance. We do not want to rust our love with untidy glimpses of each other the first thing in the morning or with grumpy breakfast faces or plunges for the same bathtub at the same time, or difference of opinion on how to cut the grass or harboring the neighbor's cat. We are clearing the matrimonial index of all the litter and

Muriel Ostriche, then with Arrow Films, was the cover girl on the January 21, 1921 issue of *Moving Picture Stories,* which had the unusual issue price of 7c.

Announcement

J. JOSEPH SAMETH
Presents

MURIEL OSTRICHE

in a series of five reel super productions, produced by SALIENT FILMS, Inc., under the personal direction of J. CHARLES DAVIS, 2nd.

"The Shadow"

The first of this series is now ready for distribution through

FORWARD FILM DISTRIBUTORS Inc
110 West 40th Street
New York City
Bryant 1361

Believed to have been Muriel Ostriche's last film, *The Shadow* was produced by Salient Films, Inc. and released in April 1921.

bothersome detail of marriage, keeping the paint clean and the sails white for the voyage of our love.

" 'In short, we have decided we can manage to preserve both our careers and our romance if we don't see each other so much every day. . . .

"We will each have our own friends as well as our mutual friends; we will each go where we please and see whom we please and do as we please—within limits, of course. These limits will be our own sense of right and wrong. As for the financial arrangements, I will keep my house and he will keep his. Certain expenses of the children we will share. I am fortunate in being able to do this, because I, too, am a money-maker. When we went into this arrangement we settled the details beforehand. He left upstairs two closets full of clothes. He will, moreover, always send his laundry home. There must ever be a tender bond between a man and a woman when he has the confidence to trust his washing to her. And I shall always want to keep a wifely eye on his socks and shirts, the old darling. He shall be mended up. So, Mr. Brady and I are very pleased with our foresight. We feel that we have really wisely crossed our bridges before we came to them. The last advantage of all is the surprise of courtship to which we have gone back. I watch the mails for his letter. Each time the telephone rings I think it might be him. . . .'

"Thus little Mrs. Brady explains her new idea of how to be happy though married. Just how her experiment will turn out, and when, if ever, Mr. Brady will insist upon coming home again to live, nobody can say. To be sure, one other well-known couple has already tried the same plan and made it succeed. The brilliant novelist, Fanny Hurst, and her husband, who only meet for breakfast once or twice a week, recently celebrated their tenth anniversary with a two week's honeymoon, taken together. The new kind of marriage has succeeded with them. This difference, though, is that Mrs. Brady had six years of matrimony before she tried her idea and Miss Hurst had none.

"However this latest experiment of the young Bradys may turn out, there is no question but what they have entered it sincerely, and they believe it will cement their very great affection. In the meantime, the children are getting older and perhaps, in a year or two, little Miss Gloria and little Miss Margot may take the reins into their own hands, and like good American children, put down their little feet and go bring Papa home to Great Neck and Mama." Reading this 1925 article in later years, Muriel Ostriche stated that the account was fiction, little in it was even remotely true, and that the differences between her and Frank Brady were just a case of incompatibility.

In December 1925, Muriel went to California. She later recalled: "I traveled with my close friend, Rita Warner, wife of Harry Warner. The Warners had just sold their home in Great Neck, and Harry had bought a home in Los Angeles. I arrived in California on New Year's Eve and stayed at the Warners' home for the next three weeks. I met with Ben Hecht, the well-known screenwriter, who offered me an acting job. After giving the matter some thought, I went back to Great Neck to be with my two daughters. By that time I was separated from Frank Brady, and our divorce was in the works."

The divorce became effective on August 27, 1926. On the same day, in Port Washington, New York, Muriel married Charles Wesley Copp, Jr. (October 28, 1902-August 19, 1957). Her attorney, witnessing the finality of her divorce and then her remarriage within a few hours, and the speed with which things were accomplished, asked Muriel: "What do you think you are doing—acting in a movie?" Immediately after the wedding ceremony the couple went to Lake Placid, New York, for their honeymoon.

Muriel later related how she became acquainted with her new husband: "I met him after a sleigh ride in January 1926, right after I came back from California. The sleigh broke down, and I walked home from it. I was in high heels and a short dress. My friends and I later went to a big dinner, where Charles Wesley Copp, Jr. was in attendance. Although I did not talk to him at all that night, I could see his eyes burning on me—it was an uncomfortable feeling and I was quite annoyed. Every time I turned around he was staring at me. Soon, he asked me for a date, for two weeks later. As the time drew near, I hadn't heard from him since he first asked me, so I decided to go somewhere else instead. But, we soon became close friends, and we got married about seven months later. I always called him Wesley or Wes, not Charles. When I met him I was still thinking about returning to films, but I soon dropped the idea. He was an architect and real estate developer. His family was from New England and, many generations earlier, was named Cope, and his ancestors went back to the Revolutionary War. Charles went to Staunton Military Academy in Virginia, then to the Massachusetts Institute of Technology."

Muriel had two children with Charles Wesley Copp, Jr. The first, Charles Wesley Copp III, was born on July 29, 1927 and met a tragic death in a cave-in at the age of four. The second, a daughter, Jean, was born on September 9, 1932.

After her second marriage, Muriel had little contact with the movie industry. By this time, most of production was in California, far from her home on Long Island. Most of the people she had known in her acting days had either moved to California or had left the field. She concentrated on raising her children. For a period of seven years, her husband served as mayor of Manorhaven, Long Island.

Her second daughter, Mollie, recalled that little contact was maintained with Muriel's first husband: "My sister Gloria and I saw very little of our father, Frank A. Brady. My first recollection is having luncheon with him in New York City, then going to a Strauss operetta afterwards. I was probably eleven or twelve years of age. I next saw him when I was fifteen or sixteen. He was married and called his wife Margot. I don't know whether that was really her name, or just a favorite name with him. He died when I was in high school. In March 1965, I sent to the City of New York for a copy of my birth certificate. When I received it, I was shocked to learn that my registered name was Francine Brady. There had always been discussion as to whether I was named Margot or Mollie (which I have always been called). I was raised using my step-father's last name, Copp, even though I was never legally adopted. It was no easy task getting a passport, and more difficult convincing the man at Social Security that Francine Brady and Mollie Copp were the same person!"

In a conversation with the author, Muriel Ostriche reminisced: "After I left the movies, the only movie person with whom I kept in regular touch was Mollie King Alexander. We used to exchange cards each year. She moved to Chevy Chase, Maryland, then to Fort Lauderdale and Palm Beach. One of her sons, Kenny, married an actress and moved to the Virgin Islands. The other, Bobby, went to Kentucky and bred horses.

"Our home in Sands Point, Long Island, was set on about 15 acres of land, so we had no close neighbors. Port Washington, the nearest large town, was three miles away. I have always liked the theatre, and I would often go in to New York City to see shows.

"I also played bridge a lot. Sometime around 1950 I was playing bridge at a local club, when a lady came by to sell tickets for a raffle being conducted by Lighthouse, a charity for the blind. 'It is awful to solicit,' a lady at a nearby table told the ticket seller. I felt sorry for the seller, for she was trying to help a worthy cause, so I told her I would buy a ticket. 'It is my last one,' she told me when I gave her a dollar. Later, I received a telephone call. 'You are one in a million,' the caller said, 'you've won a trip for two to Bermuda.' I thought he was kidding, and then when he explained that I had won the Lighthouse raffle, I understood. Wes didn't want to go, so I went to Bermuda with Jean.

"I have always liked knitting, and sometimes I would knit all day long. For many years I would make sweaters and other things for my family and friends. I always like to keep busy, and even now at my age I always like to have something to do. Now that I have cable television, I watch a lot of that; particularly C-SPAN, with all of the congressmen. The other day I saw John Sununu, the governor of your state, on the C-SPAN network. He made a good appearance, and what he said made sense."

After the 1957 death of Charles Wesley Copp, Jr., Muriel lived near her third daughter, Jean, in Virginia, then in Florida. When the author met Muriel Ostriche Copp for the first time in 1986, her memory was sharp concerning many details of the old days, and hazy concerning others.

As the book neared completion in early 1987, the author visited Muriel in Florida, to find her spry, in good health, and filled with enthusiasm. Asking the question, "Now that you have read the manuscript of the book, can you think of any other information which might be of interest to those reading it?" Muriel and her daughter Jean mentioned several topics.

Today, Muriel's favorite screen personalities are Kathleen Turner and Tom Cruise. Long ago, Mary Pickford was a favorite, then Clark Gable. "I don't like obsenity in today's pictures. This is something we can do without. I like epic pictures, in particular *Gone With the Wind*. In addition to attending the movies regularly, I used to go to the ballet and opera whenever I had a chance. In fact, I still go.

"I have loved swimming all my life, and I still swim when the pool is warm, although I prefer the Atlantic Ocean. Baseball is one of my favorite sports, and for years I followed the St. Louis Cardinals, although it's a shame they haven't done anything lately. In his time, Frank Shields was one of my favorite tennis stars. Today, I like Ivan Lendl. When I lived on Long Island I used to go to the West Side Tennis Club at Forest Hills every year and would stay there for a week to 10 days watching the tournament. I also enjoy watching golf, and Arnold Palmer is my favorite.

"I still do the *New York Times* Sunday crossword puzzle each week. A friend of mine mails it to me.

"My favorite foods? I still love lobster. I also love candy—and would rather have candy and ice cream sodas than dinner. I also like parties, and years ago people used to call me 'the Perle Mesta of Port Washington.'

"My friends from years ago in show business have died. I do keep in touch with one of my friends who wasn't in show business, but she did write the song *Scarlet Ribbons*—Evelyn Levine, who is from Fort Worth. She is my closest living friend from years ago.

"I can't imagine anyone being interested in my history," Muriel said modestly—quite reminiscent of interviews she gave to motion picture writers 70 years earlier.

Mr. Charles Wesley Copp, Jr.

and

Mrs. Muriel Ostriche Brady

announce their marriage

on Friday the twenty-seventh of August

Nineteen hundred and twenty-six

Port Washington Long Island

Charles Wesley Copp, Jr. and Muriel early in their marriage, relaxing in the Adirondacks. To the left is the text from their marriage announcement.

Charles Wesley Copp, Jr. as a young man. He married Muriel on August 27, 1926.

Muriel and Charles in their Sands Point, New York home in the 1950s.

This snapshot from the 1920s shows Muriel's young daughters, Mollie and Gloria, with an unidentified nurse.

A photograph taken on the beach in the late 1920s shows Muriel to the left, holding her infant son Charles. At the center and right are her friend Mollie King Alexander and her two sons, Kenny and Robert.

Two of Muriel's daughters, Mollie and baby Jean, in the early 1930s.

Studio photo of Muriel and her son, Charles Wesley Copp III, who was known as "Bootsy."

Muriel's three daughters in a circa 1939 portrait (left to right): Gloria, Jean, and Mollie.

The Copp family Christmas card, circa 1940.

Muriel Ostriche Copp and the author at the Florida home of Muriel's daughter, Jean Geoly, February 1987, just before Muriel celebrated her 91st birthday.

Muriel's daughters—Jean Geoly, Mollie Demarest, and Gloria Hewitt—photographed by the author, February 1987.

Muriel's daughter Gloria, (who married Charles Hewitt on December 1, 1945) as a bridesmaid at her sister Mollie's wedding on April 5, 1945.

Muriel's grandson, Richard Hewitt, age 20.

Muriel's grandson, William Hewitt, age 21, as a graduate from the New York State Maritime Academy.

Muriel with her grandson, Robert Hewitt, in the late 1940s.

Gloria with son Richard.

Gloria with son Richard.

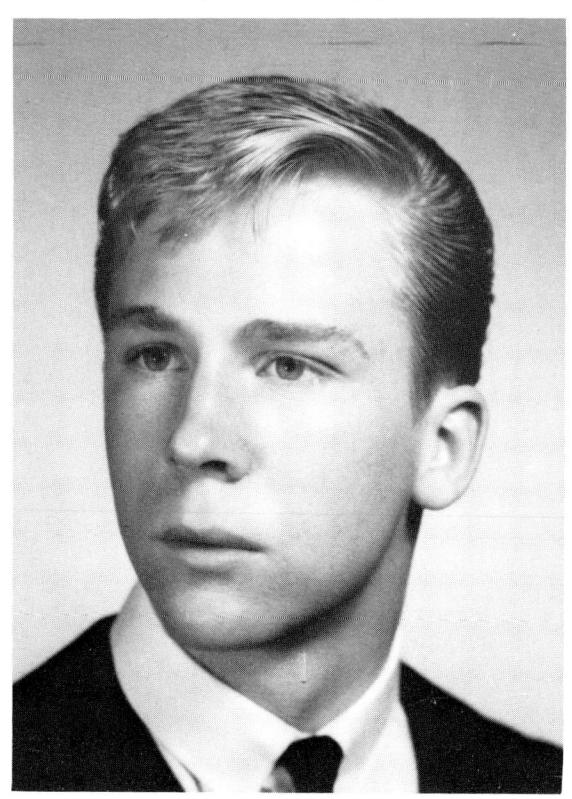

Robert Hewitt at age 18.

Muriel's daughter Mollie (who was designated Francine on her birth certificate) as a young lady. Mollie was named after Muriel's friend Mollie King Alexander, a film actress.

A page from the Demarest family album, spring 1959, with Muriel's daughter Mollie and her husband, Calvin Demarest, with their three daughters (left to right) Laura (born April 18, 1949), Susan (February 22, 1951), and Wendy (July 13, 1954).

Susan, Laura, and Wendy Demarest, Muriel's granddaughters, in the summer of 1984.

Daughter Jean, who married Charles Geoly on February 2, 1957. They had two children: Charles Andrew (September 2, 1961) and Thomas Edward (November 16, 1968).

Muriel on May 3, 1986, with her daughter, Jean Copp Geoly, and two of her grandsons, Thomas and Charles Geoly.

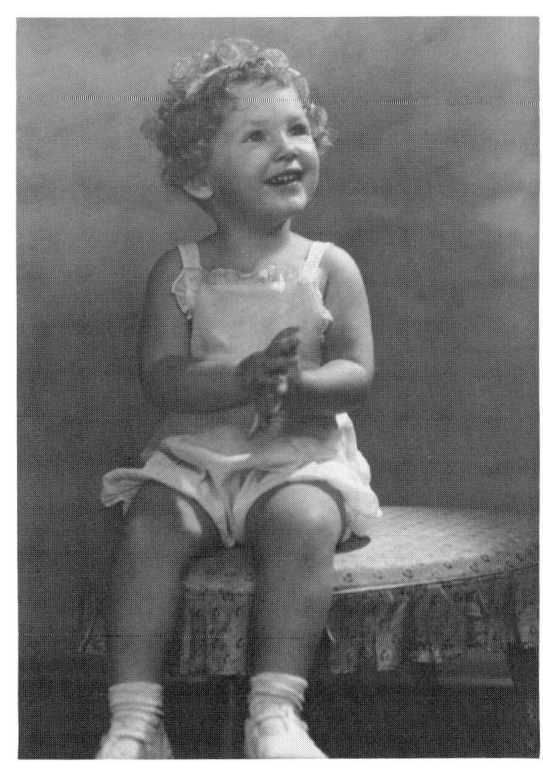

Daughter Jean in the mid 1930s.

APPENDIX ONE

Filmography

The following listing constitutes films in which Muriel Ostriche is *definitely* known to have appeared. It is presumed that she appeared in many other features as well, particularly those produced by Eclair, Thanhouser, and the Princess Department of Thanhouser, but in the absence of specific information linking her to a production, such films are not listed.

In instances in which Muriel Ostriche is listed alone, it is a virtual certainty that there were other players as well, and perhaps Muriel Ostriche was not the most important. The order of cast members listed follows that given in studio publicity, news releases, and other published sources. In instances in which Muriel Ostriche does not appear among the first two or three players, it can be assumed that she had a supporting or minor role.

Directors, screenplay writers, and cameramen are listed only when their identities are definitely known. It can be presumed, for example, that Lloyd Lonergan, Philip Lonergan, and John W. Kellette wrote many of the unattributed Princess scripts, but in the absence of specific verification they are not so identified. Similarly, when filming locations are definitely known they are listed. It can be presumed that most otherwise unattributed Eclair and World films were produced in or near Fort Lee, New Jersey, and that Thanhouser and Princess films were produced in or near New Rochelle, New York. Although several trade publications noted that Muriel Ostriche appeared in films made on the West Coast, in actuality all of her acting was done on the East Coast, without exception, although a number of her films have footage of West Coast or other scenic locations cut in. Dates given are release (not review) dates.

A TALE OF THE WILDERNESS
(American Biograph)
January 8, 1912
2 reels
Director: D. W. Griffith
Cameraman: Billy Bitzer
Cast: Dorothy Bernard, Charles Hill Mailes, Edwin August, Edna Foster, William J. Butler. Muriel Ostriche was an extra playing the part of a fort defender.
Note: Filmed in Coytesville, New Jersey

(TITLE UNKNOWN)
(American Biograph)
Circa January-February 1912
Note: Muriel Ostriche recalled that she, Priscilla Dean, and a boy were walking down a road and had to step aside to allow mounted policemen to pass.

A BLOT IN THE 'SCUTCHEON
(American Biograph)
January 29, 1912
1,500 feet
Director: D. W. Griffith
Screenplay: Linda Arvidson Griffith, from the poem by Robert Browning
Cameraman: Billy Bitzer
Cast: Dorothy Bernard, Edwin August, Miriam Cooper, Charles Hill Mailes, Claire McDowell, William J. Butler, Charles H. West, Edna Foster, Edward Dillon, Harry Hyde, Joseph Graybill, W. Christy Cabanne, J. Jiquel Lanoe. Priscilla Dean and Muriel Ostriche were pages.
Note: Filmed in the Biograph studio and New Jersey.

(TITLE UNKNOWN)
(Powers)
Early 1912
Cast: Muriel Ostriche in minor part

(TITLE UNKNOWN)
(Pathé Freres)
Early 1912
Cast: Crane Wilbur, Muriel Ostriche (substituting for Pearl White, who failed to appear)

THE LETTER WITH THE BLACK SEALS
(Eclair)
April 2, 1912
1 reel
Director: Etienne Arnaud
Screenplay: Etienne Arnaud
Cast: John Troyano, George Larkin, Muriel Ostriche, John Adolfi
Note: First film in the "Kid, Kit and Kittie" series. Filmed in Fort Lee.

THE WHITE APRONS
(Eclair)April 4, 1912
1 reel
Director: Etienne Arnaud
Screenplay: Katherine G. Maher
Cast: Featuring Muriel Ostriche
Note: Filmed in Fort Lee, New Jersey

OH, YOU RAGTIME!
(Eclair)
April 18, 1912
1 reel
Director: Etienne Arnaud
Screenplay: Etienne Arnaud
Cast: Guy Oliver, Julia Stuart, Alec B. Francis, Muriel Ostriche, Mathilde Baring
Note: Filmed in Fort Lee, New Jersey

THE LEGEND OF SLEEPY HOLLOW
(Eclair)
April 23, 1912
Director: Etienne Arnaud
Screenplay: From Washington Irving's story of the same name.
Cast: Lamar Johnstone, John Troyano, Edward Lawrence, Muriel Ostriche, John Adolfi, Alec B. Francis, George Larkin, Louis R. Grisel, Julia Stuart, Isabel Lamon
Note: Filmed in Fort Lee, New Jersey and Tarrytown, New York

THE EASTER BONNET
(Eclair)
April 25, 1912
1 reel
Cast: Muriel Ostriche (in two roles simultaneously, by split image photography), Dorothy Gibson

REVENGE OF THE SILK MASKS
(Eclair)
April 30, 1912
1 reel
Director: Etienne Arnaud
Screenplay: Etienne Arnaud
Cast: Dorothy Gibson, Muriel Ostriche, and others
Note: Filmed in Fort Lee, New Jersey.

THE RAVEN
(Eclair)
May 15, 1912
2 reels
Screenplay: Adapted from works by Edgar Allan Poe
Cast: Large cast, including Muriel Ostriche
Note: Muriel Ostriche is buried alive in a casket. Filmed in Fort Lee, New Jersey, and at the Poe Cottage at Fordham.

FEATHERTOP
(Eclair)
May 28, 1912
Screenplay: Adapted from Hawthorne's story of the same name.
Cast: Large cast, including Muriel Ostriche
Note: Filmed in Fort Lee, New Jersey.

THE HOLY CITY
(Eclair)
June 27, 1912
Director: Etienne Arnaud
Cast: Large cast, including Muriel Ostriche

ROBIN HOOD
(Eclair)
August 22, 1912
3 reels
Directors: Etienne Arnaud and Herbert Blaché
Screenplay: Adapted from stories based on English ballads
Cast: Robert Frazer, Barbara Tennant, Alec B. Francis, Julia Stuart, Mathilde Baring, Isabel Lamon, Muriel Ostriche, Guy Oliver, Charles Hundt, George Larkin, John Troyano, Arthur Hollingsworth, Lamar Johnstone, John Adolfi, et al
Note: Filmed in Fort Lee, New Jersey

MAKING UNCLE JEALOUS
(Eclair)
October 24, 1912
Cast: Alec B. Francis, George Larkin, Isabel Lamon, Will E. Sheerer, Muriel Ostriche, the Eclair Kid (Clara Horton), Mrs. Davis, Miss Knowland
Note: Filmed in Fort Lee, New Jersey

SILENT JIM
(Eclair)
November 5, 1912
2 reels
Cast: Alec B. Francis, Robert Frazer, Barbara Tennant, Lamar Johnstone, Will E. Sheerer, Mr. Kelley, George Larkin, Muriel Ostriche

THE HONOR OF THE FIRM
(Eclair)
November 12, 1912
1 reel
Cast: Robert Frazer, Fred C. Truesdell, Mr. Vaughn, Muriel Ostriche

THE VENGEANCE OF THE FAKIR
(Eclair)
December 19, 1912
2 reels
Directors: Messrs. Arnaud and Vernot
Cast: Alec B. Francis, Will E. Sheerer, George Larkin, Mildred Bright, Muriel Ostriche, Lamar Johnstone, Paul Bourgeois, Julia Stuart, Eileen Hume

A TAMMANY BOARDER
(Eclair)
January 2, 1913
Director: Etienne Arnaud
Screenplay: Etienne Arnaud
Cast: Miss Hobbs, J. Gunnis Davis, Muriel Ostriche, Alec B. Francis, Lamar Johnstone, Julia Stuart, Denton Cardow, Alice Kibbe, Alice Knowland, Jennie Ambretta, "Princess" (Bengal tiger)
Note: Filmed in Fort Lee, New Jersey. The title was undoubtedly inspired by the "Tammany Tiger," which cartoonist Thomas Nast created in the 19th century to represent the New York City political machine.

AN ACCIDENTAL SERVANT
(Eclair)
January 7, 1913
1 reel
Cast: George Larkin, Guy Hedlund, Eleanor Parker, Mildred Bright, J. Gunnis Davis, Alec B. Francis, Muriel Ostriche, Will E. Sheerer, Julia Stuart

THE SPECTRE BRIDEGROOM
(Eclair)
January 23, 1913
2 reels
Director: Etienne Arnaud
Screenplay: Adapted from Washington Irving's story of the same name
Cast: Julia Stuart, Muriel Ostriche, Fred C. Truesdell, Clara Horton, Mildred Bright, Will E. Sheerer, Eileen Hume, Gladys Briggs, Sue Willis, Lillian Kingsbury, Helen Marten, Billy Baer, M. Barbara, Alec B. Francis, Edmund Steele, J. Gunnis Davis, J. W. Johnston, Guy Hedlund, M. E. Hannefy, Charles Morgan, H. E. Guys, Arthur Ellery, Little Edna

THE LOVE CHASE
(Eclair)
February 6, 1913
2 reels
Cast: Barbara Tennant, Julia Stuart, Muriel Ostriche, Mildred Bright, Miss Davis, Lamar Johnstone, George Larkin, J. Gunnis Davis, Louis R. Grisel
Note: Filmed in Fort Lee, New Jersey, Niagara Falls, New York and New York City

THE CRIMSON CROSS
a.k.a. THE MYSTERIES OF THE ROSARY
(Eclair)
March 5, 1913
3 reels
Cast: Julia Stuart, Alec B. Francis, Grace Moreland, Mary Sennison, Gladys Briggs, J. Gunnis Davis, Laurie Mackin, Mildred Bright, Will E. Sheerer, Charles Morgan, Barbara Tennant, Alice Knowland, Evelyn Fowler, Helen Marten, Muriel Ostriche (as an angel), Isabel Gonzales, Guy Hedlund, J.W. Johnston, Fred Truesdell, Lou Wood, Mildred Tiernan, Helen Drew, Clara Horton, Willie Cottrell

FOR BETTER OR WORSE
a.k.a. FOR BETTER OR FOR WORSE
(Eclair)
March 19, 1913 (rescheduled from March 5, 1913)
3 reels
Cast: Julia Stuart, Alec B. Francis, Mildred Bright, Helen Marten (designated as Helene Merten in numerous Eclair announcements), Ann Warrington, Barbara Tennant, Hattie Delaro, Eileen Hume, Clara Horton, Denton Cardou, Muriel Ostriche, J.W. Johnston, Fred C. Truesdell, Lamar Johnstone, Will E. Sheerer, J. Gunnis Davis, Guy E. Hedlund, Ed Steele, Louis R. Grisel, Dora Ford, Mabel Ford

THE BAWLEROUT
(Reliance)
April 30, 1913
3 reels
Director: Oscar C. Apfel
Screenplay: From a story by Forrest Halsey
Cast: Edgena de Lespine, Irving Cummings, Sue Balfour, Ralph Lewis, Muriel Ostriche, Thomas R. Mills, George Siegmann, E. P. Sullivan

THE BIG BOSS
(Reliance)
May 14, 1913
2 reels
Director: Frederick Sullivan
Screenplay: Lu Senarens
Cast: George Siegmann, Irving Cummings, Muriel Ostriche, A. Balfour, E. P. Sullivan

MISS MISCHIEF
a.k.a. LITTLE MISS MISCHIEF
(Thanhouser)
June 8, 1913
1 reel
Screenplay: Lloyd Lonergan
Cast: Featuring Muriel Ostriche
Note: Muriel Ostriche's first film for Thanhouser. Filmed in New Rochelle, New York

FRAZZLED FINANCE
(Thanhouser)
August 31, 1913
1 reel
Cast: Includes Muriel Ostriche

FLOOD TIDE
(Thanhouser)
September 19, 1913
1 reel
Cast: The Thanhouser Kid (Marie Eline), Muriel Ostriche, Eugene Moore

THE FARMER'S DAUGHTERS
(Thanhouser)
September 28, 1913
1 reel
Cast: Muriel Ostriche, Jean Darnell, Billy Noel, Nolan Gane

LOBSTER SALAD AND MILK
(Thanhouser-Princess)
October 24, 1913
1 reel
Screenplay: Lloyd Lonergan
Director: Carl Gregory
Cameraman: Carl Gregory
Cast: Muriel Ostriche, Marie Eline
Note: Muriel Ostriche's first Princess film

ALGY'S AWFUL AUTO
(Thanhouser-Princess)
October 31, 1913
1 reel
Director: Carl Gregory
Screenplay: Lloyd Lonergan
Cameraman: Carl Gregory
Cast: Featuring Muriel Ostriche
Note: Filmed in New Rochelle, New York

FRIDAY, THE THIRTEENTH
(Thanhouser-Princess)
November 7, 1913
1 reel
Director: Carl Gregory
Screenplay: Lloyd Lonergan
Cameraman: Carl Gregory
Cast: Muriel Ostriche, Boyd Marshall
Note: Filmed in New Rochelle, New York. Believed to have been Boyd Marshall's first motion picture role, although John W. Kellette, in an article in the *New Rochelle Pioneer*, October 31, 1914, stated that Marshall's first film was *The Campaign Manageress*.

LOOKING FOR TROUBLE
(Thanhouser-Princess)
November 9, 1913
1 reel
Director: Carl Gregory
Screenplay: Lloyd Lonergan
Cameraman: Carl Gregory
Cast: Muriel Ostriche, Marie Eline

A CAMPAIGN MANAGERESS
(Thanhouser)
November 11, 1913
1 reel
Director: Carl Gregory
Screenplay: Lloyd Lonergan and Carl Gregory
Cameraman: Carl Gregory
Cast: Muriel Ostriche, Marie Eline, Boyd Marshall

BREAD UPON THE WATERS
(Thanhouser-Princess)
November 14, 1913
1 reel
Director: Carl Gregory
Screenplay: Lloyd Lonergan
Cameraman: Carl Gregory
Cast: Muriel Ostriche, Boyd Marshall

THE HOUSE IN THE TREE
(Majestic)
November 23, 1913
1 reel
Screenplay: Lloyd Lonergan
Cast: Muriel Ostriche, William Garwood, Billie West, Vera Sisson, Victory Bateman, Howard Davies
Note: One of several films for which Muriel Ostriche was "loaned" to Majestic, a company controlled by Charles J. Hite.

HER RIGHT TO HAPPINESS
(Thanhouser-Princess)
November 28, 1913
1 reel
Director: Carl Gregory
Screenplay: Lloyd Lonergan
Cameraman: Carl Gregory
Cast: Muriel Ostriche, Boyd Marshall, Fannie Gregory

THE LITTLE CHURCH AROUND THE CORNER
(Thanhouser-Princess)
December 5, 1913
1 reel
Director: Carl Gregory
Cameraman: Carl Gregory
Cast: Muriel Ostriche, Boyd Marshall
Note: With many scenes filmed in Manhattan

RICK'S REDEMPTION
(Majestic)
December 7, 1913
Cast: Muriel Ostriche, William Garwood

HIS IMAGINARY FAMILY
(Thanhouser-Princess)
December 12, 1913
1 reel
Director: Carl Gregory; Claude Seixas, assistant
Cameraman: Carl Gregory
Cast: Muriel Ostriche, Marie Eline, Boyd Marshall, Arthur Bauer
Note: Filmed in New Rochelle, New York

THE LAW OF HUMANITY
(Thanhouser-Princess)
December 19, 1913
1 reel
Director: Carl Gregory; Claude Seixas, assistant
Cameraman: Carl Gregory
Cast: Muriel Ostriche, Marie Eline, Boyd Marshall, Catherine Webb, Claude Seixas, Dorothy Benham, Arthur Bauer, Mrs. Hool, Morgan Jones
Note: This film is a drama. Up to this time, all Princess films were comedies. After this point, comedies, dramas, and scenic features were made. Filmed in New Rochelle, New York

CUPID'S LIEUTENANT
(Thanhouser-Princess)
December 26, 1913
1 reel
Director: Carl Gregory; Claude Seixas, assistant
Cameraman: Carl Gregory
Cast: Muriel Ostriche, Marie Eline, Boyd Marshall, "50 bright children"
Note: Filmed near New Rochelle, New York

HELEN'S STRATAGEM
(Majestic)
December 28, 1913
Cast: Lamar Johnstone, Ernest Joy, Vera Sisson, Muriel Ostriche, Demetrio Mitzoras, Howard Davies

A RURAL FREE DELIVERY ROMANCE
a.k.a. A ROMANCE OF THE RURAL ROUTE
(Thanhouser-Princess)
January 2, 1914
1 reel
Director: Carl Gregory; Claude Seixas, assistant
Cameraman: Carl Gregory
Cast: Muriel Ostriche, Boyd Marshall, Morgan Jones, Claude Seixas
Note: Filmed in New Rochelle, New York

THE TEN OF SPADES
(Majestic)
January 6, 1914
Director: Carl W. Gregory; Claude Seixas, assistant
Cameraman: Carl W. Gregory
Cast: William Garwood, Vera Sisson, Muriel Ostriche, J. H. Horsey, W. A. Lowery, Victory Bateman, Metta White, Joseph E. Swickard, C. E. Rogers

A CIRCUMSTANTIAL NURSE
(Thanhouser-Princess)
January 9, 1914
1 reel
Director: Carl Gregory; Claude Seixas, assistant
Cameraman: Carl Gregory
Cast: Muriel Ostriche, Boyd Marshall, Morgan Jones, Catherine Webb, Dorothy Benham

WHEN THE CAT CAME BACK
(Thanhouser-Princess)
January 16, 1914
1 reel
Director: Carl Gregory; Claude Seixas, assistant
Cameraman: Carl Gregory
Cast: Muriel Ostriche, Boyd Marshall
Note: Filmed in New Rochelle, New York

THE VACANT CHAIR
(Thanhouser-Princess)
January 23, 1914
1 reel
Director: Carl Gregory; Claude Seixas, assistant
Cameraman: Carl Gregory
Cast: Muriel Ostriche, Boyd Marshall, Morgan Jones, Carey L. Hastings
Note: Filmed in New Rochelle, New York

THE PURSE AND THE GIRL
a.k.a. THE LOSER WINS
(Thanhouser-Princess)
January 30, 1914
Director: Carl Gregory
Cameraman: Carl Gregory
Cast: Muriel Ostriche, Boyd Marshall, Marie Eline, Fan Bourke, Arthur Bauer
Note: Filmed in New Rochelle, New York

WHERE PATHS DIVERGE
a.k.a. WHERE PATHS DIVERGED
a.k.a. WHEN PATHS DIVERGED
(Thanhouser-Princess)
February 6, 1914
1 reel
Director: Carl Gregory; M. Perry Horton, assistant
Cameraman: Carl Gregory
Cast: Muriel Ostriche, Boyd Marshall, Catherine Webb, Eddie Ford, Morgan Jones
Note: Filmed in New Rochelle, New York

PERCY'S FIRST HOLIDAY
(Thanhouser)
February 8, 1914
Director: Carl Gregory; M. Perry Horton, assistant
Screenplay: Lloyd F. Lonergan
Cameraman: Carl Gregory
Cast: Muriel Ostriche, W. S. Percy, Justus D. Barnes, Fan Bourke, Babe Wallace, Charles Van Hout, Boyd Marshall, Ed Ford, Arthur Bauer, Grace Eline, Lydia Mead

THE TANGLED CAT
(Thanhouser-Princess)
February 13, 1914
1 reel
Director: Carl Gregory; M. Perry Horton, assistant
Cast: Muriel Ostriche, Boyd Marshall, Fan Bourke, Eddie Ford, Carey L. Hastings, J. F. Schubert

ALL'S WELL THAT ENDS WELL
February 20, 1914
(Thanhouser-Princess)
1 reel
Cast: Muriel Ostriche, Boyd Marshall, Catherine Webb, Eugene Redding, Morgan Jones, Miss Pike, Miss Keyes
Note: Filmed in New Rochelle, New York

THE HOLD-UP
(Thanhouser-Princess)
February 27, 1914
1 reel
Cast: Muriel Ostriche, Boyd Marshall, James Ayres, Catherine Webb, Joe Sparks

HER WAY
(Thanhouser-Princess)
March 6, 1914
1 reel
Screenplay: John W. Kellette
Director: Carl Gregory
Cast: George T. Welch, Boyd Marshall, Morgan Jones, Muriel Ostriche, Janet Clendenning-Henry

BILLY'S RUSE
(Thanhouser-Princess)
March 13, 1914
1 reel
Screenplay: John W. Kellette
Cast: Muriel Ostriche, Boyd Marshall, Fan Bourke, Catherine Webb, Charles Emerson, Eugene Redding, Billy Noel

THE GRAND PASSION
(Thanhouser-Princess)
March 20, 1914
1 reel
Cast: Muriel Ostriche, Morris Foster (as "Boyd, secretly in love with Muriel"), Nolan Gane, Fan Bourke, James Dunne, Mrs. Minnie McCoy. Having Morris Foster play a role under the name of "Boyd" seems illogical, in view of Boyd Marshall's strong identification with Princess films. It may be that certain Princess publicity is incorrect, and that Boyd Marshall played the part.

HER FIRST LESSON
(Thanhouser-Princess)
April 3, 1914
1 reel
Cast: Muriel Ostriche, Nellie Williams, Dorothy Benham, Madeline Thompson, Morris Foster, Nolan Gane

TOO MUCH TURKEY
(Thanhouser-Princess)
April 10, 1914
1 reel
Cast: Muriel Ostriche, Nolan Gane, Morgan Jones, Virginia Waite, Charles Horan

HER AWAKENING
(Thanhouser-Princess)
April 17, 1914
1 reel
Cast: Muriel Ostriche, Nolan Gane, Morgan Jones, Charles Horan

THE STRIKE
(Thanhouser)
April 21, 1914
2 reels
Director: Henry Harrison Lewis
Cast: Muriel Ostriche, Morris Foster, George Walsh, Fan Bourke

POLITENESS PAYS
(Thanhouser-Princess)
May 1, 1914
2 reels
Cast: Muriel Ostriche, Nolan Gane

IN HER SLEEP
(Thanhouser-Princess)
May 15, 1914
2 reels
Cast: Muriel Ostriche, Madeline Fairbanks, Morgan Jones, Charles Horan, Mrs. Arthur Ellery (Marie Rainford), Eugene Redding, Marion Fairbanks (?—mentioned, possibly inaccurately, in *Reel Life*), Miss Keyes.

A CIRCUS ROMANCE
(Thanhouser-Princess)
May 23, 1914
1 reel
Cast: Featuring Muriel Ostriche
Note: Different film from similarly-titled Equitable release of February 5, 1916.

A TELEPHONE STRATEGY
(Thanhouser-Princess)
May 29, 1914
1 reel
Screenplay: Philip Lonergan
Cast: Muriel Ostriche, Boyd Marshall
Note: Filmed in New Rochelle, New York

HIS ENEMY
(Thanhouser-Princess)
June 5, 1914
1 reel
Screenplay: Philip Lonergan
Cast: Featuring Muriel Ostriche

THE TOY SHOP
(Thanhouser-Princess)
June 12, 1914
1 reel
Screenplay: Philip Lonergan
Cast: Muriel Ostriche, Boyd Marshall, James Dunne, Maurice Stewart
Note: Filmed in New Rochelle, New York

THE LITTLE SENORITA
(Thanhouser-Princess)
June 19, 1914
1 reel
Screenplay: Lloyd Lonergan
Cast: Muriel Ostriche, Boyd Marshall

PROFESSOR SNAITH
(Thanhouser-Princess)
June 26, 1914
1 reel
Screenplay: Philip Lonergan
Cast: Featuring Muriel Ostriche
Note: Erroneously designated as "Professor Smith" in several trade notices

THE DECOY
(Thanhouser-Princess)
July 3, 1914
1 reel
Screenplay: Philip Lonergan
Cast: Featuring Muriel Ostriche

THE GIRL OF THE SEASONS
(Thanhouser-Princess)
July 10, 1914
1 reel
Cast: Featuring Muriel Ostriche

THE VETERAN'S SWORD
(Thanhouser-Princess)
July 17, 1914
1 reel
Screenplay: Philip Lonergan
Cast: Includes Muriel Ostriche

THE TARGET OF DESTINY
(Thanhouser-Princess)
July 31, 1914
1 reel
Cast: Includes Muriel Ostriche

HER DUTY
(Thanhouser-Princess)
August 7, 1914
1 reel
Cast: Muriel Ostriche, Boyd Marshall

A RURAL ROMANCE
(Thanhouser-Princess)
August 14, 1914
1 reel
Director: Arthur Ellery
Cast: Muriel Ostriche, Boyd Marshall
Note: *Moving Picture World* erroneously attributed the script to Thomas B. Ince and R. B. Spencer and erroneously gave the length as two reels.

THE BELLE OF THE SCHOOL
(Thanhouser-Princess)
August 21, 1914
1 reel
Director: Arthur Ellery
Screenplay: Lloyd Lonergan
Cast: Muriel Ostriche, Boyd Marshall, Reenie Farrington

THE KEEPER OF THE LIGHT
(Thanhouser-Princess)
August 28, 1914
1 reel
Director: Arthur Ellery
Cameraman: Charles Van Houten
Cast: Muriel Ostriche, Boyd Marshall
Note: Filmed on City Island (Bronx, New York); Execution Light on Long Island Sound

THE VARSITY RACE
(Thanhouser)
September 22, 1914
2 reels
Director: Carroll Fleming
Screenplay: Philip Lonergan
Cast: Muriel Ostriche, Irving Cummings, Arthur Bauer, Nolan Gane, Carey L. Hastings, Ethel Jewett, Bill Noel, Edward Hoyt, Walter Cameron
Note: Filmed in Philadelphia (but an account in *Moving Picture World* places the location as Poughkeepsie).

THE DIAMOND OF DISASTER
(Thanhouser)
October 13, 1914
2 reels
Director: Carroll Fleming
Screenplay: Philip Lonergan
Cast: J. S. Murray, Justus D. Barnes, Ernest Ward, Morgan Jones, John Richards, Muriel Ostriche, Irving Cummings, Carey L. Hastings, David Thompson

A MADONNA OF THE POOR
(Thanhouser)
October 27, 1914
2 reels
Director: Carroll Fleming
Screenplay: John W. Kellette from a vaudeville sketch by Carroll Fleming
Cast: Muriel Ostriche, John Reinhard, David Thompson
Note: Produced in July and August 1914

THE TURNING OF THE ROAD
(Thanhouser)
November 3, 1914
2 reels
Director: Carroll Fleming
Screenplay: Based on a story by Elizabeth Gaskins
Cast: Muriel Ostriche, Frank Wood, John Reinhard, Ethyle Cooke, Ernest Ward, Carey L. Hastings, Arthur Bauer, Perry Horton

KEEPING A HUSBAND
(Thanhouser)
November 8, 1914
1 reel
Cast: Muriel Ostriche, Carey L. Hastings, Ernest C. Ward
Note: Filmed in New Rochelle, New York

MRS. VAN RUYTER'S STRATAGEM
(Thanhouser)
November 24, 1914
2 reels
Director: Carroll Fleming
Screenplay: Philip Lonergan
Cast: Muriel Ostriche, J. S. Murray, Lydia Mead, Ethyle Cooke, Harry Benham, Helen Badgley, Fan Bourke, Ed Hoyt, Carey L. Hastings

THE AMATEUR DETECTIVE
(Thanhouser)
December 6, 1914
1 reel
Director: Carroll Fleming
Cast: Carey L. Hastings, Muriel Ostriche

THE READER OF MINDS
(Thanhouser)
December 8, 1914
2 reels
Director: Carroll Fleming
Screenplay: Philip Lonergan
Cast: Muriel Ostriche, Harris Gordon, Carey L. Hastings

THE WHITE ROSE
(Thanhouser-Princess)
December 25, 1914
1 reel
Cast: Muriel Ostriche, Boyd Marshall, Ernest Ward

WHEN FATE REBELLED
(Thanhouser-Princess)
January 1, 1915
1 reel
Director: Jack Harvey
Screenplay: Jack Harvey (his first script)
Cast: Muriel Ostriche, Boyd Marshall, Frank Wood, Madeline and Marion Fairbanks (the Thanhouser Twins)

CHECK NO. 130
(Thanhouser-Princess)
January 8, 1915
1 reel
Director: Jack Harvey (?)
Cast: Muriel Ostriche, Boyd Marshall
Note: Erroneously as "Check No. 30" in several press notices and in at least one official Thanhouser news release.

THE SPEED KING
(Thanhouser)
January 12, 1915
2 reels
Screenplay: Philip Lonergan
Cast: Muriel Ostriche, Arthur Ashley, Ethyl Jewett, Carey L. Hastings, Morgan Jones
Note: Some scenes in the second reel were filmed at Brighton Beach, near Coney Island.

PLEASING UNCLE
(Thanhouser-Princess)
January 15, 1915
1 reel
Cast: Muriel Ostriche, Boyd Marshall, Ethel Jewett, John Reinhard

AN INNOCENT BURGLAR
(Thanhouser-Princess)
January 22, 1915
1 reel
Cast: Muriel Ostriche, Boyd Marshall, Reenie Farrington
Note: Some notices omit Muriel Ostriche and mention Reenie Farrington as the co-star with Boyd Marshall.

THE HEARTBREAKER
(Universal—Big U)
April 8, 1915
2 reels
Director: Lorimer Johnston
Screenplay: Raymond L. Schrock
Cast: Muriel Ostriche, Charles Ogle, and others

WHEN IT STRIKES HOME
(Charles K. Harris Feature Film Corp.—World)
May 17, 1915
5 reels
Director: Perry N. Vekroff
Screenplay: Charles K. Harris
Cast: Grace Washburn, Edwin August, Muriel Ostriche, William Bailey, Claire Mersereau, Harry Knowles, George Henry, Walter Fenner, Gladys Peck, J. Albert Hall, Claude Cooper
Note: Filmed at the Mittenthal Brothers' Studio, Yonkers, New York

CELESTE
(Universal—Big U)
May 20, 1915
Cast: Muriel Ostriche, Earle Foxe, Charles Ogle

WHAT'S OURS?
(Vitagraph)
June 24, 1915
1 reel
Director: S. Rankin Drew
Screenplay: Winona Godfrey
Cast: Muriel Ostriche, Anders Randolf, Louise Beaudet, Donald McBride, Raymond Bloomer, Billy Billings

MORTMAIN
(Vitagraph)
September 6, 1915
5 reels
Director: Theodore Marston
Screenplay: From a novel by Arthur Train
Cast: Robert Edeson, Donald Hall, Edward Elkas, Muriel Ostriche, Joseph Weber, James Morrison, Karin Norman, J. Herbert Frank, Claude James, Roland Osborne, Helen Pillsbury
Note: Many scenes were filmed in J. Stuart Blackton's New York City apartment

FOR THE HONOR OF THE CREW
(Vitagraph—Broadway Star)
November 9, 1915
3 reels
Director: William P.S. Earle
Screenplay: William P. S. Earle
Cast: James Morrison, Edward Elkas, William B. Davidson, Muriel Ostriche, Hattie Delaro, Charles Cook
Note: Filmed in Poughkeepsie, New York

A DAUGHTER OF THE SEA
Working title: THE FISHER GIRL
(Equitable for World)
November 22, 1915
5 reels
Director: Charles Seay
Screenplay: Russell E. Smith from *The Fisher Girl*, by Frances Marion
Cast: Muriel Ostriche, William T. Tooker, Clara Whipple, Catherine Calhoun, Clifford Grey, Roy Applegate
Note: Filmed on Block Island, Rhode Island

A CIRCUS ROMANCE
Working title: BABETTE OF THE BALLYHOO
(Equitable for World)
February 5, 1916
5 reels
Director: Charles M. Seay
Screenplay: Betty T. Fitzgerald from a story by Frances Marion
Cast: Muriel Ostriche, Edwards Davis, Jack Hopkins, Catherine Calhoun, George Larkin, Charles Brandt, Mollie King, Al Hombourg, Raymond Agnell
Note: Filmed in Albany, Georgia with the Con. T. Kennedy Circus and in Florida.

KENNEDY SQUARE
(Vitagraph)
February 21, 1916
5 reels
Director: S. Rankin Drew
Screenplay: From a novel of the same name by F. Hopkinson Smith
Cameraman: Arthur Quinn
Cast: Antonio Moreno, Charles Kent, Muriel Ostriche, Tom Brooke, Dan Jarrett, Raymond Bloomer, Hattie Delaro, Harold Foshay, Herbert Barry, Logan Paul, Katherine Lewis
Note: Many scenes were filmed in the historic Jumel mansion, New York City

BY WHOSE HAND?
Working title: WHO KILLED SIMON BAIRD?
(Equitable for World)
April 17, 1916
5 reels
Director: James Durkin
Screenplay: Channing Pollock and Rennold Wolf
Cast: Edna Wallace Hopper, Charles J. Ross, Muriel Ostriche, Nicholas Dunaew, John Dillon, James Ryley
Note: Many scenes were filmed in the Adirondacks

SALLY IN OUR ALLEY
Working title: MOLLIE O' PIGTAIL ALLEY
(Peerless for World)
July 17, 1916
Director: Travers Vale
Screenplay: George Yohalem
Cast: Carlyle Blackwell, Muriel Ostriche, Pat Foy, Walter D. Greene, Jean Shelby
Note: Filmed in Fort Lee, New Jersey. One trade notice erroneously stated a location in the Midwest.

THE MEN SHE MARRIED
(Peerless for World)
November 27, 1916
5 reels
Director: Travers Vale
Screenplay: From a story by Harold Vickers
Cast: Gail Kane, Muriel Ostriche, Montagu Love, Arthur Ashley, Louise M. Bates

A SQUARE DEAL
Working title: THE PARASITES
(Peerless for World)
February 19, 1917
5 reels
Director: Harley Knoles
Screenplay: Frances Marion from *The Parasites*, a story by Louis V. Jefferson
Cast: Carlyle Blackwell, June Elvidge, Muriel Ostriche, Henry Hull, Charlotte Granville, Charles Charles

THE SOCIAL LEPER(?)
(Peerless for World)
March 19, 1917
5 reels
Director: Harley Knoles
Screenplay: Frances Marion from a story by Florence C. Bolles
Cast: Carlyle Blackwell, June Elvidge, Arthur Ashley, Evelyn Greeley, Muriel Ostriche (?), Eugenie Woodward, George MacQuarrie, Isabelle Berwin, Edna Whistler
Note: World Films advertising seen by the author, except for a glass slide made by the Excelsior Illustrating Co., omits mention of Muriel Ostriche, nor is she mentioned in reviews in *Moving Picture World*, *Variety*, or other publications seen. If Muriel Ostriche was in the film, her part was minor. The scenario involves a man who marries a worthless woman and subsequently divorces her, to later find one of his friends is in love with her. The divorced woman finds cause to blackmail her former husband. She is choked to death by her boyfriend, but her ex-husband arrives on the scene and is arrested for the murder.

MORAL COURAGE
Working title: THE WIT OF A WOMAN
(Peerless for World)
May 14, 1917
5 reels
Director: Romaine Fielding
Screenplay: From *The Wit of a Woman*, a story by Stanley Dark
Cameraman: Philip Hatkin
Cast: Muriel Ostriche, Arthur Ashley, Johnny Hines, Alec B. Francis, Edward Elkas, Clarence Elmer, Robert Forsyth, Julia Stuart, Richard Turner, Edmund Cobb

YOUTH
Working title: THE WASTER
(Peerless for World)
July 30, 1917
Director: Romaine Fielding
Screenplay: From *The Waster*, a story by Roy S. Sensabaugh
Cameraman: William S. Cooper
Cast: Carlyle Blackwell, June Elvidge, Johnny Hines, George Cowl, Muriel Ostriche, Victor Kennard, Henrietta Simpson, Henry West, Robert Broderick

THE DORMANT POWER
(Peerless for World)
October 22, 1917
5 reels
Director: Travers Vale
Screenplay: Clara S. Beranger from a story by Florence C. Bolles
Cast: Ethel Clayton, Montagu Love, Joseph Herbert, Edward Langford, Muriel Ostriche, George Morgan
Note: Most scenes filmed in Fort Lee, New Jersey and Palm Beach, Florida, but with some outdoor scenes filmed in the West.

THE GOOD FOR NOTHING
Working title: THE LADDER OF FAME
(Peerless for World)
December 10, 1917
5 reels
Director: Carlyle Blackwell
Screenplay: From *The Ladder of Fame*, a story by Alexander Thomas
Cast: Carlyle Blackwell, Muriel Ostriche, Evelyn Greeley, Kate Lester, Charles Duncan, William Sherwood, Eugenie Woodward, Katharine Johnston

THE VOLUNTEER
a.k.a. THE LITTLE VOLUNTEER
(World)
December 24, 1917
5 reels
Director: Harley Knoles
Screenplay: Julia Burham
Cameraman: René Guissart
Cast: Madge Evans, Henry Hull, Muriel Ostriche, Victor Kennard, Jack Drumier, Kate Lester, Charles Charles, and cameo appearances by Kitty Gordon, Ethel Clayton, June Elvidge, Evelyn Greeley, Carlyle Blackwell, Montagu Love, Harley Knoles, William A. Brady
Note: Filmed at the World Studio in Fort Lee, New Jersey

THE WAY OUT
(Peerless for World)
March 25, 1918
5 reels
Director: George Kelson
Screenplay: Clara S. Beranger from a story by Jack O'Mara
Cameraman: Jacques Monterau
Cast: Carlyle Blackwell, June Elvidge, Kate Lester, John Bowers, Muriel Ostriche, Jack Drumier, Marie Pagano
Note: Filmed in Fort Lee, New Jersey, with additional scenes of the beach at Trouville and battlefields, in France.

THE PURPLE LILY
(World)
April 22, 1918
5 reels
Director: George Kelson
Screenplay: Archer MacMackin
Cameramen: Lewis Ostland and Lucien Tainguy
Cast: Kitty Gordon, Frank Mayo, Muriel Ostriche, Charles Wellesley, Clay Clement, Henry West, Howard Kyle, John Dudley, Carl Axzell

LEAP TO FAME
(World)
April 24, 1918
5 reels
Director: Carlyle Blackwell
Screenplay: From a story by Raymond L. Schrock
Cameraman: Lucien Tainguy
Cast: Carlyle Blackwell, Evelyn Greeley, Muriel Ostriche, Alec B. Francis, Frank Beamish, Philip Van Loan, Lionel Belmore, William Bailey, Benny Nedell

JOURNEY'S END
(World)
May 13, 1918
5 reels
Director: Travers Vale
Screenplay: Roy S. Sensabaugh
Cameraman: Mark Schneider
Cast: Ethel Clayton, John Bowers, Muriel Ostriche, Jack Drumier, Louise Vale, Frank Mayo, Victor Kennard, Jean Loew
Note: Filmed in Fort Lee, New Jersey and Palm Beach, Florida

TINSEL
(World)
July 8, 1918
5 reels
Director: Oscar C. Apfel
Screenplay: Wallace C. Clifton from *Adele*, a story by Fred Jackson
Cameraman: Lucien Tainguy
Cast: Kitty Gordon, Muriel Ostriche, Frank Mayo, Anthony Merlo, Bradley Barker, George DeCarlton, Marie Nau, Ann Dearing, Ralph Graves

MERELY PLAYERS
(World)
August 19, 1918
5 reels
Director: Oscar C. Apfel
Screenplay: Adapted by Wallace C. Clifton from a story by Lulu Case Russell
Cast: Kitty Gordon, Irving Cummings, George MacQuarrie, Pinna Nesbit, Muriel Ostriche, Johnny Hines, Florence Coventry, Dore Davidson

THE ROAD TO FRANCE
(World)
October 14, 1918
6 reels
Director: Dell Henderson
Screenplay: From a story by Harry O. Hoyt
Cameraman: Louis Ostland
Cast: Carlyle Blackwell, Evelyn Greeley, Jack Drumier, Muriel Ostriche, George DeCarlton, Jane Sterling, Richard Neill, Inez Shannon, Henry West, Alex Shannon, Joseph Smiley, James Davis, Elizabeth Kennedy

HITTING THE TRAIL
(World)
December 2, 1918
5 reels
Director: Dell Henderson
Screenplay: Harry O. Hoyt from a story by Roy Somerville
Cast: Carlyle Blackwell, Evelyn Greeley, Joseph Smiley, George MacQuarrie, Mabel Bunyea, Muriel Ostriche, Walter Green, Edward Elkas

WHAT LOVE FORGIVES
(World)
January 6, 1919
5 reels
Director: Perry N. Vekroff
Screenplay: George D. Proctor from a story by Gardner Hunting
Cameramen: Sol Polito and Philip Hatkin
Cast: Barbara Castleton, Johnny Hines, John Bowers, Bobby Connelly, Florence Coventry, Muriel Ostriche, Joseph Smiley, Hazel Coates

THE BLUFFER
(World)
January 20, 1919
5 reels
Director: Travers Vale
Screenplay: Clara S. Beranger
Cameraman: Philip Hatkin
Cast: June Elvidge, Irving Cummings, Frank Mayo, George MacQuarrie, Muriel Ostriche, Elizabeth Garrison, Louis Grisel, Jack Davidson, Jack Raymond

THE MORAL DEADLINE
(World)
February 24, 1919
5 reels
Director: Travers Vale
Screenplay: Lucien Hubbard from a story by Earle Mitchell
Cameraman: Philip Hatkin
Cast: Fred Mayo, June Elvidge, Ned Burton, Muriel Ostriche, Grace Stevens, Alice Weeks, Gertrude Webber, Louis Grisel, Louise DuPre, Joseph Smiley, Jane Sterling

THE HAND INVISIBLE
(World)
March 17, 1919
5 reels
Director: Harry O. Hoyt
Screenplay: Clara S. Beranger from a story by Wallace C. Clifton
Cast: Montagu Love, Virginia Hammond, William Sorelle, Marguerite Gale, Martha Mansfield, Kate Lester, George LeGuere, Muriel Ostriche

THE SACRED FLAME
(Schomer-Ross)
November 8, 1919
6 reels
Director: Abraham S. Schomer
Screenplay: Abraham S. Schomer and George Roland
Cameraman: Andre Barlatier
Cast: Emily Stevens, Muriel Ostriche, Maud Hill, Violet Axzelle, Earl Schenck, Lionel Adams, Frederick Clayton, James P. Laffey
Note: Some scenes filmed in the Biograph Studio, New York (in the later facility in the Bronx)

LOVE BIRDS(?)
(Arrow)
Circa July 1920(?)
2 reels
Director: Arvid Gillstrom
Cast: Featuring Muriel Ostriche
Note: It is not certain if this film was ever released, or if it was, if another title was used. Filmed in Fort Lee, New Jersey. Muriel Ostriche stated that one of her Arrow films was produced in Atlanta; possibilities include this or one of the next several.

BETTY SETS THE PACE
(Arrow-Muriel Ostriche Productions)
July 1920
2 reels
Director: Arvid Gillstrom
Screenplay: Vide Dudley
Cast: Featuring Muriel Ostriche
Note: Presented by Garnette Sabin. Filmed in Fort Lee, New Jersey

BETTY'S GREEN-EYED MONSTER
(Arrow-Muriel Ostriche Productions)
July 1920
2 reels
Director: Arvid Gillstrom
Screenplay: Vide Dudley
Cast: Featuring Muriel Ostriche
Note: Presented by Garnette Sabin. Filmed in Fort Lee, New Jersey

MEET BETTY'S HUSBAND
(Arrow-Muriel Ostriche Productions)
July 1920
2 reels
Director: Arvid Gillstrom
Cast: Featuring Muriel Ostriche
Presented by Garnette Sabin. Filmed in Fort Lee, New Jersey (after which it was announced that all remaining Muriel Ostriche comedies would be produced on the West Coast—but none was).

(TITLE UNKNOWN)
(Arrow-Muriel Ostriche Productions)
Late 1920(?)
2 reels
Cameramen: Lucien Tainguy and Ollie Leach
Note: *Moving Picture World*, October 9, 1920, reported: "Word has been received at the Arrow offices from Mrs. Garnette Sabin . . . that Lucien Tainguy and Ollie Leach have been engaged to photograph the next Muriel Ostriche comedy, the production of which has begun." No further information is known to the author.

THE SHADOW
(Forward Films-Salient Films)
April 1921
5 reels
Director: J. Charles Davis, Jack W. Brown
Screenplay: J. Charles Davis
Cast: Muriel Ostriche, Walter Miller, Harold Foshay, Helen Courtenay, Jack Hopkins, Dorothy Blackbourne
Note: Reissued circa October 1927

THE CALL OF THE OPEN
(Salient Films)
1921(?)
5 reels
Director: J. Charles Davis
Cast: Including Muriel Ostriche
Note: It is uncertain if this film was made

APPENDIX TWO

Muriel Ostriche Chronology

1896, March 24. Born in New York City to Miriam and Abram Oestrich.
1911, autumn. Joins American Biograph.
1912, January 8. First film, *A Tale of the Wilderness*, released.
1912, early. Works with P.A. Powers.
1912, early. Works with Pathé.
1912, March. Joins Eclair Studio.
1913, circa February-March. Joins Reliance.
1913, circa May. Joins Thanhouser.
1913, July. Elected the second most popular (after Alice Joyce) screen actress in America by readers of *Motion Picture Story Magazine*.
1913, October 24. First Princess film, *Lobster Salad and Milk*, released.
1914, August 22. Charles J. Hite's death alters the destiny of the Thanhouser Company.
1915. Muriel Ostriche publicized as the Moxie Girl, which would continue to about 1920.
1915, January. Joins Independent Moving Pictures Co. (IMP).
1915, February-March. Works with Charles K. Harris Feature Film Corporation.
1915, March 22. Joins Vitagraph.
1915, September. Joins World Films.
1918, January 28. Marries Frank A. Brady.
1919, March and July. Publicity tours in New England.
1919, September. Joins Schomer-Ross Productions.
1919, October 13. Stage show, *Dream Girl*, opens.
1920, circa May. Joins Arrow Film Corporation.
1921, circa April. Joins Salient Films.
1922, September 26. Daughter Gloria born. Gloria married Charles B. Hewitt on December 1, 1945. The following children were born to the union: Robert Blackman (April 22, 1948), William Wesley (June 27, 1950), Richard Bruce (December 19, 1953).
1923, October 28. Daughter Mollie (Francine on birth certificate, occasionally called Margot in her youth by her father) born. Married Calvin Shand Demarest on April 5, 1945. The following children were born to the union: Laura (April 18, 1949), Susan (February 22, 1951), Wendy (July 13, 1954).
1926, August 27. Divorce from Frank A. Brady becomes final. Marries Charles Wesley Copp, Jr. (October 28, 1902-August 19, 1957) the same day.
1927, July 29. Charles Wesley Copp III born. Lives to the age of four.
1932, September 9. Daughter Jean born. Jean married Charles Geoly on February 2, 1957. The following children were born to the union: Charles Andrew (September 2, 1961), Thomas Edward (November 16, 1968).

Bibliography

Agnew, Frances. *Motion Picture Acting*. New York: Reliance Newspaper Syndicate, 1913.

Alvarez, Max Joseph. *Index to Motion Pictures Reviewed by Variety, 1907-1980*. Metuchen. New Jersey: The Scarecrow Press, Inc., 1982.

Altomara, Rita Ecke. *Hollywood on the Palisades*. New York: Garland Publishing, Inc., 1983.

Balshofer, Fred J. and Arthur C. Miller. *One Reel a Week*. Berkeley and Los Angeles, California: University of California Press, 1967.

Billboard, The. Cincinnati, Ohio. Various issues 1912-1921.

Bowers, Q. David. *The Moxie Encyclopedia*. Vestal, New York: Vestal Press, 1985.

— *Nickelodeon Theatres*. Vestal, New York: Vestal Press, 1986.

Bowser, Eileen (introduction by). *Biograph Bulletins 1908-1912*. New York: Octagon Books division of Farrar, Straus and Giroux, 1973.

Brownlow, Kevin. *Hollywood - The Pioneers*. New York: Alfred A. Knopf, 1979.

Brownlow, Kevin. *The Parade's Gone By*. New York: Alfred A. Knopf, Inc., 1968.

Catalog of Copyright Entries, Motion Pictures 1912-1939. Washington, D.C.: Copyright Office, Library of Congress, 1951.

Eclair Bulletin, The. Fort Lee, New Jersey. Various issues 1912-1913.

Exhibitors Herald. Chicago. Various issues 1916-1921.

Exhibitor's Trade Review. New York. Various issues 1916-1921.

Graham, Cooper C. et al. *D.W. Griffith and the Biograph Company*. Metuchen, New Jersey: The Scarecrow Press, Inc., 1985.

Grau, Robert. *The Theatre of Science*. New York: Broadway Publishing Co., 1914.

Hulfish, Davis S. *Cyclopedia of Motion Picture Work*, Volumes I and II. Chicago: American Technical Society, 1911.

Lauritzen, Einar and Gunnar Lundquist. *American Film-Index 1908-1915*. Stockholm: Film-Index, 1984.

Lauritzen, Einar and Gunnar Lundquist. *American Film-Index 1908-1915*. Stockholm: Film-Index, 1976.

Macgowan, Kenneth. *Behind the Screen*. New York: Delacorte Press, 1965.

Morning Telegraph. New York. Various issues 1912-1915.

Motion Picture Classic. New York. Various issues 1915-1920.

Motion Picture Story Magazine (later, *Motion Picture Magazine*). New York. Various issues 1912-1918.

Motion Picture Studio Directory. New York: Motion Picture News, Inc. 1916, 1918, 1919, and 1920 editions.

Motography. Chicago. Various issues 1912-1918.

Moving Picture News (later, *Motion Picture News*). Various issues 1912-1921.

Moving Picture Stories. New York. Various issues 1913-1921.

Moving Picture World. New York. Various issues 1912-1921.

Munden, Kenneth (editor). *The American Film Institute Catalog of Motion Pictures Produced in the United States; Feature Films 1921-1930*. New York: R.R. Bowker Company, 1971.

New Rochelle Pioneer, The. Various issues 1913-1915.

New York Clipper, The. New York. Various issues 1912-1916.

New York Dramatic Mirror, The. New York. Various issues 1912-1918.

Photoplay. Chicago. Various issues 1912-1921.

Photo-Play Journal, The. Various issues 1918-1919.

Ramsaye, Terry. *A Million and One Nights*. New York: Simon and Schuster, 1926.

Schickel, Richard. *D. W. Griffith—An American Life*. New York: Simon & Schuster, Inc., 1984.

Slide, Anthony. *Aspects of American Film History Prior to 1920*. Metuchen, New Jersey: The Scarecrow Press, Inc., 1978.

Slide, Anthony. *Early American Cinema*. New York: A.S. Barnes & Co., 1970.

Slide, Anthony. *International Film, Radio, and Television Journals*. Westport, Connecticut: Greenwood Press, 1985.

Smith, Albert E. *Two Reels and a Crank*. Garden City, N.Y.: Doubleday & Co., Inc., 1952.

Spehr, Paul C. *The Movies Begin*. Newark, N.J.: The Newark Museum, 1977.

Variety. New York. Various issues 1912-1921.

Vitagraph Bulletin, The. New York. 1915.

Wagenknecht, Edward. *The Movies in the Age of Innocence*. Norman, Oklahoma: University of Oklahoma Press, 1962.

Weaver, John T. *Twenty Years of Silents 1908-1928*. Metuchen, N.J.: The Scarecrow Press, Inc., 1971.

Wid's Year Book 1920-1921. New York: Wid's Films and Film Folks, Inc., 1920. Also, the separate 1921 edition.

Other sources: Studio flyers and film publicity sheets; articles cited in the text.

Index

A

Accidental Servant, An, 40
Actor and the Rube, The, 127
Actor's Children, The, 52
Adams, Lionel, 198
Adler, Bert, 58, 102, 108, 115, 119, 127
Adolfi, John, 35
Adventures of Billy, The, 19
Adventures of Dolly, The, 19
After the Ball, 148
Agnell, Raymond, 163
Aitken, Harry E., 54, 72, 87, 108
Aitken, Henry A., 50
Alden, Mary, 147
Alexander, Kenneth, 201
Alexander, Kenny, 205, 209
Alexander, Mollie King, (see: King, Mollie)
Alexander, Robert, 209
Alexander's Ragtime Band, 51
Algonquin Hotel, 190
Algy Forfeits His Claim, 67
Algy on the Force, 67
Algy the Watchman, 67
Algy's Awful Auto, 67, 69
Alice Brady Pictures, Inc., 175
Alice in Wonderland, 116, 147
All's Well That Ends Well, 86, 90
Amateur Detective, The, 122
Ambrosio Films, 23
American Film Manufacturing Company, 23, 56, 79, 87, 127, 147
American Mutoscope and Biograph Company, (see: Biograph Company)
American Weekly, The, 201
Anderson, G.M., 90
Anderson, Mignon, 24, 50, 54, 58, 83, 94, 99, 122, 127
Apfel, Oscar C., 49, 185
Applegate, Roy, 162
Archer, Frank M., 141, 146
Arnaud, Etienne, 29, 31, 37, 40
Arrow Film Corporation, 129, 198, 199, 200, 201
As it Was in the Beginning, 24
Ashley, Arthur, 122, 123, 164, 168 169, 171, 173, 174
Aspects of American Film History Prior to 1920, 94, 120
Atwell, Ben H., 107
August, Edwin, 22, 23, 149
Avenging Conscience, The, 151
Axzelle, Violet, 198
Ayers, James, 90

B

B.A. Rolfe Productions, 130
Babette of the Ballyhoo, 163, 165
Badgley, Helen, 122
Baggot, King, 87, 122
Balfour, A., 50
Balfour, Sue, 49, 109
Baluser, Grover, 122
Baring, Mathilde, 31
Barker, Bradley, 183
Barnes, Justus, 90, 92, 119
Barnum, P.T., 146
Bauer, Arthur, 75, 77, 83, 89, 92, 93, 116, 120
Baumann, Charles O., 49
Bawlerout, The, 49, 109
Beach, Alice, 169
Beacon Hall, 133, 136
Beating Back, 105
Beaudet, Louis, 151
Beautiful Snow, 93
Belle of the School, The, 115
Benham, Dorothy, 74, 76, 77, 97
Benham, Harry, 58, 99, 122
Bernard, Dorothy, 22, 23
Bernhardt, Sarah, 174
Bernstein, Isadore, 159
Betty Sets the Pace, 198, 199
Betty's Green-Eyed Monster, 199
Betty's Husband, 199
Big Boss, The, 49, 50
Big U, 147
Billboard, The, 20, 31, 33, 54, 56, 127, 163, 197
Billy Banks Medicine Show, 83
Billy's Ruse, 93
Billy's Stratagem, 22
Biograph Company, 19, 20-23, 44, 52, 56, 67, 79, 101, 126, 151, 171
Birth of a Nation, The, 19, 147, 151, 168
Bison Company, 23, 146
Bitzer, Billy, 20
Blaché, Herbert, 37
Blackton, J. Stuart, 25, 56, 79, 149, 152, 154
Blackwell, Carlyle, 168, 169, 170-177, 180-182, 186, 190
Blaisdell, George, 87
Blinn, Holbrook, 169
Bloomer, Raymond, 151, 156
Blot in the 'Scutcheon, A, 23
Bluffer, The, 186
Bolles, Florence E., 173
Bonnie-B (imported hair net), 193
Boston American, 146
Boston Post, 190
Bourgeois, Paul, 39
Bourke, Fanny, 83, 88 90, 92, 94, 96, 122
Bowers, John, 182, 186
Bracy, Sidney, 122, 127
Brady, Alice, 161, 168, 174, 175
Brady, Frank A., 176, 180, 204
Brady, Gloria, 201, 204, 208, 211 (see also: Hewitt, Gloria)
Brady, John Casper, 180
Brady, Mary, 180
Brady, Mary Alexander, (see: Brady, Mollie)
Brady, Mollie, 201, 204, 208, 209, 211, 216 (see also: Demarest, Mollie)
Brady, Thomas Joseph, 180, 197
Brady, William A., 161, 168, 170-173, 176, 177, 180
Brandt, Charles, 163
Bread Upon the Waters, 72
Bright, Mildred, 37, 39, 40, 43, 44

Briscoe, Lottie, 90
Broadway Rose Gardens, The, 107, 108, 115, 116, 126
Broderick, Robert, 175
Broncho Films, 56, 93
Browning, Robert, 23
Brulatour, Jules, 33
Brunette, Fritzi, 90
Bryan, William Jennings, 83
Bunny, John, 81, 83, 90
Bunyea, Mabel, 186
Burglar on the Roof, The, 49
Buried Alive, 35
Burns, Paul E., 197
Bushman, Francis X., 90
Butler, Henry J., 185
Butler, William J., 22, 23
By Whose Hand?, 165, 167, 190, 197

C

C.J. Hite Moving Picture Company, 79
Cabanne, W. Christy, 19, 20, 22, 23
Cabiria, 107, 151
Cahill Films, 25
Calhoun, Catherine, 162, 163, 166
Call of the Open, The, 201
Cameron, Walter, 116
Campaign Manageress, The, 67, 72
Captive, The, 151
Carlisle, Alexandra, 164
Carlton Motion Picture Laboratories, 79
Carnegie Hall, 168
Carpathia, 33
Carroll, Frank, 180
Castleton, Barbara, 186
Cavalry at Ft. Meyer, The, 110
Celeste, 146, 147
Century Motion Picture Corp., 147
Chamberlin, Riley, 116
Chambers, Robert W., 147
Champion Films, 23
Chaplin, Charlie, 146, 168, 171
Charles K. Harris Feature Film Corporation, 148
Charleson, Mary, 164
Check No. 130, 123
Chicago Board of Censors, 147
Chicago Daily News, 24
Child of the West, A, 24
Christian Science, 45
Christian, The, 151
Cinderella, 37
Cines Films, 23
Circumstantial Nurse, A, 85
Circus Romance, A, 101, 165, 166, 175, 190, 197
Clancy, Tim, 180
Clark, Jack, 81
Clayton, Ethel, 85, 169, 175, 182
Clayton, Frederick, 198
Clendenning-Henry, Janet, 98
Clysmic Waters, 116
Codfish Industry, 22

— 235 —

Cohan, Jeanette, 105
Columbia Theatre Building, 148
Comet Film Company, 54
Commercial Club of Brockton, 25
Common Law, The, 147, 168
Con. T. Kennedy Carnival Company, 163, 166
Condon, Mabel, 101, 116, 119, 148
Coney Island, 54
Connelly, Bobby, 152
Cooke, Ethyle, 120, 122
Cooper, Miriam, 23
Copp, Charles Wesley, Jr., 204, 205, 206, 207
Copp, Charles Wesley, III, 204, 210
Copp, Jean, 204 205, 209, 211 (see also: Geoly, Jean Copp)
Corrigan, Emmet, 164
Corsair, The, 26
Costello, Maurice, 81, 90
Course of True Love, The, 22, 24
Courtenay, William, 164
Cowell, George, 175
Crane, Dixie, 69
Crazy Quilt, The, 54
Crimson Cross, The, 44
Criterion Theatre, 149, 151
Cruise, Tom, 205
Cruze, James, 56, 58, 74, 94, 99, 116, 119, 122, 181
Crystal films, 146
Crystal Theatre, 176
C-SPAN, 205
Cullison, Webster, 159
Cummings, Irving, 49, 50, 90, 94, 116, 119, 185, 186
Cupid's Lieutenant, 74, 77

D

D.W. Griffith-An American Life, 23
D'Annunzio, Gabriele, 107
Dark Cloud, 22
Darnell, Jean, 64
Daugherty, Mr., 20
Daughter of the Sea, A, 160-163, 165, 190, 197, 201
Davidson, Jack, 186
Davidson, William B., 152
Davies, Howard, 74
Davis, Edwards, 163, 165, 166
Davis, Gunnis J., 40
Davis, J. Charles, 199, 201, 203
Davis, Lloyd, 180
Dawn of a Tomorrow, The, 151
Dawson, Ely, 197
Dean, Priscilla, 22, 23
Dearing, Ann, 183
DeCarlton, George, 183, 185
Decoy, The, 107
Delaro, Hattie, 152
de Lespine, Edgena, 49, 90
Delightful Dolly, 119
Delta Theatre Corporation, 107
Demarest, Calvin, 217
Demarest, Laura, 217
Demarest, Mollie, 217 (see also: Brady, Mollie)
Demarest, Susan, 217
Demarest, Wendy, 217
de Maupassant, Guy, 35, 152
Dempsey, Jack, 180
Descent into the Maelstrom, A, 35
Destiny is Changeless, 24
Diamond of Disaster, The, 119
Dickens, Charles, 52
Dillon, Edward, 23
Dillon, Gregory, 52
Dixie Theatre, 171
Dormant Power, The, 175
Dr. Jekyll and Mr. Hyde, 23
Drako Film Company, 147
Dream Girl, 197, 198
Drew, John, 44
Drew, S. Rankin, 151, 156
Drew, Mr. and Mrs. Sidney, 152
Drumier, Jack, 182, 185
Dudley, Vide, 198
Dull, Clarence, 74
Duncan, Bud, 72
Dunne, James, 105

E

Earle, P.S., 152
East Lynne, 23, 24, 25

Eastman Kodak, 33
Eclair Bulletin, The, 44
Eclair Film Company, 20, 23-25, 29-31, 33-37, 39, 40, 43, 102, 126, 146, 171
Eclair Kid, 39, 43, 54
Eddy, Nelson, 175
Edeson, Robert, 151-155, 159
Edison Company, 19, 22, 23, 25, 44, 56, 151
Eline, Grace, 92
Eline, Marie, 54, 67, 69, 74-77, 83, 88, 99
Elkas, Edward, 152, 154, 186
Ellery, Arthur, 120
Ellery, Mrs. Arthur, 94
Elvidge, June, 171-176, 182, 186, 188
Emerson, Charles, 96
Empire Trust Company, 19
Empress Picture Corp., 147
Enoch Arden, 19
Epoch Producing Company, 147
Equitable Motion Pictures Corp., 159, 161-165, 167
Equitable-World Films, 166
Escape, The, 151
Essanay, 23, 24, 151
Essemar Film Company, 147
Eternal City, The, 151
Evans, Madge, 176, 186
Evening Mail, The, 127
Evils of Impure Literature, The, 22
Excelsior Illustrating Company, 173
Exhibitors Film and Service Company, 201
Exploits of Elaine, 25

F

Fairbanks, Madeline, 54, 94
Fairbanks, Marion, 54, 94
Falstaff Department, 127
Famous Players, 151, 171, 201
Farmer's Daughters, The, 64, 67
Farrington, Frank, 116, 127
Farrington, Reenie, 87, 116, 123, 126, 127
Fatal Wedding, The, 35
Fatherless Children of France Fund, 193
Fealy, Maude, 58, 74, 99, 119
Feathertop, 35
Feist, Felix, 159
Ferdie Fink's Flirtations, 127
Ferdinand, King, 148
Fiddlers Three, 197
Fielding, Romaine, 52, 53, 175
Fields, Lew, 197
Film Supply Company of America, 79
Finch, Flora, 81
Fischer, A.A., 130
Fischer, Margarita, 159, 164
Fisher Girl, A, 161
Fisher, Harrison, 193
Five Faults of Flo, The, 54
Fleming, Carroll, 74, 116, 119, 120, 122
Flood Tide, 58, 83
For Better or Worse, 44
For the Honor of the Crew, 152
For the Love of Mike, 24
Ford, Eddie, 86, 90-92
Fordham University, 180
Fortescue, Muriel, 22
Forward Film Distributors, Inc., 199, 201, 203
Foster, Edna, 23
Foster, Morris, 50, 93, 94, 99, 127
Fox, Della, 119
Fox Film Studio, 186
Foxe, Earle, 146
Francis, Alec B., 31, 35, 37, 39, 40, 43, 44, 171
Frank, J. Herbert, 152, 154
Franklin Park Theatre, 190
Frazer, Robert, 37, 39,
Frazzled Finance, 58
Frederick McKay Productions, 147
Freuler, Mr., 108
Friday the Thirteenth, 69, 119
Friml, Rudolf, 175
From the Manger to the Cross, 151
Frontier films, 146
Fugitive, The, 54
Fuld, Horace A., 83
Fuller, Mary, 79, 87

G

Gable, Clark, 205
Gane, Nolan, 64, 93, 94, 98, 116
Gardner, Helen, 90
Garrison, Elizabeth, 186
Garwood, William, 72
Gauntier, Gene, 81
Gem Company, 146
General Film Company, 152
Geoly, Charles, 218
Geoly, Charles Andrew, 218, 219
Geoly, Jean Copp, 213, 218 (see also: Copp, Jean)
Geoly, Thomas Edward, 218, 219
Gerhardt, Charlie, 148
Gibson, Dorothy, 33, 35
Gillstrom, Arvid, 198, 199
Girl of the Season, The, 107
Gish, Dorothy, 168
Gish, Lillian, 168
Godfrey, Winona, 151
Gold Bug, The, 35
"Gold Rooster" (label), 129
Golden, Joseph, 159
Gone With the Wind, 205
Good For Nothing, The, 176, 177
Goodman, Daniel Carson, 58, 73, 119, 126, 129
Goosman, Max F.C., 199
Gordon, Harris, 122,
Gordon, Kitty, 169, 176, 183, 185
Gorman, James, 198
Gould, E.W., 171
Grand Passion, The, 93, 98
Grandin, Ethel, 81
Graustark, 151
Graves, Ralph, 183
Graybill, Joseph, 23
Great Northern films, 23, 93
Greeley, Evelyn, 173, 176, 177, 185, 186
Green, William, 25
Gregory, Carl, 56, 67, 81, 83
Gregory, Fanny, 83
Grey, Clifford, 161, 162
Griever Productions, 201
Griffith, D.W., 19, 20, 22, 50, 93, 129, 147, 148, 151, 168, 171
Griffith, Linda Arvidson, 23
Grisel, Louis R., 35, 37, 186

H

H & H Films, 54, 87
Hall, Donald, 152, 154, 155
Hall, Lindsay, 43, 44
Hall, Mayre, 116, 119
Halsey, Forrest, 49, 109
Hammond, Virginia, 188
Hand Invisible, The 188
Hansell, Howell, 74, 94
Harris, Charles K., 148
Harris, Elmer, 58
Hartman, Howard, 193
Harvesting Ice, 110
Hastings, Carey L., 83, 116, 119, 120, 122
Hawley, Ormi, 90
Hawthorne, Nathaniel, 35
Heart of the King's Jester, The, 24
Heart Breaker, The, 146, 147
Hearts Adrift, 151
Hearts in Exile, 151
Hecht, Ben, 204
Hedlund, Guy, 40, 43, 44
Helen's Stratagem, 74
Henderson, Dell, 186
Henderson, Lucius, 74, 120
Her Awakening, 94
Her Duty, 110
Her First Lesson, 93, 97
Her Right to Happiness, 72
Her Way, 90
Herbert, Joseph, 175
Hesser Motion Picture Corp., 147
Hewitt, Charles B., 214
Hewitt, Gloria, 214 (see also: Brady, Gloria)
Hewitt, Richard Bruce, 214, 215
Hewitt, Robert Blackman, 214, 215
Hewitt, William Wesley, 241, 215
High Jinks, 175
Hill, Maude, 198
Hines, John, 169, 171, 185, 186
Hirshberg, Dr. Leonard Keene, 94
His Enemy, 104

— 236 —

His Imaginary Family, 74, 75, 83
His Winning Way, 116
Hite, Charles J., 50, 54, 56, 58-60, 62, 67, 72, 74, 79, 85, 87, 94, 105, 107-110, 115, 116, 119, 122, 126, 129, 137
Hite, Marjorie, 115
Hite, Muriel, 115
Hitting the Trail, 186, 190, 197
Hold-Up, The, 90, 95
Holden, John, 52
Holland Film Manufacturing Company, 119
Holy City, 37
Homan, Gertrude, 52
Hombourg, Al, 163
Home of Silence, The, 87
Honeymoon at Niagara, A, 44
Honor of the Firm, The, 39
Hool, Mrs., 77
Hopkins, Jack, 163, 166
Hopper, Edna Wallace, 167
Horan, Charlie, 94
Horsfall Productions, 199
Horsley, David, 24
Horton, Clara, 37, 39, 43, 44, 54
Horton, Perry, 120
Hotel Wellington, 201
House in the Tree, The, 72
House That Jack Moved, The, 127
Howe, Selma, 180
Hoyt, Edward, 116, 122
Hudson River Day Line, 152
Huff, Louise, 186
Hull, Henry, 171, 172
Hume, Eileen, 39
Hunt, Gussie, 24
Hurley, Edward M., 185
Hurst, Fanny, 204
Hutchinson, S.S., 87
Hyde, Harry, 23

I

I Don't Care, 147
Illinois Theatre, 107
IMP, 23
In Her Sleep, 94
In the Chorus, 52
Ince, Jonn, 159
Independent Moving Pictures Company, 23, 119, 120, 146
Innocent Burglar, An, 123
Intolerance, 168
Irving, Walter, 197
Irving, Washington, 35
Island of Regeneration, 151
Ismay, Bruce, 33
Itala Film Company, 23, 107, 151

J

Jack and the Beanstalk, 37
Jack, the Good For Nothing, 176
James, Claude, 154
Jasbo, 94
Jealous Husband, The, 19
Jealous Julia, 24
Jennings, Al J., 105
Jewett, Ethel, 116
Johns Hopkins University, The, 94
Johnson, Arthur, 81, 90
Johnson, Bayard, 52
Johnson, H.C., 176
Johnson, Tefft, 81, 90
Johnston, J.W., 43, 44
Johnston, Lorimer, 147
Johnston, W. Ray, 94, 108, 126
Johnston, Mrs. W. Ray, 115
Johnstone, Lamar, 35, 37, 39, 43, 44, 74
Joker films, 146
Jones, Morgan, 77, 83, 86, 88, 91, 94, 119
Jourjon, Charles, 171
Journey's End, 182, 190, 197
Joy, Ernest, 74
Joyce, Alice, 52, 53, 69, 90,
Judith of Bethulia, 151
Juggernaut, The, 151

K

Kaelred, Katherine, 159, 164
Kalem Films, 20, 23, 52, 146, 151
Kane, Gail, 164, 168, 169, 171
Kay-Bee Films, 56, 93
Keeper of the Light, The, 116
Keeping a Husband, 118, 120
Kellette, John W., 81, 83
Kennard, Victor, 175
Kennedy, Jeremiah J., 19
Kennedy Square, 156
Kent, Charles, 156
Kenyon, Doris, 169
Kerr, George F., 107
Kerrigan, Warren, 53, 68, 90
Kessel, Adam, 49
Keystone Films, 56, 67, 93
Kid, Kit, and Kittie, 29, 35
Kimball, Ingalls, 108
Kimberly, Paul, 74
Kinemacolor, 148
Kinetic Films Company, The, 147
King, Charles, 49
King, Mollie, 49, 163, 169, 201, 216
King, Nelson, 163
Kirkwood, James, 49
Kleine, George, 108, 151
Knabe Ampico (reproducing grand piano), 187
Knickerbocker Theatre, 107, 171
Knoles, Harley, 172, 173
Knowland, Miss, 37
Knowlton Feature Films, 147
Kolker, Henry, 164
Kruh, Regina B., 188, 190, 193

L

LaBadie, Florence, 50, 52, 54, 58, 73, 83, 94, 99, 122, 126, 127, 129,
Ladder of Fame, The, 176
Laemmle, Carl, 23, 25, 35, 119, 146
Laffey, James P., 198
Lakeshore Theatre, 176
Lamon, Isabel, 33-35, 37-39
Landry, A.O., 175
Langford, Edward, 175
Langtry, Ethel, 160
Lanoe, J. Jiquel, 23
La Provence, 58
Larkin, George, 31, 35, 37, 39, 40, 43, 44, 163, 165, 166
Last Days of Pompeii, The, 151
Law of Humanity, The, 74, 76, 77, 83
Lawrence, Edward, 35
Lawrence, Florence, 90
Lawson, Elsie, 176
Leach, Ollie, 199
Leap to Fame, 182
Legend of Sleepy Hollow, The, 35
Lendl, Ivan, 205
Leonard, George, 197
Leonard, Marion, 90
Leoni, Gene, 197
Lester, Kate, 182
Letter With the Black Seals, The, 31, 32
Letters of a Lifetime, 83
Levine, Evelyn, 205
Lewis, Hattie, 185
Lewis, Ralph, 109
Lewis, William J., 185
Liberty Theatre, 147
"Lieutenant Moxie," 141
Life Among the Navajos, 56
Life Films, 159
Lighthouse (charity), 205
Lincoln, E.K., 81
Little Church Around the Corner, The, 72
Little Girl Next Door, The, 122
Little Senorita, The, 105
Livingston, Crawford, 54, 87, 126, 130
Lobster Salad and Milk, 67
Lodge, Sir Oliver, 190
Loew Theatre circuit, 120, 199
Lonedale Operator, The, 19
Lonely Romeo, A, 199
Lonergan, Lloyd S., 50, 58, 81, 105, 119, 122, 127
Lonergan, Philip, 50, 81, 105, 107, 116, 119, 120, 122, 123
Looking for Trouble, 67, 69
Lorens, Bobbi, 197
Lorraine, Lillian, 164

Los Angeles Board of Motion Picture Censors, 147
Loser Wins, The, 87
Love Birds, 198
Love Chase, The, 44
Love, Montagu, 186, 188
Love's Sunset, 151
Lowe, Albert E., 148
Lubin Manufacturing Company, 19, 23, 34, 35, 37, 52, 56
Lubin, Siegmund, 37
Lucas, Wilfred, 20
Luporini Brothers, 199
Lux, 23, 146
Lyceum Theatre, 197

M

Mabel Condon Exchange, 101
Macbeth, 24
MacBride, Donald, 151
MacKenzie, Lillian, 146
MacQuarrie, George, 185, 186
Madame Rex, 19
Madonna of the Poor, A, 120
Maher, Katherine G., 29
Mail Order Wife, The, 24
Mailes, Charles Hill, 22, 23
Maire, Henry J., 39
Majestic Motion Picture Company, 23, 54, 56, 72 85, 87, 93, 104, 119, 122, 146
Making Uncle Jealous, 37-39
Marion, Frances, 161
Marshall, Boyd, 69, 70, 72-77, 81, 83, 85-96, 101, 105, 107, 110, 112, 115, 116, 119, 123-127
Marston, Theodore, 151
Marten, Helen, 44
Marvin, Henry, 19
Massachusetts Institute of Technology, 204
Master Shakespeare, 54
Maurice Tourneur Film Company, 40
Mayo, Frank, 183, 185, 186, 188
McAvoy, Justice, 185
McCardell, Roy, 105
McCue, Mr., 25
McCutcheon, George Barr, 44
McDowell, Claire, 23
McGrath, Harold, 119
McNamara, Walter, 159
Mead, Lydia, 92
Méliès, 23, 101
Melton, Barry, 197
Men She Married, The, 168
Merely Players, 185
Merlo, Anthony, 183
Mesta, Perle, 205
Mignon, 24
Million and One Nights, A 19
Million Bid, A, 151
Million Dollar Mystery, The, 52, 54, 83, 94, 105, 107, 108, 115, 116, 119, 120, 126
Minter, Mary Miles, 49, 168
Miser's Heart, The, 19
Miss Mischief, 56-58, 67, 147
Mitzoras, Demetrio, 74
Mlle. Modiste, 119
Mollie o' Pigtail Alley, 168
Monroe, Tom, 201
Montague Love, 168, 175
Moore, Eugene, 58
Moore, Owen, 90
Moral Courage, 171, 174, 175, 190, 197
Moral Deadline, The, 188
Moreno, Anotonio, 156
Morgan, George, 175
Morning Telegraph, The, 127
Morning Tribune, The, 94
Morrison, James, 152, 154
Mortmain, 151-153, 155, 165, 201
Motion Picture Classic, 175
Motion Picture Exhibitors' Association of Greater New York, 122
Motion Picture Magazine, 83, 99, 102, 123, 151, 161, 163, 168, 193
Motion Picture News, The, 81, 105, 107, 110, 112, 115, 116, 119, 120, 122, 123, 127, 146, 147, 156, 163, 168
Motion Picture Patents Company, 23
Motion Picture Sales Company, 23, 87
Motion Picture Story Magazine, The, 25, 37, 42, 44, 45, 52, 53, 68, 71, 79, 83, 90, 93
Motion Picture Studio Directory, 147
Motography, 37, 101, 107, 108, 116, 122, 126, 127, 129, 148, 152, 159, 161, 163, 165, 168, 171, 176, 182, 185

Moving Picture News, The, 44 (see also: *Motion Picture News, The*)
Moving Picture Stories, 163, 202
Moving Picture World, 20, 22-24, 29, 31, 33, 35, 37, 39, 44, 49, 50, 56, 58, 64, 67, 69, 72, 74, 79, 81, 85, 87, 94, 100, 101, 105, 107, 110, 115, 116, 118-120, 122, 123, 126, 127, 129, 147-149, 151, 160, 161, 163, 165, 168, 171, 175, 176, 180, 182, 185, 186, 188, 197-201
Moxie, 141, 143, 144
Moxie Company, 141, 142, 145, 146
Moxie Girl, 190, 192, 193
Mrs. Van Ruyter's Stratagem, 120
Murders in the Rue Morgue, The, 35
Muriel Ostriche Productions, 199, 200
Murray, J.S., 119
Museum of Modern Arts, 20
Mutual Educational, 56
Mutual Film Corporation, 43, 50, 52, 54, 56, 79, 87, 107, 127, 129, 151
Mutual Girl, The, 90
Mutual Program, 67, 72, 93-95, 97
My Official Wife, 151
Mysteries of the Rosary, The, 44

N

Nashua Country Club, 190
Nashua Telegraph, 190
National Amateur Rowing Regatta, 116
National Press Club, 107
Nau, Marie, 183
Naylor, Hazel Simpson, 161, 175
Nelson, Frances, 169
Neptune's Daughter, 151
Nestor Films, 23, 24, 67, 146
New Majestic Film Company, 74
New Rochelle Pioneer, 50, 54, 69, 102, 110, 122
New Rochelle Standard-Star, 130
New York Clipper, 25, 56, 163, 165
New York Dramatic Mirror, 20, 23, 31, 35, 37, 39, 40, 74, 79, 90, 94, 107, 116, 122, 123, 127, 148, 149, 151, 152, 159, 161, 163
New York Hippodrome, 149
New York Morning Telegraph, 44
New York Picture Corporation, 87, 107
New York Sunday Telegraph, 37
New York Times, 205
New York World, 105
Niagara Honeymoon, A, 23
Noel, Billy, 64, 96, 116
Norman, Karin, 154
Normand, Mabel, 22
North Avenue Theatre, 107, 126

O

Oestrich, Abram, 22
Oestrich, Cora, 141
Oestrich, Miriam, 22, 104, 201
Ogle, Charles, 147
Oh Boy, 197
Oh, You Beautiful Doll, 29
Oh, You Ragtime!, 31
Old Excuse That Worked, An, 22
Oldfield, Barney, 81
Oliver, Guy, 31
Onyx Club, 85
Osborne, Roland, 154
Ostriche, Muriel, solicited for a part in the movies by W. Christy Cabanne, 19; interviewed by D.W. Griffith at Biograph 20; joins Powers Company, 25, joins Pathé as a replacement for Pearl White, 25; joins Eclair Film Company, 29; experience with Reliance, 49; joins Thanhouser, 50; scores high in nationwide popularity contest, 52; friendship with Florence LaBadie, 52; Princess Department set up, 67; "A Picture Play Ingenue" article, 67; Boyd Marshall becomes her leading man in Princess, 69; at the International Picture Exposition, July 1913, 79; Screen Club Ball, January 1914, 87; speaks to New Rochelle club, 93 interviewed by Mabel Condon, 101; wins trophy at Second International Exposition of the Motion Picture Arts, June 1914, 105; biography in *Reel Life*, 109; recalls Charles J. Hite's death, 116; in Thanhouser multiple-reel releases, 116; rejoins Princess, 123; featured in Moxie soft drink advertising, 141; joins Independent Moving Pictures Company (IMP), 146; difficulties with Julius Stern at the IMP studio, 146; joins the Charles K. Harris Feature Film Corporation, 148; joins Equitable and World, 159; Essay on relationships between director and actor, 160; recollections concerning *A Daughter of the Sea*, her favorite film, 161; recalls Rudolf Friml, 175; recalls Rudolph Valentino, 176; marries Frank A. Brady, 176; recalls Jack Dempsey, 180; gives a party for children, 180; wrongly named in suit involving William J. Lewis, 185; hires publicist, 188; travels in New England, 190; joins Schomer-Ross Productions, 197; in a stage play, *Dream Girl*, 197; joins Arrow Film Corporation, 198; Garnette Sabin produces Muriel Ostriche Comedies, 199; signs with Salient Films, 179; recalls Babe Ruth, 201; daughters Gloria and Mollie born, 201; divorces Frank A. Brady, marries Charles Wesley Copp, Jr., 204; Charles Wesley Copp III and Jean born, 204; family photograph album, beginning page 206; filmography, beginning page 223.

P

Pagano, Marie, 182
Palmer, Arnold, 205
Panama-Pacific International Exposition, 119
Panzer, Paul, 81
Paragon Studio, 186
Parasites, The, 171
Park Theatre, 190, 193
Parker, Eleanor, 40, 43, 44
Patents Company, 79, 81
Pathé Frères, 23, 25, 29, 44, 49, 74, 83, 101, 104, 126, 129
Pathé's Weekly, 25
Peerless Studio, 159, 168, 174-176
Pennington, Ann, 146
Pepperday Inn, 136
Pepperday, Mary, (Mrs.) 136
Percy, Eileen, 146
Percy, W.S. 90, 92
Percy's First Holiday, 90, 92
Perils of Pauline, 25, 26
Peters, House, 169
Photoplay Company, 201
Photo-Play Journal, 187, 188, 193
Photoplay Magazine, 163, 186
Photoplayer's Review, 163
Pickford, Jack, 19, 25
Pickford, Lottie, 25
Pickford, Mary, 25, 52, 90, 122, 168, 205
Pillsbury, Helen, 154
Pippa Passes, 23
Pit and the Pendulum, The, 35
Plaza Hotel, 168
Please Remit, 22
Pleasing Uncle, 123, 125
Poe, Edgar Allan, 35, 40, 69, 152, 155
Poison Fang, 52
Politeness Pays, 94
Pollard, Harry A., 159
Pollock, Channing, 167
Polychrolatin Film Corporation, The, 147
Pop Rock, 108, 149
Popular Productions, 197, 198
Power, Tyrone, 25
Powers Motion Picture Company, 23, 25, 44
Powers, Pat A., 25
Pre-Eminent Films, 147
Preferred Picture Corporation, 147
Princess Department, 67, 87, 116
Princess Films, 69, 70, 74, 76, 77, 81, 85, 88-91, 93, 95, 97, 101, 103-105, 107, 109, 110, 112, 115, 116, 119, 122, 123, 126, 127, 190
Princess (tiger), 40
Pritchard, Frances, 146
Professional Diner, The, 152
Professor Snaith, 107
Profits of the Business, The, 37
Prohibition Film Corporation, 147
Providence Bulletin, 193
Purple Lily, The, 182
Purse and the Girl, 87-89

Q

Quirk, Billy, 25, 90
Quo Vadis?, 151

R

Ramsaye, Terry, 19
Randolf, Anders, 151
Raven, The, 35
Raymond, Jack, 186
Reader of the Minds, The, 122
Rector's (restaurant), 176
Red Wing, 25
Redding, Eugene, 96
Redpath Lecture Bureau, 87
Reed, Florence, 164
Reel Life, 56, 67, 75, 81, 109, 127
Refugee, The, 127
Reich, Howard, 168
Reichenbach, Harry, 159
Reilley, Jack, 201
Reinhard, John, 120, 124
Reliance, 23, 44, 49, 50, 56, 72, 93, 94, 102, 107, 109, 146
Republic Films, 23
Rescued From the Eagle's Nest, 19
Revenge of the Silk Masks, 35
Rex films, 23, 146
Richards, John, 119
Riley, James, 165
Ritchey, J.V., 49
Ritchey Lithograph Company, 199
Road to France, The, 185, 186
Robertson-Cole Company, 199
Robinson, Gertrude, 49
Roland, Ruth, 68
Romance of the Rural Route, A, 76, 81
Romance of Wall Street, 24
Romola, 23
Rose Marie, 175
Rose, Miriam, 22
Rosenthal, Mr., 186
Ross, Charles J., 159, 164, 165, 167
Ross, James, 56
Ross, Walter, 168
Royal Vagabond, A, 197
Rubens, Alma, 129
Rubenstein, Leon J., 127
Rubenstein, S., 199
Rural Free Delivery Romance, A, 81
Rural Romance, A, 112
Russell, Lulu Case, 185
Russell, William, 58
Ruth, Babe, 201
Ryno films, 146

S

S and A Film Company, 147
S & O Feature Film Company, 147
Sabin, Barbara, 199
Sabin, Garnette, 199, 200
Sacred Flame, The, 197, 198
St. Louis Cardinals, 205
Sally in Our Alley, 168-170, 180
Salient Films, Inc.; 199, 203
Salvini, Alexander, 52
Sameth, J. Joseph, 199, 203
Saturday Evening Post, The, 105
Sawyer, Joan, 176
Saxe, Martin, 171
Scandals of 1919, 197
Scanlon, Matty, 197
Scarlet Ribbons, 205
Scheff, Fritzi, 119
Schenck, Earl, 197, 198
Schickel, Richard, 23
Schliesser, Michael, 74
Schomer, Abraham S., 197, 198
Schomer-Ross Productions, 197, 198
Schrock, Raymond, 147, 148
Scott, Cyril, 164
Seay, Charles W., 159-161, 163
Seixas, Claude, 76, 83
Selig films, 23, 151
Selznick, Lewis J., 159, 161, 168, 171
Shadow, The, 199, 201
Shallenberger, John F., 198
Shallenberger, W. Edgar, 127, 129, 130, 198
Shallenberger, Dr. Wilbert, 54, 79, 110, 115, 116, 126, 127, 130, 198
She Stoops to Conquer, 90
Sheerer, Will E., 37, 39, 40, 43, 44
Sheridan, Frank, 164
Shields, Frank, 205

Shot Gun Cupid, A, 72
Shrine Theatre, 146
Siegmann, George, 49, 50, 109
Silent Jim, 39
Simpson, Henrietta, 175
Sindelar, Pearl, 81
Sis, 116
Sisson, Vera, 74
Slide, Anthony, 54, 94, 120
Smalley, Phillips, 79
Smiley, Joseph, 186
Smith, Albert E., 149
Smith, F. Hopkinson, 156
Smith, Russell E., 159, 160, 161
Smithsonian Institution, The, 107, 186
Snappy Stories Magazine, 168
Snow, Marguerite, 56, 58, 74, 83, 94, 99, 119, 122
Social Leper, The, 173
Solax Company, 20, 23, 24, 146, 188
Sorerio, Thomas D., 190, 193
Spanish influenza epidemic, 186
Spartan Father, 58
Spectre Bridegroom, The, 40, 41
Speed King, The, 123
Spencer, George Soule, 164
Spiegel, Arthur H., 159, 161, 168
Spier, Martha, 25
Spoilers, The, 151
Square Deal, A, 171, 172
Stage Woman's War Relief, 197
Standard Oil Company, 112
Standard Studio, 198
Stanlaws, Penryhn, 52
Staunton Military Academy, 204
Sterling, Richard, 37
Stern, Julius, 146, 147
Sterne, Elaine, 152
Stevens, Emily, 197, 198
Stewart, Anita, 105
Stewart, Maurice, 105
Stolen Orders, 180
Stoning, The, 151
Strand Theatre, 190, 192, 193
Strike, The, 94
Stuart, Julia, 31, 35, 37, 39, 40, 43, 44
Sullivan, E.P., 49, 109
Sullivan, Frederick, 50
Sunny Jim and the Amusement Co., Ltd., 152
Sunny Jim Comedies, 152
Sununu, John, 205
Swanson, William, 25
Sweet, Blanche, 22, 68, 168
Syndicate Film Corporation, 118

T

Tainguy, Lucien, 199
Tale of the Wilderness, A, 20-23
Tammany Boarder, A, 40
Tangled Cat, The, 90, 95
Tanguay, Eva, 147
Target of Destiny, The, 110
Telephone Stategy, A, 101
Ten of Spades, The, 85
Tennant, Barbara, 35, 37, 43, 44
Tennessee River Dam project, 175
Terrible Discovery, A 20
Terris Feature Film Company, 147
Terrors of the Deep, The, 107
Tess of the Storm Country, 151
Thackery, William Makepeace, 52
Thanhouser, Edwin, 24, 50, 52, 54, 58, 64, 120, 123, 126, 127, 129, 130
Thanhouser Film Corporation, 20, 23, 44, 49-67, 69, 71-73, 79-81, 83, 85, 87, 90-94, 98, 102-105, 108-111, 115-140, 180, 197
Thanhouser, Gertrude, 126
Thanhouser Kid, 54, 58, 67, 69
Thanhouser Kidlet, 58
Thanhouser, Lloyd, 64
Thanhouser Players Photoplays, 126
Thanhouser Players Theatre, 126
Thanhouser Poodle, 54
Thanhouser Syndicate Corporation, 120, 127
Thanhouser Twins, 54, 101, 122, 124
Than-O-Play, 129
Theby, Rosemary, 81
Theosophy, 45
Thirty Leagues Under the Sea, 116
Thomas, Olive, 193

Thompson, Dr. Augustin, 141
Thompson, David, 94
Thompson, M., 176
Thompson, Madeline, 97
Three Fishers, The, 23
Tincher, Fay, 147
Tinsel, 183, 185, 190, 197
Titanic, 53
Too Much Turkey, 94
Tooker, William H., 159, 161, 162, 164
Toy Shop, The, 105
Train, Arthur, 151, 155
Tramp and the Bear, The, 22
Traymore Hotel, 1880
Triangle Studio, 37, 159
Troyano, John, 31, 35
Truesdell, Charles, 39
Truesdell, Fred, 43, 44
Tunis, Fay, 197
Turner, Joseph, 108
Turner, Kathleen, 205
Turner, Muriel, 37
Turning of the Road, The, 118, 120
Twenty Million Dollar Mystery, The, 120, 127
Tynan, Brandon, 164

U

Ulrich, Lenore, 164
Uncle Tom's Cabin, 25
Underwood & Underwood, 176
United States Shipping Board, 185
Universal Film Manufacturing Company, 25, 35, 37, 107, 146, 148, 151, 171, 186
Urban Eclipse, 23

V

Vacant Chair, The, 85, 88
Vale, Travers, 170, 186, 188
Valentino, Rudolph, 176
Valley of Regrets, The, 24
van den Broek, John, 40
Van Houle, Charles, 92
Van Trump, Jessalyn, 74
Variety, 147, 156, 163, 165, 168, 171, 185, 186
Varsity Race, The, 116, 119
Vekroff, Perry N., 148, 186, 187
Vengeance of the Fakir, The, 39
Vernot, Director, 39
Veteran's Sword, The, 110
Vickers, Harold, 168
Victor films, 146
Victor Theatre, 175
Vitagraph Company, 19, 20, 22-25, 52, 56, 79, 101, 108, 149-153, 156, 163, 180, 197
Vitagraph Theatre, 153, 156, 163
Vitagraph-Lubin-Selig-Essanay Motion Picture Company, 149
Volunteer, The, 176

W

Wagenknecht, Edward, 20
Walker, Laura, 146
Walker, Lillian, 81, 90
Wall, Dave, 90
Walsh, George, 94
Walsh, Raoul, 23
War and the Woman, 129
War Film Corporation, 147, 148
Ward, Ernest, 119, 120
Warner Bros., 149
Warner, Harry, 204
Warner, Rita, 204
Warner's Features, Inc., 25
Warwick, Robert, 169
Washburn, Grace, 148, 149
Waster, The, 175
Way Out, The, 182
Wayne, Daphne, 22
Webb, Catherine, 77, 86, 90, 91, 95, 96
Weber, Joseph, 154
Weil, M.J., 176
Wells, Mae, 43, 44
West, Charles H., 23
West, Henry, 175
West Point Military Academy, 104
West Side Tennis Club, 205
Western Film Exchange, 87
What Love Forgives, 186
What's Ours, 150, 151

When Fate Rebelled, 123, 124
When It Strikes Home, 148, 149
When the Cat Came Back, 85, 86
When the Studio Burned, 44, 56
Where Paths Diverge, 86, 90, 91
Whipple, Clara, 162, 164, 169
Whirlwind Melody, The, 49
White Aprons, 29, 31
White, Pearl, 25, 26, 83 181
White Rose, The, 123
White Way Theatre, 176
Who Killed Simon Baird?, 165
Wilbur, Crane, 25, 26, 68, 90, 191
Wildflower, 151
Williams, Earle, 52, 53, 68, 81
Williams, Laura Jane, 163
Williams, Nellie, 93, 97
Williamson brothers, 107, 116
Willie Stayed Single, 152
Wills, Nat M., 25
Wilson, Francis, 108, 115, 137
Wilson, Fred H., 146
Wilson, Hal, 43, 44
Wilson or the Kaiser, 191
Winter Garden, 108, 146
Wit of a Woman, The, 171
Wolf, Rennold, 167
Woman in White, The, 129
Woman's Club of New Rochelle, 90, 93
Wood Frank, 120, 123
World Film Corporation, 37, 49, 106, 151, 159, 161, 163-165, 168-173, 175, 180, 182, 183, 185, 186, 188, 190, 192, 197
Wurlitzer Hall, 198
Wurlitzer Hope-Jones Unit Orchestra, 149
Wyman, Bruce, 58

Y

Young, Brig, 190
Young, Clara Kimball, 81, 122, 130, 159, 163, 168, 169, 171, 181
Young, James, 81, 161
Younge, Lucille, 43, 44, 74
Youth, 175

Z

Zudora, 54, 83, 119, 120, 122, 126, 127

Muriel Ostriche and the author, May 8, 1986 (photo by Gloria Hewitt)

ABOUT THE AUTHOR

Q. David Bowers is the author of over two dozen books on various historical subjects, including *The History of U.S. Coinage* (for The Johns Hopkins University), *The Encyclopedia of Automatic Musical Instruments*, and other works which have become standard references in their fields. His *Nickelodeon Theatres* (Vestal Press, 1986) was the first book ever written expressly on the subject of the early exhibition of motion pictures in America, 1896-1916.

The author's interest in cinema history dates from the 1960s. Since then, he has built an archive of periodicals and publications, including many items formerly the property of George Kleine, Martin Quigley, William Fox, and other notables in the industry. He is currently gathering data for a detailed history of the Thanhouser Company, its films and its people.

A 1960 graduate of the Pennsylvania State University, Q. David Bowers was given the Alumni Achievement Award by that institution's College of Business Administration in 1976. With Raymond N. Merena he is co-owner of Bowers and Merena Galleries, Inc., a worldwide business based in New Hampshire.